Coolidge

· ·

Coolidge

....

An American Enigma

Robert Sobel

Regnery Publishing, Inc.
Washington, D.C.

Library of Congress Cataloging-in-Publication Data

Sobel, Robert, 1931 Feb. 19–
    Coolidge : an American enigma / Robert Sobel.
      p. cm.
    Includes bibliographical references and index.
    ISBN 0-89526-410-2 (acid-free paper)
    1. Coolidge, Calvin, 1872–1933. 2. Presidents—United States—
Biography. 3. United States—Politics and government—1923–1929.
I. Title.
    E792.S64 1998
    973.91'5'092—dc21
    [B]   98-14826
                                                   CIP

Published in the United States by
Regnery Publishing, Inc.
An Eagle Publishing Company
One Massachusetts Avenue, NW
Washington, DC 20001

Distributed to the trade by
National Book Network
4720-A Boston Way
Lanham, MD 20706

Printed on acid-free paper.
Manufactured in the United States of America

10 9 8 7 6 5 4 3 2 1

Books are available in quantity for promotional or premium use. Write to Director of Special Sales, Regnery Publishing, Inc., One Massachusetts Avenue, NW, Washington, DC 20001, for information on discounts and terms or call (202) 216-0600.

Other Books by Robert Sobel

*Dangerous Dreamers: The Financial Innovators
from Charles Merrill to Michael Milken*

The Life and Times of Dillon Read

The New Game on Wall Street

RCA

ITT: The Management of Opportunity

N.Y.S.E.: A History of the New York Stock Exchange

Herbert Hoover at the Onset of the Great Depression

The Great Bull Market: Wall Street in the 1920s

Contents

For

Elizabeth Rose Sobel and Lauren Michelle Sobel

Had he been simply mediocre and commonplace, one would have gained no clearer impression of him at all. But just as a man may be so picturesquely ugly as to attract attention, so Coolidge's personality was apparently so negative that it at once challenged human interest. In appearance he was splendidly null, apparently deficient in red corpuscles, with a peaked, wire-drawn expression. You felt he was always about to turn up his coat collar against a challenging east wind. As he walked there was no motion of the body above the waist. The arms hung immobile, with the torso as inflexible as the effigy of a lay figure.

In his enigmatic character he has been compared to the Sphinx. From the enigma standpoint the comparison is inexact; but like the Sphinx, he seemed to look out with unseeing eyes upon a world which held no glow, no surprises. Desert sand blown by the wind—endless, tantalizing dust.

—Alfred Pierce Dennis, 1931

1

Meet Calvin Coolidge

It was my desire to maintain about the White House as far as possible an attitude of simplicity and not engage in anything that had an air of pretentious display. This was my conception of the great office. It carries sufficient power within itself, so that it does not require any of the outward trappings of pomp and splendor for the purpose of creating an impression. Of course there should be proper formality, and personal relations should be conducted at all times with the best traditions of polite society. But there is no need for theatrics.

The Autobiography of Calvin Coolidge

AMERICAN INTELLECTUALS DO NOT so much harbor a negative opinion of Calvin Coolidge as they trivialize him. He often is dismissed as a political naif, simpleton, and lazy misfit, a relic from the nineteenth century, whose administration set the stage for the Great Depression. Most of the time, however, he simply isn't taken very seriously. Pulitzer Prize–winning historian Irwin Unger recently wrote, "Coolidge slept away most of his five years in office. During his term, the watchword of government was do nothing." This is the image of Coolidge passed on to students and others. They have come to perceive Coolidge as an accidental president who lacked an agenda, did not call for sacrifices and crusades, and did none of those things that mark presidents usually considered great.

Do historians who hold this view have a point? They might observe there was no shortage of issues Coolidge might have addressed from 1923 to 1929, had he wanted to assert presidential leadership. The coal industry was a disaster area. In foreign policy there were America's relations to the League of Nations and war debts. A response might have been mounted to the Japanese arms buildup. Harding had programs or recommendations to deal with most of these matters, and even before the Great Depression, his successor, Herbert Hoover, was a whirlwind of activity.

A major national debate centered around Prohibition. Coolidge disliked Prohibition, since he felt it could never work, but also because he generally opposed federal interferences with the ways people conducted themselves. He abhorred the Ku Klux Klan, and often spoke out for civil rights and against racism, but couldn't bring himself to condemn the Klan's philosophy and actions directly or take any actions to create more harmonious race relations. The same was true for a bill that included a ban on immigration from Japan. He opposed this part of the measure, but signed it anyway.

For the most part, however, historians are silent on these matters. Indeed, a reading of many texts discloses most are scanted or not even discussed. Rather, there seems to be three reasons for his poor reputation, one being the perception that he took no steps to prevent the Great Depression, which is to say, he lacked the ability to foresee the future—a failure he shared with all presidents, and indeed, all humans. This one doesn't merit serious consideration, and in any case, Coolidge's words and actions regarding the economy will be discussed in detail later in this book, and the reader can decide for himself or herself on the matter.

Another is the view of him as being indolent, and the business of sleeping away his time and doing nothing. Writing in 1926, Walter Lippmann touched upon this in an ironic but perceptive fashion.

> Mr. Coolidge's genius for inactivity is developed to a
> very high point. It is far from being an indolent activity.
> It is a grim, determined, alert inactivity which keeps Mr.
> Coolidge occupied constantly. Nobody has ever worked
> harder at inactivity, with such force of character, with
> such unremitting attention to detail, with such
> conscientious devotion to the task. Inactivity is a

political philosophy and a party program with Mr.
Coolidge, and nobody should mistake his unflinching
adherence to it for a soft and easy desire to let things
slide. Mr. Coolidge's inactivity is not merely the absence
of activity. It is, on the contrary, a steady application to
the task of neutralizing and thwarting political activity
wherever there are signs of life.

This is quite different from sleeping away five years in office.

C. Bascom Slemp, formerly Coolidge's private secretary, gathered together the president's thoughts on various subjects in 1926, in a work entitled *The Mind of the President*. In words that Coolidge must have approved (though he denied having anything to do with the book), Slemp wrote:

He had reversed a recent tradition of the presidential
office. For a quarter of a century our presidents have
professed democracy but have practiced benevolent
autocracy. They believed that they could advance the
welfare of the nation better than the people could
advance it. They announced what they declared to be
progressive policies and tried to convert the people to
these policies. They have tried to improve government
from the top.

While this statement appears to place Warren Harding in the progressive tradition, the concept certainly can be easily defended. Slemp went on to say that Coolidge believed progress comes from the people, and that a national leader should not try to "go ahead of this majestic army of human thought and aspiration, blazing new and strange paths." Lippmann went still further. "Mr. Coolidge, though a Republican, is no Hamiltonian Federalist," and so he extended the time line to the first secretary of the treasury at least through Woodrow Wilson, during which the tendency of Hamiltonians and Republicans was toward centralization. This matter will be discussed on several levels in the pages that follow.

Finally, Coolidge is portrayed as one whose major concern while in office was to assist business, especially big business. It is upon this issue more than any other, and Coolidge's supposed rhetoric rather than his actions, that they base their conclusions. One of the objects of this book is to demonstrate that his words and actions were more complicated on the matter than is commonly thought, and also to examine and defuse other myths that have gathered around him.

Upon examination the case for Coolidge being a servant of big business is weak, at least when he is compared with those presidents who preceded him. Virtually all presidents, Democrat as well as Republican, believed that without a strong business sector all would suffer—labor, farmers, consumers. This was true from Abraham Lincoln onward, and under Republicans took the forms of high tariffs, aid to internal improvements, legislation to press for strong banks, lax regulation, and the promotion of education. Even Theodore Roosevelt, generally considered highly critical of big business, was on generally good terms with Wall Street and the tycoons of his time, receiving financial contributions from the likes of J.P. Morgan and E.H. Harriman during his successful 1904 presidential campaign. There were two Democratic presidents in this period, Grover Cleveland and Woodrow Wilson. Wilson indeed was a reformer and an activist, but Cleveland considered the role of the president to be that of executing legislation passed by Congress and vetoing those measures of which he did not approve, which is what he did. Cleveland also brought a large measure of honesty to a Washington that had undergone a long period of corruption. Of all the presidents, an argument might be made that Coolidge resembled Cleveland more than any other. Yet Cleveland has generally received high grades from historians.

Businessmen certainly approved of much of what Coolidge said, stood for, and did. Coolidge asked for and got tax cuts, balanced budgets, lower government spending, and high tariffs. He supported the highway program, wanted a strong merchant marine, and advocated railroad consolidation. His intervention in alleviating distress during the Mississippi floods was a precedent-breaker, but he grudgingly used federal muscle to assist Americans in this time of trouble. It would be a stretch to consider this pro-business; in fact he initially opposed flood aid because he feared most of it would go to business interests. Coolidge fought against direct federal assistance to farmers, and a later generation assumed he was therefore prepared to see their suffering continue. But he was also in favor of high tariffs on imports of farm goods and low ones on equipment farmers purchased. Moreover, his reasoning regarding such aid was vindicated when the policies he opposed were put into place and created a clumsy and unsatisfactory situation.

Certainly Coolidge favored high tariffs, all but abandoned antitrust prosecutions, and did not name activist commissioners to the regulatory agencies. The Commerce and State Departments vigorously assisted American businesses expanding overseas. All of this was known and generally approved at the time, and for good reason: rarely had businessmen's reputations been so high as in the 1920s. The men who had been called "robber barons" during the progressive era were then dubbed "captains of industry." Bruce Barton, who had written glowingly of Coolidge, was also the author of a 1924 best-seller, still quite popular in 1929, *The Man Nobody Knows*, who was Jesus Christ. Barton was repelled by interpretations of Jesus as a dreamer, a person uninterested in worldly matters. Instead, said Barton, he was a hail-fellow-well-met, popular with his friends, able to tell a good story. He was a man who "picked up twelve men from the bottom ranks of business and forged them into an organization that conquered the world." "Some day," wrote Barton, "someone will write a book about Jesus. Every businessman will read it and send it to his partners and his salesmen. For it will tell the story of the founder of modern business." In Barton's reading of the Bible, business was moral, selling was akin to prayer, and God meant us to enjoy ourselves. This was not considered blasphemy by approving readers. Indeed, Barton was elected to Congress in 1936, the year of the Franklin D. Roosevelt landslide.

Others thought the same. Fred French, one of the decade's major real estate operators, said, "The best example of a sales talk is the life of Jesus Christ. He was the best salesman of his time. He said, 'Knock and it shall be opened to you.' What he meant was 'Keep knocking until the door is opened and if it isn't opened pretty soon kick down the door!' That's my philosophy, too."

In this book I contend that the reason for current treatments of Coolidge is a generalized ignorance on the part of those who hold such views. Like most people, Coolidge was quite complicated; although he possessed a strong and clear intellectual core, he was capable of holding dissonant views on some subjects. Moreover, again like most people, his ideas evolved as he aged and the issues changed. Coolidge, the state politician in Massachusetts, was a strong force in the Republican Party, a progressive leader, and an activist. As vice president he was a cipher, as were most who held that office before him. Moreover, he came to that position against the wishes of the national party's leader, and doubtless would have been dropped from the ticket had President Warren Harding lived to run again in 1924.

While president for the remainder of the Harding term, he dedicated himself to carrying out the agenda his predecessor had put in place. He wanted the presidency in his own right, and maneuvered skillfully to win the nomination against the wishes of the party leaders but very much in line with the desires of the general population. And he managed to carry it off.

Then tragedy struck, in the form of the death of his son, and Coolidge fell into a depression. He was a different person after that. This is the Coolidge most nonspecialists know. But even then, there was more to his presidency than is generally known or considered.

What of the country during the Coolidge years? Coolidge presided over an America in which consumerism was filtering down to the masses, enriching their lives. The numbers of automobiles, radios, household appliances, and other amenities rose sharply. Electrification proceeded apace; indoor plumbing became standard. The arts flourished; in music there were Jerome Kern, Irving Berlin, Sigmund Romberg, George and Ira Gershwin, Richard Rodgers, and Cole Porter. The Harlem Renaissance captured the attention of the world, and American blacks achieved high rates of economic growth and low rates of illegitimacy. This was the golden age of sports— Babe Ruth, Jack Dempsey, Bill Tilden, and Red Grange, among others, were in the public spotlight. Charles Lindbergh flew the Atlantic.

What did Coolidge have to do with all of this? Not a thing. But then, he never indicated he was responsible for developments having little or nothing to do with his administration. Indeed, he would often go out of his way to disclaim credit for his supposed accomplishments. When Coolidge was vice president–elect and in New York to receive a medal for his efforts in the Boston police strike, he remarked:

> If it had not been for the clear insight and the determination of Edwin U. Curtis, a former mayor and then police commissioner of the City of Boston, the question that came to me would never have come. It was because he decided that question right in the first instance that I had the opportunity of supporting him in the second.

The public nodded approval when they read Coolidge's last address to Congress in 1929, shortly before he left office. He began this way:

> No Congress of the United States ever assembled, on surveying the state of the Union, has met with a more pleasing prospect than that which appears at the present time. In the domestic field there is tranquility and contentment, harmonious relations between management and wage earner, freedom from industrial strife, and the highest record of years of prosperity. In the foreign field there is peace, the good will that comes from mutual understanding, and the knowledge that the problems which a short time ago appeared so ominous are yielding to the touch of mutual friendship.

But he did not claim this for his administration. The next day there were no protests of exaggeration in the nation's newspapers. Coolidge was stating a simple truth that most Americans realized.

Had he wanted another term in 1928, Coolidge would have had no trouble getting the nomination and being elected. On leaving office he noted that the country was in excellent shape, and most agreed. The market crash came half a year later. By then Coolidge was back in Massachusetts, in the half of a rented two-family house he had lived in while a Massachusetts legislator, engaged in a remarkable amount of writing on a wide variety of subjects.

Was Coolidge intelligent? This may be a criterion for assessing him, though some of our better presidents weren't particularly bright, and several of the brainiest presidents did not perform very well. Arguments will be presented here to indicate he was quite intelligent, but, perhaps more important for the presidency, was unusually astute politically. Coolidge appreciated the temperament required of a politician in his time, and had concluded he filled the bill. In 1915, when still fairly obscure, he reflected on the matter:

> If an individual finds he has a liking and capacity for his
> work in politics, he will involuntarily find himself
> engaged in it. There is no catalogue of such capacity.
> One man gets results in his life in one way, another in
> another. But, in general, only the man of broad and deep
> understanding of his fellow men can meet with much
> success in politics.

A lawyer by training, Coolidge had been admitted to the bar in 1897, whereupon he opened a small practice in Northampton, Massachusetts. He handled just about anything that came across the trestle, but from the first, much of his practice was politically related or generated. Coolidge was elected to the city council as a Republican two years later, and there followed a series of other elective posts in the state that culminated with his election to the governorship. In all, Coolidge ran for political office nineteen times and held one appointive post, for positions ranging from city solicitor to president of the United States, and he won seventeen of these contests. He served continually in office, with minor breaks between moving from one to the other, from 1898 to 1929. Once asked whether he had any hobbies, Coolidge replied, "Yes. Running for office."

As Coolidge edged higher on the political ladder in Massachusetts, he made the proper contacts, won over the right sponsors, and learned swiftly and well the ways to please the powerful and retain the confidence of the electorate. He was an acclaimed politician, which is to say he was aware of the needs of constituents and of the consequences of his actions. Coolidge appealed not only to Republicans but also to voters who considered themselves Democrats. Three-quarters of a century before there were Reagan Democrats, there were Coolidge Democrats. His was hardly the record of a person who did not understand politics. One might easily argue that he was one of the most experienced and successful politicians ever to become president.

Coolidge was more loquacious than he is credited with being, and preferred short, simple, declarative sentences. A statistician with time on his hands once computed that Coolidge's sentences averaged 18 words, compared to Lincoln's 26.6, Wilson's 31.8, and Theodore Roosevelt's 41. This is a testament to Coolidge's ability to be concise.

Much (but certainly not all) of Coolidge's nonofficial prose is a pleasure to read. H.L. Mencken, who was scathing in his characterization of most politicians' writings, said of Coolidge, "He has a natural talent for the incomparable English language," which was high praise indeed from the author of *The American Language*. Yet Heywood Broun, who was not a Coolidge admirer, called his writings and use of the language "one hundred percent wooden," which was a common belief at the time. "He seems to me the least gifted author the White House has known in many generations."

How may one explain this sharp difference of opinion between two perceptive writers? One reason is that most presidents make so many speeches and do so much writing that one can find felicitous phrases amid dull stretches. After all, not all of Lincoln's state papers come up to the level of the Second Inaugural and the Gettysburg Address, and this holds true for Coolidge. Throughout this book are scores of Coolidge quotes, and the reader can decide for himself or herself. Take this one, for starters:

> No man was ever meanly born. About his cradle is the
> wondrous miracle of life. He may descend into the
> depths, he may live in infamy and perish miserably, but
> he is born great. Men build monuments above the graves
> of their heroes to mark the end of a great life, but
> women seek out the birthplace and build their shrine,

not where a great life had its end but where it had its
beginning, seeking with a truer instinct not the common
source of things in that which is gone forever but in that
which they know will again be manifest. Life may
depart, but the source of life is constant.

Coolidge isn't very attractive to a generation raised on the constant din of motion pictures, stereos, and especially radio and TV. To
them he must appear exotic, and a good deal of this can be ascribed
to his upbringing compared to that of today's Americans. He was
reared in an area barely reached by the railroad. His youth was relatively untouched by the "modern." His home didn't have indoor
plumbing, electricity, or a telephone. Yet Coolidge had intellectual
interests, and came alive in philosophy classes at Amherst. He was
an avid reader, and some of his speeches are peppered with classical
references. When he left for his honeymoon, he was in the midst of
translating Dante's *Inferno* into English. After his death his wife
wrote that he had a small, select library. Among his books were "his
Bible, the *Life and Letters of Charles E. Garman*, the Amherst professor whose influence upon his students was so marked, and
Paradise Lost in two paper-covered volumes. These two small books
he frequently carried with him when traveling." But he didn't care to
have this known. Those who think he was humorless will be surprised to learn that he was selected by his graduating class to deliver
the Grove Oration, which by tradition had to be amusing.

His was a style that takes some getting used to by today's public,
which hears empty promises from politicians, not straightforward
prose. Not only would Coolidge have nothing to do with negative
campaigning, but he refused even to utter the name of his opponents.
The thought of Coolidge philandering, keeping an enemies list, lying,
or flip-flopping on the issues would have amazed even his political
enemies. The sleaze that characterizes much of American political
life today, in both parties, was absent in his administration.
Whatever one thinks of Coolidge, the possibility that he would sell
access to the Lincoln bedroom or divert public funds for private uses,
two of the many stories that bedevil politicians today, would have
been dismissed out of hand. In 1920, when he was mentioned for the
presidential nomination, one reporter wrote of him, "You just have

confidence in Coolidge. He may not do what you want him to, he may not do what you think he ought to do, but you know he's done his best to do right."

Of all our presidents, Coolidge was the one who couldn't care less what we thought of him—while taking pains to make sure his reputation was safeguarded. He wasn't openly concerned much about the barbs thrown his way by intellectuals, who constantly belittled him. Once, an agitated Hoover asked whether he had seen influential columnist Frank Kent's article about him in the *American Mercury*. Coolidge replied, "You mean that one in the magazine with the green cover? I started to read it, but it was against me, so I didn't finish it."

Historian Robert Ferrell, one of the most astute president-observers of our time, remarked in 1996 that only three presidents in the twentieth century did not contract "Potomac Fever," which is to say, become so enamored of high office as to be willing to sacrifice a great deal to obtain it. These, said Ferrell, were Truman, Harding, and Coolidge. Whether Coolidge really belongs in this short roster will be left for the reader to decide.

Coolidge's reputation underwent a renaissance of sorts among conservatives and moderates with the Reagan presidency, due in no small measure to Reagan himself, who admired Coolidge. Allowing for differences in time, place, and style, their ideas are similar. Consider a typical Coolidge statement on economics, from his 1920 inaugural address, following his reelection as governor:

> The resources with which to meet taxation are dangerously near the point of exhaustion. There is a limit to the taxing power of a State beyond which increased rates produce decreased revenues. If that be exceeded intangible securities and other personal property become driven out of its jurisdiction, industry cannot meet its less burdened competitors, and no capital will be found for enlarging old or starting new enterprises. Such a condition means first stagnation, then decay and dissolution. There is before us a danger that our resources may be taxed out of existence and our prosperity destroyed.

Reagan spoke often of the need to return governmental functions to the states. So did Bush, and Clinton's welfare program did just that. Here are Coolidge's thoughts on the matter in 1926:

> While we ought to glory in the Union and remember that it is the source from which the States derive their chief title to fame, we must also recognize that the national administration is not and cannot be adjusted to the needs of local government. It is too far away to be informed of local needs, too inaccessible to be responsive to local needs.

When he arrived in the White House, Reagan strolled into the Cabinet Room, where he saw portraits of Truman, Jefferson, and Lincoln. Knowing something about his new boss, White House curator Clement Conger remarked, "If you don't like Mr. Truman, you can move Mr. Truman out." So he did. Reagan ordered the Truman portrait down, and in its place came one of Coolidge. "It's a new era," Conger murmured.

Even so, Reagan was no more a reincarnation of Coolidge than FDR was the second coming of Woodrow Wilson. The 1980s were so different from the 1920s, the problems the two men faced so disparate. In many ways, Coolidge was the last president of the nineteenth century. Reagan was the man who helped bring the twentieth century to its end with the conclusion of the Cold War.

Coolidge also was the last president who believed in a passive executive branch in times of peace and prosperity. Of those who occupied the White House in the twentieth century, Coolidge was the most Jeffersonian in philosophy and practice—a judgment those who admire Jefferson but have not delved deeply into his writings may find astonishing.

The following pages represent an attempt to introduce or reintroduce Coolidge to those to whom he is a cartoon caricature and figure of derision. Coolidge scholars will find some fresh interpretations in these pages but no major revelations. Coolidge destroyed his private papers, and scholars have pored over the public ones, to the point that what remains to be learned is the filling in of minor portions of the man and his times. This book is not based on original research. Moreover, I do not intend to present a complete picture of the Coolidge presidency, and certainly not that of his era. Rather, this book is about a man I have found to be extraordinary in his simplicity and notable in his complexity, which is to say, an unusual human being who merits serious consideration.

2

....

Growing Up

The town of Plymouth lies on the easterly slope of the Green
Mountains, about twenty miles west of the Connecticut River
and somewhat south of the central part of Vermont. This part
of the state is made up of a series of narrow valleys and high
hills, some of which rank as mountains that must reach an
elevation of at least twenty-five hundred feet.

The first paragraph in *The Autobiography of Calvin Coolidge*

MOST AMERICANS DURING the Coolidge era didn't know much
more about him when he left the White House in 1929 than they
did when he arrived there in 1923. Careful readers of the press could
learn about his youth, education, and legal career, how he rose in
politics, about his family, the workings of his presidency, and his
ideas as expressed in speeches and interviews. And at least a dozen
biographies of Coolidge—all of them idolatrous—were written
before and while he was in office. Virtually all Americans had heard
Coolidge jokes. The vast majority of Americans also knew they liked
him, and he was considered an able if not a great president. But they
weren't sure why and how they had come to this conclusion.
Coolidge, to put it simply, was puzzling—which was the way he
wanted it.

Many remarked on the enigmatic nature of our thirtieth president, who rose to the highest office in the land without the familiar
attributes of the successful politician. Writing of him at the time,

journalist Sherwin Cook, who called Coolidge one of the "two great enigmas of the first third of the twentieth century" (the other being the popularity of the play "Abie's Irish Rose"), commented:

> If before he had become prominent in the public eye,
> the portrait of a man with the attributes of Coolidge
> had been sketched to any political leader and that
> leader had been asked what such a man's availability
> was, the answer would have invariably been, "A
> political impossibility." Coolidge's unimpressive
> physique, his reticence, his lack of florid speech, his
> utter want of social attributes, his entire aloofness, are
> proverbial. How could such a man ever been elected to
> a municipal council?

Michael Hennessy, the dean of Boston journalists and a veteran "Coolidge watcher," came to a similar conclusion:

> He was not a back-slapping politician and was woefully
> deficient in most of the arts of the office seeker, but
> people liked him because he kept his word and was
> scrupulously honest. He inherited from his Vermont
> ancestors their characteristics of plain living and high
> thinking, thrift, taciturnity, and humor. He was not a
> brilliant man, was sparing of his words, and had a mind
> of his own.

Gamaliel Bradford, a prominent biographer of Coolidge's era, agreed, adding:

> The truth is, it was not in his temperament to enjoy
> glory or anything else. That temperament was the
> inherited, cumulative, aggravated temperament of New
> England, in which the sense of duty is the overriding
> force, and an uneasy conscience suggests that we are not
> in this world mainly to have a good time, or even to
> have a good time at all, but for some higher purpose.

Always there is that New England face, with all its
subtle implications, and the face seems peculiarly out of
keeping with merry-making or any of the riot of set
publicity, most of all with the ludicrously inappropriate
decorations which were resorted to in Coolidge's
Western surroundings. There is the garish cowboy rig,
and in the midst of it the chilly Vermont countenance,
wondering painfully and wearily what it was all about.
Those people were not working: why should anybody
want to do anything but work?

Certainly Coolidge's public performances—which is what they
were, performances—were geared to create this image. But there was
more than this to the man. He seemed aloof and even uncaring, but
in reality Coolidge could be quite emotional about some subjects.
Consider these words about the state in which he was born and raised:

Vermont is my birthright. Here one gets close to nature,
in the mountains, in the brooks, the waters of which
hurry to the sea; in the lakes, shining like silver in their
green setting; fields tilled, not by machinery, but by the
brain and hand of man. My folks are happy and
contented. They belong to themselves, live within their
incomes, and fear no man.

Vermont is a small state geographically and demographically.
The 1870 census indicated it had a population of slightly more
than 330,000, not much different from a quarter of a century earlier. The swelling ranks of immigrants to America—Irish and
German in the 1840s and 1850s, eastern and southern European
later in the century—barely touched the state. The tough and stub-
born men and women remained there to eke out hard livings. The
more easily discouraged and the more ambitious would stay a
while, and then move on. It was not unusual to find a village in
which practically all the inhabitants could trace their lineage there
prior to the American Revolution. Writing of the pre–Civil War
generation, Coolidge noted:

> They were some hardy self-contained people. Most of
> them are gone now and their old homesteads are
> reverting to the wilderness. They went forth to conquer
> where the trees were thicker, the fields larger, and the
> problems more difficult. I have seen their descendants
> scattered all over the country, especially in the middle
> west, and as far south as the Gulf of Mexico and
> westward to the Pacific slope.

Vermont was a rural state when Calvin Coolidge was growing up. The rocky soil and harsh winters dictated small, subsistence farms and working the maple forests for sugar and syrup. There were some important extractive industries, especially limestone, marble, and granite, and some iron and quartz.

Vermont was well forested, with maple, birch, and pines. Isolated from the transportation, communications, and industrial forces that were shaping other parts of the country after the Civil War, the state did not participate in the changes brought by iron, coal, and railroads, and even less by those wrought by petroleum and natural gas. Life was much slower in Montpelier, and certainly Plymouth Notch, than in Boston or New York. While there may have been drawbacks, there were also benefits. Or at least, so Coolidge believed toward the end of his life. Writing in 1932, he said:

> Experience was sufficiently meager so that it could be
> carefully considered and digested. Contemplation was
> possible. There was nothing to suggest to a boy that
> conditions would change violently. I never mistrusted
> that history was not all made, public questions about all
> decided, and the world—at least our part of it—was not
> destined to go on indefinitely as it was then going. Each
> year brought the same seasonal routine.

John Calvin Coolidge (who was named after his father but soon dropped the John) was born on July 4, 1872, in Plymouth Notch, which was in Plymouth township, a community on the eastern foothills of the Green Mountains. The Stage Road went through the township, and close by were the hamlets of Frog City, Tyson

Furnace, and Five Corners. Tyson Furnace was named after an iron foundry that had been there in a more prosperous and hopeful period. The nearest large town was Ludlow, some twelve miles away.

The Notch itself had only three public buildings—a school, a church, and a general store—and three dwellings. J.W. Stickney, a friend of the Coolidges, tried to present the township's qualities in a favorable light in 1887:

> In Plymouth there are no large villages; the population
> is widely scattered among its hills; the churches are
> too small to make trouble with one another and too
> weak to have troubles among themselves—which gives
> the town a quietude unknown to places of strong
> churches with large memberships. The absence of
> railroads, and of a foreign population consequent
> upon railroad towns, is escaped, and no real cause
> exists here for trouble.

This is not to say that Plymouth was completely isolated. The railroad ran to Ludlow, a two-hour drive in those days, and Notch dwellers could go from there to Boston and other major cities. Few did. One of those who made the trip, at least twice yearly, was John Coolidge, Calvin's father, a shopkeeper and farmer, who drove the family buggy to Ludlow to take the train to Boston, where he would arrange for shipments of supplies. Writing of him in the first chapter of his *Autobiography*, Coolidge said:

> My father, John Calvin Coolidge, ran the country store.
> He was successful. The annual rent of the whole place
> was $40. I have heard him say that his merchandise bills
> were about $10,000 yearly. He had no other expenses.
> His profits were about $100 per month on the average,
> so he must have sold on a very close margin.
>
> He trusted nearly everybody, but lost a surprisingly
> small amount. Sometimes people he had not seen for
> years would return and pay him the whole bill....
>
> He was a good businessman, a very hard worker, and
> he did not like to see things wasted.

John Coolidge must have earned a decent living, because he helped support his son into his thirties. When he died in 1926 he left an estate of $70,000, a sizable amount in those days. Interestingly, in the shortest of all presidential memoirs, Coolidge told again about his father's abhorrence of waste:

> My fundamental idea of both private and public
> business came first from my father. He had the strong
> New England trait of great repugnance at seeing
> anything wasted. He was a generous and charitable
> man, but he regarded waste as a moral wrong.

So would his son.

John Coolidge was much more than a shopkeeper and farmer, however. He served in a wide variety of public offices—constable, justice of the peace, tax collector, and pound keeper. In addition he was a member of both the state house of representatives and senate, serving in the latter body while his son was climbing the political ladder. He was commissioned a colonel on the staff of the governor of Vermont in 1900, and for the rest of his life was called "Colonel Coolidge." John Coolidge was also an insurance agent, dabbled in real estate, and wrote credit reports for R.G. Dun & Company. He was handy with tools and machines. John Coolidge was, in short, one of the most prominent people in the district, the prototypical big fish in a little pond. He was impressive physically, a powerfully built man with an impassive square face. "If there was any physical requirement of country life which he could not perform," wrote Coolidge, "I do not know what it was."

Calvin was close to his father, one of the few people to whom he opened his heart completely. To judge from the frequent letters they wrote each other over a period of more than forty years, Calvin held his father in deep respect, high esteem, and abiding love. As a boy and young man he strove to impress him by working long hours and succeeding in whatever he attempted. They would kiss whenever they met, even after Coolidge was president and dogged by reporters. His letters to his father while governor and president indicate how pleased Calvin was to have honored his father in such a way. John Coolidge rarely prodded Calvin on to new heights, but the son knew that they would please his father, and to do so was one of his chief goals in life. "I was exceedingly anxious to grow up to be like him," Coolidge wrote in his *Autobiography*. In an interview published soon after John Coolidge's death in March 1926, Coolidge said:

> My father had qualities that were greater than any I possess. He was a man of untiring industry and great tenacity of purpose.... He always stuck to the truth. It always seemed possible for him to form an unerring judgment of men and things. I cannot recall that I ever knew of his doing a wrong thing. He would be classed as decidedly a man of character.

The Coolidges had arrived in America in the early years of the Massachusetts Bay Colony. Calvin Coolidge's great-great-grand-father, John Coolidge, had come to Plymouth around 1780 with his young wife, the former Anne Priest of Marlboro, giving the family deep roots in the town. The Coolidges, of both Massachusetts and Vermont, were sturdy and stolid for the most part, and John Coolidge was a fine example of the breed. Most of them remained there, and several became important forces in industry, banking, and government. T. Jefferson Coolidge became president of the Old Colony Trust Company of Boston, was an early backer of the telegraph and later on the telephone, and was one of American Telephone & Telegraph's (AT&T) most important figures in the 1890s.

As close as Calvin was to his father, he was closer still to his mother, Victoria Moor Coolidge. "She was of a very light and fair complexion with a rich growth of brown hair that had a glint of gold in it," he wrote in his *Autobiography*. "Her hands and features were regular and finely molded. The older people always told me how beautiful she was in her youth." The Moor family had moved to the Notch in 1849, and Victoria attended the local schools and had a year in Black River Academy, a private school in Ludlow. Apparently she loved literature, and instilled this in her children.

Victoria Coolidge was an invalid when she bore Calvin and his younger sister, Abigail. She died in 1885, probably of consumption, at the age of thirty-nine, when Calvin was twelve years old. Recalling her almost half a century later, Coolidge wrote:

> Whatever was grand and beautiful in form and color
> attracted her. It seemed as though the rich green tints of
> the foliage and the blossoms of the flowers came for her in
> the springtime, and in the autumn it was for her that the
> mountain sides were struck with crimson and with gold.

"The greatest grief that can come to a boy came to me," he continued. "Life was never to seem the same again." When president, he drifted into a friendly relationship with Edmund Starling, who was a member of the Secret Service assigned to the White House. They would walk together often, and occasionally they would sit at night, smoking cigars, while Coolidge rambled on about his youth. Sometimes he reminisced about his mother. "I wish I could speak with her," he said one evening. "I wish that often." He carried a portrait of his mother wherever he went. It was on his dressing table every night. It was in his breast pocket when he died. But he never spoke of these matters in public.

The young boy was never quite the same after his mother died, one of several deaths that affected him while growing up. He had been a favorite of his grandfather, Calvin Galusha Coolidge, who died when the boy was six years old, and his paternal grandmother, Almeda, who helped raise the boy. He was particularly close to his sister, "Abbie," a plump, friendly, intelligent girl, who died in 1890, at age fifteen, when Calvin was eighteen.

None of this was unusual for the time and place. The life expectancy at birth at the time was forty years; among the leading causes of death were tuberculosis, influenza, and gastritis, and among women, birthing. In Vermont in the 1880s, tuberculosis accounted for 16 percent of all deaths. And Calvin did not inherit his father's robust physique, but rather he favored his mother's branch of the family—and quite a few Moors had died of tuberculosis.

Young Calvin Coolidge was small, slender, and delicate. The only thing close to flamboyant about him was his bright red hair, which contrasted with his pale, freckled skin. The frail boy seemed destined for a short life. Calvin often came down with colds, some of which would debilitate him for weeks, and he had asthma as well. Death stalked Calvin Coolidge then and later.

Calvin cared little for sports or other activities that interest boys, although he did like to ride horseback, usually by himself, and in the winter he would go sledding with friends. He was not mischievous or adventuresome, and was uncomfortable in large groups. Calvin did his chores about the store, tended the farm animals, helped with the plowing, and attended school when it was in session.

Calvin's favorite avocation was reading. In those early years he may have been shy, because friends later remarked how little he engaged in classroom discussions, how difficult it was to draw him out on any subject. His wife, Grace, wrote that he once told her, "I am as much interested in human beings as one could possibly be, but it is desperately hard for me to show it." To his closest friend, Frank Stearns, he later confided:

> When I was a little fellow, as long as I can remember, I would go into a panic if I heard strange voices in the house. I felt I just couldn't meet the people, and shake hands with them. Most of the visitors would sit with Mother and Father in the kitchen, and it was the hardest thing in the world to have to go through the kitchen door and give them a greeting. I was almost ten before I realized I couldn't go on that way. And by fighting hard I used to manage to get through that door. I'm all right with old friends, but every time I meet a stranger, I've got to go through the old kitchen door, back home, and it's not easy.

Even so, he had fond memories of his childhood, which he portrayed in almost bucolic terms:

> It would be hard to imagine better surroundings for the
> development of a boy than those which I had. While a
> wider breadth of training and knowledge could have
> been presented to me, there was a daily contact with
> many new ideas, and the mind was given sufficient
> opportunity to thoroughly digest all that came to it.
>
> Country life does not always have breadth, but it has
> depth. It is neither artificial nor superficial, but is kept
> close to the realities.

While much of this might have set young Calvin apart in some other places and other times, few of these qualities were remarkable for the rural Vermont of the 1880s. He was, in other words, a fairly ordinary boy, hardly one who seemed destined for an important role in history.

In elementary school Calvin performed well enough, but not outstandingly. "He was not an inquisitive boy. He seldom asked for an explanation of anything we had in hand," recalled one of his first teachers. "He seemed to understand every question that came up in class. He always seemed to be thinking of something." Another of his teachers, Carrie Brown, was to become John Coolidge's second wife. In a small town like Plymouth, such closeness was common.

At the age of fifteen, in 1887, Calvin was registered in Black River Academy in nearby Ludlow. The switch from local public school to a private boarding school was not unusual; quite a few Plymouth boys had preceded him there. The fees were $7 a term, and room and board were another $3 a week. Coolidge figured the total came to $150 a year, at a time when the average family income in America was approximately $360. John Coolidge could afford that amount. He drove Calvin there in the family buggy, along with a calf he was sending to Boston to be sold. Coolidge recalled the trip and his thoughts vividly in his *Autobiography*.

> My whole outfit went easily into two small handbags,
> which lay in the straw in the back of the traverse
> sleigh beside the fatted calf that was starting to
> market. The winter snow lay on the ground. The

weather was well below freezing. But in my eagerness these counted for nothing.

I was going where I would be mostly my own master. I was casting off what I thought was the drudgery of farm life, symbolized by the cowhide boots and every-day clothing which I was leaving behind, not realizing what a relief it would be to return to them in future years. I had on my best clothes and wore shoes with rubbers, because the village had sidewalks.

I did not know that there were mental and moral atmospheres more monotonous and more contaminating than anything in the physical atmosphere of country life. No one could have made me believe that I should never be so innocent or so happy again.

As we rounded the brow of the hill the first rays of the morning sun streamed over our backs and lighted up the glistening snow ahead. I was perfectly certain that I was traveling out of the darkness into the light.

According to one version of the story, the Coolidges said little as they rode to the academy. When they parted, the father said to the son, "Well, good-bye Cal. You may some day, if you work hard, get to Boston. But this calf's going to beat you there."

Ludlow was hardly a metropolis, but unlike Plymouth, it qualified as an urban location. Waterwheels on the Black River provided power for several red brick mills, of the type that can still be seen in New England towns, and which were the reason for Ludlow's existence. Yet it did not have electricity, a sewer system, or concrete sidewalks, nor would these appear for years after Coolidge left.

Calvin took a room east of the business district, a short distance from what was called B.R.A., then celebrating its fiftieth anniversary. The school itself occupied three rooms on the first floor of an erstwhile church, but had been taken over by the town for municipal purposes. In late 1888 B.R.A. moved to larger quarters in a new building. The curriculum included mathematics, English and American literature, American and world history, and—for those hoping to go on to college—Latin, Greek, and classical literature.

There were three terms a year, and students might attend any of them they selected, since the boys might be needed on the farms during the other two, and the girls could work as elementary school teachers during the spring term. The student body numbered 125 or so, and drew students from many parts of the area.

Coolidge did not do well that first year, probably because he had stiffer competition at B.R.A. than at Plymouth. In addition, his letters indicate homesickness, which was relieved in part when in 1888 Abbie joined him at the school. Now and then there would be a social, often held in the meeting room upstairs. Calvin attended, but he didn't dance or mix with the others. When he felt lonely, he would walk four miles to the home of an aunt and uncle, the Pollards, in Proctorsville. They had three sons with whom Calvin would socialize and then, on Sunday afternoon, after a large dinner, he would return to Ludlow. Other times he would travel to Plymouth, also on foot, and visit with his father. Occasionally he would work on Saturdays in a nearby toy factory.

> I worked there some on Saturdays, so I came to know
> how toys and baby wagons were made. It was my first
> acquaintance with the factory system, and my approach
> to it was that of a wage earner. As I was employed at
> piece work my wages depended on my own ability, skill,
> and industry. It was a good training. I was beginning to
> find out what existence meant.

This was Coolidge's first exposure to a small part of industrial America, and to industrial workers. It also was his last. Never again would he have direct contact of this sort with the new kind of nation that was emerging.

During this period, the nation's railroad network was remaking the face of American industry, and gasoline was supplementing the age of steam. Little of this touched Coolidge directly. He did not visit Boston until he was a college upperclassman. He didn't take his first automobile ride until 1904, when he was thirty-two years old. His driver recalled that Coolidge was quite shaken by the experience. "It's wonderful to ride in a horseless wagon," he told the driver. "But it won't amount to much." All his life, he remained a product of rural Vermont. "The chief industry of the town was a woolen mill, that always remained a mystery to me." So it was.

Later, when he became president, some of his classmates were asked about what he was like in this period. As might have been expected, all were quite positive about him, but from their answers it appears clear he was not a leader in sports or academics. Calvin had difficulties with mathematics and Greek, but excelled in Latin and history. In his *Autobiography* he gave special thanks to two of his teachers—George Sherman, who was also principal at the school, and Belle Challis—both of whom lived to see him enter the White House. In an uncharacteristically florid statement, he wrote:

> Under their guidance I beheld the marvels of old Babylon, I marched with the Ten Thousand of Xenophon, I witnessed the conflict around beleaguered Troy which doomed that proud city to pillage and flames. I heard the tramp of the invincible legions of Rome, I saw the victorious galleys of the Eternal City carrying destruction to the Carthaginian shore, and I listened to the lofty eloquence of Cicero and the matchless imagery of Homer. They gave me a vision of the world when it was young and it is almost impossible for those who have not traveled that road to reach a very clear conception of what the world now means.

Calvin discovered Cicero in his last year at B.R.A., and was entranced by his orations against Cataline. He read all he could by Cicero, and became fairly fluent in Latin as a result. In this period in which Calvin's political consciousness was being molded, Cicero—a political moderate who looked to law and reverence for tradition to preserve stability and liberty—was a profound influence. Calvin became known as an able speaker. Word of his accomplishments spread through the small school, and at the end of his junior term, he was selected to write and deliver the traditional farewell speech to the graduates.

Coolidge devoured the classics at B.R.A., but in time he turned to history and political science. Later, after Coolidge became president, John Coolidge was constantly badgered by reporters who wanted to know more about the enigma. "My boy was always shy and quiet-like and never put himself forward," John reminisced. "I thought the boy had the makings of a good doctor, but he told me he didn't care particularly; all he wanted was a good education." Afterward, in his junior year in college, Coolidge told a friend that he might return to Plymouth and become a storekeeper like his father, and spend his spare time reading. That is, he did not attend school to better himself socially or financially, although he was always aware that money could purchase security and freedom. But he was also too practical to be an intellectual who enjoyed simply playing with ideas.

The boys had to wear coats, ties, and stiff collars, but Calvin went overboard, wearing a derby, a starched dickey, and carrying a cane, perhaps in order to draw attention to himself. Not only did he become something of a fashion plate, but he also started a small business of selling mail order jewelry to his classmates.

Abbie died, apparently from appendicitis, in March of his senior year, less than three months from graduation. She had always been a healthy girl, and had been ill for only a week. Calvin was depressed, as he had been when his mother died. "It is lonesome here without Abbie," he wrote his father. Two years later, he wrote again about her, telling John Coolidge, "We must think of Abbie as we would of a happy day, counting it as a pleasure to have had it but not a sorrow because it could not last forever."

In the spring of 1890, Calvin graduated in a class of five boys and four girls. Part of the ceremony consisted of brief speeches by each graduate, and Calvin elected to talk on the subject of "Oratory in History," alluding to Peter the Hermit, Martin Luther, John Cobden, John Bright, James Otis, Patrick Henry, Daniel Webster, William Lloyd Garrison, and Wendell Phillips, as well as Cicero, indicating the breadth and depth of the education he had received at B.R.A.

The school did not have the privilege of certifying students for college, and by then Calvin had decided he wanted to apply to

Amherst College, largely because George Sherman had gone there and had urged Calvin to consider enrolling. In this period B.R.A. was a "feeder" school for Amherst. John Coolidge was quite willing to see his son attend the school. Now that Abbie was gone, he had only Calvin to pin his hopes on, and he wanted to do all he could to assure his son a good life. Besides, he had asked Carrie Brown to become his wife, and she had accepted. She was an attractive, intelligent, and warm woman, who in addition to having been a teacher had also clerked in the store John once owned. Calvin instantly took to Carrie. And while she did not take Victoria's place in his affections, the two became very close.

In the autumn of 1890, Calvin traveled to Northampton, Massachusetts, to take the entrance examination for Amherst. He had a cold which got progressively worse as the day of the test approached, and it may have affected his performance. In any event, he could not complete the examination, and returned home, where the illness persisted into early winter.

At Sherman's suggestion, he entered St. Johnsbury Academy, a leading preparatory school some ninety miles from Plymouth. After two months there the headmaster was willing to certify that he merited admission to Amherst—which in those years sufficed. So on September 17, 1891, little more than a week after his father remarried, Calvin entered Amherst.

At the time, Amherst was a small, well-regarded school, drawing most of its students from the region. The enrollment was 336, of which 259 were from New England and New York, and almost all were sons of professionals or businessmen. In this period few expected to attend any institution of higher learning. In 1890 only 16,700 of 63 million Americans were awarded bachelors' degrees.

The college was a respected institution, but hardly an academic powerhouse. Rather, it concentrated on teaching in small classes. The student–faculty ratio in those days was ten to one, which meant the students not only knew their teachers well, but more important, received individual attention.

The nature of academia was changing in the 1890s. Though Amherst was more immune to the changes occurring than were the major universities, the school Calvin Coolidge entered was somewhat different from the one George Sherman had graduated from ten years earlier. In Sherman's time most graduates became teachers or ministers; by 1890, many more aspired to be lawyers or businessmen. Among the major alterations taking place in American higher education was the curriculum. While the classics still held sway in the 1890s, philosophy, Latin, and Greek—the hallmarks of an educated man—were being replaced by the social sciences. Even at Amherst, students were starting to go to schools in order to make "contacts." When Sherman attended, about half the students belonged to fraternities; by 1890 the figure was closer to 80 percent.

Rather than take a room in the ramshackle dormitories, Coolidge moved into a rooming house not far from the school. He intended to remain there until he was pledged by one of the fraternities, after which he could live there. Since there were nine fraternities for the small student body, it would be difficult not to be rushed. But Coolidge was passed over, and the disappointment showed. "I don't seem to get acquainted fast," he wrote to his father in October, and, as had been the case at Black River Academy, he soon became homesick. "A drabber, more colorless boy I never knew than Calvin Coolidge when he came to Amherst," wrote one of his fellow students to Coolidge biographer Claude Fuess. "He was a perfect enigma to us all. He attended class regularly, but did not show any great interest."

There really was no mystery to this behavior. Coolidge, shy, withdrawn, awkward, and insecure, didn't know how to meet or talk with girls. He couldn't dance or make small talk. He certainly didn't know how to flirt. If he had a girlfriend or if any of the girls at nearby Smith, Mount Holyoke, or some other school were the objects of his affections, we don't know of it. He didn't drink in his freshman year, and seldom smoked. And he was a grind, at a time when this was neither admired nor emulated.

That first year came and went, and Coolidge returned home for the summer to help with the work around the farm and house. The sophomore year was more of the same. Coolidge derived satisfaction from his courses, especially those dealing with the classics, and his grades were good if not outstanding. He was getting the education he wanted, but not much more.

Things seemed to take a turn for the better in the spring of 1892. A chapter of Phi Gamma Delta, a large national fraternity, was going to be established at Amherst, and two of the founders invited Coolidge to join. Coolidge was customarily cautious. "I don't know but I would," was his reply. But nothing happened because the founders didn't follow up. He finally received a firm invitation in his last year at Amherst. This he accepted quite willingly, perhaps the natural reaction of a reticent young man eager to become part of a larger group. But Coolidge didn't move into the fraternity house; he remained a boarder for the remainder of his college career.

Coolidge was never a joiner. Even though it would have been useful politically and professionally, as an adult he never became a Mason, an Elk, a Red Man, an Odd Fellow, or a member of any other fraternal organization. Though he was always a religious person and a nominal Congregationalist, he was not a regular churchgoer either. For his entire life he was a strong, even passionate, believer in individualism. When asked to identify himself, he usually said he was a Republican, and a regular one at that. This was the extent of his willingness to submerge his identity into a large organization.

Those who consider the later Coolidge a somber, inarticulate president will be surprised that during his college years he became known on campus as a public speaker. After being one of the losers in a traditional footrace, he was obliged to deliver a short speech and contribute toward an oyster stew and beer dinner for the winners. Coolidge's speech was a success, and he was on his way toward distinction as a wit and speaker. Encouraged, he participated in debates, and in his junior year he was the cowinner of the J. Wesley Ladd prize for the best oration. Now his letters home were peppered with enthusiasm regarding his victories in debates. In 1894 he wrote:

> I had a debate yesterday as to whether a presidential or
> parliamentary form of government is the better. I had
> the parliamentary side, which is not particularly popular
> inasmuch as it is really to show England's form of

government is better than our own, and I spoke against
Pratt of Brooklyn, who is a very good debater, being
captain of our football team. But the parliamentary side
won by a large majority when the question was decided.

Coolidge was at Amherst during one of the nation's most severe
depressions. The year after he entered the college the long, violent
Homestead strike took place, during which the manager of the
works, Henry Clay Frick, barely escaped assassination. In his
junior year, there was a major financial panic on Wall Street, various bank closings, and the heating up of the drive for a bimetallic
currency. When Coolidge was a junior, in 1894—the year of the
historic Pullman Strike in Chicago—more than 750,000 workers
went on strike. The year he graduated, the United States government had to be bailed out by J.P. Morgan, who narrowly saved
the nation's credit.

Surely Coolidge must have thought about these issues, but his
letters and future writings offer no hint of it. He was against
bimetallism, but what of his other convictions while a student?
True, Coolidge was a charter member of the Amherst Republican
Club, but this was not surprising; almost all Amherst students
were Republicans. This had also been the case at B.R.A., where
seventy students supported the Republican Benjamin Harrison
against nineteen for Democrat Grover Cleveland in the 1892 presidential election.

The isolation of western Massachusetts from the developing
industrial economy of the period helps explain Coolidge's silence on
the great issues of the time. Chicago and Pittsburgh had their
strikes, but not Plymouth or Northampton. The depression of the
1890s reached these places, but not with the impact it had in the
industrial and commercial cities. Wall Street, too, seemed quite a
distance from Amherst, especially since at the time only the wealthy
had bonds and only speculators played with stocks, which excluded
the parents of Amherst students.

Coolidge's grades at Amherst during his first three years were
good although not outstanding, but this too was about to change.
By then he had developed a liking for modern languages, especially

French and Italian, and for modern history, political science, and philosophy. In his senior year he placed among the Hyde Fifteen, the top orators in his class, and an intercollegiate jury awarded him the gold medal for his essay on the American Revolution.

In Coolidge's junior and senior years he took courses with two of Amherst's most popular teachers, Anson Daniel Morse and Charles Garman, who affected him profoundly. Recalling these teachers, Coolidge later wrote:

> As I look back upon the college I am more and more impressed with the strength of its faculty, with their power for good. Perhaps it has men now with a broader preliminary training, though they then were profound scholars, perhaps it has men of keener intellects, though they then were very exact in their reasoning, but the great distinguishing mark of all of them were that they were men of character. Their words carried conviction because we were compelled to believe in the men who uttered them. They had the power not merely to advise but literally to instruct their students.

Morse, who taught history, was a specialist on the subject of political parties, which to him "were by far the most important of the agencies through which the crude first thoughts and blind first feelings of the people are transformed into rational thinking and feeling, which is public opinion." Morse hewed to the traditional Whig interpretation of history as a steady march of progress and expansion of liberty, from barbarism to civilization. "The whole course was a thesis on good citizenship and good government," Coolidge wrote in his *Autobiography*. "Those who took it came to a clearer comprehension not only of their rights and liberties but of their duties and responsibilities."

While Morse's influence on Coolidge's development was important, that of Garman was even more profound. This was so not only for Coolidge, but also for generations of Amherst students. Garman was one of those rare teachers capable of encouraging students to think independently, while through force of intellect and personality at the same time able to inspire them to accept his philosophy of life and religious ideals. To his students, Garman was a prophet and guide. He had such a profound influence on Coolidge that it is impossible to understand the sources of Coolidge's philosophy without referring to Garman.

Garman was the son of a Congregationalist minister, and he took his Christianity seriously, if not literally—for a while he was enrolled at Yale Divinity School. Garman attended Amherst and returned to his alma mater after serving for a while at other schools. He was named to the Amherst faculty in 1882, when he was thirty-two years old, and was in his prime when Coolidge was a student. At different times he taught mathematics, natural sciences, and philosophy, which in that period encompassed psychology as well, but his most famous course was an eclectic combination of philosophy and religion, which appeared to have been derived from American transcendental thinkers.

Garman was unique in that he had a national reputation for his work in the classroom, and not his research and publications. "We looked upon Garman as a man who walked with God," Coolidge wrote. Fellow student Dwight Morrow, who was to carve out a career as a banker and diplomat, and was considered a star student, wrote to Garman in 1894, "I don't believe, Professor, that you can fully appreciate what a strong hold you have on Amherst today. It isn't only with the senior class with whom you come into contact. Underclassmen go to the seniors for advice continually because they know the seniors have something which they have not." Another student, Charles Burnett, wrote that "Garman made us feel the tremendous importance of philosophy; and we became docile learners. A recalcitrant among his students was a rarity, and any opposition seemed outrageous." To which Coolidge could add, "It has always seemed to me that all our other studies were in the nature of a preparation for the course in philosophy." From this it might seem Garman created acolytes, but this wasn't so. Many students testified to his unwillingness to come to conclusions, to accept nothing on authority, and to be skeptical—even of himself.

Coolidge spoke and wrote of Garman on many occasions, but usually in generalities.

Ever since I was in Amherst College I have remembered how Garman told his class in philosophy that if they would go along with events and have the courage and industry to hold to the main stream, without being washed ashore by the immaterial cross currents, they would some day be men of power. He meant that we should try to guide ourselves by general principles and not get lost in particulars. That may sound like mysticism, but it is only the mysticism that envelopes every great truth. One of the greatest mysteries in the world is the success that lies in conscientious work.

On one occasion, however, Coolidge was more specific about what he had taken away from those philosophy classes, quoting his teacher at length:

Our late Dr. Garman recognized this limitation in one of his lectures, where he says: "Critics have noticed three stages in the development of human civilization. First: the let-alone policy; every man to look out for number one. This is the age of selfishness. Second: the opposite pole of thinking; every man to do somebody else's work for him. This is the dry rot of sentimentality that feeds tramps and elect laws that excite the indignation of Herbert Spencer. But the third stage is represented by our formula: every man must render and receive the best possible service, except in the case of inequality, and there the strong must help the weak to help themselves; only on this condition is help given. This is the true interpretation of the life of Christ. On the first basis He would have remained in heaven and let the earth take care of itself. On the second basis He would have come to earth with His hands full of gold and silver treasures satisfying every want that unfortunate humanity could have devised. But on the third basis He comes to earth in the form of a servant who is at the same time a master commanding His disciples to take up their cross and

follow Him; it is sovereignty through service as opposed
to slavery through service. He refuses to make the world
wealthy, but He offers to help them make themselves
wealthy with the true riches which shall be a hundred-
fold more, even in this life, than that which was offered
them by any former system."

Such thoughts would inform Coolidge's actions as politician.
Perhaps he would have come to these conclusions without Garman,
for these kinds of ideas were in the air at the time. Andrew Carnegie
said as much when he said he opposed charity and supported phil-
anthropy, as did many more leading figures. As it happened,
Coolidge obtained his strong belief in service to humanity and in
the barrenness of materialism via Garman.

Garman used no textbook, but rather wrote essays on the subjects
he covered in class, ran them off on his own printing press, and distributed them to students, with the proviso they be returned. He did
not publish any of them, although some were collected and privately
printed by his wife after his death. Garman utilized the Socratic
method in his teaching. And he might be considered a Hegelian, in
that he viewed history as a struggle between opposing forces out of
which mankind and the individual achieve progress. In his teaching he
liked to set up ideas and then demolish them, confusing his students
but at the same time forcing them to think. Among his favorite sayings
were: "Carry all questions back to fundamental principles," "The
question how answers the question what," "Weight the evidence,"
and "Define your terms." According to his students, he was skilled in
nudging students into debates, which he refereed. Sometimes the students would continue their discussions long after the class was over,
even well into the night. In a letter to a student, he wrote:

Each man must solve his own problems if he is to perfect
himself. Others can only furnish the appropriate
conditions for him to work in. Now that at once makes
the unit of our thought not the race but the individual. It
requires eternity for the individual to work out his own
perfection.... The individual is the only conceivable unit
of thought.

In other words, Garman believed everyone had to work out his own destiny, and could not permit others to think for or control his life or thoughts. He emphasized the importance of work, and the doctrine of service to one's fellow man. Beyond that, Garman stressed spirituality. One historian of Amherst wrote of him, "Every student, he believed, must some time make a choice between a spiritual and a material world. That was the critical point in his life."

There were strains of this in Coolidge's statements and actions after he left Amherst, but there was also a shrewd political sense that could not have derived from a man like Garman. Like many of Garman's students, while he idolized the man and teacher, he was not an acolyte of the philosophy, but rather of his methodology and religious impulses. In the end, he came away affected by Garman's personal convictions, which included stress on character and honesty, progress, and a belief in Christian ideals. These thoughts would appear in many of his state papers while governor and president. Of Garman, Coolidge wrote:

> His course was a demonstration of the existence of a
> personal God, of our power to know Him, of the Divine
> immanence, and of the complete dependence of the
> universe on Him as the Creator and Father "in which we
> live and move and have our being." Every reaction in
> the universe is a manifestation of His Presence.

He added, "To Garman was given a power which took his class up into the high mountain of spiritual life and left them alone with God. What he revealed to us of the nature of God and man will stand. Against it 'the gates of hell shall not prevail.'"

Coolidge did well in that last year at Amherst. While hardly a leader or celebrity, at least he was recognized as intelligent, humorous, and of "sound judgment." He had honed his convictions, in part through contact with Garman and Morse, but, more than he might have known, from Plymouth Notch and his family. Amherst merely annealed what already was there and enabled Coolidge to mature, to recognize his innate qualities. No longer did he talk and write about returning to Plymouth to work on the farm or in the store. In January 1895 he wrote to his father about a change in plans: "I have not decided what I shall do next year, shall probably go into the store or go to law school at Boston or New York." Coolidge was offering his father a way out. Law school would be expensive; if John Coolidge didn't want to pay for professional school, his son would be willing to return to Plymouth Notch. But he knew his father well. John Coolidge wasn't going to permit his only surviving child to wither away in a store.

Even so, the expense was worth considering. In this period one could become a lawyer by entering a law firm as an unpaid clerk, reading for the law, and then taking the bar examination. This was completely respectable, the way Abraham Lincoln had become a lawyer. But by the 1890s, given the professionalization of law, those taking this route could not hope for an exalted position in a major city. Still, if Coolidge intended to practice in Plymouth or some similar place, reading law was an inexpensive way of entering the profession.

At first, Coolidge rejected this notion. He had been spoiled by contacts with Garman and Morse and yearned for the stimulation afforded by contact with superior intellects. This emerges in his letter to John Coolidge of June 19, and also in the cagey way he seemed to be advocating law school:

> I am surprised that the lawyers do not know more about law schools. Of course if they do not know they are not in a position to judge. No doubt most of them are biased by their personal experience. But as a matter of fact the best law offices will not take in a man to do office work, such as the ordinary student does in the country office, unless he had been to a law school.

Coolidge had decided to compete for selection as Grove Orator, the graduate selected to deliver a humorous speech at graduation with many references to students and faculty, complete with heckling, and won by a vote of 52 to 18. Now he would be one of the six men to speak at the Class Day celebration, clearly indicating that he had overcome the obscurity of his freshman year.

John and Carrie Coolidge traveled to Amherst for the graduation ceremonies that spring, and they heard the Grove Oration, which was a big success. Coolidge delivered it with a straight face and a monotone, which brought howls of laughter from his fellow students. Writing of this in his *Autobiography*, Coolidge took care to note that "While my effort was not without some success, I very soon learned that making fun of people in a public way was not a good method to secure friends, or likely to lead to much advancement, and I have scrupulously avoided it."

Even so, the Grove Oration marked a high point in Coolidge's college career, and it would have an important impact on his future as well. In the audience were many Amherst graduates, some with local distinction. Henry P. Field was one of these, and he was quite impressed with the speech.

Coolidge graduated *cum laude*, missing Phi Beta Kappa by a hair. Dwight Morrow was named by his fellow students the member of the class most likely to become famous, and later Morrow claimed he had voted for Coolidge—but this seems unlikely. Jay Stocking, another class leader, offered this assessment of the Calvin Coolidge of 1895:

> I was not one of those who expected Coolidge to have
> any spectacular career. I did not think he would become
> famous. The last place in the world I should have
> expected him to succeed was politics. He lacked small
> talk, and he was never known, I suspect, to slap a man
> on the back. He rarely laughed. He was anything but a
> mixer. The few who got in personal contact with him
> had to go the whole way.

Stocking couldn't fathom that the wonder of Coolidge was that he accomplished all he did without the usual trappings of politicians. He meant to be accepted on his own terms, and so he was.

At that graduation were several young men destined for success. In addition to Morrow, there was Herbert Pratt, who became president of Standard Oil of New Jersey; George Olds, future president of Amherst; and Harlan Stone, the future attorney general and Supreme Court justice—named to both posts by President Coolidge. Coolidge could not have hoped to achieve such distinction. He might have had the making of a successful country attorney, drawing up wills, handling some estates, poring over real estate transactions, and, perhaps, serving as a selectman, or even going to Boston as a member of the legislature. But more?

After the ceremony was over, Coolidge and Morrow went for a last walk together and talked of their futures. By then both had decided on the law. Morrow said he thought he would go to Pittsburgh or some other city with a large law school. As it turned out, he clerked in a Pittsburgh law firm for a year before enrolling in Columbia Law School. Coolidge said this was not for him—no Coolidge had ever gone west. "Well, where do you think you *will* go?" asked Morrow. Coolidge paused, and then replied, "Northampton is the nearest court house."

Characteristically, Coolidge didn't let on to the extent of his ambitions. On August 30, shortly after he graduated, Coolidge wrote to former Vermont Governor William P. Dillingham, who was one of the major reform politicians of the region, and was then practicing law in Montpelier, asking whether there might be an opening in his office. Dillingham was out of town and couldn't respond, so Coolidge had to find another place to read the law. Had Dillingham responded promptly, Coolidge might have wound up as a fine lawyer or politician in Vermont, and given his proclivities, might even have become governor. But he wouldn't have been in Boston in 1919, a watershed in his life.

One of his classmates, Ernest Hardy, had found a slot at the law firm of Richard Irwin in Northampton, and he knew the partners at the offices of John C. Hammond and Henry P. Field, both Amherst graduates—and, of course, Field had heard the Grove Oration. They offered Coolidge the opportunity to read law with them, and he accepted. Hammond, the senior partner, had the reputation of being the best lawyer in town, while Field, whom Coolidge later characterized as "a man of engaging personality and polish," dabbled in politics and was then an alderman.

Hammond & Field handled wills and estates, real estate transfers, and minor suits. Whenever possible they tried to settle disputes out of court; reputations for fairness and evenhandedness, not for being litigious, counted in 1895 Northampton. This was in the tradition of none less than Abraham Lincoln, who said, "Persuade your neighbors to compromise whenever you can. Point out to them how the nominal winner is often a real loser—in fees, expenses, and waste of time. As a peacemaker the lawyer has a superior opportunity of being a good man. There will still be business enough." Court appearances in advocacy roles were for "big city lawyers," not the Hammonds and Fields.

This suited Coolidge's personality. He felt uncomfortable making a case for a client to the exclusion of contrary evidence. He had a judicial rather than lawyerly temperament. In his *Autobiography*, he wrote approvingly of Stephen S. Taft, a Springfield attorney who was "the best lawyer I ever saw," because "if he was trying a case before a jury he was always the thirteenth juryman, and if a trial was before the court he was always advising the judge." Coolidge added, "But he did not win these cases." Paraphrasing Lincoln, Taft told Coolidge, "Young man, when you can settle a case within reason you settle it. You will not make so large a fee out of some one case in that way, but at the end of the year you will have more money and your clients will be much better satisfied."

Coolidge's future was to be in Massachusetts, not Vermont. Not that Northampton was so different from Plymouth. Northampton was closer geographically and culturally to Vermont than it was to Boston.

Why did Hammond and Field offer Coolidge the spot? Many years later, when Coolidge was president, Field told a writer, "I liked to laugh and Calvin Coolidge was very funny."

3

....

Law and Politics

[W. Murray Crane] confirmed my opinion as to the value of a silence which avoids creating a situation where one would otherwise not exist, and the bad taste and the danger of arousing animosities and advertising an opponent by making an attack upon him. In all political affairs he had a wonderful wisdom, and in everything he was preeminently a man of judgment, who was the most disinterested public servant I ever saw and the greatest influence for good government with which I ever came in contact. What would I not have given to have had him by my side when I was president!

The Autobiography of Calvin Coolidge

WHILE HARDLY A METROPOLIS, Northampton was larger than Amherst or Ludlow. In 1895 the city, with a population of 15,000, was the commercial center for the region, to which farmers and inhabitants of smaller places went for supplies and entertainment. Like Amherst, it was a college town, and held Smith, Mount Holyoke, and several smaller schools, including the Clarke Institute for the Deaf; education was an important "industry" there.

Northampton was the kind of place where an ambitious, able lawyer could do well for himself in a modest sort of way, and given interest and ability, expect a fairly decent political career, winding up as, say, a judge. This was probably in the back of Coolidge's mind. Henry Field had that kind of life, becoming a judge in 1919. Field was interested in local politics, and he urged Coolidge to "get involved." Coolidge had every intention of doing so. He was diligent, trustworthy, and intelligent, qualities Field noticed even while he must have been disappointed when Coolidge didn't deliver on the anticipated rib-cracking humor. In referring to Coolidge, he once remarked to Hammond, "I guess we've added the Sphinx to our staff." Yet Field was attracted to Coolidge, as some of his teachers had been. Coolidge had several mentors, and Field was next in line after Garman and before Winthrop Murray Crane. From Field he learned about local politics, and the need to service constituents, as well as how to become a successful small-town lawyer and politician.

Coolidge read law at Hammond & Field for a little more than a year and a half. In this period he impressed everyone with the way he prepared for all contingencies. In his *Autobiography*, Coolidge said that one of the first things he did was "to divest myself of the college fashion of long hair." He was at the office at 8:00 AM and left at 6:00 PM. He read *Kent's Commentaries*, prepared writs, deeds, and wills, and did whatever Hammond and Field bid him do.

> My evenings I gave to some of the masters of English composition. I read the speeches of Lord Erskine, of Webster, and Choate. The essays of Macauley interested me much, and the writings of Carlyle and John Fiske I found very stimulating. Some of the orations of Cicero I translated, being especially attached to the defense of his friend the poet Archias, because in it he dwelt on the value and consolation of good literature. I read much in Milton and Shakespeare, and found delight in the shorter poems of Kipling, Field, and Riley.

Those who recalled Coolidge's apprenticeship thought that he was dependable and sound, but they didn't use words like "brilliant" or "imaginative" to describe him. One of his earliest admiring biographers wrote of the beginning of his public career:

> Two qualities, not extraordinary in themselves but powerfully effective when maintained consistently, explain

much of Mr. Coolidge's success in politics. They are the
quality of cold judgment and the quality of doing the work
immediately at hand. Neither of these is a magic attribute
of character; each can be developed by almost any person.
He began their development young, and he persevered.

Although he was as reserved as ever, he did make some friends,
among them Jim Lucey, an Irish-born shoemaker whom he first met
while a student at Amherst. When he felt the need for recreation
and company, Coolidge would stroll to the shoemaker's shop, take
a seat, and listen to the stories Lucey and his cronies would relate.
He would do the same in a local barbershop, and occasionally, he
would go to a nearby beer garden for a solitary draft. He purchased
cigars at a local drug store, and sat quietly there, taking a few puffs
before going to the office or home. Coolidge also became friendly
with Dick Irwin, a prominent Northampton lawyer who had served
in the state senate. He had other friends and acquaintances in var-
ied walks of life, Democrats as well as Republicans, Catholics as well
as Protestants, at a time when such differentiation mattered.
Coolidge even joined a local canoe club, and on balmy Sundays went
out on the lake. He seemed to have had no romantic attachments
while at Hammond & Field, probably because as disciplined a person as he would have realized he could not afford to get married,
and mere dating might have seemed frivolous.

On June 29, 1897, with Field as his sponsor, Coolidge applied
for admission to the bar. He was a few days short of his twenty-
fifth birthday, and he was prepared to go into the world and make
a living for himself. While he had made a favorable impression at
Hammond & Field, it was understood from the first he would not
join them. Small-town practices did not encourage expansion.

Coolidge intended to open an office of his own, and do the best he
could, patterning himself after Field. "I fully expected to become
the kind of country lawyer I saw around me, spending my life in the
profession, with perhaps a final place on the bench." These words
were written, of course, after Coolidge left the White House. At the
time, however, he was not as sanguine. In a letter to his father on
July 12, he expressed his trepidations about his prospects:

> I do not know as there is a "good opening" for a young
> lawyer anywhere. I knew of one once but in a few
> months the young lawyer was requested to get out of
> town. There is nothing here but a general law practice.
> No partner. I estimated for you the cost of fitting up an
> office. I judge I could live on a total expense of about
> $500 a year. I have been obliged to live for two years in
> entire seclusion. I do not judge that would be a wise
> course for a lawyer whatever it might be for a student—I
> presume one gets business by "getting in" with people,
> by associating with them in their clubs and in various
> walks of life and social organizations.

Apparently, in an earlier letter, John Coolidge had suggested that
his son might try to get a job in an office doing clerical work, perhaps at Hammond & Field, a prospect that must have been crushing.

> A man well trained in a law school might be of some use
> in an office. At present I am still trying to learn a little
> law. It is hardly possible that I could stay in this office
> and make such "business acquaintances" that I could
> leave the office and draw away its practice with me....
> Your plan of my being an office boy does not appeal
> to me. Still I have tried to do the best I could by my
> feeble efforts to carry out other plans which did not
> appeal to me very strongly and if I have sometimes
> faltered, if I have failed to meet with the success you
> desired, forgive me—I think I tried my best. And now if
> you are of the opinion that I have the making of a good
> office boy in me it is my pleasure to try to perform such
> duties to the best of my ability.

More can be learned about Coolidge's thoughts, fears, hopes, and
dreams from these letters than from any of his public utterances.
He was completely at ease with John Coolidge, as with no other person he would ever know.

For a while Coolidge considered relocating to Great Barrington, some fifty miles to the northeast of Northampton, and he toyed with the idea of going to Boston. He seriously considered Lee, Massachusetts, which was near Pittsfield and had a population of four thousand. Pittsfield itself had a population of twenty thousand, and there weren't many lawyers there. There was no indication he ever intended to return to Plymouth, or any other place in Vermont. Coolidge was wedded to Massachusetts. In the end, on February 1, 1898, he hung up his shingle in Northampton.

By then Coolidge had become more active in politics than in the law, perhaps because he felt that his prospects in private practice were dismal, or that he could get the right "contacts" in politics to benefit his law practice, a thought not unusual then. The 1896 national election campaign began while he was still at Hammond & Field. The Republican convention in St. Louis selected William McKinley for the presidency. The Democrats, in a wild convention in Chicago, nominated the young, charismatic William Jennings Bryan as their candidate, and the Populists chose Bryan shortly thereafter. This was an election with important policies at stake, the first since the Civil War in which there was a clear and distinct demarcation between the candidates.

Paramount among these was the currency issue. McKinley was for the gold standard and Bryan for bimetallism, the free and unlimited coinage of silver. The distinction was presented and viewed as the creditor versus the debtor, industrial America versus agrarians, but of course it was more complicated than that. More than three decades after the end of the Civil War, Americans throughout the nation still voted with their hearts on that conflict, and there were local considerations as well.

There was no doubt where Vermont and Massachusetts stood on the issues or the election; the states were solidly Republican. Coolidge was already active in party affairs in a small way. The previous year Henry Field had accepted the local party's nomination for the mayoralty of Northampton, while Hammond ran for district attorney. These were not onerous or even full-time positions; Field and Hammond would continue their practice no matter the outcomes. Coolidge participated in the campaign. He attended the state Republican convention as an alternate, and returned home to work for McKinley. Coolidge attended local Republican meetings, and volunteered to do whatever he could to assist Field. Not that this was needed; while Democrats occasionally won the office, they did so more on personal contacts than ideology. In any case, Field wasn't seriously challenged. Coolidge handed out flyers, and he spoke with his friends at Jim Lucey's and other places about Field's qualities and character.

Not only was Northampton solidly Republican, but the town was also—outside of the Smith College faculty and some students—strongly for the gold standard. Making the best of a bad situation, Democrat John O'Donnell, a popular figure and a former Northampton mayor, published a defense of Bryan and free silver in the local Democratic newspaper. At Field's suggestion, Coolidge wrote a reply that was published in the Republican newspaper. Although it was hardly a keen analysis of the money question, the article did demonstrate the skills he had honed as a debater. It was uncharacteristically sarcastic, and out of keeping with the kind of image Coolidge would later adopt.

> And finally we come to that most specious device of the advocate. All discussion of the merits of free silver is dropped, and we are asked to content ourselves with reading testimony to the character of its prime agitator. His private virtues are so attractive! And what are they? Merely a few conventional decencies which all the funeral orations since the memory of man have claimed as the attributes of each departed spirit. William J. Bryan is accused of financial heresy and we are told that his morals are orthodox. He is censured for an attempt to debauch the monetary system of America and the defense is "a personal character as pure as a woman." He is charged with desiring to pollute the sacred shrine of the public credit, and we are calmly informed that he says his prayers every night.

After 1896 Coolidge never again denigrated his opponents in political races, and in most races he didn't even mention his opponent by name. As chairman of the Northampton Republican Committee, he wrote of an unsuccessful campaign in 1904 he helped manage: "We made the mistake of talking too much about the deficiencies of our opponents and not enough about the merits of our own candidate. I have never again fallen into that error."

Coolidge was as good as his word. He was gracious in victory, and went out of his way to make certain the losers in those campaigns in which he was involved knew he bore them no enmity.

In addition to campaigning locally for McKinley, Coolidge traveled to Plymouth Notch to visit his father, and while there delivered an address supporting the candidate. If other political appearances were made in Northampton, we have no record of them. Coolidge was still a neophyte. Attention was afforded him, but not much.

The Bryan nomination and the money issue divided the Democratic Party badly, and many Democrats voted Republican. McKinley defeated Bryan in Massachusetts by a margin of more than two to one, while incumbent GOP Governor Roger Wolcott, who had succeeded on the death of Governor Frederic Greenhalge only eight months before the election, won over his Democratic opponent by a vote of 260,000 to 104,000. Since Field won handily in Northampton, Coolidge started his political career with a winner.

In 1897 Coolidge received his first political "reward," being selected as a member of the Republican City Committee for Ward Two. The following year he served as delegate from Ward Two to the Republican State Convention.

In December 1898 Coolidge won his first election. The position was modest: he was to be one of the three councilmen for Ward Two. Coolidge came in second out of six candidates in the race for the two seats, receiving 207 votes. As expected, all three of the top finishers were Republicans, the bottom three, Democrats. Quite simply, Coolidge won because of his party designation, not because he had entranced the electorate. Almost immediately, he demonstrated political acumen. An Irish–American Democrat had died, and Coolidge introduced a motion to honor his memory. Already thought of favorably by Irish–Americans in the city as a result of hanging around barbershops and the shoemaker's shop, he was now solidifying his support with the political opposition. It was one of earliest instances in his long political career in which Calvin Coolidge used his political astuteness to achieve results—avoiding the glad-handing that politicians normally employ.

On many occasions in the coming years he observed that anytime a Democrat voted for him, the vote counted as two—one less for his opponent, one more for him. Certainly, Coolidge was not nonpartisan, but he did solicit the good will of his opposite numbers. He was unfailingly courteous to the Democrats, whether voters or politicians. It paid off. Few Massachusetts politicians were more popular with members of the opposition party than was Coolidge. In a 1929 book entitled *Presidents I've Known and Two Near Presidents*, journalist Charles Thompson wrote of this appeal: "When he began to stir about in the politics of Northampton the bewildered Republicans in that city learned there was a body of voters there whom they came to classify as 'Coolidge Democrats.' He first went to the Legislature from a Democratic district, and as he spread out locally the Coolidge Democrats spread out too—spread out all over Northampton."

Coolidge dutifully attended all meetings of a legislature that didn't have much responsibility. He introduced a motion to employ a Northampton architect rather than an outsider to draw up the plans for an extension to the schoolhouse, and voted for an appropriation of $350 to defray the expenses of a visit by President McKinley. It was that kind of body. The following year Coolidge became a delegate to the Republican State Convention, and he was well on his political path before he was welcomed to the bar. Coolidge wrote that he worked very diligently in this period, so much so that he wasn't able to visit his father for three years. Later, when his practice was growing, he credited his success to following Stephen Taft's dictum:

> People began to feel that they could consult me with
> some safety and without the danger of being involved
> needlessly in long and costly litigation in court. Very few
> of my clients had ever to pay a bill of costs. I suppose

that they were more reasonable than other clients, for
they usually settled their differences out of court. This
course did not give me much experience in the trial of
cases, so I never became very proficient in that art, but it
brought me a very satisfactory practice and a fair
income.

In his first full year in practice Coolidge earned $1,200. This was
the amount he *earned*, but not all of it was received; his total take was
less than half that sum. In that time and place, clients paid lawyers'
fees slowly, often over a period of years. As a result, Coolidge wrote
often to his father, asking for small sums to tide him over. "I shall
want $22 to pay my board June 1," he wrote on May 25, 1898. "My
business has been good this month, I judge it will amount to about
$350, but in cash I have had only $17 and my incidental expenses
have just about covered that sum." And: "I am short of money again
and think I shall have about $40 before the first of February,"
Coolidge wrote to his father on January 13, 1899: "I will write you
again when I know what I must have." Whenever Coolidge asked
for money, his father complied and never complained. In 1917, when
he was lieutenant governor of Massachusetts, Coolidge wrote to
thank his father for a $20 check.

Coolidge spoke and wrote about how he had always tried to save
money while a lawyer and working his way up in politics, and there
is no reason to doubt him on this score. But, all the same, he had a
loving, generous father on whom he could count for anything he
needed. Indeed, Coolidge relied upon his father financially as well
as emotionally, indicating the warmth of family feeling he possessed—which, along with other aspects of his private life, he
attempted to keep carefully hidden from the public.

Matters improved. In 1899 he was appointed counsel and vice
president at the newly organized Nonotuck Savings Bank, and his
earnings came to $1,400. In 1900 Coolidge ran successfully for the
post of city solicitor, which was selected by the city council, meaning
that Coolidge won it by lobbying the members, not by facing the
general electorate. The post carried a salary of $600, but more
important, it brought him greater professional and political expo-

sure. "I wanted to be city solicitor because I believed it would make me a better lawyer," he wrote. "The training in this office gave me a good grasp of municipal law that later brought some important cases to me." The work wasn't onerous, and didn't interfere with Coolidge's private practice. He won reappointment in 1901. Writing to his father on January 28, he did not sound triumphant, but rather spoke once again of his worries.

> There were a couple of Irishmen after the job. They made me some trouble but they did not get votes enough. I have business enough to get a fair living, but there is no money in the practice of law. You are fortunate that you are not having me to support. If I ever get a woman some one will have to support her, but I see no need of a wife so long as I have my health.

Coolidge lost his bid for a third term to Democrat Theobald Connor, perhaps one of those Irishmen to whom he referred in his letter to his father. The loss was due not to any mishaps on his part; rather, he lost because the council had a tradition of rotation in office, and so turned him out. Indeed, two of the Republicans on the council voted against him, probably for that reason. In effect, Coolidge was asking for something he knew he shouldn't have. It was a mistake he would not repeat.

The following year Coolidge bounced back, when on the death of the incumbent he was appointed temporary clerk of courts for Hampshire County, a political post paying a salary of $2,300. This was a much sought-after position, a fine career move that could easily lead to a judgeship down the line. Coolidge considered this "the greatest compliment ever paid my professional ability," but realized this was not for him. For all of his fears regarding the law, he thought there were more possibilities—political as well as financial—in private practice.

Coolidge was named chairman of the Republican City Committee, worked at the clerkship, and continued handling private cases. He had reason for satisfaction. "My earnings had been such that I was able to make some small savings. My prospects appeared to be good. I had many friends and few enemies. There was a little more time for me to give to the amenities of life." Which was his ever-practical way of saying he could now consider marriage.

Whether Coolidge courted anyone before he met Grace Anna Goodhue is a matter of some conjecture. Her biographer writes of an "infatuation for a red-haired Northampton girl who refused to marry him," but didn't go into details. What seems more certain is that Coolidge decided early on not to think seriously of marriage until his professional and financial situations were secure, and then he cast about for a proper mate. As with so many important aspects of his life, Coolidge was fortunate in the time, the place, and the person.

At the time Coolidge was rooming at Round Hill, at the home of Robert Weir, the steward of the nearby Clarke Institute for the Deaf, where Grace Goodhue worked. She came from a good family, and, like Coolidge, was a Vermonter—her family lived in Burlington, approximately one hundred miles northwest of Plymouth. Her father, Andrew Goodhue, was a steamboat inspector for the Champlain Transportation Company. Goodhue was a Democrat, obtaining his job through political pull. Grace's mother, Lemira Barrett Goodhue, was a reserved and somewhat dour housewife. Grace herself was in stark contrast to Calvin Coolidge: friendly, gregarious, and vivacious. She attended the University of Vermont, where she was a popular figure on campus. Upon graduation in 1901 she took a course in lip reading and obtained the requisite skills to apply for a position at the Clarke School, arriving there in 1902.

According to Grace Coolidge, she first saw her future husband as she walked past Round Hill. He was standing at a window, shaving, with his hat on, in a union suit. Coolidge saw her, too, and according to one account, decided on the spot he would ask her to marry him. He spoke with Weir about her, and learned she was a teacher at the school. Weir introduced the two soon after. She mentioned the business with the hat, and he explained that he had a lock of hair that always got in the way when he shaved, and so before taking up the razor he would wet his hair, comb it, and then don the hat.

The two dated—streetcar rides, picnics, church socials, walks, and the like. They must have seemed an unlikely pair. Grace was quick to smile and laugh, while Coolidge was tight-lipped and not given to banter, sometimes cranky and, in public at least, undemonstrative. Two months before their marriage, they visited a college classmate of Grace's, and Coolidge just sat in a corner, looking straight ahead, saying nothing. After a while he stood and said, "We'll be going now." Privately the friend said, "My land, Grace, I'd be afraid of him." As they drove back to Northampton, Grace remarked, "Now, why did you act like that? She thinks that you are a perfect stick and said she'd be afraid of you," to which Coolidge replied, "She'll find I'm human." But Coolidge would never be able to banter with strangers—or even friends, for that matter. Perhaps Grace understood this early in their relationship. In any case, she cheerfully put up with this kind of behavior. When in the White House someone remarked on her vivacity, she laughed and said, "Well, I have to talk for two."

It was quite clear almost from the first that he considered Grace's education inadequate, and he would not talk with her about politics and his work. In her memoir of their lives together, she wrote:

> Sometimes I wonder if Mr. Coolidge would have talked
> with me more freely if I had been of a more serious turn
> of mind. I do not think that he was very favorably
> impressed with my education. As a matter of fact, he
> definitely cast aspersions upon it when he asked me one
> evening, out of the blue, when Martin Luther was born.
> I had no more idea than the man in the moon, and I said
> so; whereupon he asked, "Didn't they teach you
> anything where you went to school?"

After the birth of their first child, Mrs. Coolidge purchased a book entitled *Our Family Physician*, for $8.00, but was too scared to tell her husband. Several weeks later she picked up the book and glanced at the flyleaf, to discover Calvin had written: "Don't see any recipe here for curing suckers! Calvin Coolidge."

Grace later wrote, "If I had any particular interest, I am sure I should have been properly put in my place." What a lively, inquisitive person like Grace Goodhue saw in Coolidge is difficult to imagine. Of course he was hardworking, honest, decent, and trustworthy. Of all the presidents of the twentieth century, Coolidge is the most difficult to imagine as a philanderer. Almost undoubtedly, Grace was the first woman he thought seriously about marrying. Also quite certainly, Coolidge went about it methodically. He would not marry unless and until he felt himself financially capable of supporting a wife, and then he would go shopping. There was nothing impulsive about Coolidge, at any time of his life. Yet he did have a sentimental side, which he kept carefully hidden from public view. Coolidge unquestionably loved her deeply. In his *Autobiography*, he wrote:

> I have seen so much fiction written on this subject that I may be pardoned for relating the plain facts. We thought we were made for each other. For almost a quarter of a century she has borne with my infirmities, and I have rejoiced in her graces.

Grace even learned to appreciate his sense of humor, perhaps because, being from Vermont, she understood it. After they married, he presented Grace with fifty-two pairs of socks that needed mending, telling her that when she finished, he would have some others. Apparently he had saved them up against the time he would have a wife to do such tasks for him. Later, Grace asked if he married her to get his socks mended, and he answered, "No, but I find it mighty handy."

This relationship was not unusual for the time. It was a period in which a man's home was his castle—his castle, that is, not his wife's.

Calvin and Grace visited the Coolidge and Goodhue families. The Coolidges took to Grace immediately, and Andrew Goodhue got along well with Coolidge once he became accustomed to his quiet ways. But Lemira Goodhue was wary about Coolidge, perhaps because he was somewhat like her, and they never became anything more than correct with one another. Although she attended his inauguration in 1925, she visited the White House for only ten days while the Coolidges were in the White House.

One day, in the spring of 1905, Coolidge appeared uninvited at the Goodhue residence in Burlington. When Mr. Goodhue entered his living room, he found Coolidge sitting there, reading a magazine. "Hello Calvin, what are you doing in Burlington? Got some business here?" he asked. "No," Coolidge replied. "Came up to marry Grace." "Why, have you spoken to her yet?" the father asked, to which Coolidge said, "No, I can wait a few days if it's any convenience to you."

Coolidge asked Grace to marry him soon after. Or to be precise, he declared, "I am going to marry you." She accepted. At the time, he was thirty-three years old, and she was twenty-six. This was not the marriage of two impulsive youths. Mrs. Goodhue, unhappy at this turn of events, tried to talk her daughter into quitting her job and returning home for a year, perhaps hoping the separation and time would lead her to reconsider. But Grace was certain of herself and refused. They married in the Goodhue residence in Burlington on October 4, 1905. There was a small party the night preceding the wedding, and one friend, who arrived late, observed Calvin in a corner, looking on, saying nothing. Knowing Grace was a teacher of the deaf and dumb, she asked, "That young man standing by himself in the corner—is he one of Grace's pupils?"

They went to Montreal for their honeymoon, intending to see the sights for two weeks, but even then, Coolidge had other things on his mind, and they returned to Northampton after only one week. He had decided to run for a place on the Northampton School Board, a nonpaying post but one that would keep him involved in politics and in a position to meet future constituents. Ordinarily he would have had an easy time of it, but another Republican, S.D. Drury, entered the race so that Democrat John Kennedy won, with 934 votes to Coolidge's 840 and Drury's 762. It was hardly a major setback. Indeed, had Coolidge known of the second Republican candidate he would have withdrawn from the race, but when he returned it was too late. Coolidge showed style. When he ran into Kennedy during the campaign, the

Democrat said, "Calvin, I think I've got you beat." Coolidge replied, "Well, either way they'll have a good man." Several weeks later a Republican in the district told him that he had voted for Kennedy, because the Democrat had children in the public school and Coolidge did not, to which Coolidge replied, "Might give me time."

Three years later, when Kennedy ran for reelection, he did so with Coolidge's support. When asked how he could recommend that Republicans vote for a Democrat, Coolidge replied that he had a good record.

After living for a brief time in a nearby hotel, Coolidge rented a seven-room duplex, half of a two-family house at 21 Massasoit Street, and retained the lease almost to the end of his life. They lived frugally; while there they had a party line telephone. Now that he was married with responsibilities, Coolidge's earlier confidence in his future was again replaced by the familiar doubts. Afterward, he wrote of his thoughts in this period:

> Of course my expenses increased, and I had to plan very
> carefully for a time to live within my income. I knew
> very well what it means to awake in the night and
> realize that the rent is coming due, wondering where the
> money is coming from with which to pay it. The only
> way I know of to escape from that constant tragedy is to
> keep running expenses low enough so that something
> may be saved to meet the day when earnings may be
> small.

In microcosm this is, in fact, the Coolidge presidential philosophy. His ideas on government finance were conservative; he had gotten them from his father, his teachers, and his readings—from the very air of Vermont and western Massachusetts. His views combined political philosophy with the lessons of personal experience.

Grace quickly became pregnant, and their first son, John, was born on September 7, 1906. Coolidge was married and a father, thirty-four years old, a practicing attorney, and he still had to rely upon occasional remittances from his father.

By then Coolidge had started to consider a race for the Mass-achusetts House of Representatives, the lower house of the state legislature known as the General Court. The pay was meager, only $750 a year plus mileage, meaning Coolidge could be home week-ends. The term was for one year, so candidates had to be perennial campaigners. The legislature met from January to June, leaving members free to pursue other interests the rest of the time, which most did.

This was considered an entry position for those interested in advancement. House members could meet politicians from other parts of the state, trade favors, win reputations, and perhaps go on to the state senate, or even to Washington. A diligent and clever rep-resentative could catch the eye of businessmen and enter the com-mercial world. A lawyer might come into contact with future clients. The shrewd Coolidge surely considered such possibilities.

In his *Autobiography* Coolidge wrote that he was still learning the law and reading literature. "Because I thought the experience would contribute to this end I became a candidate for the Massachusetts House of Representatives." Maybe, but for more than ten years he had been cultivating the Northampton electorate and earning a reputation for probity, fairness, and integrity. He did not make promises and pledges he would not and could not keep. Even those who ran against him had good words for Calvin Coolidge. On the other hand, outside of conventional Repub-licanism, he stood for no cause, and displayed little enthusiasm for the political issues of the time.

Coolidge was cagey about running, as he was in all of his subse-quent races. He took no chances, and made certain in advance that even if rejected, he would come out ahead in terms of respect for his loyalty and, perhaps, additional clients. On September 15, 1906, a shrewd reporter for the *Daily Hampshire Gazette* wrote an item entitled "Calvin Coolidge Willing But Not Anxious." Only seven days before filing, Coolidge had still not made up his mind.

> He says he would like to go to the legislature sometime.
> At present, he thinks, because of business conditions, he
> would prefer to wait, but adds there will always be

something of that kind, so perhaps now would be as favorable for him as any time. He says he does not care enough about it to fight for the nomination, and that if some prominent party men such as ex-mayors Hallett or Mather want the nomination he would gladly stay out and put his shoulder to the wheel. And even then, if he doesn't have to fight for the nomination, he adds that he cannot say whether he would accept. "If the party wants me, however, I will consider the matter," says Mr. Coolidge.

The party wanted him; there was no rival in the field. This was the Coolidge way in politicking; he replicated it in all of his other state campaigns.

The Democrats renominated Moses Bassett, who in the previous election had barely squeaked out a victory and was considered a weak candidate. In addition, Bassett had been feuding with Michael McCarthy, who had opposed him for the nomination in 1905 and who now vowed to work against his reelection. The *Hampshire Gazette*, nonetheless, seemed to think Bassett would win the election.

Coolidge campaigned vigorously. Field prepared a short biography that was mailed to every Northampton voter, and the candidate carried on a door-to-door campaign, concentrating on Democratic households. He was a speaker at a Republican rally attended by the party's candidates for governor and the House of Representatives, Curtis Guild, Jr., and Frederick Gillett, respectively. He made several campaign speeches, the first of his life in his own behalf. It was a successful campaign, and Coolidge won by a margin of 1,329 to 1,065, a large increase over the party's vote the previous year. It was a Republican year, as Guild defeated Democrat John B. Moran by a margin of 222,518 to 192,295. Guild had been lieutenant governor under his predecessor, William L. Douglas, and according to tradition in the state, had moved up a notch in the next election.

Winning election to General Court marked the true beginning of the Coolidge political career, for those earlier positions—Republican delegate, city councilman, city solicitor, clerk of courts—were either ancillary or nonpolitical.

He took the new position quite seriously. Dick Irwin, who had campaigned for Coolidge, provided him with a letter of introduction to Speaker of the House John T. Cole. "Like the singed cat, he is better than he looks. He wishes to talk with you about committees." Henry Field, who knew his way about the legislature, accompanied Coolidge to Boston and introduced him to some of his fellow legislators. This done, Coolidge took a small room at the Adams House, an inexpensive hotel in a line of buildings on Washington Street, whose time of glory had been in the 1870s, when it was one of Boston's leading hostelries. By the early twentieth century it was faded, favored primarily by legislators like Coolidge—those from the provinces seeking cheap lodgings. His room had hot and cold running water, but no bath or toilet and only a small window looking out on an inner court.

Those who have never seen the House chambers in Boston might be forgiven for thinking it a grand place. It was not. The room was small—some might think it "cozy"—which made for close contacts. The members all knew one another quite well. Even so, Coolidge was an inconspicuous figure in the legislature that year. Martin Lomasney, a leading Boston Democrat, remarked, "This fellow is either a schoolteacher or an undertaker from the country. I don't know which." Coolidge served on the mercantile affairs and constitutional amendments committee, neither of which was important, and rarely was heard from on the floor. He tended to vote the straight party line, and didn't make waves or an impression. Coolidge voted for the direct election of U.S. senators and came out in favor of the Women's Suffrage Amendment. And, despite his later conservatism, Coolidge at this time was viewed as one of the more *progressive* Republicans. One of his legislative colleagues, Roland D. Sawyer, later on wrote that Coolidge was "uncomfortably progressive for some of his constituents in Northampton."

Coolidge did not have the kind of temperament to enter any political fray without calculating costs and benefits. But he did have more inviolable principles than most politicians, then and now, and many of these might be classified as advanced. The trouble with the term "progressive" is that it is often used as shorthand for a wide variety of concepts and programs. Coolidge understood this and eschewed labels, refusing to be so categorized. He best expressed his views on the subject in a 1924 press conference:

> I don't think I can give any definition of the words "reactionary" and "progressive" that would be helpful…. Sometimes the person is not well thought of and he is labeled as a reactionary. Sometimes he is well thought of and he is called a progressive. As a matter of fact all the political parties are progressive. I can't conceive of a party existing for any length of time that wasn't progressive, or of leadership being effective that wasn't progressive.

Coolidge took his seat in the Massachusetts House of Representatives at the flood tide of Rooseveltian Progressivism, and the state GOP reflected it. But it might be more accurate to say that, in some ways, Theodore Roosevelt represented forces long at work in Massachusetts, which had been a national leader in social legislation. At the time a child labor amendment to the federal Constitution was being debated; Massachusetts had child labor legislation in 1836. It passed the first factory inspection act in 1866, and in 1874 limited the workday for women and minors to ten hours. The state had pure food and drug laws before Roosevelt recommended them to Congress. And it had laws for the recall of judges. Reflecting on this in 1914, Roosevelt wrote, "It is rather funny to think that if the Massachusetts and Vermont methods of electing and removing judges were advanced by men, I should be denounced as almost a communist." Governor Guild spoke out and worked for civil service reform, further regulation of utilities, limitations on campaign expenditures, and state laws to protect savings accounts. Most important from Coolidge's standpoint, Guild favored economy in government, and cut the state's debt by 12 percent his first year in office.

Around this time Coolidge met and became friendly with Winthrop Murray Crane, who was a former Massachusetts governor and current junior senator. Crane lived long enough to see Coolidge elected vice president in 1920, and five years later, when he was in the White House, Coolidge wrote the preface for a Crane biography. It was one of Coolidge's characteristically opaque pieces, but he did touch upon Crane's most important trait:

> Ever since I have been in Massachusetts I have known of Mr. Crane, but I did not come into personal relation with him until I had entered public life in Boston. The more I saw of him the more I came to admire him. This was the almost unbroken experience of every person that came into contact with him. He was a most difficult person to describe. His influence was very great, but it was of an intangible nature. I do not recall that he ever volunteered any suggestion to me in relation to any public duty which I had to perform. He never made any request concerning legislation. He never recommended anyone for appointment. Yet I think everyone who knew him recognized that he was a positive influence for sound legislation and the selection of qualified persons to fill public office. His actions were never moulded to serve any private interest of his own, but always with a desire to promote what he believed to be the public welfare.

This giant that Coolidge and others described was a small, sad-eyed, and balding man, unimpressive and forgettable in looks, quiet and calm in demeanor. A friend of both men thought Crane made Coolidge look positively gabby. A Washington newsman said, "He never writes if he can talk, and he never talks if he can nod."

Nevertheless, Crane had remarkable abilities and influence. New York Senator Chauncey Depew, who served in Congress from 1900 to 1911, wrote, "He never made a speech. I do not remember that he made a motion. Yet he was the most influential member of that body." President William Howard Taft seconded this, saying that, although Crane entered the Senate without legislative experience, "he became its most influential member." Michael E. Hennessy, a perspicacious contemporary observer of the Massachusetts political scene, added, "Mr. Crane was a unique figure in Massachusetts politics. He lacked much of what people generally regard as necessary in a successful man in politics. He had not a commanding presence nor was he given to the glad hand habit, so common among public men, but he possessed many attractive personal qualities which endeared him to his neighbors and friends."

Crane was admired and courted by many young legislators. This was the period when state political bosses were dominant figures, ruling their domains like feudal barons, often but not always in alliances with business interests. Crane was such a boss, but different from the others. He was not power hungry or venal, did not make demands on his allies and followers, and was not personally ambitious. Perhaps because of this he was able to sway others to his way of thinking by force of character rather than through promises and threats. He usually tried to resolve differences with compromise, often behind the scenes. Crane cared little whether a suggestion was progressive or conservative, whether it came from a Republican or Democrat. If he thought it sensible, he would support it. By seeming nonpartisan, however, Crane was able to advance Republicanism more than had he been a doctrinaire partisan. He would not, moreover, move on a matter unless he was certain he was right. Often he would say to those who asked his advice, "Do nothing." His credo was, "It is more important that the law be permanently fixed than that experiments in new legislation should be tried." This was Crane's *modus operandi*—and would become Calvin Coolidge's as well.

Crane was a member of one of the most distinguished families in western Massachusetts. In 1799 one of his forebears founded a paper mill in Dalton, some thirty miles from Northampton. Having decided not to attend college, Murray Crane (as he was known) entered the family business, and several years later won the contract to provide the federal government with paper used to produce currency, which it still retains. Crane also became involved in AT&T and Otis Elevator.

Crane's *bêtes noires* were the aristocrats of eastern Massachusetts. The state's senior senator was Henry Cabot Lodge, whose very name dripped Massachusetts history, an austere man who guarded his power and privilege and brooked no challenges. Certainly not from the likes of Crane, a man from the provinces who was in trade, and thus not a true gentleman. Not only hadn't Crane attended Harvard, he wasn't even a college man.

Like his father and grandfather, Crane was active in politics, and in 1892 was made a member of the Republican National Committee, on which he served for more than twenty years. In 1896 he was elected lieutenant governor, and then served as governor from 1900 to 1902, achieving a reputation for businesslike actions in government. Only thirty-seven years old when he took office, Crane's inaugural address was the first time he had spoken before a public assembly of this kind.

Crane's three terms as governor showed his concern with economy in government and efficiency. In the progressive tradition of Massachusetts, he strengthened the pure food and drug laws, further limited the hours worked by women and children, and handled teamsters' and railroad workers' strikes by bringing the sides together in marathon negotiations. Crane was so successful in this that President Roosevelt called on him to help resolve the coalminers' strike, and employed the Crane techniques himself. A few months after leaving office Crane went to Washington as senator to replace the deceased Walter Hoar.

Crane was, for Coolidge, the ideal. Of course, Crane wasn't his first mentor. There had been his father, whom Coolidge would always love and cherish, but he did not want to be a small-town tycoon. At Black River Academy he had been influenced by George Sherman, but Coolidge was not attracted to secondary education. The impact of Charles Garman on him was certainly important, but he did not intend to embark upon a life of philosophical contemplation. Henry Field was a fine counselor, and but his reach did not extend beyond local politics. It isn't possible to understand Coolidge without realizing the kind of men he modeled himself after. From his father to Crane they all were of a type—stolid, conservative, distrusting of government but willing to participate in the political process, patriotic, trusting of the American individual, and above all, reluctant to act until all expedients were exhausted. Most curious, none of these men made strenuous attempts to win Coolidge to a particular philosophy. Rather, they did so subtly, by example.

By 1907 Coolidge was in Boston, the center of the New England universe, hobnobbing with men whose exploits he had read about in Northampton but had never expected to meet. Now he was one of them, a minor figure to be sure, ignored or joked about, but he was used to this. Crane took note of him; the two men consulted on state matters. Murray Crane, the powerful businessman and national political figure—it must have been heady for Coolidge. His future was in politics, tied to the coattails of Murray Crane.

Despite his social, educational, and geographic differences with Lodge, when Crane entered politics he did so with Lodge's support and even friendship. Not until 1912, when Crane endorsed William Howard Taft for a second presidential term while Lodge dithered over the Roosevelt candidacy, did their relationship become strained, and it was never the same, especially after Crane came out for the League of Nations.

In his prime Crane was a greater power in Massachusetts than Lodge. In part this was due to his grip on western Massachusetts, where there were few Democrats, while Lodge had to worry about the immigrant and Irish threats, embodied in the Democratic Party, in the east. By 1900 more than 60 percent of the Massachusetts population was foreign born or of foreign-born parents, and most of them were in the eastern part of the state. There had been socialists in the General Court and socialist mayors of towns—like Haverhill and Brockton, both in eastern Massachusetts. The Republican position in the eastern end was being challenged, and demography was on the side of the Democrats. But for the moment, the GOP was able to capture a large share of the Irish–American vote outside of Boston, which was typified by Coolidge's popularity with them in Northampton.

Crane was a more judicious politician than Lodge, who offended people with his imperious ways. Lodge's friendship with Roosevelt was legendary; but TR offered Crane the positions of secretary of the treasury, postmaster general, and secretary of the interior, all of which he rejected. Moreover, when Lodge died, a Crane protégé, William Butler, took his place in the U.S. Senate.

In 1907 Coolidge, with Crane's support, ran for a second legislative term. His opponent, Alfred Preece, a Northampton alderman, was considered a weak candidate. Coolidge ran on the record of his votes, including several pro-labor measures:

> If there are any body of our citizens who ought to feel satisfied with my efforts in their behalf, it is our working people. I have no doubt they are. I have never heard a word of complaint from a union man. It has all come from someone who desires to ride into office through their dissatisfactions. I have no doubt the workingmen of Northampton are too well informed to be caught by misrepresentation.

The Northampton *Daily Herald*, a Republican newspaper, came out for him. "Mr. Coolidge is entitled to the thanks of the wage laborers of his district for his manly defense of their interests." In those years, when Theodore Roosevelt was in the White House, Calvin Coolidge acted, talked, and voted like a Rooseveltian. He won reelection, and, more secure and confident, and with some seniority and Crane's support, he was able to obtain a position he wanted on the Judiciary Committee. Coolidge now spoke out in favor of and voted for laws requiring employers to provide their workers with a six-day work week, a measure restricting the hours of labor for women and children, another to provide half-fares on streetcars for schoolchildren, and other "progressive" measures. In a period when there was some doubt regarding the future of the Massachusetts GOP, Coolidge may have been hedging his bets, as would almost any prudent politician.

Coolidge at times took action that displayed his progressivism. Thomas Hisgen, a prominent member of a reform organization known as the Independent League, ran against Guild in 1907. Hisgen was a petroleum dealer who tangled with Standard Oil, and he petitioned the General Court to pass legislation outlawing the Standard Oil practice of charging lower prices to force competition from the field, and then raising them when the others had fled. Hisgen's approach was Rooseveltian; not only did Coolidge support Hisgen, but he also sponsored the measure in the legislature. "You forbid a labor union to injure a man's business," he said, "but a giant corporation can do exactly the same thing." Coolidge concluded that "havoc, spoil, and ruin follow these 'aggregations of capital.'" Theodore Roosevelt could not have put it better.

But this is not the Coolidge who became president in 1923, and who is remembered today. Simply put, he mutated. From the vantage point of 1931, Coolidge reflected on how he had changed since that period:

> Serving on the Judiciary Committee, which I wanted
> because I felt it would help me in my profession, I
> became much interested in modifying the law so that an
> injunction could not be issued in a labor dispute to
> prevent one person seeking by argument to induce
> another to leave his employer. This bill failed. While I
> think it had merit, in later years I came to see that what
> was of real importance to wage earners was not how
> they might conduct a quarrel with their employers, but
> how the business of the country might be so organized as
> to insure steady employment at a fair rate of pay. If that
> were done there would be no occasion for a quarrel, and
> if it were not done a quarrel would do no one any good.

What caused these changes? Might it have been the maturing of a young reformer? Or could it have been his later experiences in the executive branch years? While a Massachusetts legislator and governor, Coolidge reflected that state's political realities, and while president he echoed the conservative disposition of the nation during the 1920s. Was Coolidge a political chameleon or an opportunist? Perhaps it was the influence of Murray Crane, quiet, steady, patient, and reasonable. Coolidge remained a Crane man, and was proud to be one of the several young men the senator was placing in important state positions. But he also was able to think for himself, as he demonstrated in the legislative years.

4

....

To the Statewide Scene

It was at this time that my intimate acquaintance began with
Mr. Frank W. Stearns.... In the spring he suggested that he
would like to support me for lieutenant governor. He was a
merchant of high character and very much respected by all who
knew him, but entirely without experience in politics. He came
as an entirely fresh force in public affairs, unhampered by any
of the animosities that usually attach to a veteran politician. It
was a great compliment to me to attract the interest of such a
man, and his influence later became of large value to the party
in the commonwealth and nation.

The Autobiography of Calvin Coolidge

JUST AS IT WAS CUSTOMARY for the Massachusetts lieutenant
governor to move up a notch to run for the governorship, so it was
the tradition in those years for representatives to step down after two
terms. Accordingly, Coolidge departed the legislature in 1908 and
contemplated a full-time law practice, which would certainly grow
due to his political experiences and the patronage of powerful men
in the state. This was all the more necessary since his second son,
Calvin Coolidge, Jr., was born on April 13. Coolidge was by no
means wealthy. A month later he wrote to his father, the letter beginning with, "Your letter and check received. It is correct." Apparently
Coolidge still relied upon him for financial support.

As it happened, there was no hiatus in his electoral career. The mayor of Northampton, Democrat James O'Brien, intended to retire, and Coolidge agreed to run for the post.

The Democrats named Henry E. Bicknell, a prominent local merchant, who came out for Prohibition. By then one of Coolidge's clients was a local brewery, and perhaps because of this he was "wet." Thus, the normally anti–Prohibition but Democratic Irish and French residents of Northampton were faced with a conundrum, which Coolidge exploited. As he had in his two legislative runs, Coolidge wooed the Democrats assiduously, knocking on doors, shaking hands, and saying, "I want your vote. I need it. I shall appreciate it." He avoided personalities, another of his practices. Reporting on his method, the *Gazette* wrote, "There is one thing we like about candidate Coolidge; he does not say anything about the other candidate. At the Democratic rallies they keep telling what a poor man Coolidge is, how little he ever did that was good and how much he did that was bad." Commenting on Democratic criticisms in a speech before a largely Irish audience, Coolidge said, "I never could satisfy the other party. These seemed like the British at the battle of Bennington who complained that the Green Mountain boys took aim in battle. It is of great consequence to me that my fellow citizens may say of me, 'He has conducted a clean, honorable campaign and borne himself like a man.'"

According to one often repeated story, some Democrats were offering odds of two to one that Bicknell would capture the Irish Ward Seven. Coolidge gave $100 to a friend and asked him to bet half of it on him, and with the other half, buy beer and cigars for the residents. As he predicted, the Seventh went for him, and thus turned the $50 into $150, of which Coolidge gave $50 to his friend for his help. But as it really happened, the ward went for Bicknell by a margin of 159 to 151.

Coolidge won the election by a vote of 1,597 to 1,409. The following day, according to one of those many stories that surfaced later, he met a Democratic friend, who congratulated him on his victory. "I see you're elected mayor—but I didn't vote for you." To which Coolidge was supposed to have replied, "Well, somebody did." Soon after he sent this message to Bicknell:

My dear Harry:

My most serious regret at the election is that you cannot share the entire pleasure of the result with me. I value your friendship and good opinion more than any office and I trust I have so conducted the campaign that our past close intimacy and good fellowship may be more secure than ever.

Respectfully,
Calvin Coolidge

On the day after the election, the *Gazette* praised Coolidge. "Congratulations, cool Calvin!" This was probably the first time "cool" was attached to "Calvin" in print. It would soon become commonplace.

That December, Coolidge wrote to his father, noting the arrival of another check. "We are very thankful for it. I could not have been mayor without your help." He noted the salary was $800, but there was some talk of raising it to $1,200. The actual raise was to $1,000, but Coolidge refused to accept the extra $200 on the principle that he should receive the salary existing on Election Day.

The mayoralty of Northampton was a small office, but it provided Coolidge with his first executive experience, and his political thinking continued to evolve. In his brief inaugural address, Coolidge hinted that he intended to be an activist mayor: "Northampton has reached the point where citizens are demanding more than material welfare." He proposed the creation of a Public Improvement Commission to advise on necessary projects. "It would be their province to formulate a very broad and general plan of improvement, the details of which could be cojointly worked out from year to year by our various departments—each year as it can be afforded, much or little, but always working toward the consummation of a definite plan."

This was one of the first instances of municipal planning in Massachusetts. The commission was given Coolidge's agenda, which included paving streets and sidewalks, "each section of work to be part of a scheme for dealing with all our streets as a unit, filling in the parts in the light of the whole plan. In short, I recommend that the care of our streets and sidewalks be treated as a manufacturing proposition rather than a parceling out of municipal utilities."

Modest enough by today's standards, the plan was quite forward-looking for the time. The first concrete sidewalk had been laid in Bellefontaine, Ohio, in 1891, and such improvements had barely started at the turn of the century. In 1910 a project of this sort was quite "up-to-date" in Northampton. Similarly, the concepts of comprehensive programs for public improvements were just then appearing in municipal governments, and here too, Coolidge was in the vanguard, though happenings in a small place like Northampton were not noticed in the larger world. The wonder of it all was that Coolidge not only got his program approved and started in that first year, but he also did so without resort to a bond issue or new taxes. During his first term, Coolidge increased teachers' salaries, lowered the tax rate from $17 to $16.50, and affected a modest decrease in the city's debt.

After he became president of the United States, many Northamptonites were asked about his performance as mayor. Unsurprisingly, most replies were quite positive. "A man of the people," said one Smith College professor. Elihu Grant, another Smith professor who lived across the street from Coolidge, was positively effusive:

> His capacity for hard and continuous work, his
> unwillingness to commit himself to any position which
> he had not thought out, his economies in the
> administration of the city's business, and his
> exceptional success in gaining the suffrage of his
> fellow-citizens of both parties without any of the usual
> public manifestations of the vote-getter, already
> marked him off from other political figures. Others had
> their ups and downs in the political game. He was
> always going up. People had confidence in him and he
> never went backward from any position which he held
> in the respect of his fellow-townsfolk. He always
> seemed to have his object clearly in mind and went

straight for it. His method was one of industry and persistence. If a nomination was to be secured, he often made his major efforts before the possible opposition had begun. By the time of the election, he seemed to have the whole matter discounted in his own mind so that he was fully ready to attend to business as soon as he was invited to take charge.

His performance attracted some attention outside of Northampton, but, of even more importance, was monitored by Murray Crane. According to one story told much later, when a friend mentioned he was going to visit his daughter at Smith College, Crane told him, "Find out all you can about a young man named Coolidge. You'll save trouble in looking him up later. There is one of the coming men of this country."

A glimpse of Coolidge's political thoughts in this period comes through in a letter to his father. In June 1910 John Coolidge was nominated for the Vermont senate, a seat he won that September. Congratulating his father, Coolidge offered advice based on his experiences. "You need not hesitate to give other members your views on any subject that arises. It is much more important to kill bad bills than to pass good ones." That thought would recur in different forms throughout his career. Coolidge deeply believed that there were enough laws on the books, and that new ones should be considered cautiously; perhaps the desired goal could be achieved by enforcing some statute already on the books. One of his biographers, William Allen White, noted, "Coolidge, in those days and always, distrusted reformers." So he did, but Coolidge did not distrust *reform* itself, but rather the sources from which ideas for change emanated. He instinctively withdrew from men he labeled "world beaters" and "wonder boys"—those convinced that there were cures for every political ailment and that they could prescribe and administer any problem.

Coolidge distrusted legislators and executives who had agendas rather than philosophies. As legislator and executive, Coolidge often initiated and supported specific reforms that he might have rejected had the idea emanated from the likes of Senator Robert

La Follette, Theodore Roosevelt, or later on, Herbert Hoover. And always it would be piecemeal reform. In this period he supported not only the wages and hours legislation, but also a minimum wage for women, pensions for widows whose husbands died while employed, women's suffrage, workmen's compensation for crippling injuries while on the job, legalized picketing, and the popular election of U.S. senators—all of which were at the time considered "progressive" measures.

Coolidge won reelection in 1910, again defeating Harry Bicknell, this time by a margin of 256 votes. He knew this would be his last term, for the tradition against third terms extended to mayoralties. There was talk of an appointment as state secretary of state, but this was apparently nothing but a rumor. Besides, he had his eye on the next step on the ladder: the state senate.

Republican Allen Treadway, the current senator for Northampton, was considering stepping down, and wished to see his seat taken by Coolidge, a fellow Amherst man. When they spoke of the matter, Treadway expressed his wishes, to which Coolidge replied that while he hoped to enter the senate someday, he wasn't in that much of a hurry. Treadway opted to make a run for Congress; while he lost that race, he won election two years later. In any event, in 1911 the way was open for Coolidge to attempt to replace him in Boston. He obtained the nomination, and in an easy race against Alfred Preece, who earlier had been defeated for the House seat, Coolidge won by a vote of 5,541 to 4,061.

The Massachusetts senate had only forty members, and the senators were less anonymous than the House members. The chamber, in which the members sat around a circular table, was even smaller than the House. Coolidge immediately became chairman of both the Committee on Legal Affairs and the Committee on Agriculture, which occupied a good deal of his time.

Of greater immediate importance than either was his role in resolving a strike that began on New Year's Day, 1912, at the American Woolen Company's facility at Lawrence, where laborers under the age of eighteen worked fifty-six hours a week and were paid for fifty-four hours. The factory managers refused to meet with the workers to discuss the situation, and hadn't even notified them in advance of this change in payment. Not only did this seem unfair, but it also violated a state law mandating a maximum of fifty-four hours for eighteen-year-olds.

As a result, fourteen thousand workers walked out. Making matters more complicated, the strike spread to other facilities, and the radical International Workers of the World (IWW)—the "Wobblies"—participated in the walkouts. The IWW was known to advocate violence, and there were justifiable fears of riots in Lawrence.

It was a touchy matter, and Coolidge was selected as chairman of a General Court committee established to attempt conciliation between the parties. It was not a "plum" assignment—senior legislators attempted to avoid it. A decision either way was bound to create political enemies. In writing of his assignment to his stepmother, Coolidge said:

> I am chairman of the committee to see if any
> conciliation can be brought about at Lawrence. The
> leaders there are socialists and anarchists, and they do
> not want anybody to work for wages. The trouble is not
> about the amount of wages; it is a small attempt to
> destroy all authority whether of any church or
> government.

These private views notwithstanding, Coolidge and his committee heard all the evidence. In the end, the committee recommended a wage increase of up to 25 percent, and time and a quarter pay for overtime, which the company accepted. The strike ended peacefully, and Coolidge received favorable press coverage. He was still a freshman senator, and didn't seem much more than able.

In 1912 Republican politicians throughout the country faced a major problem—on February 21, Theodore Roosevelt announced his intention to challenge William Howard Taft for the GOP nomination. If defeated, there was a good chance TR would run as a third party candidate. Earlier on, Senator Robert La Follette had thrown down the gauntlet to Taft and obtained the Independent League's support. Now most members deserted to Roosevelt.

These developments threw the Massachusetts Republicans into disarray, and created wounds that would take more than a generation to heal. Roosevelt had the support of the progressive element, and some conservatives, believing he was the only candidate who might win, were leaning toward him as well. But then, as Roosevelt's talk turned to what at the time seemed radical programs, the moderates and conservatives returned to Taft. In any event, there was bound to be a party split.

Massachusetts was one of twelve states that held primary elections in 1912. Taft defeated Roosevelt there by a margin of 87,000 to 83,000, splitting the GOP down the middle. When Taft won the nomination that June, Roosevelt walked out to form the Progressive Party, whose nomination he accepted in August. The Democrats, who had gone through a similar partition in 1896, knew that this gave them a good chance to recapture the White House for the first time since Grover Cleveland had been elected to a second term in 1892, and that divisions on the local level might result in a Democratic House of Representatives and sweeps in some state houses and legislatures.

At the time, Eugene Foss was completing his second term as Massachusetts governor, and he intended to run for a third. A Republican who had switched to the Democratic Party, Foss was the sort of politician who appealed to Roosevelt followers. As his opponent, the Republicans nominated Joseph Walker. The Progressives selected Charles Bird, who once had been a Democrat, voted for Taft in 1908, and now was a Roosevelt supporter.

To complicate matters further, Crane announced his intention to retire from the U.S. Senate, setting off a struggle within the Republican ranks that caused more heat than even the presidential race, since by then it was assumed that Democratic presidential nominee Woodrow Wilson would gain the White House. In the end, the Republican leaders backed John Weeks for the nomination. Weeks was a wealthy banker and a Crane man, a dull speaker, a staunch opponent of women's franchise, a supporter of Prohibition, and a critic of organized labor, none of which was popular in the eastern part of the state. Sensing these weaknesses, the charismatic Samuel McCall, who was more liberal on these issues, challenged Weeks.

McCall came close to winning the nomination, but after a bitter struggle Weeks prevailed.

As the election neared, the thought of a Roosevelt presidency, and what it would mean to the state Republican Party, led a large number of GOP voters to conclude that they would be better served by a Wilson victory than another Roosevelt term. With no little disgust, they intended to vote Democratic, many for the first time in their lives. The split gave Wilson the Massachusetts electoral votes. Wilson received 174,000 votes, Taft 156,000, and Roosevelt 142,000. Weeks won the Senate seat against Democrat Sherman Whipple, with the support of Crane—and Coolidge. As expected, Foss won reelection with 193,000 votes to Walker's 144,000 and Bird's 123,000. The split vote thus gave him a rare third term. The state legislature remained Republican.

Coolidge easily won reelection to the state senate by a vote of 6,211 against Democrat Herbert Joyner's 4,222. The Progressives had intended to run a candidate in this race, but, perhaps because the party realized they couldn't defeat Coolidge, none appeared. Writing to his father after the election, Coolidge said he was "gratified" by the vote. "I was sorry that Taft could not win but am glad TR made so poor a showing. I doubt if Wilson will be a man the Democrats like. A large number of Democrats voted for Taft here. It was the Republicans voting for Wilson to kill TR that brought about the result." Even so, on the basis of his record and statements, during this period Coolidge was closer to Roosevelt than Taft; he had supported labor legislation, wages and hours laws, medical care for the indigent and chronic sufferers, factory legislation, higher wages for teachers, and even unionization. These were the Progressive programs of 1912, and Coolidge was clearly in line with these thoughts.

Coolidge was a party regular. There never was a possibility of him bolting the GOP. He might be a reformer on the stump and in his votes, but only so long as his constituents and political supporters were interested in reform and change. This was the way it had been while TR was president. He remained progressive during the Taft years, because Taft was not the conservative he was painted to be in the 1912 canvass. But as the Republican Party shifted ground, so did

Coolidge—but slowly, cautiously, and not completely until he felt it absolutely necessary, and never as fast or as far as the true conservatives would have liked. It was a Coolidge trait, on display throughout his political life.

Coolidge was one of the big winners in that election, not so much for the large vote he received, but for the perch he had achieved within the party and the legislature. "I have been placed in a position of great influence this year," he told his father, "being one of the three leaders and not the least of them." In his *Autobiography* he indicated that this was not an idle boast to a parent. "It was in my second term in the senate that I began to be a force in the Massachusetts legislature." He became chairman of the important Committee on Railroads and took a seat on the still more important Committee on Rules. Coolidge was a coming man within the party. While not a member of the inner circle of distinguished and powerful GOP stalwarts, he was admitted to the fringe, where he was recognized by and conversed with the likes of Senators Lodge and Weeks, party boss Guy Currier, Justice Walter Perley Hall, and his distant cousin, Louis A. Coolidge—and, of course, Crane.

His path to the top was now clear. Coolidge would next attempt to become president of the senate, and from there would seek the lieutenant governorship, which was directly in line for the State House. In 1912, at the age of forty, Coolidge could aspire to so high a position. After that, he could have a greatly enhanced law practice, membership on the boards of corporations, and a comfortable life, freed at last from needing those checks from his father. This, however, was probably the limit of Coolidge's ambition at the time. But who can tell? He told Dwight Morrow, "One should never trouble about getting a better job. But one should do one's present job in such a manner as to qualify for a better job when it comes along."

The way Coolidge became president of the Massachusetts senate was yet another example of the uncanny good fortune that marked his entire political career. Of course good fortune, or luck if you will, wasn't the only ingredient, for without shrewd calculations and the help of friends, Coolidge probably would have returned to Northampton and obscurity.

First, Coolidge had to run for a third term as state senator, which defied tradition—the two-term rule also applied there. Were it not for the possibility of the senate presidency, he might not have considered another term. But he knew that senate president Levi Greenwood, an extremely conservative politician, was interested in the lieutenant governorship, which would create the vacancy. On this possibility, the GOP organization in Northampton was willing to give Coolidge the third chance, undoubtedly expecting patronage rewards if he did become senate president. He set about meeting with senate colleagues in an attempt to line up votes. Then Greenwood decided to abandon the race for lieutenant governor, and instead sought another senate term.

Greenwood did not take into account the extent of the lingering effects of the 1912 party split. He must have believed that while 1913 would be a Democratic year, his district was safe. If so, he was only partially right. Amid the rancor, Democrat David Walsh was elected governor, becoming the first Irish–Catholic to win a statewide race in Massachusetts; moreover, the entire Democratic slate was carried into office. In addition, the flamboyant James Curley, the Irish–Catholic son of a hod carrier, was elected mayor of Boston. Greenwood, who was an active opponent of women's suffrage, lost his reelection bid when his opponents—led by suffragette Margaret Foley—united around a single candidate. As for Coolidge, he won reelection to the senate by a larger margin than before, with 5,140 votes against Democrat Joseph Malony's 3,721 and Progressive George Pettee's 927.

Coolidge has often been portrayed as slow and reluctant to act. True enough, but when the odds were in his favor and swift action was needed, he could be decisive and even bold, as he was in this case. The next day, Wednesday, Coolidge went to Boston, first to meet with Crane, and then to renew his lobbying campaign for the senate presidency. By Monday, with Crane's help and the support of the business interests whom Crane represented, Coolidge was able to line up more than enough supporters for the nomination, which he received with a unanimous vote. The *Springfield Republican* wrote of the selection, "It was nothing short of wonderful the way he walked right into the ring and took the prize before the public could realize there was a contest." Remarking on the election in his *Autobiography*, Coolidge said:

> The senate showed the effects of the division in our
> party. It had twenty-one Republicans, seventeen
> Democrats and two Progressives. When the vote was
> cast for president on the opening day of the General
> Court, Senator Cox the Progressive had two votes,
> Senator Horgan the Democrat had seven votes, and I
> had thirty-one votes. I had not only become an officer
> of the whole commonwealth, but I had come into
> possession of an influence reaching beyond the confines
> of my own party which I was to retain so long as I
> remained in public life.

These lines, written after Coolidge's successful tenure as president of the *United States*, indicate the pride he continued to feel about that day in the Massachusetts senate. He did not directly mention that ten Democrats had voted for him. While senate president, Coolidge would occasionally hand the gavel to a ranking Democrat when he had to leave for other business. This may have been nothing more than a gesture—it extracted no real price. But it paid dividends in the form of Democratic support for several of his key programs.*

His was a popular choice. The following Sunday a *Boston Sunday Globe* writer said, "Coolidge will make a good presiding officer. He doesn't need to consult a specialist when anything bobs up that requires nerve. He can state a humorous legislative proposition without smiling."

---

* Strangely, this practice is not common. Republican Senator John McCain of Arizona realized the importance of such symbols. In 1997, while chairman of the Senate Commerce Committee, he left the chair and turned it over to a surprised Senator Ernest Hollings, a Democrat from South Carolina. Hollings quickly recovered, and said, "John, I'd be delighted to take it, but some of your colleagues might object," to which McCain replied, "Screw that." In recounting the story, Hollings added, "I do admire that John McCain."

Coolidge assumed the senate presidency on January 7, 1914. John Coolidge was present to see and hear his son take office, and was both proud and apprehensive: "You would be surprised to see the power Calvin seems to have," he wrote to his wife. "Everyone seems ready to carry out his wishes when he makes them known, he receives letters of congratulation from all quarters. I hope he makes no mistakes...."

On this occasion he delivered an acceptance speech that came to be known as "Have Faith in Massachusetts." It was short, really a series of simple, declarative sentences, and Coolidge clearly selected his words with care. If the ideas are unremarkable, they also are crystal-clear, and presented in typical Coolidge style.

Hereafter Coolidge would deliver two kinds of speeches. The first type was filled with facts, programs, recommendations, and concrete suggestions—his State of the State and State of the Union addresses often followed this format. The second, which he preferred, was marked by generalities and revealed his political and social philosophy as derived from Garman. Both were terse, but some of the more graceful were among the latter. Moreover, they offer insight into this reticent figure.

In this speech before the state senate, after the obligatory salute, Coolidge said:

> This commonwealth is one. We are all members of one body. The welfare of the weakest and the welfare of the most powerful are inseparably bound together. Industry cannot flourish if labor languish. Transportation cannot prosper if manufactures decline. The general welfare cannot be provided for in any one act, but it is well to remember that the benefit of one is the benefit of all, and the neglect of one is the neglect of all. The suspension of one man's dividends is the suspension of another man's pay envelope.
>
> Men do not make laws. They do but discover them. Laws must be justified by something more than the will of the majority. They must rest on the eternal foundation of righteousness. That state is most fortunate in its form

of government which has the aptest instruments for the discovery of laws. The latest, most modern and nearest perfect system that statesmanship has devised is representative government. Its weakness is the weakness of us imperfect human beings who administer it. Its strength is that even such administration secures to the people more blessings than any other system ever produced. No nation has discarded it and retained liberty. Representative government must be preserved.

Coolidge spoke of the courts as guardians of liberty, and of the limitations of government:

The people cannot look to legislation generally for success. Industry, thrift, character, are not conferred by act or resolve. Government cannot relieve from toil. It can provide no substitute for the rewards of service. It can, of course, care for the defective and recognize distinguished merit. The normal must care for themselves. Self-government means self-support.

In these words we see the Coolidge whom Ronald Reagan admired—the Coolidge who has been lost to the caricature of "Silent Cal." What followed was the most often quoted statement in the address:

Do the day's work. If it be to protect the rights of the weak, whoever objects, do it. If it is to help a powerful corporation, do that. Expect to be called a stand-patter, but don't be a stand-patter. Expect to be called a demagogue, but don't be a demagogue. Don't hesitate to be as revolutionary as science. Don't hesitate to be as reactionary as the multiplication table. Don't expect to build up the weak by pulling down the strong. Don't hurry to legislate. Give administration a chance to catch up with legislation.

We need a broader, firmer, deeper faith in the
people—a faith that men desire to do right, that the
commonwealth is founded upon a righteousness which
will endure, a reconstructed faith that the final
approval of the people is given not to demagogues,
slavishly pandering to their selfishness, merchandising
with the clamor of the hour, but to statesmen,
ministering to their welfare, representing their deep,
silent, abiding convictions.

Coolidge concluded, typically, with an appeal to the spiritual.
Though this is a common technique, Coolidge was more graceful
than most in his peroration:

Statutes must appeal to more than material welfare.
Wages won't satisfy, be they ever so large. Nor houses;
nor lands; nor coupons, though they fall thick as the
leaves of autumn. Man has a spiritual nature. Touch it,
and it must respond as the magnet responds to the
pole. To that, not to selfishness, let the laws of the
commonwealth appeal. Recognize the immortal worth
and dignity of man. Let the laws of Massachusetts
proclaim to her humblest citizen, performing the most
menial task, the recognition of his manhood, the
recognition that all men are peers, the humblest with
the most exalted, the recognition that all work is
glorified. Such is the path to equality before the law.
Such is the foundation of liberty under the law. Such is
the sublime revelation of man's relation to man—
Democracy.

The legislature had been treated to the kind of speech Coolidge
would often deliver, in his own distinctive style. In 1923, for
instance, Vice President Coolidge delivered a speech at Wheaton
College entitled "The Things That Are Unseen," which echoed the
cadences of "Have Faith in Massachusetts":

We do not need more material development, we need
more spiritual development. We do not need more
intellectual power, we need more moral power. We do
not need more knowledge, we need more character. We
do not need more government, we need more culture.
We do not need more law, we need more religion. We do
not need more of the things that are seen, we need more
of the things that are unseen. It is on that side of life that
it is desirable to put the emphasis at the present time. If
that side be strengthened, the other side will take care of
itself. It is that side which is the foundation of all else. If
the foundation be firm, the superstructure will stand.
The success or failure of liberal education, the
justification of its protection and encouragement by the
government, and of its support by society, will be
measured by its ability to minister to this great cause, to
perform the necessary services, to make the required
redeeming sacrifices.

The next day's newspapers praised the new senate president
highly for the speech. Reporters singled out several phrases for special attention, in particular Coolidge's call for slowing down legislation: "Give administration a chance to catch up with legislation."
Coolidge, who was deliberate in selecting his words, probably meant
that there was sufficient legislation on the books, and implementation was now needed. While running for lieutenant governor in 1915
he said as much: "We do not need more legislation. Repeal is even
unnecessary. What Massachusetts needs—what the nation needs—
is wise administration of the law. Look not to the legislature for
relief; look to the executive."

Throughout his political career, Coolidge believed strongly in the
separation of powers between the two branches, believed that
the chief duty of the executive was to carry out the laws passed by
the legislature, and that in Massachusetts this was a prime necessity. He would return to this thought on numerous occasions. In his
second inaugural as governor in 1920, Coolidge said, "In general, it
is time to conserve, to retrench rather than to reform; a time to sta-

bilize the administration of the present laws rather than to seek new legislation." Of course, the nation would witness the concept on the larger scale of federal government in the 1920s.

Coolidge was pleased at the reception of the "Have Faith in Massachusetts" speech. Writing to his stepmother, he somewhat boastfully noted, "My speech has come back to me from many places and some of the best papers in the state have printed it in their editorial columns." Within days, the Massachusetts press was busily musing about Coolidge's gubernatorial possibilities. In part this was due to his record and the speech, but even more to the way he had managed his election to the presidency. Also, all senate presidents were considered likely lieutenant governor nominees—and the path to the governorship lay in that direction. In 1914 Coolidge seemed on the way to the next two steps up the political ladder in a normally Republican state. His prospects were pleasing, his future apparently assured.

Letters of congratulation poured in, and in order to capitalize upon the reception, Coolidge sent copies to many people on the national scene as well as the local. Former President Taft congratulated Coolidge, thanking him for "sending it to me and for giving me an opportunity to read it." There was a long, gracious letter from Senator Lodge. Lodge knew Coolidge was a Crane man, but did not as yet see him as a threat. At the time the two men had not yet met. The Lodge letter indicates that the senator considered Coolidge a consequential figure in state politics, and one to be courted, if only in a minor way. But Lodge's eye was ever on the national scene, and Coolidge could have no place there.

> I am much obliged to you for sending me the *Journal of the Senate* for January 7th, because it has given me the opportunity to read again your speech which I had already read in the newspapers. I am more struck with it on the second reading even than I was with it on the first. It is not only able but you have put the propositions with epigrammatic force and often in a very original way. That is saying much, for you are stating what you and I believe to be fundamental truths.

What I like best of all is the courage with which you
state those fundamental truths which it is the fashion
just now to put aside and hide. For some years past
political leaders, great and small, have been talking to
the people as though these truths did not exist. For
example, directly and indirectly it has been continually
declared that everybody would be made happy and
successful by legislation, a most pernicious doctrine.
Then again, the whole trend of the national legislation
and the Democratic Party has been toward the
destruction of property, entirely forgetting the fact that
the rights of property—and property as such possesses
not rights in this country—and the human right to have
property which are two totally different things. As a
citizen of Massachusetts I congratulate myself that we
have a president of the senate who not only is able but
who is ready to make such a speech.

This was high praise from the man known as "the scholar in politics." Coolidge couldn't have helped but be flattered by the apparent seriousness with which Lodge took the speech. He sent this letter
on to his stepmother too, adding that when she finished reading it,
she should return it.

Coolidge remained as discreet as ever, and his instinct for correct
behavior, reinforced by his strongly held sense of what was right,
remained intact. When the Massachusetts government set about
naming a delegation to attend the San Francisco Exposition, a clear
example of a political junket, Coolidge was named as a member. It
was a chance to see the country from a first class train, and might
have been exciting for someone who had travelled so little. "Well,
Calvin, you have a very enjoyable trip in prospect," said one of his
colleagues. "Not going" was the reply. "Not going? How unfortunate. It would really be one of the opportunities of a lifetime."
Coolidge reflected, and then said, "See Massachusetts first." As it
happened, the news of the frivolous trip hit the newspapers, and
embarrassed those who had gone.

The following year Coolidge did travel to Washington for the first
time. He saw the usual sights, and met with several politicians,

Lodge among them. Once more, the senator was gracious to his "country cousin," and patronized and flattered him during their meeting. Coolidge, by now a seasoned politician, realized what was happening, and took it all in as part of the game.

John Coolidge had probably been quite accurate in observing the extent of his son's power. Coolidge was the leader of the senate, and the highest elected Republican in the state, but at the time he seemed like most other senate presidents. Governor Walsh, on the other hand, was quite novel. Like Curley, he was a man of modest means, the son of a combmaker, in a period when such individuals weren't elected to any but local positions. He appeared a true reformer, moreover, pushing for many progressive programs. For instance, Walsh called for a state constitutional convention to consider adopting the initiative, referendum, and recall of elective officers; he favored greater home rule for the cities; he spoke out for women's suffrage, the expansion of workmen's compensation, and even a line item veto. And Walsh managed to get many of his recommendations accepted during his first term. The newspapers wrote that Walsh and Curley represented the new spirit in Massachusetts.

Meanwhile, quietly, often behind the scenes, Coolidge accumulated power and influence. Walsh's victories were due in part to Coolidge's successful attempts to work with the Democrats, his willingness to accept Walsh's agenda when he could, to modify bills when he felt this necessary, and to reject them occasionally and then with reluctance.

Coolidge devoted much of his time to party business, especially the problems of bringing the Progressives back into the GOP and lining up candidates for the 1914 election. The party selected Samuel McCall to run for governor. McCall, who had earlier lost the senatorial nomination to Weeks, was a retired congressman who had been a Mugwump—a bolter from the party—when the Republicans divided over the nomination of James G. Blaine in 1884, and was generally considered a reformer. After a stint as a newspaper editor he served in the General Court, and in the U.S. House of Representatives from 1893 to 1913, after which he opened a law office. McCall remained in the party in 1912—he did not desert to the Progressives—and so he won the support of the regulars. Clearly, McCall was nominated as a unity candidate.

The platform was quite progressive, due largely to Coolidge, who was chairman of the Resolutions Committee. It called for wages and hours legislation, health and safety measures in the workplaces, and safeguards for child welfare. In a section written by Coolidge, the platform called for continued support

> [of] every means of compulsory and public education, vocational and technical; merited retirement pensions, aid to dependent mothers, healthful housing and fire protection, reasonable hours and conditions of labor, and amplest protection to the public health, workingmen's compensation and its extension to interstate railroads, official investigation of the price of necessities, pure food and honest weight and measure, homestead commission, city planning, the highest care and efficiency in the administration of all hospital and penal institutions, probation and parole, care and protection of children and the mentally defective, rural development, urban sanitation, state and national conservation and reclamation, and every other public means for social welfare consistent with the sturdy character and resolute spirit of an independent, self-supporting, self-governing, and free people.

This amounted to an endorsement of the Progressive platform. It was political prudence at the time—and Coolidge was ever prudent.

Walsh, who was a popular governor, won by only a narrow margin, indicating that the breach with the Progressives within the GOP was healing, with some of the dissidents returning. Republican Grafton Cushing was elected lieutenant governor, and did better than McCall among the voters. On good terms with the former Progressives, Cushing was considered a potential nominee for higher office sometime later on. Coolidge won reelection in 1914 against Democrat Ralph Staab by a vote of 6,381 to 3,596, his largest margin yet. Once again he was to be senate president, this time by a unanimous vote. Those who recalled his first address gathered to hear the second. They were disappointed, even though it concluded with a typical example of Coolidge humor:

> My sincerest thanks I offer you. Conserve the firm
> foundations of our institutions. Do your work with the
> spirit of a soldier in the public service. Be loyal to the
> commonwealth and to yourselves and be brief; above all
> things, be brief.

Coolidge was involved in a bit of business that would help alter his life. It was to bring him into contact with a man who could not be considered his next mentor—no, by now Calvin Coolidge had become a mature thinker in his own right. Rather, this man became an associate with whom Coolidge would have an unusual and fruitful relationship.

In the spring of 1912, Frank Stearns, an Amherst trustee, had been asked to see Coolidge regarding a bill dealing with sewage disposal in the town. Stearns arrived at Coolidge's office the following year, only to be told by the senator, "I'm sorry. It's too late." Stearns departed, angered at being so rudely treated by a fellow alumnus. Coolidge, however, did not forget, and in 1915 he used his influence to have the measure passed, without telling Stearns.

Versions of what happened next differ. According to one, Dwight Morrow, by then a coming man on Wall Street, spoke with Stearns about Coolidge. "I have a classmate in Boston who is quite a fellow—named Coolidge. Do you know him?" Stearns said he did not, to which Morrow replied, "You ought to—I will tell him that he ought to know you."

A group of Amherst men soon met to consider whether to back one of their classmates for higher office, in the hope of countering Harvard's influence in the state house. Judge Field, Coolidge's legal mentor, mentioned him to Stearns as a man the Amherst contingent should get behind. Stearns was displeased. "Well, if you say Coolidge, it's Coolidge. But the only time I ever met him he insulted me." Field then told of Coolidge's role in the bill's passage, and of the unusual way Coolidge got things done. They met again, and at first Coolidge was uncommunicative, but then he approached Stearns and said, "Ever anything you want up on the Hill come up and see me." And Stearns did come see Coolidge in the senate chamber.

> While I sat there, three different senators, one after another, stuck their heads in the opening in the portieres, saying, "Mr. President, I think we ought to do so-and-so." In each case he answered, "No," and the senator simply said, "All right, just as you say." This entire absence of effort to impress me was different from the action of any politician that I had ever met, and it finally interested me so much that I began to look him up.

Stearns was hooked, and quickly became Coolidge's most important confidant and aide. After Coolidge became president of the United States, Stearns wrote to Grace Coolidge:

> You and I have one thing in common, at any rate. You picked out Calvin Coolidge some years ago and gave him your endorsement; more recently I picked him out and gave him the most emphatic endorsement I know how to. Of course many others can claim to have picked him out, but amongst them all I think we can shake hands over the proposition that yours was the most important endorsement and mine comes next.

In 1915 some within the Coolidge circle thought he might go all the way to the State House. Stearns believed that Coolidge—then only president of the Massachusetts senate, and barely known anywhere outside the state—was the greatest contemporary American political figure and was destined to wind up in the White House. To anyone but Stearns, the thought was preposterous at the time, but to him, it was inevitable. In all matters concerning Calvin Coolidge, he was a true believer.

Frank Stearns was an intelligent, able man, but, to casual acquaintances, he seemed by no means exceptional. He was fifty-nine years old in 1915, with a head of grey hair and a moustache to match. Of medium height, thick-set, and generally grave, he looked like the prosperous Boston merchant that he was. The dry goods store of R.H. Stearns and Company had been founded by his father in 1847. After graduating from Amherst in 1878, Stearns went to New York, where he worked for a year in the wool business. Stearns returned to Boston in 1880, and soon became president of the family store. In 1905 Stearns began work on a large department store in Boston Common, which opened in 1909 and quickly became the most popular in the city. In the years that followed he divided his time between expanding the store and tending to his family, and to Amherst, to which he was devoted.

Until he met Coolidge, Stearns had next to nothing to do with politics. Then he plunged into it with gusto. It must have seemed strange to professionals like Murray Crane and William Butler, who saw Stearns laboring away for Coolidge, providing him with funds and raising more from others, and never asking for favors in return. This was not the way political sponsors were supposed to behave. They had memories of Mark Hanna, William McKinley's chief operative, who took his payment in the form of favorable legislation, power within the party, and recommendations for appointments, and who eventually wound up in the Senate. In his time Hanna was one of the most commanding figures in the GOP, and he relished the role of kingmaker. Stearns, on the other hand, did not yearn for public office. He shrank from power. He was unique—a man wholly and completely devoted to the career of another man, for reasons of civic pride and patriotism.

Although Stearns would offer advice and ideas, he almost never volunteered his thoughts on legislation or political appointments. Once, however, while Coolidge was governor, Stearns was approached by a friend who asked his help in obtaining a judicial appointment. Stearns replied, "I have never made a recommendation for an appointment to the governor, and I never shall," but later that day he did mention the applicant's name to Coolidge.

"Mr. Stearns, what do you know of this gentleman's legal and judicial training?"

"I'm afraid that I don't know very much about it except that he's a fine man and a staunch supporter of yours."

"Mr. Stearns, I don't think that you ought to interfere in matters about which you are so badly informed."

And that was that. Stearns did not repeat the mistake. Later, another supplicant approached him, saying, "You have great influence with the governor." Stearns replied, "Yes, perhaps more even than you think, but it will last just as long as I don't try to use it, and not one minute longer."

Some historians have suggested, without offering evidence, that Stearns was a sort of surrogate older brother for Coolidge. However, neither man ever talked about their relationship in more than generalities, so the idea is mere conjecture. Much has been made of a statement by Stearns that one of Coolidge's earliest biographers quoted: "In a social way I feel a father to Calvin Coolidge. In a political way I feel a son to him." Others thought Stearns was a Machiavellian who preferred to operate behind the scenes, manipulating Coolidge for his own ends—but they neglect to indicate what those ends might be.

Clearly Stearns, like Coolidge, was a rarity. The urge among historians to ascribe selfish motivations to him is understandable, for other presidents besides McKinley have had their amanuenses and close associates—Wilson had his Colonel House; Harding had Harry Daugherty; Franklin D. Roosevelt had a host of them, starting with Louis Howe and Harry Hopkins; and of course, there were the Kennedy brothers. But these men, and many others, were quite visible figures in their own right, for they wanted it that way. Even Clark Clifford, who remained in the background while he assisted Harry Truman, emerged as a public figure in his own right. Likewise, Bill Moyers was a dutiful detail man for Lyndon Johnson, but after he left the White House he became an important media figure.

This visibility did not appeal to Stearns. He was utterly without public conceit. He would have fallen on a sword for Coolidge, and not asked anything concrete in return from his idol or posterity. After Coolidge died, he faded away. He was not a politician or public figure. Stearns was a close friend of this one man, and when he left the scene, there was no role he cared to play. He assisted others in their writings on Coolidge, but he would not make his own contribution. Instead, he joined the boards of many philanthropic organizations, remained out of the spotlight, and died barely noticed in 1939. Suffice it to say, Frank Stearns was an enigma, much like the man to whom he was devoted.

In 1931, after receiving copies of the president's collected letters, Stearns wrote a letter expressing his devotion to Coolidge. Their political careers apparently over, Coolidge inscribed the volumes to the man "who really brought me to the position making this book possible." To which Stearns replied, "I cannot think of anyone in the history of this country who had anything so much to be prized, unless by chance either George Washington or Abraham Lincoln saw fit to say something of a similar kind to some devoted friend of his." This was nothing new; almost from the time he got to know Coolidge in 1915, Stearns told all who would listen of his virtues.

Could it have been that Stearns, who was not a simpleton, truly believed Coolidge belonged in the pantheon of American saints? Clearly he admired Coolidge, and considered him an exceptional individual—honest, forthright, and intelligent. But there was another quality Coolidge possessed that attracted Stearns: Coolidge was an Amherst man, and Stearns loved the school. On July 23, 1915, in a letter to Dr. George Olds, one of Coolidge's classmates and a member of the Amherst faculty, Stearns revealed his ambition for Coolidge:

> Just for a minute it does not seem best to push him for anything higher than lieutenant governor of Massachusetts, but later, of course, he must be governor and still later president. *Just think what a time we will have at commencement when the president of the United States, a graduate of your Class, '95, comes back to commencement!*" [emphasis added].

In that time, the loyalties graduates felt for their colleges and fraternities ran deep. Stearns's dedication to Coolidge may have derived, in part at least, from his passion for his school.

In 1935 Grace Coolidge asked a group of those who had known her by-then deceased husband to write their recollections of him, to which she appended comments. Stearns provided anecdotes, but little else. In her notes, Mrs. Coolidge said:

> Mr. Stearns knew and understood the president as no other man knew and understood him. He stood by in his quiet, self-effacing way, eager to help, but never offering advice unless it was sought. Sometimes they had long talks together in the president's study, at other times days would pass in which few words were exchanged.
>
> In the early days the newspaper correspondents thought Mr. Stearns might prove to be a source of ready information, but they soon learned that as a contact man he was an excellent Boston merchant; they welcomed him when he came upon a group of them gathered in an outer room of the executive offices not as a man who had great secrets locked within his breast, but as a friend who trusted them.

Coolidge himself wrote this of Stearns in his *Autobiography*:

> While Mr. Stearns always overestimated me, he nevertheless was a great help to me. He never obtruded or sought any favor for himself or any other person, but his whole effect was always disinterested and entirely devoted to assisting me when I indicated I wanted him to do so. It is doubtful if any other public man ever had so valuable and unselfish a friend.

So, in 1915, after falling under Coolidge's sway, Stearns set about organizing the Amherst alumni for his candidate, and a series of fundraising events followed. Coolidge must have been aware of just how important such funds and connections could be for his political future. In a letter to his father after one of these affairs, he wrote, "I think you would have been proud of the character of the men who came to honor me."

Although Stearns was a conservative Republican, he refused to talk about the specific details of his ideology. Clause Fuess, one of the most astute Coolidge biographers, suggested that Coolidge's public utterances became more conservative after he met Stearns. The man who earlier had shown compassion for workers, the unemployed, child and women labor, now told reporters, "If a man is out of a job it's his own fault"; "The state is not warranted in furnishing employment for anybody so that that person may have work"; and "Anybody who is not capable of supporting himself is not fit for self-government." But his progressive statements continued as well. Overall, Coolidge was consistent throughout this period—there was no dramatic change in philosophy. In a letter to a friend, he said, "I think I have a reputation of being conservative, which I am, because I do not make so loud a noise as some others. [But] I think I have been in sympathy with practically all legislation intended to improve living conditions."

As far as Stearns was concerned, any change in Coolidge's attitudes was part of his maturity. In a letter to a business associate, Robert Maynard, on August 16, 1916, Stearns wrote:

> He told me once that when he first went into the legislature he supposes he was considered a radical, especially along the lines of legislation in favor of social betterment. There came a time around the middle of his legislative experience when he came to the conviction *not* that his previous ideas were wrong but that Massachusetts, at any rate, was going too fast. As he put it, legislation was outstripping the ability to administer. He felt that unless we were willing to get into serious trouble that would take years to rectify, a halt must be called; and he faced about and was probably then considered a conservative.

Encouraged by Stearns, his traditional friends, and the Amherst alumni, Coolidge prepared to run for lieutenant governor. His public statements became far more restrained, perhaps because Coolidge realized that Samuel McCall would get the gubernatorial nomination and that he was positioning himself to balance the ticket by being to the right of the leader. Or, as Stearns suggested, his restraint in this time might reflect the gradual alteration of his own philosophy. Coolidge's attitudes on public matters had developed when Progressivism was a potent force on the state scene, but by 1915 it seemed certain TR would return to the GOP and the Progressive Party would disintegrate.

Republican Grafton Cushing, who had been president of the senate and then lieutenant governor, might have stayed on in the latter post, but in this period he had ambitions for the governorship itself. Were this not the case, Coolidge would not have made the race, given his cautious nature and the style of Massachusetts GOP politics. But Cushing opened the way for Coolidge to run for lieutenant governor.

During the next few months Coolidge conferred with Crane, Field, and Stearns, among others, about his chances. He would not make the move until and unless the odds were strongly in his favor—Coolidge did not relish the idea of a losing campaign. There is some evidence that he sought a backup position, selection for one bureaucratic job or another if the bid failed. But finally, on June 20, he went to see Stearns, and handed him a note:

> I am a candidate for lieutenant governor.
> Calvin Coolidge

His more formal announcement soon after was almost as spare.

> I am a candidate for lieutenant governor. This
> announcement is made for the purpose of informing my
> fellow-citizens of my plans. I shall discuss my reasons
> for being a candidate and place before the voters an
> expression of my views upon those issues which
> confront the people of Massachusetts.

A trifle miffed, Stearns asked Coolidge why he hadn't made the announcement while the senate was in session, in order to maximize the impact and give him more time to electioneer. Coolidge's reply indicated how sophisticated he had become in the ways of Massachusetts politics:

I could not have acted like myself if I had announced my candidacy during the session. No matter what I did or said, it would have been misconstrued, and there would have been thirty-nine candidates to succeed me as president of the senate. It would have interfered with the public business of the senate.

As noted, the candidates for both governor and lieutenant governor would be selected through the primary process, which meant that they had to appeal to the electorate rather than the party bosses, which suited Stearns. He sprang into action, sending off his missives throughout the state, drumming up support. Coolidge did the same, with behind-the-scenes help from William Butler and the powerful Crane organization. A committee was established to take charge of the campaign, with Stearns as chairman and representatives from all parts of the state. Stearns made it quite clear that he was willing to spend large amounts in Coolidge's behalf. But it wasn't necessary; as Coolidge wrote in his *Autobiography*, "[T]he expense [of my campaign for lieutenant governor] was within the allowed limit of $1,500, which was contributed by numerous people. I was thus under no especial obligation to any one for raising money for me."

Coolidge's major adversary was Guy Ham, a Boston lawyer and an old-fashioned orator who had Rooseveltian overtones, with Prohibitionist proclivities. Although Ham had served in the General Court, he lacked the leadership role Coolidge possessed. The leading gubernatorial candidate was Samuel McCall, now sixty-six years old. He again intended to appeal to former Progressives to return to their old home. His opponents included Cushing, who had strength only in eastern Massachusetts, and Eugene Foss, the erratic former governor whose party switches both confused and irritated the electorate. In the gubernatorial nomination the party members had a known quality in McCall versus the unknown and the capricious, while the race for the nomination for lieutenant governor was between the solid Coolidge and the flamboyant Ham. On September 28, a week after the primary, while the ballots were still being counted, Coolidge wrote to his father, telling him that all was well, and that it looked as though he had won. He added a few words about Stearns. "I do not know why he has been so interested in my success but he has been very much so. He has never taken any part in politics before. He is a great worker."

On another occasion Coolidge wrote again to his father about his chances for the nomination:

> The campaign is coming to a close and while it is impossible to tell what is going to happen the outcome seems to be good. I think I have been making very large gains in the past two weeks. Every newspaper of importance in the state is supporting me. The business interests also appear to be on my side. Whatever the outcome may be my support has been such that I am very proud of it and feel that I shall be a gainer by having been a candidate even if I am not nominated.

Coolidge defeated Ham by a lopsided vote of 75,000 to 50,000, and McCall won the gubernatorial nomination over his two rivals with 66,000 votes to Cushing's 60,000 and Foss's 10,000. As anticipated, the Democrats renominated Walsh and ran the colorless former lieutenant governor Edward Barry—who had preceded Cushing in that office and had lost to him in 1913—against Coolidge.

It was a vigorous campaign. McCall and Coolidge campaigned together, and the contrast between the flamboyant gubernatorial candidate and the drab Coolidge was striking, but they complemented one another nicely. Their stump styles were a study in contrasts. William Allen White wrote that "McCall could fill any hall in Massachusetts and Coolidge could empty it." McCall would appeal to the reform elements, while Coolidge was there to assure the regulars of "sound government." If Coolidge had the Amherst contingent hard at work in his behalf, McCall, who was a staunch and active member of the Dartmouth alumni association—he had once been offered the presidency of the college—could count on support from that quarter.

Stearns led the campaign for Coolidge as though he were running for national office. He flooded the state with copies of "Have

Faith in Massachusetts," and the Coolidge campaign may have even cost more than McCall's. Stearns brought in some outside speakers to assist his candidate, including Senator Warren Harding of Ohio. Walsh was harmed by allegations that he would support Prohibition, a major source of contention, but in fact none of the four candidates was a Prohibitionist.

This time, unlike in the primary, Coolidge was quite confident of the results. On October 10 he wrote to his stepmother about his prospects: "I would not be surprised if I got the most votes of anyone on the ticket"—which indeed was the case. McCall defeated Walsh by a vote of 235,000 to 229,000, while Coolidge's margin was more than 52,000. Coolidge wrote to his father, "I have no doubt that my being on the ticket elected Mr. McCall." The *Boston Herald* appeared to agree. "The election has given the Republican Party a new leader in its lieutenant governor–elect, Calvin Coolidge of Northampton." The *Daily Hampshire Gazette* seconded the thought, but took note of several important aspects of the races:

> Calvin Coolidge is the great vote-getter, and will be governor in time. He was fortunate in the man he had against him, while McCall was unfortunate. Walsh was popular, and it was a wonder people voted against him. Barry was not popular. Coolidge had this to help him and McCall had opposite conditions to pull against him. But Coolidge has positive qualities which attract votes. He is efficient. He understands the state business and has made one of the best senate presidents on record. His speeches are gems, and have attracted more attention than those of any man in public life for many years. There is a real basis for the popularity of Mr. Coolidge, and it will last.

Stearns was ecstatic. Replying to Coolidge's rather formal letter of thanks, he wrote:

> As I look at it, your campaigns have only had an auspicious opening. They are in their early stages as yet.

> As long as I have health and strength, you can count on
> me.... I am almost staggered by the realization that
> every step now must be taken with great care, because
> the opportunity is wonderful and the need is almost
> beyond words.

World War I had begun, and by the time Coolidge was inaugurated on January 6, 1916, it was apparent that dreams of a short war would not be realized. It was the beginning of a presidential year, in which Woodrow Wilson would campaign on the slogan "He Kept Us Out of War," and then, after he won the election, would ask for a war declaration. The world was changing rapidly, and in Massachusetts, the solid, dependable, old-fashioned Calvin Coolidge, a man whose values and outlook were so well attuned to the prewar period, was the most striking politician in the state of Massachusetts—a near-certain future nominee for the governorship.

5

....

Governor Coolidge

It was no secret that I desired to be governor. Under the
custom of promotion in Massachusetts a man who did not
expect to advance would scarcely be willing to be lieutenant
governor. But I did nothing in the way of organizing my
friends to secure the nomination. It is much better not to press
a candidacy too much, but to let it develop on its own merits
without artificial stimulation. If the people want a man they
will nominate him, if they do not want him he had best let the
nomination go to another.

The Autobiography of Calvin Coolidge

MASSACHUSETTS WAS NORMALLY a Republican state, and it
was customary for the GOP to permit governors to remain in office
for three one-year terms. So when Coolidge administered the oath of
office to Samuel McCall, he was likely looking ahead to 1919, when
it would be his turn. Perhaps his time would come even sooner, given
the advanced age of the new governor and his supposed senatorial
ambitions.

In fact, McCall was aiming even higher. In December 1915 he
asked Frank Stearns's opinion as to whether he should run for the
presidency the following year. This may have been an oblique way of
learning whether Stearns would lend an organizational and financial
hand, knowing that McCall's early departure for Washington would
open the way for Coolidge in Boston. But Stearns told McCall he did

not think much of the idea, and he probably mentioned it to Coolidge, as well.

The slippery pole of this kind of politics was not for Coolidge. He would have realized the next three years would be dull. For him, or almost anyone else, the senate presidency was more desirable than the lieutenant governorship. As president of the senate, especially with a Democrat in the governor's chair, he had wielded real power. As lieutenant governor he would fill in for McCall when he was out of state and would be a member of the Governor's Council. That was all, except for a salary of $2,000.

In ordinary times Coolidge would have watched and waited, but these were not ordinary times. Because of the war and President Wilson's method of mobilizing the nation, the governors were on call for special assignments, and were asked to work with the War Industries Board to coordinate the procurement effort. Part of the reason for this was Wilson's own experience as governor of New Jersey, but also his innate distrust of central power, even when fostering it. Whatever the reason, McCall often had to be in Washington, and on these occasions, Coolidge took over in Boston.

Unsurprisingly, Coolidge was loyal to McCall, deferring to him on all occasions. Once, while acting-governor, he had occasion to do a favor for a constituent, and took care to remind him that McCall deserved the credit, and not he, who was merely the governor's "temporary agent."

Coolidge delivered speeches around the state, which was expected of all lieutenant governors. In these he called upon government to assist in creating a fairer society. In August he said:

> Good government cannot be found on the bargain counter. We have seen samples of bargain counter government in the past when low tax rates were secured by increasing the bonded debt for current expenses or refusing to keep our institutions up to the standard in repairs, extensions, equipment, and accommodations. I refuse, and the Republican Party refuses, to endorse that method of sham and shoddy economy.

In September Coolidge specifically addressed the matter of a new hospital that was being blocked by some local Democratic politicians. Hospitals and aid to the mentally troubled and feeble-minded were appropriations Coolidge had always supported. "I feel that the time has come when the people must assert themselves and show that they will tolerate no delay and no parsimony in the care of our unfortunates," he said. Then, in what seemed an echo of his "Have Faith in Massachusetts" speech, he went on to reassert his philosophy of government:

> I repeat that this is not partisan. I am not criticizing individuals. I am denouncing a system. When you substitute patronage for patriotism, administration breaks down. We need more of the Office Desk and less of the Show Window in politics. Let men in office substitute the midnight oil for the limelight. Let Massachusetts return to the sound business methods which were exemplified in the East by such Democrats as Governor Gaston and Governor Douglass, and by such Republicans as Governor Robinson and Governor Crane.

Other lieutenant governors attended to their business and professional affairs while in office, but Coolidge decided this was not for him. He had thought it all out carefully. In the summer of 1915, before the election, he invited to his office a young Northampton attorney, Ralph Hemenway, and asked him to join his practice. Hemenway said he would do so if he were made a partner, and not an associate. "Draw up the papers," said Coolidge, which Hemenway did, providing for an equal division of the profits after the second year. Later Coolidge told Hemenway, "If I ever become governor, the business is yours." Hemenway later revealed the papers were never signed. "They had no validity whatever—except that best validity of all by which a man's word is as good as his bond."

It was always "Mr. Coolidge" and "Mr. Hemenway," though their relationship was warm. Once, when Coolidge returned to

Northampton and the law office after leaving the presidency, Hemenway was short of funds due to the closing of a local bank during the hard times of 1931. Coolidge walked into his office and placed a check for $5,000 on the desk. As he walked away, Coolidge remarked, "And as much more as you want."

With Hemenway installed in the Northampton office, Coolidge turned his back on the law for good. Later, when Coolidge was nominated for the vice presidency, Hemenway indicated the extent to which Coolidge had removed himself from the practice: "He could, no doubt, have made me rich by reason of his influence and position, but I can truthfully say that in those five years [that we have been partners] Mr. Coolidge has not turned over a dollar's worth of business through political influence or pull."

McCall and Coolidge ran for reelection in 1916, when Senator John Weeks was Massachusetts's favorite son contender for the presidential nomination. The Democrats nominated Frederick Mansfield for governor and Associate Judge of the First District Court Thomas P. Riley for lieutenant governor. Although he was gradually becoming more conservative in this period, Coolidge still ran what was considered a progressive campaign, especially on the social issues. In a speech at Riverside on August 28, he said:

> We cannot curtail the usual appropriations or the care of mothers with dependent children or the support of the poor, the insane, and the infirm. The Democratic programme of cutting the state tax, by vetoing appropriations of the utmost urgency for improvements and maintenance costs of institutions and asylums of the unfortunates of the state, cannot be the example for a Republican administration. The result has been that our institutions are deficient in resources—even in sleeping accommodations—and it will take years to restore them to the old-time Republican efficiency. Our party will have no part in a scheme of economy which adds to the misery of the wards of the commonwealth—the sick, the insane, and the unfortunate; those who are too weak even to protest.

Coolidge then indicated his priorities.

> Because I know these conditions I know a Republican
> administration would face an increasing state tax rather
> than not see them remedied.
> The Republican Party lit the fire of progress in
> Massachusetts. It has tended it faithfully. It will not
> flicker now.

Coolidge won in a landslide, by a vote of 283,000 to Riley's
199,000. Not only did he outpoll McCall, but he received more
votes than any other statewide candidate.

In his inaugural address, McCall asked for a comprehensive
health insurance program. "I am strongly of the opinion that there
is no form of social insurance that is more humane, sounder in principle, and that would confer greater benefit upon large groups of
our population and upon the commonwealth as a whole than health
insurance." He also asked for legislation to extend old age benefits
and the abolition of capital punishment, then and now a litmus for
liberalism. In all of this, as with everything else, Coolidge supported
his chief.

This was too much for Stearns, who wrote to Coolidge, "Young
man, you are going to get yourself into trouble. You are backing
the governor in things that you know are unwise." Coolidge, who
recognized what his responsibilities—and his limitations—were as
lieutenant governor, wrote back:

> I apprehend that I was elected by the people of
> Massachusetts to do a definite job, second in the
> administration, a long ways behind the first. I accepted
> the office and my duty is perfectly clear—to back up the
> administration to the limit, whether I like it or do not
> like it. If this position should ever be so bad that I
> positively cannot do this, then my duty is equally clear—
> to keep my mouth shut. If any protests are to be made,
> they must be made by the rest of you.

Coolidge's tone perfectly conveyed how he viewed his position in the most practical of terms. This response offers insight into how Coolidge would perform as vice president under Warren G. Harding.

Stearns admired Coolidge because of his principles, and here the lieutenant governor was demonstrating constancy and respect for the political pecking order—which of course was political pragmatism, as well. Although Coolidge indicated that McCall's ideas were not his, he implied that when he became governor, things would be different. In the meantime he would be as still as possible and permit others to voice objections. In this way, Coolidge could be the loyal subaltern and yet maintain his principles.

The nation edged toward war, but Coolidge continued to deliver speeches on local and state matters. He said little about national affairs, and when he criticized the Wilson administration, it tended to be for its domestic rather than foreign policies. In any case, the big issue in the state was neither economic nor political, but constitutional. McCall wanted a state constitutional convention, and one was arranged to begin on June 6, 1917. Coolidge was not a candidate for delegate, but he did attend some of the meetings. There were three sessions, the final one on August 12, 1919. In the end the electorate ratified the new constitution, but then the Massachusetts Supreme Judicial Court set it aside. Some changes were accepted, as well as a provision for the consolidation of many state commissions, meaning the next governor or the one taking office in 1921 would have to dismiss quite a few officeholders, and in addition, starting in 1920, serve a two-year rather than a one-year term.

The team of McCall and Coolidge entered the lists once again in 1917. There was a rumor that Coolidge would oppose McCall in the primary, but the *Boston Evening Transcript* editorialized that there was nothing to it. After McCall won the primary, the paper wrote:

> Calvin Coolidge... who has shown himself one of the shrewdest "politicians," in the best sense of that oftentimes abused word, and one of the biggest vote getters that Massachusetts has even seen, is one big reason for the McCall "landslide."... Whatever he may have individually done to accomplish yesterday's result,

there is no doubt that his hosts of friends throughout the
commonwealth, regardless of their personal sentiments
about McCall, did all they could to renominate His
Excellency. They were determined to leave nothing
undone that would prevent the side-tracking of Coolidge
as Governor McCall's successor next year in the
gubernatorial chair; and with that end in view, they were
a large factor in the result.

McCall once again faced Mansfield in the general election, while
Coolidge's opponent was Bostonian Matthew Hale, a former
Progressive who hoped to woo some of those voters from the GOP.
Coolidge did not appear too troubled by the prospect. The *Boston
Herald*, always favorable to Coolidge, supported him again, and predicted he would win easily, which he did. Coolidge won with a mar-
gin of 102,000, again more than McCall, whose margin was 85,000.
Coolidge even came within 2,500 votes of winning in Democratic
Boston. "I told you the Irish vote would probably be for me," he
wrote to his father after the votes were counted. "It was the same
story in all the cities. This is not to be repeated. No one knows what
will happen in a year's time, but it looks as though I would be nominated for governor." Referring to the Boston vote, the *Daily
Hampshire Gazette* wrote:

> The astonishing way in which the man from
> Northampton cut down the Boston man's vote in even
> his own city, from the normal for a Democratic
> candidate in the biggest Democratic stronghold of the
> state, is simply another evidence of Calvin Coolidge's
> ability as a vote getter, and is an augury of what will
> happen next year.

Within a few months McCall told Coolidge he did not intend to
try for a fourth term, leaving the way open for Coolidge to start
campaigning for the nomination. McCall was stepping down for two
reasons: tradition, and the slim chance he might replace John Weeks
as the GOP senatorial nominee, and in this way, avenge his defeat by

Weeks six years earlier. Weeks was not particularly popular. His anemic showing as a favorite son contender for the presidential nomination in 1916 wasn't any help, especially since David Walsh indicated an interest in the Democratic nomination. Nevertheless, Weeks had sufficient power—with Crane's support—to throw back any challenge, and in the end McCall abandoned his ambitions for the U.S. Senate.

Coolidge announced his candidacy for governor on June 23, 1918, by which time the United States had entered the war. As expected, the news from France received more attention than the gubernatorial race, as American troops engaged in battle for the first time on a large scale. The Soviet Revolution in Russia prompted fears of Bolshevism, and resulted in passage of a Sedition Act, the beginning of what would later become the Red Scare. By autumn the influenza pandemic hit America, and by October the death rate in Boston, which was particularly hard hit, had risen more than 700 percent. All of this pushed thoughts of the forthcoming election to the back burner.

Coolidge received the gubernatorial nomination without opposition, and Channing Cox, a Boston-based lawyer, was selected over Guy Ham for the lieutenant governorship. Cox had been Speaker of the Massachusetts House of Representatives in 1915, and had attended Dartmouth and the Harvard Law School. The Democrats had a large field, and in the end settled on Richard Long, the owner and manager of a large shoe factory in Framingham, who was to finance his own campaign, which was instrumental in his nomination. Long was a former Republican who had switched to the Democrats in a failed bid to be Walsh's running mate in 1914, after which he returned to the GOP. His eagerness for the gubernatorial nomination had much to do with a running feud Long had with the United Shoe Manufacturing Company that involved patent infringement. That company was a staunch supporter of the Republicans, hence Long's willingness to return to the Democrats. Such switching had not been unusual in state politics since the Republican split in 1912, but it did lead many to question Long's sincerity. To balance him, the Democrats chose Joseph O'Neal of Boston, a banker and devoted Democrat, for the lieutenant governorship.

Coolidge ran on the McCall record, which is to say, moderate political progressivism combined with fiscal conservatism, a vague opposition to Prohibition and support for women's suffrage, and backing for the war. The Democrats also came out for the suffrage, and called for an eight-hour workday and old age pensions. In addition, they supported the initiative and referendum, a central issue at the constitutional convention, and public ownership and control of utilities.

On the surface, Coolidge seemed to have a relatively easy time of it in 1918. The threat of a McCall candidacy was gone, and Crane's grip on the state remained strong. Stearns was working full-time lining up voters, and his purse and those of his friends were at Coolidge's disposal. The party was solidly behind him, and Lodge supported Coolidge, thinking quite naturally that the governorship was the height of ambition for this provincial lawyer. Lodge even wrote to Theodore Roosevelt about Coolidge on October 7:

> Calvin Coolidge, our present lieutenant governor, is our candidate for governor. He is a graduate of Amherst, a very able, sagacious man of pure New England type. He is not only wise and tolerant, but he also has an excellent capacity for firmness when firmness is needed. He has been ardently for the war from the beginning. He has been in thorough sympathy with your views and mine, and in his campaign he has not been talking for himself at all but just making war speeches.

This prompted TR, who favored the war and criticized President Wilson for taking too soft a line, to endorse Coolidge on October 28. Though of the boilerplate variety, the endorsement was important:

> Mr. Coolidge is a high-minded public servant of the type which Massachusetts has always been honorably anxious to see at the head of the state government; a man who has the forward look and who is anxious to secure genuine social and industrial justice in the only way it can effectively be secured, that is, by basing a jealous insistence upon the rights of all, on the foundation of legislation that will guarantee the welfare of all.

Even with such strong support, Coolidge faced a host of problems. The dissension caused by the Weeks–McCall contest divided their supporters. McCall had been a fine if not electrifying campaigner, while Weeks was drab; the contrast was striking, just as it was between the personable Long and the dry Coolidge—which did not help the Republicans' chances. Coolidge and Weeks differed on Prohibition and labor issues, which created more problems. As Lodge indicated, Coolidge supported the war and on the stump spoke more often of patriotism than state issues, but he could go no further than endorsing the McCall record. In an atypically passionate speech, Coolidge said:

> The past four years has shown the world the existence of a conspiracy against mankind of a vastness and a wickedness that could only be believed when seen in operation and confessed by its participants. This conspiracy was promoted by the German military despotism. It probably was encouraged by the results of three wars—one against Denmark which robbed her of territory, and one against France which robbed her of territory and a cash indemnity of a billion dollars. These seemingly easy successes encouraged their perpetrators to plan for the pillage and enslavement of the earth.

Since there was only a small German–American population in Massachusetts, Coolidge need not have worried about losing votes from such a stance. But the Boston Irish could not have been particularly pleased with this strong rhetoric, for to them it implied approval of the despised United Kingdom.

By 1918 industrial eastern Massachusetts had grown larger than the bucolic western part of the state, due in part to the influx of industrial workers from Europe and the movement to the factories. The Democratic voters were increasing in number, while the Republicans were standing still. The full impact of these changes would not be felt for more than a decade, but the signs were there, and they troubled Coolidge and his followers. Just before the primaries, Coolidge wrote to his stepmother about his prospects:

There is no occasion for you or father to worry about
the election. It looks very favorable; but of course it is
impossible to forecast it, as elections are always very
uncertain. I have been handsomely treated in
Massachusetts, whether I happen to secure this election
or not.

It was a difficult campaign, for Long proved a slashing candidate, attacking Coolidge as a reactionary and tool of the McCall
interests. Long also supported the war, and promised the returning
veterans a bonus of $360. Beyond that, he would abolish the poll tax
and increase taxes on the wealthy.

Most of the newspapers supported Coolidge. The *Boston Herald*
came out for him, contrasting "Coolidge the Constructionist" with
"Long the Profiteer." This referred to the accusation that Long had
charged the government exorbitant prices for shoes for the military.
Coolidge said nothing on the matter. As with his other statewide
campaigns, he refused to mention his opponent in public.

Just before Election Day, Coolidge again blasted the Germans.
As he had throughout the campaign, he wrapped himself in the flag,
which he could afford to do since he was clearly ahead. Long, as
the underdog, hammered away at state problems, while Coolidge
simply ignored him and them:

America has been performing a great service for
humanity. In that service we have arisen to a new glory.
The people of the nation without distinction have been
performing a great service for America. In it they have
realized a new citizenship. Prussianism fails.
Americanism succeeds. Education is to teach men not
what to think but how to think. Government will take
on new activities, but it is not more to control the
people, the people are more to control the government.

Of course none of this had anything to do with the issues of the
contest, and was dismissed by the Democrats as blather, while
Republicans noted that Coolidge never offered comfort to the

Wilson administration. Rather, his remarks on the war were conventional, patriotic, and vague. When he did discuss state policies, it was in generalities:

> The duties of governor of the commonwealth are not intricate or burdensome if a man looks upon their discharge as a public function and not as a personal prerogative. If chosen to be your governor, I shall try to conduct the duties of the office so as to merit the sincere endorsement of men of fair minds and in all parties. I can promise nothing more. I would not deem myself worthy of your support if I promised anything less.

If Coolidge would not delve deeply into the issues, he also refused to return the attacks leveled at him by the Long forces. The Democrats printed an advertisement alleging that Coolidge did not completely support the Wilson war programs and had no record to speak of. Angered, Stearns prepared a counter-advertisement featuring the endorsement of prominent public figures, and showed it to the candidate. In writing of the episode to his son, Stearns said that Coolidge remarked, "It is a good advertisement, but I will not get into a controversy of that kind. I will not attack an individual. If the people of Massachusetts do not know me well enough to understand the animus of such advertisements and are not willing to elect me without my answering every indiscriminate attack, then I would rather be defeated." In his last speech of the campaign, however, he did refer obliquely to the Long campaign:

> We need to say a word of caution and warning. I am responsible for what I have said and what I have done. I am not responsible for what my opponents say I have said or say I have done either on the stump or in untrue political advertisements and untrue posters. I shall not deal with these. I do not care to touch them, but I do not want any of my fellow-citizens to misunderstand my ignoring them as expressing any attitude other than considering such attempts unworthy of notice when men are fighting for the preservation of our country.

Coolidge defeated Long by the narrow margin of 214,000 to 197,000, the smallest in his statewide career—a plurality of only 17,000. This was the same plurality by which Walsh defeated Weeks, becoming Massachusetts's first Democratic senator since the Civil War. Walsh's election also indicated that, despite his earlier defeat by McCall, he remained a popular figure in the state, so much so that he was the only Democrat to win a statewide race.

Something seismic was happening in Massachusetts. It wasn't only Walsh's popularity, but also the turning of the tide toward the immigrants he represented. Astute politician that he was, Coolidge must have known what this implied. He would have to seek either stronger support from the conservative elements of the state or a way to appeal to the newcomers, who were more liberal than he.

The world was changing as he watched. In a relatively short period Coolidge had come from the insular Plymouth Notch to the larger environment of Northampton, and had adjusted with ease to a place of new sidewalks and street lamps. Then he learned how to appeal to the quite different population of eastern Massachusetts, with its immigrants and factory workers. The changes continued. Coming from a place untouched by the railroad, Coolidge had had to accommodate himself to one in which the automobile was becoming commonplace. Lieutenant Governor Coolidge did not own a motorcar, and he became the last president not to have flown in an airplane. At a time when the United States was becoming a major factor in world politics, Coolidge had never traveled west of the Mississippi—or the Appalachians, for that matter. The thought of going overseas had not entered his mind. Nor would it. Other than that week-long honeymoon to Montreal, the only time Coolidge left the United States was for a short trip to Havana in January 1928, where he went to address the opening session of the Sixth International Conference of American States—and he left as soon as he could.

Coolidge was inaugurated as governor of Massachusetts on January 1, 1919, the day the War Industries Board closed down. The Great War was over, and President Woodrow Wilson was in Europe trying to put together a durable peace and create a League of Nations. The nation was in the grip of a postwar depression, as military contracts were suddenly canceled and soldiers and sailors dismissed from the armed services, all of which affected Massachusetts more than most states. The war had ended less than two months earlier, and now the state had to face the problems posed by reconversion to peacetime activities and the returning servicemen. His speech on this occasion was another in the tradition of "Have Faith in Massachusetts." Coolidge concentrated on those by-then-familiar homilies; turning to the members of the General Court, he asked questions but provided no answers:

> It is your duty not only to reflect public opinion, but to lead it. Whether we are able to enter a new era in Massachusetts depends upon you. The lessons of the war are plain. Can we carry them on into peace? Can we still act on the principle that there is no sacrifice too great to maintain the right? Shall we continue to advocate and practice thrift and industry? Shall we requite unswerving loyalty to our country? These are the foundations of all greatness.

And his generalities revealed a man who was still progressive on many social issues:

> Each citizen must have the rewards and opportunities worthy of the character of our citizenship, a broader recognition of his worth and larger liberty, protected by order—and always under the law. In the promotion of human welfare, Massachusetts happily may not need much reconstruction, but, like all living organizations, forever needs continuing construction. Let there be a purpose in all your legislation to recognize the right of a man to be well born, well nurtured, well educated, well employed, and well paid. This is no gospel of ease and selfishness, or class distinction but a gospel of effort and service, of universal application.

Coolidge had campaigned for office without a specific, well-defined legislative agenda, or to be more precise, with the view that the legislature's job is to legislate, and his to administer. As president of the senate he had proposed measures and blocked others. Now he suggested that he would permit the General Court to make the new rules, should any be needed, and he would either accept or veto them. Nonetheless, he exerted a measure of leadership and spoke out on the issues—on which he was by no means conservative, even by today's standards.

The programs Coolidge backed reveal a politician who was not the passive conservative—or, worse, the mossback reactionary—that historians portray. Coolidge pushed for—and helped pass—pay raises for teachers, saying, "We compensate liberally the manufacturer and merchant; but we fail to appreciate those who guard the minds of our youth." The man who was later portrayed as an admirer of materialism also said, "We have lost our reverence for the profession of teaching and bestowed it on the profession of acquiring." He worked for legislation to ease the housing shortages caused by the war; he also sponsored bills that fought profiteering by landlords (an act that slightly resembled later rent control measures), gave the courts the power to stay eviction proceedings for six months, fined deadbeat landlords, prevented collusion by price fixing, and encouraged managements to raise wages to help employees cope with the rising cost of living. Coolidge remained a consistent leader in the campaign to improve the state services for mentally retarded children, to provide for maternity nursing in rural areas, and to improve public transportation.

The governor also pushed the legislature to provide a $100 bonus to Massachusetts war veterans, and urged that they be given preference in hiring by the state. He approved a law reducing the work week from fifty-four to forty-eight hours for women and children, despite the objections of textile manufacturers who complained that this legislation would prevent them from competing effectively with southern states. "We must humanize industry, or the system will break down," he replied. Coolidge established a commission to explore the possibility of providing pensions for state employees. He even endorsed a law that stated that "a manufacturing corporation may provide by by-laws for the nomination and election by its employees of one or more of them as members of its board of directors"; although the law had little chance of being passed, he even mentioned it in a speech to the American Federation of Labor (AFL) later in the year. He also accepted a controversial measure increasing maximum weekly work-men's compensation payments from $14 to $16.

One of his few vetoes was of a measure to increase the salaries of members of the General Court from $1,000 to $1,500 and to provide some modest additions to their expense allowances; despite his objections, the bill passed over his veto. Coolidge later remarked, "I have signed every bill which had the backing of the workers, with the exception of the bill to increase the salaries of members of the legislature."

In short, Governor Calvin Coolidge was not the tool of big busi-ness that he has become in today's legend. In fact, as a result of his agenda, the remaining devotees of the somnolent Progressive move-ment viewed Coolidge as one of the more "enlightened" Republicans. He had earned their support by deeds and words. Moreover, he was an activist—within the accorded limits of his role as governor—not a person who merely spoke and let it go at that.

One of Coolidge's most important tasks that first term was to make appointments to various state posts, a matter that was com-plicated by the consolidation of offices that required him to make dismissals as well. Of course, according to the new Constitution, Coolidge might have put this off until 1921. Predictably, Coolidge rewarded the party faithful. He made many good appointments, but most were Republicans. "We have a government of parties," he observed unapologetically. "We must recognize party. A man ought to be loyal to those who have been loyal to him." But he also named Democrats to commissions, a few women to assistant commission-erships, and took care to make certain the Irish–Americans, Italian–Americans, and members of other ethnic groups got their pieces of the pie. As senate president he had treated the Democrats with respect and consideration; they might have opposed Coolidge, but also considered him fair and even generous. Now he did the same as governor.

Some executives would have taken this as a chance to reward old friends and make new allies, while punishing opponents, but Coolidge did not see it that way. "Every time a man makes an appointment he creates one ingrate and a thousand enemies," he said. Coolidge later remarked to a friend, "They say [intervening in the Boston] police strike required executive courage; reorganizing 118 departments into 18 required a good deal more."

Coolidge established a "Commission on the Necessities of Life" to alleviate suffering due to the wartime inflation. He did not oppose price increases as such, but rather those that clearly reflected gouging. As he noted to the commission,

> [t]he ordinary consumer is interested in and affected
> by retail prices. Except as these prices reflect prices at
> wholesale, he is uninterested in wholesale prices.
> While there is very little constitutional authority for
> the fixing of prices by law, it is of the utmost
> consequence that the public know that charges are
> reasonable. All kinds of wages have been increased,
> and these, of course, are reflected in the increased cost
> of materials. The public knows this and is expected to
> pay for those necessary increases.

When the retailer sought to take advantage of the situation, said Coolidge, government must act: "Government fails as an administrator of justice if it permits to go unchallenged an exorbitant charge upon the public."

In time Coolidge would be criticized for not pushing for one program or another. But critics fail to take into account the thoughts that governed his political actions. Coolidge was an atypical politician. Even more than Theodore Roosevelt did, he used the political arena as a stage to set forth a political philosophy, from which listeners could draw their own conclusions. His speeches often resembled more closely discourses on ethics and morality than agendas for action. The citizenry was never informed of what he was attempting, but the people of Massachusetts—and later on, the country as a whole—were being treated to a series of lectures on the political and social philosophy of Charles Garman, again not unlike what the legislators had heard in his "Have Faith in Massachusetts" speech. What else explains such statements as these?

> Work is not a curse, it is the prerogative of intelligence, the only means to manhood, and the measure of civilization. Savages do not work. The growth of a sentiment that despises work is an appeal from civilization to barbarism.
>
> It is conceived that there can be a horizontal elevation of the standards of the nation, immediate and perceptible, by the simple device of new laws. This has never been the case in human experience. Progress is slow and the result of a long and arduous process of self-discipline. Real reform does not begin with a law, it ends with a law. The attempt to dragoon the body when the need is to convince the soul will end only in revolt.

Many remarked that Coolidge was a clever and astute politician, but he was also a teacher of morals and ethics who believed in the innate goodness of mankind, which had been corrupted by government and other external forces. Part of that morality was a denial of materialism, a central component of Garman's philosophy to which Coolidge adhered for the rest of his life—which might surprise those who consider him a philistine. In a 1919 speech he said:

> If material rewards be the only measure of success, there is no hope of a peaceful solution of our social questions, for they will never be large enough to satisfy. But such is not the case. Men struggle for material success because that is the path, the process, to the development of character. We ought to demand economic justice, but most of all because it is justice. We must forever realize that material rewards are limited and in a sense they are only incidental, but the development of character is unlimited and is the only essential. The measure of success is not the quantity of merchandise, but the quality of manhood which is produced.

One of the major tasks of the leader was "to set an example," an idea that was never far from Coolidge's thoughts, whether he served as city councilman or president of the United States.

The election also did not change other aspects of Coolidge's life and thoughts. He did not take up Stearns's offer of financial help in renting a large house in Boston. Instead he exchanged his $1 a day room at the Adams House for two rooms for $2, and sublet his $32 a month Northampton home. Stearns suggested he send greeting cards to some state employees. Coolidge agreed, and wanted them to go out third class for a penny each in postage; Stearns talked him into using first class mail. When Stearns tried to make him a present of $5,000, he sent the check back in a flash of anger. Coolidge told him that he had put aside some savings on his $2,000 salary as lieutenant governor. On $10,000, he could certainly make do nicely.

National issues intruded upon the local scene and affected Coolidge in his first year. First the peace treaty and the League of Nations became major issues. On July 10 Wilson submitted the Versailles Treaty to the Senate and set out to work for it to the exclusion of almost all else. Then there was the growing fear of Bolshevism. Civil war continued to rage in Russia, and everyone seemed to understand that the Bolsheviks meant to spread that doctrine to the rest of Europe, and the United States as well. Finally, the country underwent a wave of strikes, which in some ways were linked in the minds of many to Bolshevism.

Taken together, these forces bred nativism and xenophobia that took many forms, from the revival of the Ku Klux Klan and its fear that a foreign pope would order American Catholics to undertake un-American actions, to race riots in Washington, Chicago, and elsewhere. There was the "Red Scare," spearheaded by Attorney General A. Mitchell Palmer, known to supporters as "the Fighting Quaker" and to critics as "the Quaking Fighter." Among other things, Palmer was certain the Communist Party, born on September 1, 1919, had infiltrated the unions. He would later write, "It is my belief that while they have stirred discontent in our midst, while they have caused irritating strikes, and while they have infected our social ideas with the disease of their own minds and their unclean morals, we can get rid of them! And not until we have done so shall we have removed the menace of Bolshevism for good."

Palmer considered the rapid growth of the AFL and the Railroad Brotherhoods signs of Bolshevism. Between 1914 and 1919 the number of trade unionists rose from 2.7 million to 4.2 million. To Palmerites it looked like an international problem; in the United Kingdom, the Labour Party came out for nationalization of coal and other basic industries. The formation of the Communist Party in America might have given rise to the thought that this was a possibility for the United States as well. Certainly the many strikes of the period had their impact. There had been 3,353 strikes in 1918 and another 3,630 in 1919, as against the 1,204 in 1914, the last peacetime year.

By spring the rash of strikes had become a flood—more than four million workers went on strike or were locked out in 1919—threatening the nation's industries. Steelworkers were considering closing down the giant U.S. Steel Corporation, and there was some talk of a coalminers' strike.

These strikes resulted in part from the inflationary economy of the period. The cost of living in late 1919 was more than 80 percent higher than it had been in 1914, with most of this rise taking place after the United States entered the war in 1917. President Wilson initiated several probes into the causes and the inability of wages to keep up with prices. In addition, labor practices a later generation would consider little short of barbaric, a vestige from the early days of industrialization, were coming under sharp criticism.

Consider the situation in steel, where many laborers had a two-shift, swing-shift arrangement. Half the 191,000 U.S. Steel workers had a twelve-hour day, and half of these worked seven days a week every other week, when they swung from one shift to the other. The average work week was sixty-nine hours. There were no vacations or sick time, and of course, fringe benefits were nonexistent. Injured workers were fired. Three out of four steelworkers were paid below the government's estimated minimums for comfort.

And this wasn't due to the company's financial problems. In 1919 the corporation's retained profits were close to half a billion dollars, up from $135 million when the war began in 1914. Like so many of the companies threatened with strikes, U.S. Steel was in excellent financial shape and easily capable of making wage adjustments.

More disturbing than a possible steel stoppage were strikes and threatened walkouts by unions of transportation workers, which could paralyze their operating areas. The National Association of Letter Carriers asked for a 35 percent pay raise in a "respectful application" to Postmaster General Albert Burleson, but Burleson turned down the request. There was even some talk of strikes by policemen and firemen, who had become increasingly militant and demanded major wage concessions.

Before the war such civil servants hadn't been organized into unions, but rather joined "benevolent societies," which engaged in bargaining but did not claim the right to strike. Now this was changing throughout the country. By 1919 thirty-seven American cities, including Washington, D.C., St. Paul, Los Angeles, and Vicksburg, had police unions, most of them affiliated with the AFL.

There had even been some police strikes, usually brief, in which the strikers were replaced by State Guard troops or scabs. Though rare, those sporadic walkouts inspired fear. All of this prompted Senator Henry Myers of Colorado, a Democrat born during the Civil War, to declare that unless Congress found some way to put a stop to the unionization of police forces, the country would collapse. "There will be no need of holding an election in 1920 to select a Republican or Democrat president; a Soviet government will have been organized by that time."

The most important test of the police unionization effort would come in Calvin Coolidge's Massachusetts. On July 26, 1919, Governor Coolidge and his family left Boston for a vacation in Plymouth, and remained there until August 18. As he packed for the trip, news about a possible police union and subsequent strike vied with reports about the debate over the League of Nations and over whether Ty Cobb, George Sisler, or "Shoeless Joe" Jackson would capture the American League batting championship. There had already been a strike of woolen workers in March, and afterwards, walkouts by silk, tobacco, marine, and buildings trade workers, with more of the same being threatened. The railroads in

California, Arizona, and Nevada had been all but completely halted by unauthorized strikes called by four railroad brotherhoods.

In late January 1919 some twenty-five thousand shipyard workers had gone on strike in Seattle, only weeks after the new mayor, Ole Hansen, took office—some took this as a preview of what was to come throughout the nation. At one time Hansen had been quite progressive, and even pro-labor, but the 1917 Soviet Revolution caused him to rethink his positions. During his 1918 campaign for mayor he had run on an antiradical and anti-union platform. Hansen denounced the strikers, and became apoplectic when a week later the area's other unions called a general strike, in which forty thousand additional workers left their jobs. It was the first time an American city had been hit by a general strike. Life in Seattle was completely disrupted—the public schools closed; newspapers ceased publication; the city's transportation system ground to a halt; restaurants were shuttered; and soup kitchens had to be organized.

Mayor Hansen took a strong stand against the action. He branded the strikers as "communists" and "radicals," and sent telegrams to newspapers throughout the nation:

> The sympathetic revolution was called in the exact manner as was the revolution in Petrograd. Labor tried to run everything. Janitors and engineers in schools were called out; everything was stopped, except a few things that were exempted.
>
> We refused to ask for exemptions from anyone. The seat of government is at City Hall. We organized 1,000 extra police, armed with rifles and shotguns, and told them to shoot on sight anyone causing disorder. We got ready for business. We had already had trouble on two instances and had completely whipped the Bolsheviki. They knew we meant business and they started no trouble.

"Any man who attempts to take over the control of municipal government functions here will be shot on sight," Hansen told reporters. He promised to swear in ten thousand additional special policemen if necessary. Meanwhile, Wilson interrupted his campaign for the League to offer federal aid. The state militia set up machine gun emplacements at the major intersections, as though expecting a repeat of the Petrograd revolution. The strikers couldn't stand this kind of pressure, and they started returning after two days. Three more days, and it was all over.

Washington Governor Ernest Lister, the only Democrat who had been elected statewide, a progressive activist who had a strong pro-labor record, said and did nothing in this situation. For one thing, he was far from the scene, and for another, he was ailing, stricken by Bright's Disease, and had relinquished his duties to conservative Republican Lieutenant Governor Louis Hart. More important, this was a municipal problem, and governors generally did not interfere in such matters.

So Hart was ignored, while Hansen was hailed as the "Fighting Mayor" and became a national figure and a target for radicals. A bomb was mailed to him two months later but was detected before it went off. Hansen charged the Bolsheviks had marked him for death because he was the symbol of a pure Americanism.

Then, on August 28, Hansen announced his resignation as mayor. Still considered a hero by his fellow Washingtonians, he said, "I am tired out and am going fishing." But this was half a year after the strike. Why did it take so long for him to resign? And why, instead of relaxing, did he embark on a national lecture tour, in which he warned against Bolsheviks and called for immigration restriction? One reason might have been the $40,000 in lecture fees he earned over a seven-month period, but the talk in Washington was that because of his new fame and the public fear of Bolshevism and unions, Hansen might become a candidate for the Republican nomination for vice president.

Coolidge undoubtedly knew of the Hansen situation, and he might have noted that talk of the vice presidential nomination stopped after a little while, perhaps because even then, no one campaigned openly for the second place on the ticket. In any case, by then the "Hansen Boom" had fizzled.

Other mayors and governors spoke out against strikes and radicalism. General Leonard Wood, the army chief of staff and a well-known national figure, brought out troops to prevent violence in the West Virginia coal fields, and did the same when a race riot erupted in Omaha. There was also a steelworkers' walkout in Gary, Indiana, which he managed to quell. "I want to make one thing clear to the workers you represent," he told the union leaders there. "The military forces are in Gary not in the interest of the steel operators and not in the interest of the strikers, but to maintain law and order." Wood, too, was talked of as a presidential possibility. "Today Leonard Wood is the political man of the hour," wrote influential journalist William Allen White on November 30. "He is the epitome of the need of America today."

The situation in Boston that spring was somewhat similar to what it had been in Seattle. In April there was a brief strike of telephone workers. Coolidge asked the White House for authority to seize the company if the strike were not ended soon. After the strike was settled, Coolidge issued a statement: "It did not appear to me that the strike should ever have been permitted."

> There is another principle involved which has received very little attention, and that is the obligation that exists on those who enter the public service to continue to furnish such service even at some personal inconvenience. This obligation reaches from the highest officer or government official to the humblest employee. *The public has rights which cannot be disregarded* [emphasis added].

Shortly before the Coolidges left for Plymouth, workers on the Boston Elevated Street Railway engaged in a brief walkout, which prompted the governor to ask both sides to seek arbitration. They accepted, and the arbitrators agreed to a tidy increase in wages. Then there was a threatened strike at the Boston Fire Department, in which Coolidge again intervened successfully.

That same January that Hansen had acted in Seattle, Coolidge had been urged to intervene on behalf of management in the textile strike at the American Woolen Company in Lawrence. This wasn't the first time Coolidge had to deal with a strike at that facility, having done so in 1912 when he was a member of the Massachusetts senate. This time he contacted F.F. Fuller, who was on the editorial staff of the *Boston American*, to ask him to go to Lawrence and report back. Fuller told Coolidge that he should know that he favored the strikers, but Coolidge knew Fuller to be honest, and urged him to accept the assignment, which he did. On the basis of Fuller's report, Coolidge refused to send in the state troops, and talked the company into negotiating with the workers.

Now it was the policemen's turn. The Boston police force complained of their lot to Commissioner Edwin U. Curtis, a man who once had been Boston's youngest mayor. Curtis was close to the Brahmin class, which had ruled Boston throughout the nineteenth century, and he had seen the city "taken over" by Irish politicians. Curtis saw this in the election of Walsh. Men like John F. Fitzgerald—best known today as John F. Kennedy's maternal grandfather but then renowned as the mayor who opened the path to municipal power for the Boston Irish—also provided their supporters with opportunities to win lucrative municipal contracts. And then there was James Michael Curley. Curtis deplored the likes of Walsh, Fitzgerald, and Curley. He had become commissioner in 1918, in the hope of stemming the Irish tide. Even so, he was a fair man, and, while he did not intend for the police to gain the upper hand over the city's political leaders, he recognized they had legitimate grievances.

At the time the pay of the Boston policemen started at $1,100 a year, from which they had to lay out $300 the first year for uniforms and incidentals. They even had to pay for bullets fired in the course of duty. The maximum pay of $1,400 was hardly munificent. The policemen worked twelve-hour shifts, six days a week. Station houses were old, in ill repair, and crowded; men slept two in a bed in some precincts. They hadn't had a raise since before the war, and the post-war inflation came down hard on them. Curtis was able to obtain a raise of $200 for them, but said there was no money for station improvements. Coolidge knew of the situation, and wrote to Mayor Andrew Peters, urging him to make the needed appropriations.

They managed to get by, because in those days, policemen who walked the beats—which is to say, most of them—had certain perquisites. One of the more important was shakedowns, especially of saloons eager to retain their licenses. The Prohibition Amendment had been ratified earlier that year, and, seemingly, an important source of policemen's earnings would vanish when it went into effect on January 1, 1920. As it happened, Prohibition introduced much more graft than ever, and corrupt cops did very well as long as it lasted. In October 1919 no one could have anticipated what would happen under the "Noble Experiment."

That summer the policemen edged cautiously toward unionization. The previous year they had organized themselves into a group they euphemistically called the "Boston Social Club." Then-Commissioner Stephen O'Meara reacted by stating that he would not countenance a police union. The following year, when the police considered unionization, Commissioner Curtis issued an order similar in content and tone to the O'Meara reaction: "I desire to say to the members of the force that I am firmly of the opinion that a police officer cannot consistently belong to a union and perform his sworn duty. I am not an opponent of labor unions, and neither was Mr. O'Meara."

In August the social club must have heard of the police strikes in London and Liverpool that ended when the policemen received raises and increased benefits. The social club applied to the AFL for a charter. Curtis then issued an addition to the department rules: "No members of the force shall join or belong to any organization, club, or body outside of the department."

Boston was not alone. In New York a strike by the Brooklyn Rapid Transit (BRT) tied up businesses in that borough, and when arbitration resulted in a wage increase, the union announced it would seek to organize all workers on New York's transportation system. Simultaneously, workers on the Interborough Rapid Transit (IRT) threatened a strike. Based on the generous settlement at the BRT, the IRT appealed to the city to boost the fare from five to eight cents to satisfy the wage demands. The IRT warned of radicals in the union movement: "If agitators are permitted to take advantage of this condition to disorganize business, inconvenience the public, intimidate and injure faithful employees, and destroy property, these warnings will have been in vain."

At the same time, shopmen at the New York, New Haven & Hartford Railroad struck and tied up that railroad, and there were signs that the engineers and trainmen would join them. Their counterparts in Chicago and Minneapolis were also on strike. It was infectious. Keystone Wire & Steel in South Bartonsville, Illinois, struck and closed down all communications with the town, leading the governor to call out the State Guard. An actors' strike had closed down several theaters in New York, and was spreading to others. By mid-August the Chicago theaters had started to close, all of which resulted in George M. Cohan's quitting both the Friars and the Lamb Clubs, famed for their associations with actors, while David Belasco announced he would never produce plays featuring members of Actors Equity. Meanwhile, the four thousand member Brotherhood of Painters, Decorators, and Paperhangers went on strike in Brooklyn. The Mason Builders' Association ran an ad in several newspapers pinning the blame on "a radical element in the Union, who had temporarily inflamed the more conservative workers."

On August 14 the New York Patrolmen's Benevolent Association "requested" consideration of an increase in wages from $1,650 to $1,800. The policemen had received a boost from $1,400 in the last four years, but had to spend $300 for uniforms and other necessities previously provided by the department. If rejected, the association planned to take its case to the Board of Estimate. There was no talk of a strike, which New York policemen presumably did not believe was appropriate behavior.

Not so their Boston counterparts. On Saturday, August 11, the AFL issued a charter to the social club, which became the Boston Police Union. The following day, the Central Labor Union of Boston passed a resolution offering the policemen "every atom of support that organized labor can bring to bear in their behalf."

These moves were not unusual for Boston. Several months earlier, Boston firemen had formed a union that affiliated with the AFL, and there had been no reaction from City Hall. Curtis now charged the police union's leaders with insubordination and prepared to conduct a hearing on possible dismissals. The union responded that if the men were punished, they would go on strike. Curtis found the men guilty, but, not wishing to push the matter too far, he suspended the sentences, indicating all would be forgiven if the relationship with the AFL was dissolved. He gave the men until September 4 to act.

Mayor Peters was more conciliatory. For one thing, he was a Democrat, as were most of the policemen. He had won the primary election against the flamboyant Curley, with the support of the reformist Good Government Association. Peters was wealthy enough not to be open to bribes, and in any case was an honest, decent person. But he was a clumsy politician who often seemed baffled by what was going on around him. Peters had run for the mayoralty out of genuine concern for the city's well being. The problem was he hadn't much of an idea how to be an effective mayor. As a result, this well-meaning dilettante presided over an administration every bit as corrupt as those of Fitzgerald and Curley—but those mayors, unlike Peters, had been effective.

Peters and Curtis came from the same social background, but otherwise were quite different. Peters was what today might be considered a typical Social Register type who sympathized with the "lower orders," and wanted more than anything else to ameliorate their conditions, but not if this required him to socialize with them. Curtis feared the new dispensation, and hoped to prevent the newcomers from taking more power than they already had. That they would have opposite views regarding a police union was evident. More than anything else, Peters wanted a solution to the problem the strikers could accept. Curtis considered the strikers dupes, and would not yield an inch to them. For the time being, Governor Coolidge was content to wait on the sidelines and watch. After all, this was an affair for Bostonians to deal with, not the governor.

Probably no governor in the nation had more experience with strikes than had Coolidge in 1919, and he was considered pro-labor. As far back as 1908, when he ran for reelection as mayor of Northampton, he had had the support of several unions. "Mr. Coolidge is entitled to the thanks of the wage laborers of his district for his manly defense of their interests," editorialized the Northampton *Daily Herald*. Then, as governor, he had to deal with the telephone strike, the strike at Boston Elevated, and the Lawrence strike. The streetcars in Salem were being challenged by jitneys, small buses that were taking some of their passengers. Because the jitneys operated in violation of an order by the municipal government, Coolidge came down on the side of the streetcar companies, whereupon one of the jitney supporters threatened, "If you do that, the labor people will go into every town in the state and crucify you politically." According to one of his early biographers, Coolidge listened calmly, and then dryly replied, "Don't let me deter you. Go right ahead." At the same meeting one member of the committee dealing with the situation remarked, "Well, about all we have done so far is to pass the buck." Coolidge stared at the man: "Try it on me. I won't pass the buck."

6

....

The Boston Police Strike

In August I went to Vermont. On my return I found that
difficulties in the Police Department of Boston were growing
serious and made a statement to reporters at the State House
that I should support Commissioner Edwin U. Curtis in his
decisions concerning their adjustment. I felt he was entitled to
every confidence.

The Autobiography of Calvin Coolidge

ON SEPTEMBER 13, after the Boston police strike had transformed
the man whom many considered the insignificant governor of
Massachusetts into a national figure, an imaginative reporter for
the *New York World* filed a story from Boston introducing his readers to the new marvel.

> To one who has never seen Governor Calvin Coolidge of
> Massachusetts, he is a sphinx or an enigma. He talks
> little. It is his silences which seem to speak loudest, for
> when one ventures to put a question to him, the answer
> comes in a tightening of the governor's lean face and the
> closing of his lips. He has a lean and hungry look, and
> the Policemen's Union and the Central Labor Union of
> Boston discovered that such men are dangerous.
>   Contrary to the accepted characteristics of the usual
> sort of politicians, "Cal" Coolidge seldom smiles, hardly

ever does any hand-shaking, and has a reputation that his word is as good as gold.

Ethnologists in search of specimens to be preserved in bronze or marble as a reminder of the type of true New Englanders for future generations should come to Beacon Hill and take the measure of this governor. He is the type of New Englander one sees on the stage—long and thin. He has red hair tinged with gray. A pair of pale-blue eyes pierce the veil of silence that usually envelops his face. Where other men may smile, "Cal" Coolidge is grave. Where home folks pretend to effervesce with enthusiasm for a visitor or the possessor of a vote, the governor is aloof and forbidding.

Generally speaking, Governor Coolidge is a living contradiction of that school of politicians anxious for a career. Massachusetts politicians, [do] not do him homage, but few, if any, have ever discovered the secret of his success. Politicians say it would be impossible to beat Coolidge in an election with a baseball bat. He is regarded as unbeatable, and has proved himself so from the moment he entered politics. He has passed without threat or fear from member of the legislature, president of the senate and lieutenant governor to governor of the state. The governor is a Republican, but it is said that the Democrats would do anything for him, many of them as much as vote for him.

The reporter might have added that seldom had a state elected a governor better qualified by virtue of experience than Calvin Coolidge in 1918. Coolidge knew the drill when it came to handling strikes. He had the experience to know when to act, but more important, when not to intrude.

Mayor Peters had no idea of how to deal with the strike threat. Casting about for a proper response, he did what politicians in his position often do to duck responsibility—he appointed a Citizen's Committee, headed by banker James J. Storrow, to investigate the situation.

The Storrow Committee met frequently with the police representatives from August 29 to September 2 and then came up with suggestions. While rejecting the notion of an AFL affiliation, it recommended compromise in all other matters. This was more than Commissioner Curtis was willing to grant, and on September 3 he rejected Storrow's request for a delay in acting against the union leaders. But Mayor Peters intervened, and asked Curtis to put off his action until Monday, September 8, which the commissioner reluctantly agreed to do.

What of the governor? When Coolidge arrived back at his office on August 19, he called in several aides to learn what was happening. Shortly thereafter he issued a terse statement: "Mr. Curtis is the police commissioner invested by law with the duty of conducting the office. I have no intention of removing him, and so long as he is the commissioner I am going to support him." That was that. It was a curious statement, however, because until then no one had suggested Curtis be removed. It was typical of Coolidge's indirect way of talking and writing.

Coolidge remained silent while the police union situation reached its boiling point. He monitored the situation carefully, which was easier for him to do than it might have been for most other governors. Massachusetts was one of those states whose capital was also its central city. The governor of New York, sequestered upstate in Albany, would have to learn about doings in Manhattan by means of newspaper, telephone, and telegraph. Washington's ailing Governor Lister had to follow the Seattle strike from his perch in Salem, more than sixty miles from the scene, but Coolidge was only a few city blocks away from those discussions.

He appeared calm and assured, but later there were reports that Coolidge had written a morose letter about the matter to his stepmother, in which he purportedly sketched his probable response—which was to support Curtis strongly—and indicated it might mean the end of his political career. He expected to be in a tough political race against Democrat Richard H. Long, the colorful and contentious Framingham shoe manufacturer who had lost narrowly to him the previous year, and his position on a strike might carry him to defeat.

Had Coolidge actually written the letter? The following month, after the crisis had passed, Coolidge wrote to Edwin Grozier of the *Boston Post*, saying, "I understood perfectly that my attitude in the police matter greatly endangered what at the time appeared my certain election. What I did then had to be done. It was of more consequence than my success at the polls. I should not have done otherwise had I known that it would bring about my certain defeat." Similarly, in his *Autobiography*, Coolidge wrote, "I fully expected it would result in my defeat in the coming campaign for reelection as governor."

Was his comment to Grozier the communication of a shrewd politician who, knowing how popular he had become, wanted to portray himself as a man of strong convictions, willing to risk all for principles? Or was this actually the case?

Whatever the answer, the governor who had intervened when the telephone, firemen, and elevated railroad workers struck or seemed on the verge of striking, and who had interceded in the American Woolen strike, said and did nothing in the police matter while the situation unraveled in early September. This was the Coolidge style: Consider the possibilities and probabilities; work out alternative plans of action; prepare to act, but hope it will not be necessary to do so; then, if necessary, act decisively. But why should he have acted at all at that point? Acting-Governor Hart had held back during the Seattle strike, as had other governors in labor disputes. Precedent was on the side of inaction.

On Monday morning, September 8, true to his word, Curtis suspended (but did not discharge) nineteen union policemen. This was his compromise, though he did not portray it as such to the union.

That day Coolidge traveled to Greenfield, where he addressed an AFL convention, not saying a word about the situation in Boston, but reiterating his belief in the right of labor to organize and receive fair wages. "Human labor will never again be cheap," he said, going on to recommend a role in management for workers. "Labor should supply wise suggestions on the future conduct of business and help direct public sentiment." Early that afternoon Frank Stearns telephoned to urge him to return to Boston. He did, and that evening he dined with Storrow and Peters. These two had devised another compromise: the policemen would be permitted to form an unaffiliated union, and if they promised not to strike, the disciplinary action against the nineteen suspended policemen would be dropped, with all other matters submitted to arbitration. Coolidge, who by then had decided to go all the way with Curtis, rejected the plan. The mayor next asked Coolidge to mobilize the State Guard, but he declined, reiterating his confidence that Curtis could handle the matter.

Afterward, Storrow wrote to a friend of the Coolidge approach. "Coolidge's instinct is in the first place to back up the man who has the immediate responsibility, even though his own subordinate.... The police commissioner was sure he had the matter well in hand, could fully control the situation, and so advised the governor." He concluded, "Coolidge never is quick on the trigger, but he keeps his mind right on the problem, and it is generally more important in public affairs to be right than quick." This was another trait that Coolidge took along to the White House: Delegate authority to a person whose judgment and abilities you trust, and then let him do his job.

According to William Allen White, one evening Coolidge had a visitor, "Diamond Jim" Timilty, the Democratic boss of Roxbury Crossing and a union leader who had served with Coolidge in the Massachusetts senate. These two men with strikingly different backgrounds and philosophies liked and respected one another. Timilty often said, "Calvin Coolidge can have anything he wants from me." The political boss, who had strong connections and influence with the other unions, was there to allay any fears the governor might have regarding the possibility of a general strike. White wrote that years later Timilty told this story to Robert Brady, a reporter for the *Boston Post*, who related it to him:

> I just went in to see my little pal and tell him not to
> worry over all this mush about a general strike. You
> know, I'm president of the largest labor organization in
> the state, the city and town laborers' organization, with
> the largest membership of any union in Massachusetts. I
> just told Cal that "we won't go out," and we have more
> votes in the central labor organization than any of the
> others. You see, Cal's my kind of guy, and he's right
> about those damned cops.

It is unclear whether this was true, exaggerated, or braggadocio. In any event, Curtis knew nothing about this visit, and that evening he told reporters, "I am ready for anything." He added a belief—or hope—that relatively few police would walk out, and that those who remained could handle things.

Coolidge already had information from Adjutant General Jesse Stevens about the availability of State Guard units. Stevens, who had tried to read Coolidge's mind, called for one mounted squadron to meet at the Commonwealth Armory. Angered, since he instantly realized the action would be inflammatory, Coolidge went to the Armory and dismissed the troops. Meanwhile, the policemen held a meeting at which they voted to strike by a whopping margin of 1,134 to 2, the operation to begin at 5:45 PM the next day, September 9.

Coolidge's lack of action did not mean that he hadn't given the matter a great deal of thought. Curtis had assured him many times that despite the vote, most police would not go out on strike. Even if they did, Curtis seemed quite confident he could handle things. In this case, as in others, the governor would interfere only when he felt it absolutely necessary. Throughout his political life, Coolidge would step aside whenever a plausible individual appeared willing to do what he himself would. That way, if the individual succeeded, Coolidge would have had his victory, be able to share the glory of success, and go on to other things. In case of failure, the other person would be blamed. Though his "inaction" would come to be lampooned by critics, Coolidge calculated his every move—or, more to the point, *whether* to move.

Mayor Peters evidently had no plan to deal with the strike. It was different with Coolidge. Perhaps he saw little to be gained from discussions with Peters; after all, he would later say, "I have never been hurt by anything I didn't say." French Strother, one of the more perceptive journalists of the time, wrote of Coolidge: "The universal testimony of those who know him is that he is always thinking. Not mind-wandering, casual consciousness, but hard, disciplined, purposeful thinking upon his problems. He is, they say, forever thinking ahead. That is why he is never caught off his guard, never excited when the moment for decision and action comes."

His actions at the time and discussions afterward reveal that Coolidge knew exactly what he was doing and trying to accomplish, although he spoke and wrote sparingly about it. His attitude toward the strike was reflected in a completely unrelated matter half a year later, when he vetoed a measure that would have permitted the production of beer, cider, and light wines, in contravention of the Eighteenth Amendment. While somewhat sympathetic to those who opposed Prohibition, Coolidge saw the issue as a matter of law versus lawlessness. "The authority of the law is questioned in these days all too much. The binding obligation of obedience against personal desire is denied in many quarters. If these doctrines prevail all organized governments, all liberty, all security are at an end." Coolidge then asked the question he might have posed in October 1919: "Can those entrusted with the gravest authority set any example save that of the sternest obedience to law?"

There were no public opinion polls in those days, but the Boston newspapers generally supported Curtis, though they were clearly fearful of what might happen if and when the police left their posts. Would there be a general strike on the Seattle model? Were the Bolsheviks masterminding the walkout? The Central Labor Union was talking as though a mass walkout was in the works.

At 5:45 PM, 1,117 of the 1,544 man force walked out wearing their uniforms, after having carefully removed their badges. Nothing untoward happened at first. Then there were reports of rowdyism. Bands of young men roamed through the downtown streets, breaking windows and accosting pedestrians. Some of them broke into a market, stole crates of eggs, and threw their contents at passers-by. A streetcar conductor was shot in the leg.

Meeting with advisors the next morning, Peters heard rumors that the firemen, telegraph operators, and railroad workers were about to join in a sympathy strike, which would close down the city as had the strike in Seattle. Now the mayor acted decisively. He mobilized the Boston State Guard, and that evening temporarily removed Curtis from control of the Police Department and replaced him with General Charles Cole. Peters also issued a communiqué stating he had received "no cooperation from the police commissioner and no help or practical suggestions from the governor." In effect, he had assumed command of the opposition to the strike, the only official up to that time willing to take a stand. Reacting swiftly, Curtis went to see Coolidge, and knowing the governor's mind, all but demanded he either be removed completely or supported.

Meanwhile, a hastily assembled volunteer police force, comprised of middle-aged businessmen, students, earnest housewives, and others, was prepared to assist the guard in maintaining order. Francis Russell, who later wrote extensively about the strike, was a boy at the time and witnessed these activities; he thought some of the volunteers believed they represented the Brahmins, taking back control of the city from the Irish.

There were many more scuffles than the previous night, as well as looting. The newspapers had a field day, conjuring the image of a city in the grips of lawless elements. In fact, the violence was minor and pretty much confined to the Scollay Square section, and involved hundreds, not thousands as the newspapers suggested. But the reports prompted nearby Cambridge to advertise in the Boston newspapers, urging businesses there to consider relocating "where you will be protected by a reliable police force." Automobile insurance companies ran advertisements notifying policyholders they were not protected against riot damages.

The stories coming out of Boston, even those in the more sensationalist newspapers, were not particularly frightening, however. Thirty young men went to a restaurant, ordered and ate meals, and then refused to pay the bill; they proceeded to strip the counter of pies and threw them at the help. A gang of south Boston rioters stole a safe from a variety store, dragged it into the street, found it empty, and left it in the middle of the road. Another group stole two barrels of whiskey, opened them up, and then poured drinks from stolen glasses, treating the mob to refreshments. Later on, the City of Boston, held liable for the damages, paid out $34,000 to the businesses involved. There also were acts of brutality. Some guardsmen mounted saber attacks, and others were obliged to use their sidearms. Three deaths resulted.

By early Thursday morning it appeared not only that the violence was abating, but also that the strikers, who earlier had been convinced of victory and outraged at their treatment, were having some second thoughts. Was it the violence, the opposition of the newspapers, the rising anger of the citizenry, or the belated but firm action taken by Mayor Peters? Might President Wilson's denunciations of the strikers have had an impact? The president certainly had been forthright on the matter: "A strike of the policemen of a great city, leaving that city at the mercy of an army of thugs, is a crime against civilization." Yet earlier Wilson had not acted forcefully when the Washington, D.C., police attempted to unionize.

One thing is fairly certain. Coolidge had done next to nothing to alleviate the distress, much less halt the walkout. On Thursday morning, if anyone came out of the situation with an enhanced reputation, it should surely have been Peters.

Coolidge learned of Peters's communiqué on Thursday morning. "I see the mayor has taken a hand in this," he told some of his associates. Those present said Coolidge was as furious as they had ever seen him. That afternoon he had lunch at the Union Club with Herbert Parker, a former attorney general and current advisor to Commissioner Curtis, and William M. Butler. While Parker was solid and consequential, as the CEO of the Hoosac and Quinsett Mills and the West End Thread Corporation, Butler was even more important. He was a veteran politician who once served as president of the state senate. Butler, who was known as Crane's "Boston man," delivered a clear and simple message. The state GOP boss thought that any further disturbances would harm Coolidge politically. As Butler later recalled, "I said that the governor should take over the situation, call out the militia, and also take charge of the police affairs of Boston." Parker seconded this.

Only then did Coolidge decide to act. The desire to reap political profits may have been a motivating force, but in addition Coolidge must have felt he could not permit Peters to implement the Storrow Committee recommendations, which included recognition of an independent police union. To him, this would have meant surrender to forces of anarchy and a negation of the concept of the rule of law.

Coolidge issued a proclamation calling out the State Guard, asking for public support, and assuming control of the Boston police force. To cap things off, he restored Curtis to his post, clearly indicating that the governor intended to treat the strikers harshly. The order to Curtis was in the typical Coolidge terse, clear style:

> You are hereby directed, for the purpose of assisting me in the performance of my duty, pursuant to the proclamation issued by me this day, to proceed in the performance of your duties as police commissioner of the city of Boston, under my command and in obedience to such orders as I shall issue from time to time, and obey only such orders as I may so issue or transmit.

James Parker, a Boston attorney quite close to Curtis, was delighted with the development, but he had some sympathy for Peters, and suggested that Coolidge might send a copy of the order to Peters. Coolidge demurred: "Let him find out about it in the papers." Even so, Peters did receive a copy by messenger.

The Central Labor Union now realized the strike had been lost, and acted to cut losses. The members voted against a general strike, and behind the scenes police representatives attempted to work out some way they could return to work without penalties. Curtis would have none of this, and he issued an order that none of the men who had failed to report for duty on September 9 could regain their jobs. He added, "Nor are they to remain or loiter on the premises of the different station houses."

Now Coolidge took center stage. Meeting with reporters, he called the strike "desertion of duty," and he indicated complete support for Curtis, whose next step was to declare that the now vacant positions on the force would be filled by new recruits. The Central Labor Union petitioned Coolidge to reconsider and reinstate the strikers, talking vaguely of the possibility of a general strike. Important Boston businessmen who may have feared violence from the dismissed strikers supported this position. When they observed that the strike might cost him his office, Coolidge snapped back, "It is not necessary for me to hold another office." But Coolidge, having carefully considered his actions, knew that his position was quite popular, and bound to win rather than lose votes.

AFL head Samuel Gompers, who was in New York attending his father's funeral, tried to contact Peters and Coolidge, in the hope of swaying them. His letter to the mayor was published in the September 13 newspapers: "No man, or group of men, more genuinely regrets the present Boston situation than does the American Federation of Labor," it began. "You have undoubtedly been apprized [sic] of President Wilson's suggestion to the commissioners in the District of Columbia who adopted a similar regulation to the one adopted by the Boston authorities, ordering policemen not to become members of or retain membership in a union affiliated with the American Federation of Labor." Since Wilson had not dismissed the Washington police, couldn't Boston do the same? If so, the policemen would be back on their beats, awaiting further discussions.

The telegram to Coolidge took a different tone. Gompers did not know the governor, nor had he read his statement in the telephone workers' strike a few months earlier; if he had, he would never have taken the stance he did.

"The question at issue is not one of law and order," Gompers wrote on September 13, "but the assumption of an autocratic and unwarranted position by the commissioner of police, who is not responsible to the people of Boston, but who is appointed by you. Whatever disorder has occurred is due to his order in which the right of the policemen had been denied, a right which has heretofore never been questioned."

The Gompers telegram provided Coolidge with the opportunity to present his case to the public, at a time when the press clearly supported his efforts. His response was reprinted in newspapers throughout the country and would be recalled during his second race for the governorship and at the Republican Convention in 1920:

> Replying to your telegram, I have already refused to
> remove the police commissioner of Boston. I did not
> appoint him. He can assume no position which the
> courts would uphold except what the people have by
> the authority of their law vested in him. He speaks only
> with their voice. The right of the police of Boston to

affiliate has always been questioned, never granted,
[and] is now prohibited. The suggestion of President
Wilson to Washington does not apply to Boston. There
the police remained on duty. Here the Policemen's Union
left their duty, an action which President Wilson
described as a crime against civilization. Your assertion
that the commissioner was wrong can not justify the
wrong of leaving the city unguarded. That furnished the
opportunity; the criminal element furnished the action.

Then followed the words that captured the public mood of the
time, a period when strikes seemed a harbinger of the coming sovi-
etization of the United States:

There is no right to strike against the public safety by
anybody, anywhere, any time.

Newspapers throughout the nation picked up on that sentence.
In New York the mayor and commissioner of police warned the
police union that it could expect the same treatment if it called a
strike. The *New York Times* editorialized: "The Boston strike has
sharpened the nation's conception of the strike problem and defined
for everyone the line upon which the public must make its fight for
self-preservation. We hope the AFL and Mr. Gompers have been
equally instructed." And the *New York Herald* wrote: "It is fortunate that Massachusetts has a governor who, like its wartime
Governor Andrews, has the determination and patriotism to stand
firm for the sovereignty and dignity of the commonwealth." The
New York World joined in: "The policemen of Boston could not at
once gain what they desired, therefore they turned over their city to
thugs and rowdies. The case was an extreme example of childish vin-
dictiveness and selfish spite. Thanks to the courage and plain speech
of Governor Coolidge, it has served to clarify the minds of all."

No one noticed a signal difference between the actions and words
of Coolidge and the by-then-forgotten Ole Hansen. Hansen spoke
first and then acted; Coolidge acted and then spoke. Hansen might
easily have been embarrassed by the developments that followed

his words. Coolidge ran no such risk. Moreover, during a period in which "red-baiting" was quite common, Hansen used inflammatory language. Coolidge never remotely suggested the Boston policemen were inclined toward Bolshevism, something that would have been easy to do and that would have enhanced his popularity. Indeed, he even showed sympathy for the policemen's plight.

There also was a difference between General Wood's and Governor Coolidge's actions against strikes. Wood was not dealing with strikes against the public, but rather those aimed at employers. In addition, Wood did not utter a memorable phrase. He was to become a dominant political figure in 1920, but not because of his actions on the strike front.

In the weeks and months that followed, Coolidge received some seventy thousand letters, telegrams, and other communications praising his stand, many calling upon him to run for national office.* President Wilson sent his congratulations.

Other signs pointed to the popularity of his stand. A group calling itself "Defenders of Public Safety," formed to aid the loyal police and the volunteers, raised more than half a million dollars in a matter of weeks. The liberal *New Republic*, which had tried to be neutral earlier, now wrote, "In spite of the substantial grievances of the strikers, their proposal to affiliate with the AFL was not compatible with the faithful execution of their regular duties." The equally liberal *Nation*, which would be critical of Coolidge throughout the rest of his political career, put a different slant on the performance:

> Governor Coolidge sat discreetly on the fence until he saw on which side public sentiment was gathering.

---

* One of the letters came from an old classmate, Elmer Slayton Newton. Coolidge replied:

Dear Newt:
    I am glad you liked what I did. I knew you would.
                    Cal

> When this had manifested itself distinctly against the police, and after Boston's danger had been averted, Governor Coolidge climbed down from the fence on the side with the crowd and issued a proclamation needlessly mobilizing the entire State Guard.

This wasn't at all the case. Coolidge would have never supported the strike. Rather, he knew what he wanted to accomplish, and searched for the best means to carry it through. Even so, he had regrets, though they would not be voiced until after he left the White House. In his *Autobiography*, Coolidge wrote, "To Mr. Curtis should go the credit for raising the issue and enforcing the principle that police should not affiliate with any outside body," but also conceded that he had waited too long before acting. Nonetheless, to allay any doubts regarding his resoluteness, on September 24, 1919, Coolidge issued a proclamation that indicated he had not budged. This was a curious document, much more belligerent in tone than the others, before or after. The familiar Coolidge cadences are lacking, as is his inherent caution.

> There appears to be a misapprehension as to the position of the police of Boston. In the deliberate intention to intimidate and coerce the government of this commonwealth a large body of policemen, urging all others to join them, deserted their posts of duty, letting in the enemy. This act of theirs was voluntary, against the advice of their well-wishers, long discussed and premeditated, and with the purpose of obstructing the power of the government to protect its citizens or even to maintain its own existence. Its success meant anarchy. By this act, through the operation of the law they dispossessed themselves. They stand as though they had never been appointed.
>
> Other police remained on duty. They are the real heroes of this crisis. The State Guard responded most efficiently. Thousands have volunteered for the Guard

and the Militia. Money has been contributed from every walk of life by the hundreds of thousands for the encouragement and relief of these loyal men. These acts have been spontaneous, significant, and decisive. I propose to support all those who are supporting their own government with every power which the people have entrusted me.

There is an obligation, inescapable, no less solemn, to resist all those who do not support the government. The authority of the commonwealth cannot be intimidated or coerced. It cannot be compromised. To place the maintenance of the public security in the hands of a body of men who have attempted to destroy it would be to flout the sovereignty of the laws the people have made. It is my duty to resist any such proposal. Those who would counsel it join hands with those whose acts have threatened to destroy the government. There is no middle ground. Every attempt to prevent the formation of a new police force is a blow at the government. That way treason lies. No man has a right to place his own ease or convenience or the opportunity to make money above his duty to the state.

Commissioner Curtis had no trouble recruiting men to replace the strikers; this was a period of widespread unemployment, and many veterans and others were eager for the jobs. But the strikers continued to hope for reinstatement. On October 15 there was a rally by strikers, their families, and friends, all but pleading for a reconsideration. Three weeks later a Massachusetts judge denied a petition to restore the nineteen leaders to their posts. They continued to work for reinstatement for several years, but eventually gave up.

Coolidge wrote in his *Autobiography*: "Later I helped these men in securing other employment," but they would never again work as policemen in Boston. As it happened, one of the strikers was William F. Regan, who eventually found work on the railroad. William and his wife, Kathleen, were in dire straits, for Kathleen had given birth to their son the previous year. The son, Donald Regan, was to be Ronald Reagan's secretary of the treasury and later his chief of staff.

While Coolidge's actions in the police strike won him the applause of both progressives and conservatives, they were later perceived as being anti-union and even reactionary, which ignores the context of the times. Actually, Coolidge's attitude toward the police was quite liberal, both by the standards of that time and today, and he spoke out in favor of "a properly compensated police force." In early 1921, while vice president–elect, Coolidge reviewed Raymond Fosdick's *American Police Systems* for the *Outlook*, and wrote:

> There is nothing so destructive of our liberties as a misuse of police power. No people will submit to it for long, least of all Americans. The worst thing that could happen would be to have the conviction abroad that police, courts, and the government were more concerned with the protection of property than with the protection of the personal rights of the individual. Under a wise and judicious leadership, a well-trained and properly compensated police force, this danger would not arise. Under a police force which is the sport of political conditions it is likely to arise at any time.

The police strike was the most important event of Coolidge's gubernatorial career, but there were other developments as well. Coolidge welcomed President Wilson on his return from the Versailles Peace Conference on February 24, 1919. By then the League of Nations had become a contentious issue in national politics. Crane favored American entry into the League, and so backed the Democratic president, while Henry Cabot Lodge was the leader of the GOP opposition. Thus, the state's Republican leadership was divided on this important issue. At the time he greeted Wilson, Coolidge seemed to support the League, which would have placed him squarely in Crane's camp, though he did so in a typically oblique fashion. In greeting Wilson, he said, "We welcome him as the representative of a great people, as a great statesman, as one to whom we have entrusted our destinies, one to whom we are sure we will support in the future in the working out of that destiny, as Massachusetts has supported him in the past."

Assistant Secretary of the Navy Franklin D. Roosevelt, who was present at the ceremony, remembered Coolidge as "a diffident little man who no one outside of Massachusetts had then heard of." He recalled that after this welcome, which was not enthusiastically received, Coolidge extemporized the following:

> We hail, moreover, a great leader of the world who is
> earnestly striving to effect an arrangement that will
> prevent another horrible war. He has gone across the
> seas to further his purpose. He has given of his strength
> and energy. I can assure him that, in all of his efforts to
> promote and preserve the peace of the world, he has the
> hearty support of the people of Massachusetts.

A year later Coolidge and Roosevelt were nominated for the vice presidency by the Republican and Democratic parties, respectively, and both would follow Wilson to the White House.

Most of the press interpreted the Coolidge statement as an endorsement of the League, but Coolidge tried to remain on the fence, not stating a clear opinion one way or the other. When finally pinned down by a reporter, who asked bluntly, "Governor, what do you think of the League?" Coolidge replied:

> I am the governor of Massachusetts. The state of
> Massachusetts has no foreign relations. If ever I should
> hold an office calling for action or opinion on this
> subject, I shall put my mind on it and try to arrive at the
> soundest conclusions within my capacity.

In addition, he had nothing to say about Prohibition, which was scheduled to go into effect in 1920, except that he would uphold the law. He did, however, veto a measure allowing for 2.75 percent alcohol content beer and wine, arguing this violated the Eighteenth Amendment.

The State Democratic Convention took place on September 23. In their platform, the Democrats asserted: "While we do not condone the policemen who left their posts of duty, we condemn Governor Coolidge for his inaction and culpability in failing to protect the lives and property of the city of Boston." As expected, the convention nominated Richard Long, who sided with the strikers, saying, "Governor Coolidge has shown himself to be the weakest, most helpless and incompetent governor that our state has ever had." Long promised to replace Curtis as Boston police commissioner and reinstate the striking policemen. The Central Labor Union came out for Long, as did other unions.

The Republicans gathered on October 4, and quietly renominated Coolidge and Cox, but the party was not completely united this time. In Washington the battle over the League continued to rage, pitting Crane against Lodge. The GOP platform included a plank endorsing the League, demonstrating the extent of Crane's power in the state.

As before, Stearns was there to organize the troops and conduct the publicity campaign for Coolidge. He did not have to raise much money; his total campaign spending came to $2,171.90. Part of the campaign chest was used to print a collection of Coolidge's speeches, entitled *Have Faith in Massachusetts*.

More attention was paid nationally to the Massachusetts elections that November than usual, since as a result of the police strike, Coolidge was being discussed as a potential dark horse presidential candidate. Even so, it was only a blip on the political horizon. Long proved a vigorous campaigner, while Coolidge was a quieter one, in part because he was ill with a severe cold in the early days of the campaign.

Coolidge won in a landslide, with 317,774 votes to Long's 192,673, the greatest electoral victory in the state's history. Long took Boston, the most Democratic city in Massachusetts, by a margin of only five thousand votes. Of the state's thirty-seven cities, Coolidge lost only two others besides Boston.

Congratulations came from all quarters—from Charles Evans Hughes and Warren Harding, among others. President Wilson telegraphed his felicitations. "I congratulate you upon your election as a victory for law and order. When that is the issue all Americans stand together." In his victory speech, Coolidge acknowledged that more than anything else, the election had been a plebiscite on his actions during the police strike.

> The attempt to appeal to class prejudice had failed. The men of Massachusetts are not labor men, or policemen, or union men, or poor men, or rich men. They are Americans first…. They are for the government. American institutions are safe in their hands…. Massachusetts is American. The election will be a welcome demonstration to the nation and to people everywhere who believe that liberty can only be secured by obedience to law.

Coolidge carried out his duties during his second term as governor with the national spotlight on him. His legislative accomplishments during his second term were greater than for the first, due largely to the ability of the state GOP machine to control the legislature.

On November 6, Edwin McKnight, president of the state senate, announced that he would be a candidate for delegate to the Republican Convention, committed to Coolidge's presidential nomination. Others followed suit. Half a year before the Republicans were due to convene in Chicago, a Coolidge boomlet was under way. It was by then almost a natural progression for the reelected governor. From Northampton his scope had enlarged to include western Massachusetts, and then he had had to appeal to voters in all parts of the state. Now he was moving to the national stage, the most complicated and difficult of them all, more so perhaps in this period than it would be toward the end of the twentieth century.

In order to better understand just what happened in 1919–1920, one must temporarily put aside Coolidge's activities and turn to the nature of presidential politics in 1920, to appreciate what was involved in obtaining the nomination of a major political party that year.

Begin by understanding that national politics in this period bore little resemblance to national politics today. For one thing, there was no truly national party in this period. Credit is sometimes given to Mark Hanna of Ohio for having created a national GOP in 1896 for the McKinley campaign, but Hanna was always first among equals, with the stress on the equals. Rather, the state organizations ruled supreme in their areas, and their leaders would come together every four years to select a national ticket and write a platform.

This was still a time when local politics was deemed more important than national politics, and there were city bosses as well as those who dominated states. The situation was changing, to be sure, especially through the actions and efforts of Theodore Roosevelt and Woodrow Wilson. Before TR, Congress was deemed the more important branch. When Admiral George Dewey made an abortive try for the presidency after the Spanish–American War, he told reporters that he was qualified because the president takes orders from Congress, and he had been taking orders all his adult life. Thomas Reed, who was an able Speaker of the House in the 1890s, once refused to consider a bid for the presidency, which he considered an inferior office to the one he occupied.

Roosevelt and Wilson shifted power to the White House, but in 1920 the legislators and the political bosses were prepared to retake power, and all the putative candidates recognized this. Independent though he was, Roosevelt understood this and courted the bosses once in office. So did Wilson. Any president who hoped to rule without their support would enter into uncharted territory.

This was the unspoken assumption that delineated the atmosphere during the primaries. The primary elections so familiar nowadays existed then as well, and indeed went back more than forty years, but there the similarity ends. Sixteen states were to have primary elections in 1920, to be conducted between March and June, but most of these were not binding. Although each state selected delegates in its own way, the primaries were more akin to popularity contests than anything else. In some of the states the primary was followed by a party convention, during which the actual delegates were selected. The convention might be informed by the primary regarding the public's preferences, but this was rarely deemed an important matter. Delegates found it possible to vote their own wills. Those few primaries in which the votes were binding were so only for the first ballot, and since most conventions went through several ballots, the primaries had little effect on the nominations except to vindicate the claims of one candidate or another. Usually only the party faithful, taken to the polls by representatives of the state machine, bothered to cast their ballots in primaries, and so the results usually reflected the desires of the leadership.

The candidates selected the primaries they entered with care. If winning did not mean much, losing might be taken as a sign of weakness. Then, too, at a time when favorite sons were quite common, it might be fatal to enter the ranks against such a candidate. Losing against the local man was very possible, while a victory would earn the anger of the state party. Most important, these primaries could be costly, eating up funds needed for the general election and prompting candidates to trade favors for donations. And when it was all over, the winners and losers would have been at each other's throats for months, thus making a reconciliation difficult if not impossible. Such had been the case with the 1912 Republican primaries, when Roosevelt and Taft so savaged one another that the experience contributed to the party split. The 1920 Republican primaries were to have a major impact on the nomination, but not in the way designers of these elections had anticipated.

The state political bosses were the key to presidential politics in this period. They represented a tradition as old as the country itself. Boies Penrose in Pennsylvania, Joseph Foraker in Ohio, Reed Smoot of Utah, and their counterparts in other states exercised grips on their parties that do not exist today. Often these men executed their powers from the Senate, as did Foraker, Smoot, and Penrose, and, for a while, Crane. In addition to them there were some lesser leaders, such as James Wadsworth of New York, the son of a respected House member; William Calder, also from New

York, who dominated downstate GOP politics; James Watson of Indiana, a party wheelhorse who, had the bosses been able to install a president by fiat, might have been their choice; Frank Brandegee of Connecticut, who succeeded to the power and office of boss Orville Platt in 1905; Medill McCormick of Illinois, who was allied to newspaper and farm machinery fortunes; and Charles Curtis of Kansas, among others.

If there was a "boss of bosses," a man who might be considered Hanna's successor, it would be Penrose. Actually, Penrose succeeded Nelson Aldrich in such prominence, while Aldrich had been elevated when Matthew Quay of Pennsylvania died. Quay had followed Hanna.

Pennsylvania was a pivotal state, with thirty-eight electoral votes and seventy-six voting delegates to the convention, second only to New York's forty-five electoral votes and eighty delegates, but this was not the reason for Penrose's power. Through force of personality and intimidating size—6'4" and 350 pounds in his prime, with a bull neck and pig-like eyes—Penrose was the kind of man who dominated a room and to whom others looked for wisdom and favors. He had been a man of enormous appetites, capable of devouring two ducks or a five-pound steak at a sitting, along with a quart of champagne or whiskey. As for clout in Washington, he was chairman of the Senate Finance Committee. Not an orator, or even particularly well-known outside of the Senate, Penrose wielded his power in committees and private meetings.

By 1920, however, Penrose was a sick man, and easily distracted. He was wasted by then, almost thin, unable to work for long stretches. He hardly ate, and his drinking was no longer on a gargantuan scale. When he could pull himself together, however, it became clear his powerful intellect had not dimmed. Nor would he relinquish power to others.

As with most of the other bosses, Penrose's attention was sharply focused on the needs of his state. In Pennsylvania that meant high tariffs. He bargained astutely on this issue and usually had his way. Penrose was known as a man who did not forgive easily and who rewarded his friends, but more important, as a man of his word. A promise from Penrose could be banked. Not only his words. After his death $226,000 in cash was found in his safe deposit box.

Perhaps all of this would have mattered little had Roosevelt been available for the nomination. In late 1919 he was the odds-on favorite. TR's record, stands on issues, personal popularity with both the rank-and-file and the leaders, reputation, and of course his electability were all in his favor. Roosevelt had started accumulating a campaign fund when he died on January 6, 1919. It seemed at the time that no one could fill the gap, though several would try, and as was often the case in such situations, there was a chance they would cancel one another out. In mid-January, as the Republican leaders pondered what would transpire without Roosevelt, they turned to Penrose for a sign.

Penrose met with several leaders to talk about the 1920 elections. Veteran reporter Frank Kent, who had attended many conventions and was considered one of the more perceptive observers of the period, thought that, in the end, Penrose would lead the other bosses into selecting the ticket. As the general public watched the candidates, Kent tried to follow the bosses. In 1923 he wrote of the nature of conventions:

> National conventions are uncertain assemblies. They are made up of delegates from every state in the Union and the average delegation is a thoroughly bossed and controlled delegation. The average delegation is made up of hand-picked men who can be swung into line when the word is given out. Notoriously, delegates to national conventions are unemotional and unswayed by public clamor or enthusiasm. The galleries go wild, but the delegates sit tight.

Since some of the leading candidates talked and acted as though they intended to be strong presidents, the bosses devoted more thought, time, and effort to stopping them than to figuring out whom they would support. As it happened, this was left to the convention's last hours.

As with most nominations of the period, this one was brokered, the only question being whether the deal would be arranged on the convention floor between the candidates and their managers, or by the bosses. Delegations hoping to bargain for their support might unite behind a favorite son, usually the governor or a senator from the state, knowing he hadn't much of a chance, but realizing that supporters of individuals were not ruining their chances with one of the front-runners.

Coolidge had little reason to expect victory under this system. He was an outsider to the politicians in the rest of the country, and he hadn't cultivated the powerful men who ruled outside of Massachusetts. Crane would back him, but Coolidge could not expect anyone else to do so. Then, too, the Massachusetts delegation was not united behind him, since Lodge led a rump group that supported Wood, and this was a sign of weakness. True, some senators came to the commonwealth to campaign for him—most notably Harding—but this counted for little. To many Americans, Coolidge was a hero for his actions and words during the Boston police strike, but in those days popularity with the masses did not count as much as it does today.

If Coolidge was known for anything, it was honesty, integrity, and incorruptibility. As far as the bosses were concerned, these hardly were the kinds of attributes they sought in a president. The bosses sought compliance from the candidate, and Coolidge was too much of a loner. The only president of the postbellum period who had Coolidge's attributes was Grover Cleveland (like Coolidge, he had served as mayor and governor), and before he left office in 1897, he had all but been read out of the Democratic Party.

Delegates pledged to Coolidge, led by Stearns, would have had little bargaining power and a lot of history to overcome. The Republican Party was strong in New England, but the heart of the party was in the Midwest, Ohio in particular. Ever since the election of Lincoln (Illinois) in 1860, triumphant Republicans had come from the nation's heartland. This was true of Presidents Grant (Ohio), Hayes (Ohio), Garfield (Ohio), Harrison (Indiana), McKinley (Ohio), and Taft (Ohio). Arthur and Roosevelt, both from New York, succeeded on the deaths of Garfield and McKinley; neither man would have been nominated on his own. James G. Blaine, who lost to Cleveland in 1884, was from Maine. It didn't seem likely that Coolidge would be the second New Englander nominated by the Republicans.

Were there any positives for Coolidge? One was a vacuum at the top of the ticket, another was that he had no dedicated enemies. What, then, might Coolidge have hoped for? In case of a deadlocked convention, the leaders would look for a compromise candidate. But there were many of these hopefuls, most of whom were more acceptable to the leaders than Coolidge. Or the political managers of the candidates might be able to hammer out a ticket among themselves and bypass the bosses, but Coolidge would have little to offer potential partners. Then, too, the delegates might revolt against dictation. This happened in 1896, when William Jennings Bryan came out of nowhere with his "Cross of Gold" speech to capture a Democratic nomination that seemed assured for Congressman Richard Bland. This wasn't likely to happen in 1920. Even had he been given a chance to address the convention, Coolidge was hardly a spellbinding orator of the caliber of Bryan, and in any case, he intended to remain in Massachusetts, and did not seek a position on the delegation.

Finally, there was the matter of Coolidge's personality. He was not a bold man, the kind who would mount a quixotic campaign. Such had never been his style. If limited to one adjective to describe him, it might be "calculated." He did not take chances, which was one of the reasons he often seemed reluctant to speak out on issues. He delayed decisions, perhaps more than he should have. As has been seen, he could be swift and decisive, but only when the odds were good. After his reelection as governor, a perceptive neighbor who preferred to remain anonymous offered this telling analysis to a reporter for *Current Opinion*:

> Calvin has been a good representative, a good senator, and a good governor. He's honest as the day, and he's got plenty of brains, a lot of experience, and all the firmness anybody needs. I'm inclined to think he'd make a good president. You see, he never makes mistakes. He has the limitations of his Vermont Yankee hereditary. He was born cautious. All great men make mistakes,

probably more mistakes than anything else. Three times
out of five that great men come to bat, they strike out.
The other two times are home runs tho. Calvin never
takes a chance and strikes out, and never hits a home
run. A base hit is his limit. He'll make that every time, to
do him justice.

This soon became a staple of stories about, and analyses of,
Coolidge.

After his overwhelming reelection as governor, a Coolidge for
President boom took off in Massachusetts. Many were drawn to his
banner, but not the governor himself. Nor would he encourage those
who boosted him for the vice presidency, presumably the next rung
on the ladder. His terms as lieutenant governor had been unsatisfy-
ing, and Coolidge wouldn't seek another post as standby equipment.

As it happened, the 1920 Republican Convention was more exciting than anyone imagined. Front-runners were toppled, and dark
horses and favorite sons remained in the background. In the end,
when it came to the top of the ticket, the expected happened. While
there is some disagreement, the weight of evidence indicates that
the bosses picked the nominee, Warren Harding of Ohio. According
to American presidential mythology, Harding was the quintessential dark horse, but his selection certainly did not come as a surprise, since he ran fourth in the early polling of delegates. The
Harding nomination was not the greatest shock at the convention—
it was how Coolidge got the nod for the vice presidency. Without
giving a speech, without being there, without the use of any of the
conventional bargaining arrangements, he pulled off the greatest
upset since Bryan's in 1896. Harding was nominated by the *political bosses*. The *party* selected Coolidge for the vice presidency, without him having to make any pledges or promises. This was at the
same time his glory, and his problem.

7

The Nominee

Massachusetts did not present my name, because my friends
knew I did not want to be vice president, but Judge Wallace
McCamant of Oregon placed me in nomination and was
quickly seconded by North Dakota and some other states. I
received about three-quarters of the votes cast. When this honor
came to me I was pleased to accept, and it was especially
agreeable to be associated with Senator Harding, whom I knew
well and liked.

The Autobiography of Calvin Coolidge

THE COOLIDGE BOOMLET gathered steam in the wake of the
1919 gubernatorial election. Newspaper reporters and magazine
writers started placing stories about him, many of which argued that
he was a different kind of politician, although they seemed unsure of
what exactly that meant. They stressed his spare but eloquent
phrases, his economy of style, and his simple life. There was always
the matter of the police strike. On November 12, the *Outlook* published one of these typical pieces entitled "Calvin Coolidge,
American," in which the author proclaimed, "The election of Calvin
Coolidge in Massachusetts is an event of national significance." The
Boston Herald exaggerated somewhat in stating, "The contest here
was watched by leading men all over the United States, and by them
regarded as transcending in importance any election that has been
held anywhere in the United States in the last decade." The *Boston*

Post, for its part, observed, incorrectly as it turned out, that the threatened split between Lodge and Crane over the League had been "called off"; the newspaper claimed they would work together in harmony on the Coolidge presidential nomination.

Coolidge had written to Lodge on February 22, 1919, asking him to moderate his criticism of the League, which was proving popular in parts of Massachusetts. Lodge replied, in a perfectly courteous letter, that he would not oblige. He then told reporters that he didn't know whether Coolidge was in the race for the Republican presidential nomination, and he wouldn't indicate whom he supported, although at the time many thought he was leaning toward Leonard Wood, TR's old comrade-in-arms from the Spanish–American War. This would have complicated matters. At the time Wood lived in Massachusetts and appeared to have substantial strength in the state. A Wood nomination would also have foreclosed any possibility of a Coolidge vice presidential run—the Constitution forbade the president and vice president being from the same state.

Coolidge wrote in his *Autobiography,* "About Thanksgiving time Senator Lodge came to me and voluntarily requested that he should present my name to the national Republican convention. He wished to go as a delegate with that understanding." Lodge confirmed this to reporters, and there was talk of a struggle between the senator and Stearns regarding tactics and strategy.

As the first prominent Republican to come out publicly for Coolidge, Lodge provided credibility to the movement. Still, he could not command the Massachusetts delegation. Lodge was an insider, but not a boss. He was considered a stuffed shirt by the men with power in their states, who had little liking for the man who gloried in being known as "the scholar in politics." His prominence in 1920 rested more on the centrality of the League of Nations issue than his political leadership.

Lodge had never before indicated much admiration for the governor, and the two men still were not close politically. Since a President Coolidge would have displaced Lodge as the most important Republican in the state, the senator could hardly have wanted him to rise that high. Even an unsuccessful Coolidge presidential bid would give him exposure, and could lead him to challenge

Lodge, if, at the age of seventy-two, the senator opted in 1922 to run for reelection. Some have suggested that the endorsement was a political ploy; Lodge might have realized that Coolidge had little hope for the nomination, and that by backing him as a favorite son, he would have a free hand once the serious bargaining began. It was a time-honored tradition for fence sitters, one that suited Lodge at that time.

Lodge might have had another thought in mind. The still-powerful Crane wanted the Massachusetts delegation to come out in favor of the League. Perhaps Crane would moderate his stand if Lodge supported his protégé.

In spite of his unwillingness to commit himself to the race, others announced for Coolidge. As expected, Crane came out for him, and Frederick Gillett followed. Stearns was actively working for the purported candidate; money was being raised; delegates were being courted; deals were being discussed.

In early 1920 Coolidge was visited by a reporter for the *New York World*, who wanted to interview this new force on the national scene. The *World* had applauded Coolidge's actions in the strike, and supported him for reelection, unusual at a time when few out-of-state newspapers took such stances. The resulting article might have been the model for the many to come.

> Coolidge is outwardly neither impressive nor expressive, and looking at him therefore is rather wasting time. It will not inform you who it is lives behind the cold mask of his lean and muscular face, and sees out of the eyes that are always looking, in the homely New England metaphor, "between the horse's ears." Nothing there will tell you what has brought him political standing and strength. He admittedly lacks all oratorical power in addressing a crowd and all personal magnetism in meeting an individual, and so ignores the charm of the plum-tree that when he became governor he retained in their positions all the efficient appointees of his predecessor. Yet for some years he has been the surest vote-getter in Massachusetts. You would never learn

why by looking at him, tho. You might notice that while he is not large-headed, the shape of his skull gives him somewhat more than average brain space; that in body and feet and hands he is of the thoroughbred type, long, slender, and sinewy; that his fingers are the fingers of a scholar, an artist, or a very deft mechanic; that his lips are thin and firmly set in a horizontal line; that his chin is very solid without squareness. Listening to Calvin Coolidge is not considered in Massachusetts likely to be much work—unless you were waiting to hear him break the long silence. If that be true, my own experience must have been unusual. I spent some three hours alone with him one evening, and could have spent three more with enjoyment. What he said was not in the main for quotation, nor did it prove much more revelatory and explanatory than the scrutiny of his record had. Listening to his friends—I could find no enemies, or at least none ready to admit it—was relaxation rather than investigation. Their comment was mainly in the form of illustrative anecdotes, and the anecdotes were good.

Bruce Barton, one of the more prolific and popular magazine writers of the time, placed a long piece dealing with Coolidge in the March issue of *Women's Home Companion*, entitled "The Silent Man on Beacon Hill," which contained a score or so of Coolidge quotations, as though to indicate he wasn't all that silent. Barton, who became a Coolidge enthusiast, concluded, "The greatest leaders we have had have been spiritual leaders. In Washington, in Lincoln and Roosevelt, in every man who has stirred America, there has been always an appeal that reached down beneath the material to something large, and unselfish, and eternal in man. And Calvin Coolidge also is a leader of that sort."

Realizing his chances for nomination were slim at best, Coolidge spoke out soon after the Barton article appeared: "I have not been and am not a candidate for president." Still hopeful, however, Stearns wanted to send an unpledged Massachusetts delegation to the Chicago Convention, and he worked for this at the GOP conclave. In the selection process on April 27, Lodge, Gillett, and Crane led in the balloting, and in the end the thirty-one person delegation was split between Coolidge and Wood, with several fence sitters.

Coolidge had nothing more to say on the matter. He had spoken, and gave the impression that he was content to play the cards he had. In his *Autobiography*, Coolidge wrote of his thoughts during this period:

> When I came to give the matter serious attention, and comprehended more fully what would be involved in a contest of this kind, I realized that I was not in a position to become engaged in it. I was governor of Massachusetts, and my first duty was to that office. It would not be possible for me, with the legislature in session, to be going about the country actively participating in an effort to secure delegates, and I was totally unwilling to have a large sum of money raised and spent in my behalf.
>
> I soon became convinced also that I was in danger of creating a situation in which some people in Massachusetts could permit it to be reported in the press that they were for me when they were not at heart for me and would give me little support at the convention. It would, however, prevent their having to make a public choice between other candidates and would help them in getting elected as delegates. There was nothing unusual in this situation. It simply was a condition that always has to be met in politics.

Here Coolidge was saying that he knew he was a long shot who might be tapped if the convention deadlocked, and that he was open to the highly unlikely possibility of a draft but didn't expect lightning to strike. Also, he was aware that his support, broad as it might be in the Massachusetts GOP, was also shallow, especially at the top. Why take risks in a situation like this?

There was another factor in the equation. Just as the deaths of his mother and sister affected Coolidge deeply, so did that of his stepmother, Carrie, on May 18. She had been married to John Coolidge for almost thirty years, and Calvin Coolidge had been very close to his stepmother. In his *Autobiography* Coolidge wrote, "I was greatly pleased to find in her all the motherly devotion that she could have given if I were her own son. For thirty years she watched over me and loved me, welcoming me when I went home, writing me often when I was away, and encouraging me in all my efforts." When she fell ill in 1908, he wrote to his father, "I am a great deal disturbed about mother. Are you sure you are doing all that can be done to help her?" and went on to say, in atypical Coolidge phrases, "*Everything* that is possible ought to be done to stop her suffering. I am afraid you may not realize how bad she might be." And now she was dead, and Coolidge might have felt that with her passing, the joys of politics were diminished. It wasn't the first time a death had caused him to become morose and withdrawn. Nor would it be the last.

Then another of those strokes of luck that often affected Coolidge's political career appeared out of nowhere. After Roosevelt's death, several contenders tried to seize his mantle, and their maneuvers, sensible as they might have seemed at the time, hurt them all. Senator Hiram Johnson, the California Progressive who had been Roosevelt's running mate in 1912, and who was a likely successor, was eager to make the race. He could count on support from former Progressives now returned to the GOP, but for that very reason was anathema to the regulars—they might accept a Roosevelt, with all his glamour and charisma, but no other Progressive. Moreover, Johnson was an ardent isolationist, even more opposed to the League of Nations than Lodge. His harsh, absolutist stand attracted zealots but repelled moderates. None of the bosses was remotely interested in Johnson.

Wood was a more likely surrogate for Roosevelt. A medical doctor who received a regular army commission in 1886, Wood rose to be personal physician to the McKinley family. He became friendly with Roosevelt in 1897; together they organized the "Rough Riders," in which Wood was the commander, and they fought side by side in Cuba. As Roosevelt went on to become governor of New York, Wood served as military governor of Cuba and then of the

Moro Province in the Philippines. From 1910 to 1914 he was the army chief of staff. In 1917 Wood was the army's senior officer, and normally would have received a command in France, but President Wilson kept Wood stateside, perhaps fearful that Wood—who had sought the Republican nomination in 1916—would ride to the White House on a military victory after the war. Thus in 1920 Wood appeared to many not only as TR's political heir, but also as Wilson's victim. Nevertheless, in a time when large numbers of voters had concluded that the United States had mistakenly entered the war, a military man was an unlikely candidate. Besides, Wood gave little indication of having a political agenda, except that he favored universal military service, hardly popular in that period.

At no time during the campaign did any of the newspapers or magazines discuss General Wood's activities in the strikes of 1919. Because of the scope of the man's career, these didn't seem important. Coolidge's more modest accomplishments were recalled in detail, and his words at the end of the police strike were often repeated. It was the measure of the two men in the context of the nomination period, and indicated not only that Coolidge seemed a minor force with minor accomplishments when placed on the national scene, but also that he was now entering the big leagues of politics.

Just as Johnson appealed to those who cherished Roosevelt's Progressive agenda, so Wood attracted those who admired the man himself—that is, the more conservative element. Members of this set provided the campaign with lavish financing. Under the leadership of William Procter, who ran Procter & Gamble Company, they formed the Leonard Wood League and hired some of the best political operatives to work on the general's behalf, including John King, who had been considered a possible manager for the Roosevelt campaign. Because of this, that winter Wood seemed a likely nominee. But the bosses certainly would not support anyone in the Roosevelt tradition, a man who would be independent of them and probably ignore their interests. Indeed, Wood would be even more dangerous than Johnson.

The same might be said for the third major candidate. Governor Frank Lowden of Illinois was a capable, intelligent, and admired individual, who entered politics while administering the estate left to his wife by her father, railroad magnate George Pullman. His record was exemplary, as were his origins. Lowden was the son of a black-smith born on a farm near Sunrise, Minnesota, but he was hardly a rustic: he erected an estate on six hundred acres in northern Illinois he called "Sinnissippi," one of the most magnificent country homes in America, open on designated days to visitors. Lowden had entered the House of Representatives in 1906, being named to fill the unex-pired term of a deceased congressman, and he served two additional terms. He remained with Taft when the Republican party split in two in 1912 and had urged the party to reunite, and so he was not tainted with the stain of political treason. In 1917 he became the governor of Illinois.

As governor, Lowden streamlined the state government, cut taxes and expenditures, and would leave the state with a $15 million sur-plus. He doubled aid to public schools, pushed through one of the nation's major road construction measures, and started work on a waterway to connect the Great Lakes to the Mississippi. After Chicago was hit by a race riot in 1917, Lowden sponsored legisla-tion to punish racial and religious discrimination. He replaced polit-ical appointees with those selected from civil service rolls, and cleaned up a corrupt statehouse. If the nation wanted an honest, effi-cient, and independent governor, untainted by Washington, Lowden seemed to fit the bill better than Coolidge. Walter Lippmann, who supported the Lowden candidacy, wrote of it in words that might have described a Coolidge race:

> There is a logic to Lowden, once you grant the
> premises. He comes from the middle of the country, he
> stands in the middle of the road, in the middle of the
> party about midway between Wood of New Hampshire
> and Johnson of California. He has risen from a farm to
> an estate, from obscurity to moderate fame, perhaps
> not quite the darling of the gods but surely one of their
> favorite sons....
> The people are tired, tired of noise, tired of politics,
> tired of inconvenience, tired of greatness, and longing
> for a place where the world is quiet and where all

trouble seems dead leaves, and spent waves riot in
doubtful dreams of dreams....

Lowden is the noiseless candidate in this campaign. I
have watched his appeal to the voters. He tells them that
he will talk only of prosaic things and he does. He
assures them that he will not bother them much as he
will not.

Lowden had congratulated Coolidge on his actions during the
Boston police strike. He supported Coolidge's reelection in 1919,
warning that his defeat would be "a repudiation of his stand in the
Boston riots." One of his aides suggested the "perfect" national
ticket for 1920 would be Lowden and Coolidge—in that order. For
Lowden it would draw delegates from New England; for Coolidge,
Lowden could be a counter to Wood and Lodge in Massachusetts.

But Lowden, too, had liabilities. He was criticized for living
ostentatiously—he seemed to fancy his nickname, "the Squire of
Sinnissippi." He clashed repeatedly with Chicago Mayor "Big Bill"
Thompson over patronage and his supposed suppression of antiwar
groups. Because of this, he could not expect a united Illinois delegation to support him. Then too—and this was close to fatal—the
state bosses didn't trust Lowden, who was independent and apparently incorruptible. Nonetheless, Lowden may have been the best
qualified Republican in 1920, or for that matter, 1924 and 1928,
as well.

By late winter there were many more announced or supposed possibilities. Herbert Hoover was a genuine hero of the war, a successful businessman, and better and more favorably known than any of
the major candidates. But he, too, was distrusted by the bosses, and
he ran an unusually inept campaign. There was Robert La Follette of
Wisconsin, the sixty-five-year-old symbol of progressivism; Nicholas
Murray Butler, the president of Columbia University, and New
York's favorite son; Governor William Sproul of Pennsylvania,
another favorite son, who most thought would hold on to the state's
votes—until orders came down from Boies Penrose. As always, there
were several very minor candidates representing special causes. For
instance, Lucy Page Gaston, a noted anticigarette crusader, entered

several primaries, telling reporters that just as Lincoln had freed the slaves, so she would free the nation from the cigarette.

In the spring of 1920, as delegates prepared to go to Chicago for the convention, they continued to wonder whom Penrose would back. The party's leaders, who had conferred with Penrose in Pennsylvania in 1919 and 1920, knew he was troubled by the lack of a candidate to represent their interests. In the summer of 1919 he considered Harding, and in a private meeting asked him, "Harding, how would you like to be president?" Harding tried to beg off—he liked being a senator and had no ambitions for the White House. In the end Penrose gave up on him. "Harding isn't as big a man as I thought he was," he said, after reading a Harding speech. "He should have talked more about the tariff and not so much about playing cymbals in the Marion brass band."

Probably so. Harding was a genial, friendly, comfortable kind of person; after graduating from Ohio Central College, he became a teacher, studied law, sold insurance, and, eventually, became a newspaper reporter. In 1884 he purchased the defunct *Marion Star*, which he nursed into a successful publication. Seven years later he married Florence Kling DeWolfe, a divorcee five years his senior, and a domineering woman ambitious for her husband. She nudged him into politics, and in 1899 he was elected to the Ohio senate, where he met Harry Daugherty, his future manager. There followed a reelection to the state senate, a term as lieutenant governor, and failed attempts to win, first, the GOP gubernatorial nomination, and then—finally succeeding in that—the general election for the governorship.

Despite this lackluster record, Harding was selected to place Taft's name in nomination at the 1912 Republican Convention, and two years later he won election to the United States Senate. Harding quickly became a popular figure in the Senate "club," and chaired the Republican Convention in 1916. In 1919 he was named to the Senate Foreign Relations Committee, though he had no experience or interest in foreign policy. Harding was opposed to the League, in favor of conservative Republican policies, and quite content with his position in life. So, he was reluctant to make the race for president, since if he did he could not also run for reelection to his beloved Senate.

Penrose would have to seek elsewhere for his candidate. He looked favorably at Pennsylvania's other senator, Philander Knox, who had served as attorney general in the McKinley cabinet, and who had been named to the Senate in 1904. He soon became a member of the GOP inner circle, and was a safe conservative. A few weeks before the convention opened, Penrose met with Knox, and asked whether he would like to be president. Knox pleaded age and ill health, but Penrose persevered. "You won't need to do much work. We'll get a good hard-working cabinet for you and you can sit at the head of the table and run the show." Knox demurred, and did his best to avoid Penrose thereafter, afraid that he might give in.

Penrose let out the word that he was ill and probably would not attend the convention. Later it came out that Penrose was actually close to death at the time, often in a coma, and that the real power over the Pennsylvania delegation was exercised by favorite son Governor Sproul. All the same, everyone seemed to believe that no one could expect the nomination without the support of Penrose and most of the other bosses.

In time the primary system would displace the bosses, but that time was not 1920. That year there were sixteen primaries, starting with New Hampshire in early March, which General Wood won. He did not, however, carry any momentum out of New Hampshire; Hiram Johnson won in North Dakota, even though the delegation included some recalcitrant Wood people. Then came South Dakota. Although South Dakota would send only ten voting delegates to the convention, Wood went there anyway, campaigning throughout the state, followed by Lowden, who hadn't intended going until Wood filed his papers.

Procter concocted this strategy, which the professionals in the Wood camp opposed. They argued that it was reckless to enter primaries in which favorite sons were running, since this would antagonize them and preclude deals at the convention. But Procter, who had no real idea how the political game was played, argued that if Wood could knock enough of them out of the contest, his resulting popularity would make him unstoppable. A large number of wealthy industrialists backed Procter because they wanted to usurp control of the GOP's policies and nominees from the party bosses. As it turned out, however, the professionals were right: Wood's actions in the primaries won him some delegates, but lost him political opportunities to work with the others.

Wood and Lowden advertised lavishly, while Johnson had a much more modest war chest. Despite the efforts of the candidates, through a series of primaries in the Midwest, no candidate emerged as a clear-cut favorite. Indeed, the leading candidates, conducting bitter campaigns, seemed to be canceling one another out.

Ohio was the bellwether state. Favorite son Harding won a close contest over Wood, but the general managed to take several delegates; Harding thus would not come into the convention with a united state delegation, which was traditionally seen as a sign of weakness. Harding was prepared to quit the race and make a try for the Senate, but his campaign manager, Harry Daugherty, talked him out of it. Daugherty told his uncertain candidate, "I think you have the best chance [of winning the nomination]." As Daugherty later recalled, he explained his logic to Harding.

> "Neither one of the leading candidates can win. General Wood is backed by a powerful group of rich men who wish a military man in the White House. They are nervous over the social disorders following the World War. They are nervous over the growing demands of labor. They wish to entrench themselves behind the invisible force of the bayonet and the machine gun. The scheme won't work. The people are sick of war. The boys who saw it in France have begun to tell tales out of school. They hate war to a man. They'll not vote for a general. The women will vote in the next election. It would be suicide on that account to name a general. The Republican convention will not do it."
>
> "Money's a powerful force in our primaries!" Harding sighed.
>
> "That's so, too. But there's not enough money in the world to buy the nomination for a man who wears epaulets in 1920."

"Lowden's a power to be reckoned with," Harding suggested.

"Sure. The best man on the list, too. I like him. He'd make a fine president. But he'll never have the prize or a nomination."

"Why?"

"Because he's too rich."

"Nonsense."

"Besides, he married Pullman's daughter. No party will name a railroad magnate for the office of president."

"Why, he's a farmer."

"Yes, but he married into the railroads. He'll never win. He and Wood will fight each other to a finish and deadlock the convention."

"Then Johnson may slip in."

"Never. They'll say he defeated Hughes in California, and the real Republicans will not forgive him."*

"Come down to brass tacks," Harding ordered. "Am I a big enough man for the race?"

"Don't make me laugh! The day of giants in the presidential chair is passed. Our so-called Great Presidents were all made by the conditions of war under which they administered the office. Greatness in the presidential chair is largely an illusion of the people."

Daugherty's analysis was on target. Despite the fact that his own career in electoral politics had been dismal—he had failed to win nomination to the posts of state attorney general, congressman, governor, and three times for senator—he was a skilled political operative.

As expected, favorite son Coolidge won the Massachusetts primary, but Wood took some delegates as well. As with Harding in Ohio, Coolidge's failure to carry all the delegates in his home state was a sign of weakness.

---

* This refers to the continuing split in the Republican Party in 1916, when Johnson's refusal to support Hughes lost him the electoral votes of that state, and with it, the presidency.

Soon thereafter Harding traveled to Boston to deliver an address. In his speech he predicted that Coolidge, who had received only a scattering of votes, would be the eventual nominee. Did this mean he was coming out for Coolidge? "If I lived in Massachusetts, I should be for Governor Coolidge for president. Coming from Ohio, I am for Harding." The speech won Harding the good will of the listeners. Harding had, of course, gone through New England earlier and had met with Coolidge, which gave Ohio party leader Newton Fairbanks an idea. Writing to a friend, he declared, "The ticket you suggest, 'Harding and Coolidge,' would sweep the country like a whirlwind, and reestablish an American government in Washington."

In the California primary Johnson decisively defeated Hoover, all but knocking him out of the race. Wood, Lowden, Johnson, and Harding contested for Indiana, with Wood winning narrowly over Johnson. Next Johnson captured Oregon, and then North Carolina.

When all the primaries were over, Wood had won 124 delegates; Johnson, 112; Lowden, 72; and Harding, 39; but in the popular votes Johnson had 966,000; Wood, 711,000; and Lowden, 389,000.

In short, there was no clear victor, and plenty of room for deals. Despite Johnson's popular appeal, he had no chance; the bosses positively despised him, and he returned the feeling. Yet the bosses weren't particularly enamored of Wood or Lowden, either.

Moreover, the front-runners had conducted such an acrimonious campaign that there was no chance that any two would unite to form a ticket. But Harding, who had angered no one and was in fourth place, was in a good situation for some bargaining. Unlike the others, neither he nor Daugherty had challenged favorite sons or attempted to pressure any of the bosses. The Harding people were perfectly willing to trade favors for votes on second, third, and fourth ballots. Coolidge, and the others who were far behind, had faint hope, since there was the possibility for deadlock. It was all in the hands of the bosses.

In February, Daugherty made what would become a famous prediction to a *New York Times* reporter:

I don't expect Senator Harding to be nominated on the first, second, or third ballots, but I think we can afford to take chances that, about eleven minutes after two, Friday morning of the convention, when ten or twenty weary men are sitting around a table, someone will say, "Who will be nominated?" At that decisive time the friends of Harding will suggest him and can well afford to abide by the results.

At the time it was considered a foolhardy prediction, but Daugherty had thought it over, and it made sense. Reporters also understood how the parties worked. On June 7 a *New York Times* reporter wrote a story about the backroom politicking that occurs at conventions:

One of the most interesting questions to be answered when the Republican Convention is over—if anyone can answer it—will be whether the presidential candidate was nominated at the Congress Hotel or the Blackstone Hotel. Formally and officially, of course, he is to be named by the delegates on the floor of the conventional hall. As a matter of fact, unless there is a genuine stampede—and political historians differ as to whether there ever has been a single Republican stampede since the beginning of things—he will be named either in the lobbies, corridors, and headquarters of the Congress or in the private rooms of the Blackstone.

As it happened, the selection *was* made in the private rooms of the Blackstone, but most Americans, who did not understand party mechanics, followed the campaign like a horse race. By spring everyone—including the presidential hopefuls—pondered one question: even if Lowden did manage to stop Wood, could he win the prize for himself? Just prior to the convention, Daugherty again sketched a scenario for a reporter:

I won't try to fool you. You can see what we've got here, it's only a shoestring. I'll tell you in confidence what's in my mind. All I'm doing is getting in touch with the leaders and delegates who are for Wood and Lowden, being friendly with them. When the convention comes, those two armies will battle each other to a standstill. When both realize they can't win, when they're tired and hot and sweaty and discouraged both the armies will remember me and this little headquarters. They'll be like soldiers after a battle, who recall a shady spring along a country road where they got a drink as they marched to the front. When they remember me that way maybe both sides will turn to Harding—I don't know—it's just a chance.

Despite fervent campaigning, the candidates said little about issues. Newspapers and candidates focused on the League of Nations as a central issue of the campaign. They ignored, however, the problems of reconversion of the economy, the recession that the nation was beginning to experience, the unfinished agenda of Progressivism, and much more, including Prohibition. Although voters learned that Johnson was an isolationist, that Wood believed in a strong America and was a bit of an authoritarian, and that Lowden was concerned with encouraging economic development, the details were not made clear. And why should they be? There would be enough time for that in the general election. In Chicago, the candidates had to win delegates, not the electorate.

By then Stearns had established a Coolidge for President headquarters in Washington, led by James Reynolds, a Capitol insider who had once served as the party's secretary. A second office was established in Chicago, the convention's site, that June. It was a modest, amateur affair. Stearns had learned his way around Massachusetts politics, but he had no experience outside of the state. Reynolds sought out his colleagues and boosted Coolidge as a sure-fire vote-getter. Lieutenant Governor Channing Cox arrived to speak out for Coolidge, and other friends and associates were there, including Dwight Morrow. Coolidge's name appeared in some of the columns as a possible compromise candidate in case of a deadlock, but this was usual talk in the age of brokered conventions.

And what did the putative candidate think of all this? He was, as usual, circumspect. Coolidge clearly wanted to be president, and he obviously believed himself qualified for the position. Did he believe he had a chance? A letter to his father, written shortly after Crane's death in October, indicated he did: "Had he [Crane] been his old self in Chicago I feel the result there would have been different. We did not know until too late that he had been physically unable there to do what we had expected of him."

Coolidge did not then consider the vice presidency. He rejected offers from several states to back him for the second post, but he also knew that the people around the presidential designee, and not the delegates, would decide the vice presidential nomination.

Stearns raised $68,000 for the Coolidge campaign, of which he contributed $12,500, and Crane another $5,000, with much of the rest coming from Massachusetts businessmen. It was a small amount, but then again Daugherty had raised only $113,000 for Harding. Soon, however, their paucity of funds seemed a blessing; Wood and Lowden, each rich in funds, maneuvered to crush one another—for one of the key issues became campaign spending. Even before the balloting, *New York Times* reporter Ernest Harview took note of the matter:

> What becomes of the enormous sums of money raised and disbursed at every recurring election for president of the United States? The sums so contributed amounted to $3 million in 1904, to $5 million in 1908, to $8 million in 1912, and to more than $12 million in 1916.
>
> The present presidential campaign is only in its primary stage, and already as testimony before the United States Senate committee had shown, between $2 million and $3 million has been expended, though neither party convention has yet been held. Is this money being used for bribery and corruption or applied to legitimate campaign expenses. What becomes of it?

Answers were soon provided.

Louis Seibold, a reporter for the *New York World*, brought to the attention of his editor, Charles Lincoln, one of Hiram Johnson's speeches condemning Wood's lavish campaign spending. The newspapermen concluded there was a story there. Lincoln contacted Johnson's manager, William Borah, one of the lions of the Senate, a cantankerous maverick. Borah was interested, and wanted to know more.

On March 27 the *World* ran a front page story listing the key contributors to the Wood campaign, which Seibold had obtained on a leak from John King—whom Wood had dismissed as his campaign manager. After being dumped by Wood, King became the eyes and ears for Boies Penrose, who wanted to block Wood.

Borah then took to the Senate floor to demand an investigation, and a subcommittee was selected from the Senate Committee on Privileges and Elections, headed by William Kenyon, an Iowa Republican who had entered the Senate in 1911, a Progressive who had come out for Johnson. There was no Lowden supporter on the subcommittee, as the other two members wavered between Harding and Wood.

The subcommittee, which began its work in late May and was still in session on the eve of the convention, soon discovered that Wood had raised $1.8 million, Lowden $414,000, and Johnson a mere $194,000. This sparked talk of how the wealthy were trying to buy elections.* For example, William Procter, who had voiced sympathy for totalitarian movements, had made the Wood campaign a $710,000 "loan," and there had been donations from such tycoons as E.L. Doheny, Dan Hanna, and Ambrose Monel.

Although the Lowden people argued that only $35,000 of the contributions to their man came from outsiders, and that the Lowdens had anted close to $400,000 of their own money, this ploy backfired—it just showed how wealthy individuals dominated presidential politics. Worse, Louis Emmerson, one of the Lowden's managers, could not account for $5,000 of the funds expended in

---

* The Kenyon Committee later disclosed that spending on the presidential campaign in 1920 cost $10.3 million, of which $8.1 million went for Harding, and $2.2 million for James Cox.

Missouri, and then two of the delegates from that state revealed that they had received $2,500 each.

But by the time of the convention, the damage had been done. Wood and Lowden, the front-runners, had been tainted by money and the stench of corruption. Johnson, however, did not benefit, either; the party regulars, who opposed him in any case, resented his attempt to smear the party as corrupt.

The newspapers for June 5 carried the betting odds offered by bookmakers on the hopefuls. Fred Schwed, a stockbroker who also booked wagers, quoted Johnson at 2 to 1, Wood at 2½ to 1, Lowden at 10 to 1, and Hoover at 7 to 1. He had Harding at 6 to 1, and Coolidge at 8 to 1. Although Lowden still had a sizable number of pledged voters, most thought that he had reached his zenith, and that in the end it would come down to a race between Wood and Johnson.

The *Literary Digest* polled its mostly middle class readers on the eve of the convention. The poll indicated that Wood was ahead with 277,486 of those questioned, while Johnson was in second place with 263,087. Then came Hoover, Lowden, Charles Evans Hughes, Harding, and Coolidge. The governor of Massachusetts received 33,621 votes, while 67,041 wanted Coolidge for the vice presidency.

Strategies changed based on the revelations leading up to the convention. In this period of brokered conventions, managers took a handful of axioms seriously, and reporters were well aware of them. The first was momentum; the candidate, if at all possible, had to show progress through the balloting. The second was that all the secondary candidates had stakes in uniting to cripple the leader. The third was that the temporary lending of delegates was perfectly acceptable. Thus delegates pledged to Candidate One could be lent for a few ballots to Candidate Two in order to block Candidate Three. Once this was done, they would be returned to Candidate One, who would then try to bowl over Candidate Two and all the others. Daugherty was a master at this game. He also knew that while all watched the delegate count, in the end the bosses, informed by what was happening on the floor, would weigh in with their choice. His task was to make Harding look good in the balloting and impress the real powers. But Frank Stearns, just a state politician, had no access to the leaders, and concentrated instead on rallying his meager forces on the floor.

Of the 984 GOP delegates in 1920, a clear majority—529—were nominally uncommitted, but actually the number was higher than that, and the deal making was on in earnest. Before the campaign opened, Daugherty later wrote, he met with Emmerson to discuss a proposition. Daugherty was willing to throw some of Harding's delegates to Lowden. "We'll form an alliance then to first beat Wood, for we can't allow Harding's vote to be too small, but we'll loan you every vote we can until you pass Wood. The minute you do this, Wood is out of the race and all friendship on the floor of the convention ceases between us—you understand that." Emmerson certainly did. He believed that when this happened, Lowden would become unbeatable, and wouldn't need the Harding delegates. For his part, Daugherty would then line up with other candidates or a single candidate to stop Lowden. It was a risky strategy, but in his position, he had to take risks.

Lodge, who as expected became temporary and then permanent chairman, opened the convention on Tuesday, June 8, and delivered a long tirade against Wilson and the League. The platform was adopted that evening, and, predictably, covered everything from the League (it hedged), to relations with Mexico (strongly opposed to that country's nationalization policies), to the high cost of living (opposed), to immigration restriction (favored). As with so many platforms, it was hardly noticed.

While Lodge spoke, the temperature in the convention hall neared 100 degrees and remained there throughout the meetings. The building, a converted prison, had thick stone walls and turrets, which were supposed to repel the heat but didn't; throughout the convention the delegates suffered in those pre–air conditioning days. They sat or meandered through the long nominating speeches for the leading candidates, the seconding speeches, the cheering and marches—close to an hour for each. Then Gillett nominated Coolidge, in a speech that took all of five minutes. "Our candidate is a man of few words, and in that respect I shall imitate him," he began. "And I only wish I could imitate his effective use of words." He ended in the traditional way. "He is as patient as Lincoln, as silent as Grant, as diplomatic as McKinley, with the political instinct of Roosevelt. His character is as firm as the mountains of his native state. Like them, his head is above the clouds, and he stands unshaken amid the tumult and the storm."

According to newspaper reports, the Nebraska delegation rose to applaud the speech, and then individual delegates from other states joined in.

Mrs. Alexandra Carlisle Pfeiffer—the only woman in the Massachusetts delegation, an amateur actress with a fine stage presence that Stearns recognized—delivered a short, well received seconding speech for Governor Coolidge. Only thirty-four years old, she was a handsome woman. Mrs. Pfeiffer was one of several women called upon to deliver seconding speeches, reflecting that this was the first election in which women would vote under the provisions of the new constitutional amendment.

Through all of this Coolidge remained in his apartment in the Adams House, where he received convention news from his secretary, Henry Long, and others. He wrote of his thoughts at the time to his father:

> Before this reaches you the nomination will be probably
> be made. Just now Johnson is out of it. Balloting was
> just beginning. Probably Wood or Lowden cannot win
> but may. If not my chance seems best. My nomination
> by Speaker Gillett was well taken with genuine
> spontaneous applause—not manufactured.

Other nominations followed. Harding was nominated by Ohio Governor Frank Willis, a real spellbinder, who started out with: "Every candidate before this convention is worthy of the honor, and the man nominated will be elected—no matter what his name." After the acrimony of the past few months, this was greeted gratefully by the delegates.

The balloting began on Friday morning. On the first ballot Wood led with 287 votes; Lowden had 211; Johnson, 133; and far behind these and some others, Harding had 65 votes, and farther behind still, Coolidge had 34, of which all but six were from Massachusetts, with seven from the state, including that of Lodge, going for Wood. The Lodge vote was no surprise; the senator had reportedly said, "I have known Calvin Coolidge only as long as it has been necessary to know him."

On the second ballot Daugherty filtered votes to Lowden, at the same time trying unsuccessfully to make Harding's vote rise. On the fourth ballot Lowden had 289 votes to Wood's 299; it seemed he had gained enough momentum to pass Wood on the next ballot and then roar on to victory. Harding then had 61½ votes, and Coolidge, 25. Lowden seemed a near-certain winner. "Running fine," one delegate wrote him. "Nomination not later than the 5th ballot."

Daugherty then shifted his attention to halting the Lowden steamroller. On the floor he tried to rally his troops to return to Harding, while the bosses prepared to settle matters their own way. Senators Lodge and Reed Smoot conferred for a moment at the platform, and then Smoot went to the podium to move the convention to adjourn until 10:00 AM. The Wood and Lowden forces, both of which thought they might win if the balloting continued, shouted their objections. When Lodge called for the vote, the "nays" erupted, followed by a scattering of "aye" votes. With this, the stunned convention adjourned. Journalist Mark Sullivan cornered Smoot and asked why he wanted the adjournment. "Oh, there's going to be a deadlock and we'll have to work out some solution; we wanted the night to think it over." This did not appear in the following day's newspapers, but newsmen like Sullivan and Frank Kent knew it meant the bosses were going to meet.

Several currents swirled around that evening. Borah had an idea what was happening and attempted to find some way to leverage the Johnson votes to strike a deal. Borah, New Hampshire Senator George Moses, and others went to see Johnson and gave him their views of the situation. Moses, who had originally supported Wood, had days earlier suggested a Wood–Johnson ticket, but Johnson did not respond. Now Moses came up with another compromise: a ticket headed by Philander Knox with Johnson for vice president. Despite Knox's advanced age—he was sixty-seven years old in 1920—and ill health, Johnson would have nothing of it. The Harding men also visited Johnson, proposing a Harding–Johnson

ticket, but Johnson also turned down this offer—he would not settle for second place with anyone.

Both tickets had appeal; either could have been elected. As it
turned out, Knox died in 1921, as did Harding two years later. Had
Hiram Johnson accepted either offer, he would have been president,
while Calvin Coolidge would have retired to Northampton and have
been forgotten. As so often happened in his political career, Coolidge
benefited from a stroke of good fortune.

When the convention adjourned neither Lodge nor Smoot knew
the next step; they had acted without consulting the party leaders.
For a while it had seemed Wood might be able to swing the vote;
over the telephone, Penrose told his representatives that Wood could
have the nomination in return for giving the bosses three cabinet
posts; Wood rejected the notion, calling it a "wicked game." That
evening Senators Charles Curtis of Kansas, Frank Brandegee of
Connecticut, and Lodge dined with George Harvey—a former
Democrat and member of the Wilson team who was now going over
to the GOP—in Harvey's suite at the Blackstone Hotel. They all
agreed Wood and Lowden would cancel each other the next day, and
that Johnson was out if it. Whoever among the others showed
strength could win on some future ballot. Several names were mentioned—Charles Evans Hughes, who had lost to Wilson in 1916;
Philander Knox; William Sproul; and Republican National Chairman Will Hays. Then they talked about Harding, who Curtis felt
had the best chance.

Curtis went to contact the bosses, while the others continued their
ruminations. Representatives of the bosses appeared from time to
time, entered the discussion, and then left. Crane was there, but what
he or any of the others said is not known. Penrose, of course,
remained in Philadelphia, but a year and a half later his physician,
Dr. H.W. Carpenter, reported his contact with the group.

> He was a very sick man. He collapsed… he had been
> unconscious for hours. But even in that condition his
> mind was subconsciously turning over the problem at
> Chicago. He came to at last… turned to Leighton C.
> Taylor, his secretary, and asked what they were doing at

Chicago. It was the first question he asked after
regaining his consciousness. Taylor answered that they
had been doing nothing, that a deadlock had been
reached. The senator lay a moment, thinking. "Call up
King," he said at last to Taylor, "and tell him to throw it
to Harding."

Again and again the conferees went over the different possibilities,
and every time the Harding gambit seemed the best. News of this
may have leaked to the Ohio senator. Described as harried and worried earlier in the day, he now was spied by a reporter who saw him
leaving the Ohio delegation headquarters with former Governor
Myron Herrick at 11:00 PM. When asked for a comment, Herrick
said, "You can say that Senator Harding will be nominated on the
first ballot tomorrow," but of course this was to have been expected
from a Harding supporter.

At around 11:00 PM the conferees in the "smoke-filled room" had
just about settled on Harding. They were tired and uncomfortable due
to the heat. Brandegee said what many of them must have thought:

There aren't any first-raters this year. This ain't 1880 or
any 1904; we haven't any John Sherman or Theodore
Roosevelt; we got a lot of second-raters and Warren
Harding is the best of the second-raters.

An hour later Harvey sent for Harding, who was expecting the
call. Harvey wanted to know whether there was anything in the candidate's background that might embarrass the Republican Party
were he nominated for the presidency. Nan Britton, the mother of his
illegitimate child, was with Harding in Chicago. There was also a
liaison with another woman, Carrie Phillips, the wife of a close
friend who had tried unsuccessfully to blackmail him into taking a
pro-German position before the United States entered the war. In
addition, there were rumors one of Harding's ancestors was black.
Harding asked for a few minutes to think it over, then said he was
clean. After this, the group broke up. While waiting for an elevator,
Senator Smoot was greeted by a reporter, George Morris of the *New*

York Telegram. "Anything decided on at your conference upstairs?" Morris wanted to know. Surprisingly, Smoot did not prevaricate: "Yes. We decided on Harding, and he will be nominated this afternoon, after we have balloted long enough to give Lowden a run for his money." Morris wired in his story, and the newspaper had the scoop of the convention. It was almost precisely at the time Daugherty had predicted it would be.

But had the smoke-filled room really selected Harding and then foisted him on the convention? Years later, when he wrote his memoirs, Daugherty denied the senatorial clique had given Harding the nomination. True, he wrote, there was a meeting, but the participants did not have the impact everyone seemed to think. Robert Murray, the premier Harding biographer, agreed with Daugherty's version of how Harding achieved the nomination, writing that "no orders ever went to convention delegates as a result of it, nor did it signify the implementation of a senatorial plan to nominate Harding." Murray notes that thirteen of the senators voted for other candidates after the meeting, and they continued to do so for several more ballots. But this would be in line with what Smoot had told the reporter, and those senators who did not vote for Harding might have had other political debts to pay. Besides, the few personal votes wouldn't have made a difference.

Finally, Claude Fuess quoted a letter from Mark Sullivan to Edward Duffield sent shortly after the convention:

> There never was any time when the Senate group was
> not in control of the Chicago Convention. I was a
> delegate there as you were and I was also a reporter and
> had the reporter's end of it, and I knew all the time what
> was going on behind the scenes. I am dead sure that I
> was not mistaken.

In other words, although the party bosses would in time lose power, in 1920 they still held an iron grip on the convention.

Messengers were dispatched to the Lowden, Wood, and Johnson headquarters, telling the hopefuls that Harding was the choice. They would not bow out gracefully, however. The following morning

Lowden and Wood met and tried to hammer out a deal. As Lowden wrote in a memo he placed in a confidential file:

> It was arranged that General Wood, in a closed car, should drive to the Michigan Avenue entrance of the Blackstone and that I should get into the car at that point. This was done, and we had a conference of perhaps three quarters of an hour, I should say. It was evident to both of us that the Senate combination was making great headway with Senator Harding. General Wood suggested that we ought to get together, and that our managers should meet at once. I concurred in this.

The deal might have resulted in a Wood–Lowden ticket—and they had the combined delegates to make it work—but Lowden's managers concluded that it would be next to impossible to convince his delegates to vote for Wood, while Lowden was unwilling to accept second place on the ticket. They could not reach an agreement, and besides, it was already too late.

The convention reconvened at 10:00 AM, and the balloting continued, with Harding gaining strength all the while. Lowden went into the lead on the fifth ballot by a margin of 303 to 299, with Harding's vote at 78, an increase over his 63½ on the fourth ballot. The two leaders tied at 311 on the sixth ballot, while Harding went to 89. On the seventh they remained almost unchanged, and Harding went up to 105. It continued that way through the ninth ballot, on which Harding received 374½ votes. He won on the tenth, with 692⅕ votes to Wood's 156 and Johnson's 80⅘. Lowden, who had released his delegates, received 11 votes. On the final ballot Coolidge received five votes, four from New York and one from Massachusetts.

Following convention tradition, shortly after 6:00 PM, the delegates made the nomination unanimous. The next day some delegates were comparing Harding to McKinley. Not Roosevelt, not Lincoln, but McKinley, as the candidate himself often did. They clearly felt the country needed a period of calm after two decades of reform and war.

Because of the turmoil surrounding the presidential nomination, most people ignored the vice presidency—except those candidates who were trying to strike deals. In order to correct this oversight, some of the men who had put forth Harding gathered under the platform to select his running mate. What they wanted, of course, was a man who would complement Harding. After a short conference, they had their man: Senator Irvine Lenroot of Wisconsin.

A close friend and associate of Harding's, Lenroot was a perfectly decent and intelligent senator. He had once been one of Robert La Follette's closest confidants, and had served as a member of the House. Then he broke with La Follette over the issue of the war, and became increasingly conservative. His selection for the number two spot made little sense, except that he was acceptable to Johnson, which might mollify some of the old Progressives. In this period of ticket balancing, having two midwesterners on the same ticket was pointless. Moreover, Lenroot had angered conservatives with his earlier iconoclasm, and hard-core Progressives with his subsequent change of heart.

Lenroot, however, was unwilling to accept the offer. He did agree to talk it over with his wife, but when he located her she agreed he shouldn't run on the national ticket. Why should he? After all, the vice presidency was a thankless post. The inhabitant of the office was, as Nelson Rockefeller would later say prior to being selected for the office, standby equipment. And what might happen if through the death of the president he did succeed to office? Five vice presidents— John Tyler, Millard Fillmore, Andrew Johnson, Chester Arthur, and Theodore Roosevelt—had filled out the terms of presidents who died in office. Of that group only Roosevelt managed to win nomination on his own for the following election, and of course Roosevelt was an extraordinary person and president. The last vice president other than Roosevelt to receive his party's nomination on his own, without succeeding on the death of the president, had been Martin Van Buren, back in 1832. The vice presidency was a dead end job; everyone knew this in 1920. In any case, while Lenroot pondered, the delegates took the decision out of his hands.

After the Harding nomination delegates started to leave the hall. Supporters of Lowden, Wood, and Johnson were disgusted, hot, and tired, and anxious to leave their expensive hotel rooms.

Many of the others had had their fill of politics. Even so, there were more than enough to make a quorum. The work of the convention continued.

On the convention floor Crane was busily trying to whip up support and votes for a Coolidge vice presidential nomination, but before he could do this another man accomplished the task for him.

When Chairman Lodge called for nominations for the vice presidency, Senator Medill McCormick of Illinois delivered a short speech of support for Lenroot. There were seconding speeches, but these efforts were greeted unenthusiastically. By then most of the delegates had heard the stories of how the bosses had named Harding, and now were trying to do the same with Lenroot. What could they do? They had seen the front-runners disposed of, the wishes of the primary voters ignored, and the back room crowd take over once again. That evening reporters filed stories discussing the feeling of letdown among delegates.

Lodge apparently did not recognize what was happening, or if he did, he paid it no mind. In addition, he, too, must have been weary, experiencing a letdown of his own now that the major work of the convention had been completed. He turned the gavel over to Ohio's former Governor Frank Willis, and left the auditorium.

Then fifty-three-year-old Wallace McCamant rose to seek recognition. Willis, who hadn't much of an idea what McCamant intended to do, presumably thought he would second Lenroot. McCamant took the opportunity, if not to become kingmaker, at least to create the convention's prince.

Although just an obscure Oregon judge, McCamant had already gained a degree of notoriety at the convention. On June 8, when the convention opened for business, the *New York Times* ran a front-page story about him under the headline, "One Oregon Delegate Refused to Support Johnson; Convention Row Likely Over State Instructions." Hiram Johnson had won the Oregon primary, which was binding on the delegates. Delegate McCamant supported Wood, and said he would vote for the general. He claimed that he had declared for Wood prior to the primary, and was still elected by the voters. The *Times*'s reporter called this "an unprecedented problem for the convention"—a problem further compounded when four delegates from Nebraska declared that they, too, would vote for Wood, despite Johnson's victory in their state. So McCamant's "Declaration of Independence" had struck fire. McCamant had his way, voting for Wood on all ten ballots, and the convention records show that as few as three and as many as five Nebraskans also voted for Wood in the balloting.

Now McCamant wanted more. He had received a copy of *Have Faith in Massachusetts*, which he read before leaving for Chicago. "I was impressed with Governor Coolidge's sterling Americanism, his fine spirit during the World War, the soundness of his thinking, and the conservative trend of his thoughts," he later told Claude Fuess. He and the others of his delegation resented having Harding rammed down their throats, and now the bosses handed out notices saying Lenroot was the choice for vice president. The delegates were tired of taking orders. McCamant described the Oregonians' reaction:

> No one of the delegates was pleased by the Lenroot suggestion. The suggestion that Coolidge's name be put before the convention was made by Honorable Charles H. Carey of Portland. He also suggested that I speak for the delegation in so doing. I asked the others whether the suggestion met with their approval. They nodded yes.

According to one version, McCamant told the convention:

> When the Oregon delegation came here instructed by the people of our state to present to this convention as its candidate for the office of vice president a distinguished son of Massachusetts [meaning Lodge] he requested that we refrain from mentioning his name. But there is another son of Massachusetts who had been very much in the public eye during the past year, a man who is sterling in his Americanism and stands for all that the Republican Party holds dear; and on behalf of the Oregon delegation I name for the exalted office of vice president Governor Calvin Coolidge of Massachusetts.

The nomination energized the convention, and in the confusion few noted that McCamant had said that his first choice had been Lodge. Had Lodge agreed to accept, and had the convention turned to him, he would have been president in 1923. On the other hand, the convention may not have accepted him over Lenroot. What they seemed to want was an outsider—like Coolidge. The applause for him was real, not manufactured and orchestrated. Several reporters wrote that the applause was louder than the cheers that had come with the Harding nomination. The delegates were aware of the deals, the campaign spending, the acrimony that threatened victory in the fall. To them Coolidge was an honest, decent, intelligent, sound-thinking, and even energetic governor who had no connections with the smoke-filled rooms and fat cat bankrolls.

McCamant's words set off a wave of seconding speeches, each from a state that was supposed to be controlled by a boss. H.L. Remmel of Arkansas, who shortly before had seconded Lenroot, rose to switch to Coolidge. A Kansas delegate nominated Governor Henry Allen, and more speeches for Coolidge followed. Then Henry Anderson of Virginia was nominated, but the clamor for Coolidge continued. The roll call came soon after, with Coolidge, 674½ to Lenroot's 146½. A motion to make the nomination unanimous was made and passed. And with this, the convention closed, at 7:30 PM.

Had there ever been anything quite like this? The *Boston Globe* had it right when it concluded, "Calvin Coolidge was the first vice president in a hundred years who was not wished on the country; the country wished him on the Republican Party." Former New York Senator Chauncey Depew, the dean of the convention at the age of eighty-six, had another view; telegraphing his congratulations to Coolidge, he said, "I have been present at every Republican convention beginning with 1856, and I have never seen such a spontaneous and enthusiastic tribute to a man as the vote for you for vice president." Other wires followed, including one from Wilson's Vice President Thomas Marshall, who wrote, "Please accept my sincere sympathy." Coolidge was now a national figure.

Writing of the experience after his retirement, Coolidge mused that he might have won the presidential nomination had the Massachusetts delegation been solidly on his side; that is, he placed the blame for his poor showing on Lodge. Perhaps this was the case, but probably not. Mark Sullivan concluded, "[I]f the Coolidge candidacy for the presidential nomination had been pressed with half the astuteness that had been behind Harding's, Coolidge would have been the nominee."

But as we have seen, there was never much chance Coolidge would run a campaign like that. Coolidge did not pursue any political office the way most men did at the time. He preferred to wait until it came to him, or when it seemed improbable that his bid would be rejected. So it worked out well for all concerned, especially for Coolidge. He later wrote:

> While I do not think it was so intended [that I be nominated for the presidency] I have always been of the opinion that this turned out to be much the best for me. I had no national experience. What I have ever been able to do has been the result of first learning how to do it. I am not gifted with intuition. I need not only hard work but experience to be ready to solve problems. The presidents who have gone to Washington without first having held some national office have been at great disadvantage. It takes them a long time to become acquainted with the federal officeholders and the federal government. Meanwhile they have difficulty in dealing with the situation.

Of course, we do not know how he felt at the time about not receiving the presidential nomination. He had followed the convention through the newspapers and telegrams and telephone calls, but not the radio, because at the time "wireless telephony" was in its infancy, and broadcasting still a dream. Calvin and Grace Coolidge were in their two-room suite at the Adams House when the news of McCamant's speech reached them. Telephone calls came in from Boston newspapers, which received information about the convention by telegraph. Grace knew something important had happened. Before the nomination, Coolidge spoke with Stearns via long distance lines, a connection that took a while to arrange. After one of the local calls, which lasted a bit longer than the others, Coolidge hung up and then turned to his wife.

"Nominated," he said.

"You aren't going to take it, are you?"

"Well—I suppose I'll have to."

There were more calls and some visits from well-wishers. Then the candidate wrote a statement which he gave to the reporters:

> The nomination for the vice presidency, coming to me unsought and unexpectedly, I accept as an honor and duty. It will be especially pleasing to be associated with my old friend, Senator Warren G. Harding, our candidate for president. The Republican Party has adopted a sound platform, chosen a wise leader, and is united. It deserves the confidence of the American people. That confidence I shall endeavor to secure.

H.L. Mencken later told a story that has become part of Coolidge lore:

> In one of the passages I encountered a colleague from one of the Boston papers, surrounded by a group of politicians, policemen, and reporters. He was making a kind of speech, and I paused idly to listen. To my astonishment I found that he was offering to bet all comers that Harding, if elected, would be assassinated before he had served half his term. Some one in the crowd remonstrated gently, saying that any talk of assassination was unwise and might be misunderstood, for the Armistice was less than two years old and the Mitchell Palmer Red Hunt was still in full blast. But the Bostonian refused to shut down.
>
> "I don't give a damn," he bawled, "what you say. I am simply telling you what I know. I know Cal Coolidge inside and out. He is the luckiest _____ _____ in the whole world!"

Many versions of the story exist. One holds that Stearns told this to Daugherty, after which he supposedly added, "Everything comes along to him [Coolidge] in a most uncanny and mysterious way."

Considering all the possibilities, all the dead ends, blunders, and flux during the duel for the nomination, the thought seemed justified. In the exuberance of the moment, those involved might have paused to consider that the only constituency Coolidge had was the convention delegates, and that they would soon disperse, leaving control of the party to the national committee, the bosses, and the Senate oligarchy, none of whom had any loyalty to Coolidge.

Theodore Roosevelt had faced something akin to this in 1900, but at least he was nominated for the vice presidency with the grudging acquiescence of Mark Hanna and the other party bosses. Coolidge didn't even have that. Had McKinley lived to complete his term, TR probably could not have been nominated on his own in 1904. In 1920 Coolidge didn't seem to have too much of a chance to remain on the ballot in 1924.

Of course each man had to win the confidence of the party and congressional powers after they assumed office. Roosevelt had managed to carry it off. Coolidge lacked Roosevelt's charisma and dynamism, but he failed for a much more fundamental reason. Coolidge was a man who had climbed the political ladder with the help of the Massachusetts machine. He had always been a machine politician, and in the age of political machines, a politician did not rise very far without the support of party bosses. Coolidge had achieved his position in Massachusetts with the aid of sponsors. Always pragmatic and deliberate, he had risen slowly, taking one step after the other up the ladder, expanding his constituency as he went. Now he would make the sudden leap to the national scene—without the help of a leader like Crane and the patronage of Crane's peers.

Therein lay the source of problems that would plague him in the coming years.

8

····················

Vice President

During these two years I spoke some and lectured some. This took me about the country in travels that reached from Maine to California, from the Twin Cities to Charleston. I was getting acquainted. Aside from speeches I did a little writing, but I read a great deal and listened much. While I little realized it at the time it was for me a period of most important preparation. It enabled me to be ready in August, 1923.

The Autobiography of Calvin Coolidge

THE NOMINATION THRUST COOLIDGE into a position just off center stage, often the place vice presidential nominees find themselves. He endured the usual rounds of honorary degrees and dinners, and continued to perform his duties as governor. At the end of the month Coolidge took the train to Washington to meet Harding, who said he would conduct a front porch campaign to reinforce the impression he was a reincarnation of sorts of William McKinley. They held a joint press conference, in which Harding told the reporters, "I have been telling Governor Coolidge how much I wish him to be not only a participant in the campaign, but how much I wish him to be a helpful part of the Republican administration." This was unusual talk about the normally dead-end vice presidency, and the press took note of it. On the whole, the image Coolidge fashioned during the campaign, and which the press generally adopted, was favorable. But little was written about him in the months that followed the convention.

Instead, interest was understandably focused on the head of the ticket. The general public greeted the Harding nomination with enthusiasm, but not so a significant segment of the press and intellectuals in general. Their impression of Harding was of warmth, friendliness, decency—and monotony, blandness, and ineptitude. In some ways, the opposition to Harding in 1920 was similar to what Eisenhower experienced in 1952; those unfriendly to "Ike" saw him as an amiable simpleton.

Most historians whose expertise is not in 1920s America now consider Harding a boob, an utter failure as president, who won the nomination only because he was willing to follow the bosses' orders, and who then presided over one of the most corrupt administrations in history. But Harding was in fact quite typical of the men who served in the Senate in this period. Legislators were expected to take care of constituent interests and work in harmony with state officials, and Harding was good at this. He was also respected and liked by his peers. He was not a cipher; in 1916 he had even been viewed as a dark horse possibility for the presidential nomination, and in 1919 Theodore Roosevelt told Daugherty that he was considering Harding as his running mate. The retrospective view of Harding's critics overlooks these details.

There is one other factor to consider before discussing what Harding did and didn't do while in office. Few presidents in all of American history had as many acolytes among intellectuals as did his predecessor, Woodrow Wilson, whose call for a democratic crusade endeared him to the opinion makers of his time, and who passed the thought down to the next generation through their classes and writings. Arthur M. Schlesinger, Jr., was an ardent admirer of Wilson, whom he saw as the president who played John the Baptist for Franklin D. Roosevelt. Schlesinger was one of those who helped fashion the legend. In *The Age of Roosevelt*, in which Schlesinger presented this thesis, he discusses the coming of the Republicans as though they were barbarians sacking Rome. In one of his more transparent passages, Schlesinger wrote touchingly of the last day in the life of Franklin K. Lane:

> The people had made their choice, but not all the
> people. From the start of the decade, there had been

another view of the New Era. In May, 1921, Franklin K.
Lane, Woodrow Wilson's Secretary of the Interior, the
close friend of Franklin D. Roosevelt, lay in his room at
the Mayo Clinic, wondering about death. "If I had
passed into that other land, whom would I have
sought—and what should I have done?" A parade of
images passed through his mind. "For my heart's
content in that new land, I think I'd rather loaf with
Lincoln along a river bank." His thoughts drifted to
the life he was leaving. "Yes, we would sit down where
the bank sloped gently to the quiet stream and glance at
the picture of our people, the negroes being lynched, the
miner's civil war, labor's hold ups, employers'
ruthlessness, the subordination of humanity to
industry—"

His scrawl broke off. The next day they found him
dead. The old Wilsonians watched the New Era in
indignation and contempt. They were men who had
known the exaltation of idealism. They had dared to act
greatly and risk greatly. They saw after 1920 a different
America moved, as they conceived it, by ignoble motives.

In his notes Schlesinger indicates his source: Ann Lane and Louis
Wall, *The Letters of Franklin K. Lane, Personal and Political*
(Boston: Houghton Mifflin, 1922).

While Schlesinger does not offer much else on Lane, it should be
said that the former secretary was an intelligent and honest public
servant, who left office with a record of accomplishment, scrupulously honest, without sufficient funds to purchase train tickets for
himself and his family to return home. After these passages, the presentation of a boorish Harding would contrast nicely with the eloquent, sophisticated Wilson. The problem is that Schlesinger
egregiously misinterpreted the meaning of Lane's words, as described
in Thomas Silver's *Coolidge and the Historians*.

For starters, whatever Lane's thoughts were on his deathbed, the
idea of the world being altered so drastically during the first two
months of the Harding administration hardly seems plausible, which
may be why Schlesinger dated the changes to 1920, in that phrase

"[t]hey saw after 1920…." That was the year Harding was elected, but he did not take office until March 4, 1921. Schlesinger would like the casual reader to conclude Lane was looking back at more than a year of Harding policy. Given this, it would appear that in actuality those evil things Lane wrote of referred to developments during the Wilson administration, not Harding's—the opposite of the impression Schlesinger attempts to create in his next paragraph. Schlesinger segues without a paragraph break from Lane's death to those old Wilsonians watching the Republicans with contempt. To the reader it certainly would appear that in this context he considered Lane one of those old Wilsonians who held this view. You might want to reread the Lane quotation and the Schlesinger comment to appreciate the effect Schlesinger wanted to have on the reader.

This raises the question of what exactly Lane thought of those first two months of the Harding era. Fortunately he set down his thoughts in a letter to Robert Lansing on May 2, 1921, a little more than two weeks before his death:

> Really, I think Harding is doing well, or rather that the
> whole administration is being supported well by the
> country. Oh, those Republicans have the art of governing,
> and we do so much better at talking! No one knows just
> what his foreign policy is, but something will work
> through that will satisfy a very tired people. There seem
> to be comparatively few out of work now. We are not out
> of the woods yet. But the Lord will take care of them. He
> may even keep [Senator Hiram] Johnson from bolting
> Harding. They will temporize through; that's my guess.

This is not to say that Lane approved of Harding or applauded his election, but these words are not those of a man despairing for the nation because the Republicans had come to power. What is more, Schlesinger had to know this when he wrote those two paragraphs. It is not from an obscure source, but rather a few pages earlier in the book from which Schlesinger had obtained his quotation.

In Schlesinger's view, which is quite typical of critics of the Republican 1920s, the period was a dismal valley between the reformist Wilsonian New Freedom and the Rooseveltian New Deal. To him and other New Deal historians, the history of the interwar period is a saga, almost an epic, in which there are heroes and villains. Woodrow Wilson appears on the scene and clearly is a hero, but then he is followed by the foolish and short-sighted trio of Harding–Coolidge–Hoover, and they in turn are succeeded by a reincarnation of Wilson in the form of Franklin D. Roosevelt. This is wholly consistent with Schlesinger's cyclical interpretation of history, as set forth in his *The Cycles of American History* (1986), in which he wrote: "One notes finally that the thirty-year cycle accounts both for the eras of public purpose—TR in 1901, FDR in 1933, JFK in 1961—and for the high tides of conservative restoration—the 1920s, the 1950s, the 1980s." As he wrote, Schlesinger believed the nation was due for another switch to reformism.

This is drama, not history. To believe the future is preordained is to assume that we can't control our destinies, that accident and humanity will play no role in history. More often than not we stumble through the present, try to make sense of the past, and wonder what the future will bring. When the future becomes the past, we then try to interpret it, usually through our own prisms, which are informed by ideology and, for some, a belief that patterns truly do exist. We are aware of our shortcomings, and try to overcome them, not to give in to the temptation to demonize and deify. Historians should know better. As Horace Walpole put it, "To be a good historian, it is necessary to be without religion, without country, without profession, and without party."

Schlesinger is not alone in presenting his tract as history and distorting the record, painting the 1920s as a terrible period in the national history. In Allan Nevins and Henry Steele Commager's *A Pocket History of the United States* (1976), which went through many editions, we find this:

> The idealism of the Wilson era was in the past; the
> Rooseveltian passion for humanitarianism was in the
> future. The decade of the twenties was dull, bourgeois,
> and ruthless. "The business of America is business," said
> President Coolidge succinctly, and the observation was apt

if not profound. Wearied by idealism and disillusioned about the war and its aftermath, Americans dedicated themselves with unabashed enthusiasm to making and spending money. Never before, not even in the McKinley era, had American society been so materialistic, never before so completely dominated by the ideal of the marketplace or the techniques of machinery.

Nevins, arguably the most celebrated American historian of the pre-Schlesinger generation, had a fixation on this matter. In his history of the Ford Motor Company, Nevins wrote about the coming of the 1920s. "The nation, as Wilson's towering vision crashed into the dust and Harding, Coolidge, and Mellon opened an era of selfish materialism, grew cynical." Ignore that nations cannot grow cynical—or idealistic—but that people do. Surely those old Wilsonians remained pure in Nevins's view. More to the point, what does this have to do with the life of an industrialist or the history of an automobile company? This is difficult to fathom unless one realizes that while a newspaperman, Nevins was an ardent Wilsonian who suspended his customary historical objectivity when it came to the Republican presidents of the 1920s, and then did the same when Franklin D. Roosevelt was president later on.

Return to one other phrase Nevins used to describe the 1920s. For him, "[t]he decade of the twenties was dull, bourgeois, and ruthless." How did it appear to average Americans, who lived through the decade that saw a better standard of living for average people than had previously been known? This isn't to suggest that Harding and Coolidge were responsible for the era's high standard of living, but rather that to intellectuals, this was a horrid period indeed. In his fair but clearly critical history of the decade, *The Perils of Prosperity 1914–1932* (1958), William Leuchtenberg wrote, in his bibliographic essay, of "the bleak intellectual mood of the period." Was the intellectual mood bleak? How does one judge such matters? It might be argued that some intellectuals, who recalled the Progressive reform era, were dismayed by a population that had elected Harding, Coolidge, and Hoover. How about the ordinary citizens? There is a portrait in Robert and Helen Lynd's *Middletown*, a study of Muncie, Indiana, published in 1929, that merits attention. Read this selection from a rather ordinary housewife, and try to imagine what her life had been before that decade—or the lives of her mother and grandmother:

> I began to work during the war, when everyone else did; we had to meet payments on our house and everything else was getting so high. The mister objected at first, but now he don't mind. I'd rather keep on working so my boys can play foot ball and basketball and have spending money their father can't give them. We've built our own home, a nice brown and white bungalow, by a building and loan like everyone else does. We have it almost paid off and it's worth about $6,000. No, I don't lose out with my neighbors because I work; some of them have jobs and those of them who don't envy us who do. I have felt better since I work than ever before in my life. I get up at five-thirty. My husband takes his dinner and the boys buy theirs uptown and I cook supper. We have an electric washing machine, electric iron, and vacuum sweeper. I don't even have to ask my husband any more because I buy these things with my own money. I bought an icebox last year—a big one that holds 125 pounds; most of the time I don't fill it, but we have our folks visit us from back East and then I do. We own a $1,200 Studebaker with a nice California top, semi-enclosed. Last summer we spent our vacation going back to Pennsylvania—taking in Niagara Falls on the way. The two boys want to go to college, and I want them to. I graduated from high school myself, but feel if I can't give my boys a little more all my work would have been useless.

One can easily imagine this woman voted for Harding in 1920. Was the intellectual mood "bleak"? Hers certainly was not. Were there more like her than like Nevins? The 1920 presidential vote would appear to indicate she was in the majority.

This is not to suggest that Harding lacked his critics in the 1920 election. In the weeks after the Republican convention, the opposition press lit into him. One editorial writer said he was the worst nominee since James Buchanan in 1856, and another dated it back to Franklin Pierce in 1852. The *Buffalo Times*, a generally Democratic newspaper, offered, "The decision at Chicago is not of the kind that can inspire enthusiasm." The *Ohio State Journal* declared, "Senator Harding's nomination is another great triumph for the Old Guard, which, its leader lying desperately sick a thousand miles away, with popular sentiment recorded against it in state primary after state primary, still proved itself all powerful in the supreme crisis." Throughout the country, even Republican newspapers called Harding the selection of the inner circle, bemoaned bossism, and in general were not particularly positive about the nomination. Puzzling it out the following week, Walter Lippmann thought that Harding considered the presidency too big a job for a single man, and that the senatorial leaders knew this.

> There is something in it. If you can't think of any way to redistribute the functions of government, then all you have to do is to find a president who will be so weak that power will leave him. That is the inner meaning of Mr. Harding's nomination. He was put there by the senators for the sole purpose of abdicating in their favor. The grand dukes have chosen their weakest tsar in order to increase the power of the grand dukes. And if he is elected the period will be known in our constitutional history as the Regency of the Senate.

Harding's Republican senatorial colleagues spoke of his sagacity and shrewdness, but before the nomination reporters had heard them talk of other qualities—his laziness, slowness to grasp ideas, and lack of imagination. Some of the senators kept it up even after the nomination. "Keep Warren at home," Penrose supposedly told King when planning the campaign. "He might be asked questions if he went out on a speaking tour and Warren's the kind of damned fool who'd try to answer them."

Progressive Republicans were dismayed at the thought of a Harding presidency. A group of them, known as the "Committee of 48," attended the convention of the new Farmer–Labor Party in Chicago on July 12 in an attempt to revive the spirit of the Progressive Party. Diehard Bull Moosers sat next to members of the Nonpartisan League, Socialists, Single Taxers, and radical labor leaders, trying to come to some kind of agreement. These true believers could not bear to compromise their beliefs, and so the small convention broke up without a nomination. The Committee of 48 withdrew, and then tried to induce La Follette to run. He refused, and they adjourned. There would be no significant third party in 1920. The Socialists nominated Eugene V. Debs, their long-time leader, who then was in a federal prison having been convicted under the wartime Sedition Acts. The Farmer–Labor Party selected Parley Christensen of Utah for their standard bearer. Lucy Gaston, the anti-cigarette crusader, called a press conference, and told the reporters that she would not run as an independent. Gaston added that Harding clearly was a habitual user of cigarettes, and would come to no good. She predicted that his administration would be laced with corruption, and that Harding would not live out his term.

A month after the Republicans left Chicago, the Democrats convened in San Francisco and hammered out a platform that disagreed with the GOP's on the matter of the League of Nations, but otherwise, like the GOP document, came out in favor of virtue, the flag, and motherhood. Bound by a rule requiring a two-thirds vote for the nominee, the Democrats went to forty ballots before the delegates selected a compromise candidate, Governor James Cox of Ohio. For the vice presidency, the Democrats named former Assistant Secretary of the Navy Franklin D. Roosevelt of New York. Roosevelt was a bright, articulate, handsome young man, but his major attribute was that magic name—the dead hero to so many of both parties. As at the GOP convention, the leading Democrats maligned one another, while the spirit of Woodrow Wilson hovered over the meetings. By 1920 many Americans thought entering the war had been a mistake, doubted the merits of the League, were bored by red-hunting, and were quite simply tired of crusades in general. In addition, they had been crushed by the postwar inflation and the depression that followed. The 1920 election came in bad economic times, never a good omen for the party in power.

Looking the candidates over, the same newspapers and reporters who opposed Harding decided that Cox was little better. The nation had to choose between two Ohio politicians, both of whom had been newspapermen. Some turned to the vice presidential nominees. More than a few decided to call the 1920 contest "the kangaroo election," indicating that the hind legs were stronger than the front ones. In this, at least, they turned out to be prescient.

After his meeting with Harding in Washington, Coolidge returned to Massachusetts, where he began preparing his acceptance address. No nominee of either party would accept the nomination at the convention until Roosevelt broke that tradition in 1932, so in 1920, a delegation from the convention went to see Coolidge and informed him officially of the designation. On this "Notification Day," July 27, Coolidge delivered an address in which he struck familiar themes:

> In a free republic a great government is the product of a great people. They will look to themselves rather than government for success. The destiny, the greatness of America lies around the hearthstone. If thrift and industry are taught there, and the example of self-sacrifice oft appears, if honor abide there, and high ideals, if there the building of fortune be subordinate to the building of character, America will live in security, rejoicing in an abundant prosperity and good government at home and in peace, respect, and confidence abroad. If these virtues be absent there is no power that can supply these blessings. Look well then to the hearthstone, therein all hope for America lies.

So, in his first public utterance after accepting the nomination, Coolidge said character was more important to the nation than fortune. He expressed the thought often in Massachusetts and repeated it in Washington. Otherwise it was not a memorable address, with the usual appeals to patriotism, the need for stability, and praise for the nation, the party, and the candidate. There was something for everyone; Coolidge was, as usual, circumspect. Toward the end he got to the key element: the League. He selected his words carefully. The proposed League—which is to say, Wilson's League—he called "subversive of the traditions and independence of America." But the Republican Party, he added, "approves the principle of agreement among nations to preserve peace, and pledges itself to the making of such an agreement, preserving American independence, and rights, as will meet every duty America owes to humanity."

Coolidge held close to what Harding had been saying, indicating support for the Lodge position. Both Crane and Lodge were in the audience; although Crane certainly opposed the position, he also knew his protégé had no choice but to take this stance. (Even so, he called Stearns to his side to complain about Lodge's presence: "He has no business here—he is not wanted.")

Crane did not live to see the Republican ticket win; he died on October 2. "He was a great man," Coolidge wrote to his father. He did not, as might be expected, indicate why he considered Crane great. Instead, he added, "I shall always remember he voted for me until the last."

Coolidge correctly assessed the situation in Massachusetts after Crane's departure. William Butler was the clear choice to take the departed boss's place, which he did. Butler and Coolidge had always been close, and would remain so. But Butler was a local politician without influence on the national scene. The shy, withdrawn Coolidge had always needed that kind of help. Now he was vice president, and the closest he had to such a person was Frank Stearns, who had no leverage with the party leaders or the Senate Republicans. Nor could he expect any help from Lodge, with whom he was estranged. Coolidge would have to make do on his own this time. In discussing Lodge off the record with a friend, Robert Brady, a *Boston Globe* reporter, Coolidge remarked,

> Now you ask about Lodge's friends. I don't think Lodge has many friends. He has a host of admirers. But there is a big difference between admirers and friends. Crane had friends and those friends will stick to Crane dead in

> state politics. Lodge's admirers will stick to him until he
> gets his first setback. When that comes you won't see
> many people sitting on the mourner's bench.

Coolidge attended the Crane funeral, as did Lodge. Photographers wanted a picture of the two of them together, and Lodge was willing. "I came here to bury my friend," Coolidge snapped. "It is no time for photographs." Lodge must have known at that moment that Coolidge would neither forgive nor forget.

As the general campaign began, Harding followed the planned front porch approach, but vigorous efforts mounted by Cox and Roosevelt forced him to take to the road, which was originally to be Coolidge's role. As it turned out, Coolidge spent less time on the stump than the other national candidates. In August he spoke before groups in Massachusetts, and in September he did so in Maine and New Hampshire as well. On September 18 the Massachusetts Republican Convention nominated Channing Cox for governor and Alvan Fuller for lieutenant governor. Coolidge, there to speak for them, said that the national Democrats offered "a mirage of false hopes and false security." In early October he left New England for the first time in the campaign to deliver a speech in Philadelphia.

The party decided to send Coolidge on a tour of Kentucky, Tennessee, Virginia, West Virginia, and the Carolinas, since the Republicans thought his style might play well in southern rural areas. Nonetheless, it wasn't a particularly hopeful expedition. Kentucky had voted Democratic in every presidential election since the Civil War, and the last time Tennessee, Virginia, and South Carolina voted Republican was during Reconstruction. The Republicans won occasionally in West Virginia, however.

By then the party realized that Coolidge was no dynamo when it came to speech-making. His Vermont twang wasn't the real problem; it was there, but it was not disconcerting or unpleasant. Rather, Coolidge was stiff and awkward, and not given to the niceties of delivery. To compensate for this, the party surrounded him with several able orators, including Lowden and Kentucky Governor Edwin Morrow.

Coolidge was hesitant to make the tour, writing to his father on October 12, "I did not want to go on a trip. I do not think it will do any good. I am sure I shall not enjoy it. A candidate should never be sent on a trip of that kind." To the Republican National Committee he wrote that he was still governor of Massachusetts, and should not be asked to desert his position for weeks on end. More important, "my abilities do not lie in that direction." As they set out, a reporter asked Coolidge if he was looking forward to the campaign. "I don't like it," was the reply. "I don't like to speak. It's all nonsense. I'd much better be at home doing my work."

The provincial Coolidge was timid about going to strange places. But he went, and appeared to be effective, even though he didn't change many minds in strong Democratic enclaves. Still, the New England Yankee was able to relate to the southern farmers, and they to him. As he traveled from place to place, delivering his set pieces, he grew increasingly restive. His speeches dealt with such matters as the need for thrift and industry, the importance of cutting taxes and reining in government. There were touches of what a later generation would call "red-baiting," along with suggestions that the Republicans would return the country to true Americanism. This reflected what Harding and other Republicans were saying but was out of character for Coolidge. Certainly Coolidge was a novice in national politics and perhaps he believed he needed to take a different approach from what he had used in Massachusetts, or perhaps at the time he believed in this idea of true Americanism.

Coolidge also talked about the League, not altering his views from Notification Day, but he did reach out to voters who supported the world organization by saying that there was more chance of America entering the body under a Republican administration than with the Democrats. Of course, he was talking about the League with reservations, which had come to be Republican dogma. In all, Coolidge did not say anything rash or unexpected during his tour. But then, that was his role. After the southern swing around the circuit he went to New York for a rally, which included leading a large parade up Fifth Avenue, and then back to Massachusetts.

On October 29 he wrote to his father: "I have been away and too busy to write. We are all well. I feel sure we shall carry the election by a good margin. It would have been a little bigger three weeks ago but it will be enough." On November 1 Coolidge again wrote to John Coolidge: "The campaign is over. Some mistakes were made, always are I suppose, but the ones this year were so foolish I do not see how they could have been made by men really trying to elect the ticket." He must have known nothing could prevent a Harding landslide. A few days before the election New York bookmakers were offering odds of ten to one on Harding–Coolidge, higher than any recorded in American history.

On November 3 Coolidge wrote asking whether his father had received a message he had sent the previous night regarding the election. Since John Coolidge's home lacked both a telephone and electricity, it would have been sent to the general store and from there relayed to him. The early returns on November 2 indicated a major Republican victory. Coolidge asked his father whether he knew how the voting had gone in Plymouth. He learned that his birthplace had given the Republican ticket 158 votes against 15 for the Democrats, not surprising, although four years earlier Hughes had only a two-vote margin over Wilson. For the nation as a whole, Harding–Coolidge received 16.1 million votes, and Cox–Roosevelt, 9.1 million. Harding's margin of victory in the popular vote was the largest since reliable records were kept. He received 404 electoral votes to Cox's 127. Debs received close to a million votes, many doubtless protest votes, since few Americans preferred the Socialists' proposition of world government to the League of Nations.

Harding won every borough in New York City, a bastion of the Democratic Party, and he also carried Coolidge's Boston, as well as every electoral district bordering the Pacific. Some saw this as a repudiation of Wilson and global idealism, and in part it was. But the country was traditionally Republican. Wilson's victories had been due to the Republican–Progressive split, not to a political change. Still, critics said repeatedly that with Harding the country was returning to the days of McKinley, the bucolic small-town and farm America so different from the urban country that was emerging even during the late nineteenth century. Many who voted for him would have agreed—that was what they wanted. Harding's appeal to a "return to normalcy" did not fall on deaf ears.

Voter participation in 1916 had been 61.6 percent of eligible voters; in 1920 the figure was 49.2 percent, the lowest since 1824. The Nineteenth Amendment had added 9.5 million voters to the roles, but not many women bothered to exercise their new right. In 1920, 26.7 million Americans voted, compared to 18.4 million in 1916, but women did not account for all of this differential, as the return of veterans also accounted for part of the difference.

As for the southern and border states Coolidge had visited, Tennessee went Republican by a margin of two thousand votes, for the first time since 1868 (it would not do so again until Eisenhower ran in 1952), but the Democrats took Kentucky, North Carolina, and Virginia. West Virginia was strong for Harding, but South Carolina was overwhelmingly Democratic.

The Republicans did well in the congressional races, too. Their margin in the old Senate had been two; now it rose to twenty. There had been 233 Republicans in the old House of Representatives; the new one would have 289, while the Democrats fell from 191 to 142. On the Massachusetts scene, Channing Cox had no trouble defeating his Democratic rival, John Jackson Walsh, by a better than two to one margin.

Coolidge delivered the obligatory victory statement, and as with his campaign speeches, he suggested the GOP—and not the Democratic Party—was the party of patriots. The Harding–Coolidge victory, he said, "means the end of a period which has seemed to substitute words for things, and the beginning of a period of real patriotism and true national honor." This theme would reappear in other Coolidge statements, some of which were quite surprising. In his *Autobiography* he would look back at the 1921 inaugural and write:

> When the inauguration was over I realized that the same thing for which I had worked in Massachusetts had been accomplished in the nation. The radicalism which had tinged our whole political and economic life from soon after 1900 to the World War period was passed. There were still echoes of it, and some of its votaries remained, but its power was gone. The country had little interest in

> mere destructive criticism. It wanted the progress that
> alone comes from constructive policies.

His referring to "constructive policies" surely overlooks the scandals that came to haunt the Harding administration. Also, by taking 1900 as the starting point for the despised "radicalism," he must have been referring to the very progressivism whose principles and some of whose policies and programs he once espoused.

The nation was undergoing a change from progressivism and internationalism to conservatism and isolationism. Coolidge's own horizon had changed sharply with the events and experiences of 1920. He would not go to extremes—this was contrary to the core of his being. But he was drifting to the political, social, and economic right in many ways. The changes perceivable in 1920 would continue into the decade.

During the interregnum in late 1920 there followed another round of honors, dinners, and meetings, and Coolidge dutifully attended all he could. He did avoid one: a dinner organized by the Roosevelt Club to honor Lodge. But the two men appeared together at a celebration of the three hundredth anniversary of the Pilgrims' landing at Plymouth Rock.

Down to the very end Coolidge maintained his full schedule as governor. It was evident from his letters to his father that he was relieved to be leaving the office and eager to take on the vice presidential duties. "This is my last Sunday as governor," he wrote on January 2. "It will be a great relief to get out of the office."

Coolidge spent a good deal of time that last week packing and appointing several aides to posts in the state government. In one of his speeches in this period he said, "I regret I am leaving Massachusetts and will have to give up my friends and acquaintances here. I hope I shall make new friends. I think I shall. But no friends are like old friends, and old acquaintances, and no place like home."

Coolidge was in Boston for Channing Cox's installation as governor, and then returned to Northampton for more packing and boning up on the duties of the vice president. After he had been governor for a week, Cox came across an envelope addressed to him. He opened the envelope and discovered it was a message from Coolidge.

My dear Governor Cox—

I want to leave you my best wishes, my assurance of support, and my confidence in your success.

Cordially yours,
Calvin Coolidge

Coolidge traveled to Atlanta to deliver a speech, and then the Coolidges went to Asheville, North Carolina, for a two-week vacation. They next returned to Northampton for more packing. On one of the last days before taking the train to Washington, Coolidge strolled up and down Main Street in Northampton, visiting one last time with some of his old friends. He would appear in the doorway, and say, "Well, I've come to say good-bye." Then, after some pleasantries, he would go on to the next stop.

The Coolidges now had to decide where to live. There was no official residence for the vice president. They soon learned—as had other vice presidential families before them—that they couldn't afford, on the vice presidential salary of $12,000, to rent a house, much less buy one. Frank Stearns offered to lease one for them, but Coolidge refused. Outgoing Vice President Marshall had an $8-a-day two-bedroom apartment at the New Willard Hotel, and offered to give it up to the Coolidges, and they accepted. They would remain there throughout the vice presidential years.

The inauguration took place on March 4. Coolidge took his oath in the Senate chamber and delivered his address there. The Coolidge speech lasted ten minutes, something of a record for brevity. After a short preamble he noted that the vice president's major task was to preside over the Senate, and he devoted the rest of his speech to praising that body. "Whatever its faults, whatever its human imperfections, there is no legislative body in all history that has used its powers with more wisdom and discretion, more uniformly for the execution of the public will, or more in harmony with the spirit of the authority of the people which has created it, than the United

States Senate." He then went to the White House to witness Harding being sworn in on the White House East Portico.

Coolidge tried to do what he said he would: make new friends, especially in the Senate. He did not succeed, largely because he had not been the senators' candidate, and was so unlike the vice presidents they had known. With one exception his twentieth century predecessors had been or became men of the Capitol. Marshall had been governor of Indiana before becoming Wilson's running mate, but he was a gregarious, hearty man, whose quips delighted his colleagues, and was accepted by them almost immediately. Taft's vice president, James Sherman, had been a congressman for sixteen years. Charles Fairbanks, who served under Roosevelt, was a senator from Ohio when tapped for the nomination. Roosevelt himself was the one who did not fit in well with the senatorial oligarchy; TR was governor of New York when he became McKinley's running mate over the objections of Mark Hanna. Roosevelt was unlike Garret Hobart, McKinley's first vice president, who though not a senator had been a party wheelhorse for many years.

As vice president, in an office without power, Coolidge had many negatives to overcome, and he wasn't up to it temperamentally. In 1921 Harding was fifty-six years old and seemed in robust good health. At the end of his first term he would be just past the age of sixty. By then the party leaders would have tried to select his new running mate, probably another senator or even Lowden, and then Coolidge could be sent back to Massachusetts, a place the party's leaders felt he should never have left.

The vice presidency of the United States proved one of Coolidge's less demanding positions. Certainly he had more to occupy himself as president of the Massachusetts senate and as governor. As lieutenant governor Coolidge often filled in for Governor McCall when he made his frequent out-of-state trips. Even as Northampton mayor he had to take care of many details and organize an agenda. Harding did, however, make good on his pledge that Coolidge would sit in on cabinet meetings. This wasn't completely unprecedented. President Taft had Sherman at some cabinet meetings, and, while Roosevelt did not ask Fairbanks to his, he had recommended a larger role for vice presidents, including representing the White House in Congress.

Coolidge attended cabinet meetings, but he was there to listen and learn, not offer ideas and make suggestions and recommendations.

Coolidge learned a great deal from observing the Harding administration. Examining Harding's approach to the office and his programs is thus critical to understanding the Coolidge presidency.

Penrose had told Senator Moses that if Harding were nominated and elected, the party leaders would make certain he was surrounded by able and conscientious men who would lighten his tasks. Harding probably didn't know of the conversation, but he seemed to want a strong cabinet. Some of his selections were highly capable, even inspired. Secretary of State Charles Evans Hughes had been a governor, a Supreme Court justice, and a presidential candidate, and he was one of the nation's most respected men. Secretary of the Treasury Andrew Mellon had been a powerful banker and industrialist. Secretary of Commerce Herbert Hoover was not only a great humanitarian and organizer, but before the war a highly successful businessman who knew the world—and he became the most energetic and imaginative individual to fill that position. At the time the Old Guard was wary of Hoover, who seemed a maverick on many issues and an amateur politician, but Harding wanted him, and he joined the team.

Some of Harding's other selections, however, were among the worst in American history. On this other extreme were Daugherty, who became attorney general; Edwin Denby, secretary of the navy; and Albert Fall, secretary of the interior. All brought disgrace to the administration, but in 1921 they did not seem like such terrible picks. Daugherty was being hailed as a political genius, and such men often were rewarded with cabinet posts. Denby had served in the navy during the Spanish–American War, and while in Congress he was on the House Naval Affairs Committee. When the United States entered World War I he enlisted in the Marine Corps as a private and was a major when mustered out. Few of his predecessors knew the navy better than he. Fall was also a Spanish–American War veteran who had been a senator from New Mexico, and was considered an expert on Mexican affairs. Charles Evan Hughes had even recommended Fall for secretary of state—before being named to the position himself. In addition, Fall had supported American entry to the League, and his presence in the cabinet brought some balance on this contentious issue. At the time it was known that Fall had been a strong opponent of TR's conservation policies, but Harding liked him—as he did Daugherty and Denby.

The incongruities among Harding's advisors would be reflected in the activities and record of the administration. In some areas Harding enjoyed great success, although this is rarely recalled. His failures, on the other hand, are remembered vividly and are the basis for Harding's public reputation.

Much has been made of the contrast between Harding and Coolidge, and they were in many ways quite different. Harding was a large, outgoing, gregarious, inquisitive man, who made friends easily, but was not particularly respected for his intellect. He had those two extramarital affairs, fathered a daughter out of wedlock, and did not have a happy marriage. He was also a chronic joiner, a member not only of the Moose and Elks, but also of the Odd Fellows, Redmen, and Hoo-Hoos. Coolidge was his direct opposite. Those who saw them together remarked on how Harding would try to hold a conversation, only to have Coolidge remain silent or reply in monosyllables.

Their similarities on their views of government and the economy were far more important, however, which explains the continuity of their administrations. Both believed in the separation of powers, which meant the executive's main task was to carry out legislation passed by Congress. In time Harding would provide legislative leadership, but Coolidge rarely did so. Both men worked hard and long, though for different reasons. Coolidge probably did so out of a sense of obligation; he had been reared to value effort. Harding, for his part, was aware of his limitations and labored away to try to grasp concepts and understand problems required of a chief executive.

Harding was a believer in compromise. At the outset he seemed to think that if he could bring together "the best minds" and let them interact, the ensuing give-and-take discussion might offer solutions to problems. If not, he could enter the picture and prod them into some kind of resolution. He did not consider himself an economic or political philosopher, or even a leader, because he didn't think this was needed. Coolidge, however, had a different approach. As president of the Massachusetts senate and as governor he had pushed for legislation, made decisions readily, and was prepared to share his thoughts with other state political figures. In Massachusetts Coolidge had relished compromise far less than did Harding.

As though to underline his intentions to be an agent of change, Harding called a special session of Congress, which convened on April 12. With two Massachusetts men seated behind him—Coolidge and Speaker of the House Gillett—Harding addressed Congress and presented his political program along with his views on many matters. He had devoted a good deal of time and effort to this speech, conferring with the powers within the GOP, his cabinet, and experts. Harding knew what his reputation was, and with this speech he set out to change that image. In the process, he presented not only an agenda for Congress in 1921, but also the Republican program for the next eight years.

Harding called for the gradual liquidation of the war debt, slashes in government spending, and tax reduction. "The most substantial relief from the tax burden must come for the present from the readjustment of internal taxes, and the revision or repeal of those taxes which have become unproductive and are so artificial and burdensome as they defeat their own purpose." Next, Harding asked for an emergency tariff increase to protect American industries and agriculture and provide additional revenue. During the primaries Lowden had made much of the way the Illinois budget bureau brought efficiencies to the state, and it was a popular theme. Now Harding asked Congress to provide a "national budget system." In a rambling section, he tried to assure business that it had no reason to fear a return to the progressive antitrust crusade: "We mean to have less of government in business as well as more business in government." He went on to demand lower railway rates. Harding also wanted a large-scale highway construction program, but indicated that he expected the financial burden and construction to be undertaken by the states, though with "federal participation," which he did not spell out. He asked for a larger merchant marine and navy, encouraged the development of aviation, both military and civilian, and spoke of the need to develop radio. Harding wanted to limit immigration, expand hospitals, pass an antilynching law, and create a Department of Public Welfare.

Harding saved the thorny question of the League for the final section of his address. He rejected the present League, but, "we make no surrender of our hope for an association to preserve peace in which we would most heartily join." These carefully chosen words were well received. After he was finished, Borah and the Irreconcilables claimed Harding was on their team, Lodge and his Reservationists did the same, and supporters of the League, who had been told by Taft and other League defenders that the only way the United States would enter that body would be through a Harding victory, were content.

The Harding program contained elements that pleased and distressed both progressive and conservative Republicans. Conservatives were troubled by the call for lower railway rates and hints of regulatory legislation, while progressives didn't like the tax and tariff proposals. All could agree, however, that the program was ambitious, comprehensive, and a marked change from the Wilson approach and agenda. The reaction and discussion that followed must have convinced Harding that his early hopes of acting as a conciliator and mediator could not get his policies accepted. He would have to become a leader, a cajoler, an arm-twister.

In this, Harding knew he had the support and confidence of the congressional Republican leaders. He understood them. He was one of them. Harding could move easily among the Senate Republicans. Listen. Joke. Cajole. Compromise. Much has been made of the Harding card games, the loose and easy way he operated. If inelegant, they were effective places to do business. Harding was, to put it simply, one of the boys. The Senate would bend over backward to accommodate him.

Coolidge was fortunate that by the time he became president, the Harding agenda was in place, along with some of the people who had helped carry it out for him, and who would do the same for Coolidge. All he had to do was complete the unfinished business. If Coolidge could weed out the cabinet rascals and replace them with his own people, then, when he left office, he could point to accomplishments that were, in part at least, the Harding legacy. Of course,

A young
Calvin Coolidge.

The new president:
a portrait taken
just months after
Warren Harding's
death.

Coolidge receiving news of his election as governor of Massachusetts, November 1918. His wife, Grace, stands behind him.

Notification Day, 1920:

(above) A crowd gathers around the Republican vice presidential nominee's house on Massasoit Street.

(below) The nominee and his family greet the crowd. From left to right: son John, wife Grace, Coolidge, son Calvin, Jr.

President and Mrs. Coolidge at the July 1924 funeral of their son Calvin, Jr. Coolidge was never quite the same after his son's death.

President Coolidge on the South Lawn of the White House.

owboys...

...and Indians.

Coolidge worked on his father's Vermont farm throughout his life, even after he became president. Note the frock, the same one his grandfather had worn.

From left to right: Harvey Firestone, President Coolidge, Henry Ford, Thomas Edison, Mrs. Coolidge, Colonel John C. Coolidge (the president's father). Standing: Russell Firestone.

Coolidge shaking hands with Hall of Fame pitcher Walter Johnson at Washington's Griffith Stadium.

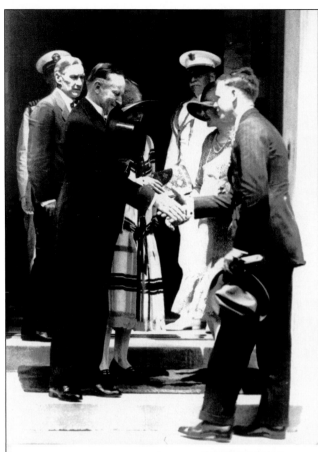

President Coolidge greets transatlantic aviator Charles Lindbergh. Lindbergh's daring 1927 flight came at what many call the high noon of the decade.

A new era was dawning in 1928: Coolidge's world was fading, while Herbert Hoover activism presaged the coming of the New Deal. From left to right: Mrs. Coolidge, President Coolidge, Republican presidential nominee Hoover, Mrs. Hoover, John Coolidge.

Coolidge did have ideas of his own, but the foundation of the Coolidge presidency had its roots in the Harding years. The sharp changes that occurred when Harry Truman succeeded Franklin D. Roosevelt and when Lyndon Johnson succeeded John F. Kennedy did not take place in the 1920s.

What might Coolidge have been thinking as he watched from his perch behind Harding? Unlike Harding, Coolidge had had the benefit of being a governor, whose responsibilities were closer to those of the president than were a senator's duties. Twice Coolidge had presented his agendas to the Massachusetts General Court, and he had a good record on getting them approved. As senate president under a Democratic governor, he had formulated programs of his own, and knew how to lead recalcitrant members of his own party and win over Democrats. Half a century later such experience in a vice president would have been an asset, but not in 1921, when, as indicated, vice presidents—even Theodore Roosevelt—were considered standby equipment. He was considered a hard worker. One Washington official told a reporter from the *Boston Sunday Post* that he had been surprised by Coolidge's industriousness.

> That's a new one on me.... I've seen vice presidents who were busy attending luncheons and dinner parties. But those other vice presidents never had much else to do. They never received any mail to talk about. Presidents seemed to forget them completely. No one ever thought of consulting them. As the weeks sped on, they became more and more forgotten. I think it must be different this time. It is different.

What did he do in office? There really wasn't much to occupy his time, except studying the issues. He must have reflected on the insignificance of the office, which vice presidents from John Adams on had remarked on. According to Pennsylvania Senator George Pepper, a great raconteur, Coolidge once related that one night a fire alarm at the Willard brought all the guests to the lobby, the Coolidges among them. When the fire was under control Coolidge started up the stairs, only to be stopped by the fire marshal. "Who are you?" he wanted to know. Coolidge replied, "I'm the vice president," to which the fire marshal replied, "All right—go ahead." But then he thought again. "What are you vice president of?" he wanted to know. "I am vice president of the United States." "Come right down," said the marshal. "I thought you were the vice president of the hotel."

In his *Autobiography* Coolidge wrote that he enjoyed studying the Senate, and soon found that it had "but one fixed rule, subject to exceptions of course, which was to the effect that the Senate would do anything it wanted to do whenever it wanted to do." As president of the Senate he possessed various powers as presiding officer. He would vote in case of a tie, which never occurred while he was there. The Constitution gave him the power to recognize whom he wished. That often meant that he could decide what business would be taken up and who would have the floor for debate at any specific time. This, of course, was the theory; in practice vice presidents didn't attempt to control events, leaving this to the majority or minority leaders. Coolidge was not a particularly strong presiding officer. Like his predecessors, if he had to be elsewhere when the Senate was in session, he would name a senator to act in his place, and he was quite bipartisan in his selection, often naming Democrats to the position.

Only one incident of significance occurred while Coolidge was the Senate's presiding officer, and it happened because he *wasn't* in the chair when he should have been. Senator George Norris, an important progressive Republican, had introduced a measure to alleviate overseas marketing problems of American farmers, but the administration favored a bill to assist domestic marketing, which was to be introduced by Senator Frank Kellogg. The vice president had told Norris he would recognize Senator Joseph Ransdell to open the debate. But just before he was supposed to do this Coolidge left the chair, turning it over to conservative Senator Charles Curtis. When Ransdell attempted to get the floor, Curtis ignored him and recognized Kellogg instead, who introduced the administration's measure, killing the Norris proposal—whereupon Coolidge reentered the chamber and relieved Curtis. The progressives believed this indicated that Coolidge would go back on his word in order to further administration wishes, and even the conservatives were upset. Though the behavior was uncharacteristic of Coolidge, and puzzling, the action poisoned his relations with the senators for the remainder of his vice presidency and into his presidency. Just as Harding was the quintessential insider, Coolidge became the archetypal outsider. Harding's exuberant personality caused senators to want to work with him; the austere Coolidge repelled them.

Coolidge, as always, kept his cards close to his vest, and we know little about what he knew or though about while vice president. Assistant Secretary of the Navy Theodore Roosevelt, Jr., wrote of him, "I do not know his policies. Though I sat more than two months in the cabinet with him, I never heard him express his opinion on major questions." Only a few of his letters to his father during this period survived, and these reveal next to nothing. He remained loyal to his chief, occasionally sending notes praising one action or another, but little else. With his experience in government, he might have learned something of the illegal and questionable activities that were taking place in the Harding administration, but Coolidge said nothing about them then or later.

The vice presidents of this period filled an important social role, freeing the presidents from the necessity of attending social functions. Writing to his father on March 17, 1921, he said, "We are out to dinners a great deal," and this would continue, at the rate of approximately three times a week. "As we were always the ranking guests, we had the privilege of arriving last and leaving first, so that we were usually home by ten o'clock." Many stories were bandied about regarding how little Coolidge said at such dinners. But in his *Autobiography* Coolidge claimed otherwise. "We found it a most enjoyable opportunity for getting acquainted and could scarcely comprehend how anyone who had the privilege of sitting at a table surrounded by representatives of the cabinet, the Congress, the diplomatic corps, and the army and navy would not find it interesting." Grace Coolidge later said that at first her husband liked these dinners, but after a while they became tedious. Once when asked why he went to so many dinners, Coolidge replied solemnly, "Got to eat somewhere." So the Coolidges continued to dine out regularly, but they did not enter into the Capital's social whirl.

Vice presidents were in demand for speeches, and Coolidge was no exception. He traveled throughout the country, mostly east of the Mississippi, delivering talks on a wide variety of topics, many of them historical, such as "Theodore Roosevelt" (in New York City), "Andrew Carnegie" (Pittsburgh), "Ulysses S. Grant" (Washington), "Great Virginians" (Frederickburg), "Our Heritage from Hamilton" (Chicago), "The Place of Lincoln" (Springfield, Illinois), and "William McKinley" (Cambridge, Massachusetts). Unsurprisingly, he had nothing but praise for his subjects. There were also inspirational addresses, dealing with such topics as "The Power of Moral Law" (Springfield, Massachusetts), "The Purpose of America" (Baltimore), "Thought: The Master of Things" (Philadelphia), and "The Needs of Education" (Reynoldsville, Pennsylvania). Missing from his topics were talks dealing with current politics, legislation, world affairs, and related topics.

The speeches read well, but almost all are devoid of originality. Seldom did Coolidge say anything contentious or bold. But it did happen. On August 2, 1922, he was in Wellesley Hills to deliver an address at an industrial conference. In it he spoke of the need for more worker ownership of shares in the companies at which they were employed. "In the ideal industry, each individual would become an owner, an operator, and a manager, a master and a servant, a ruler and a subject. Thus, there would be established a system of true industrial democracy." He continued:

> In very many industries this is already taking place. Employees are encouraged to purchase stock in the corporation and are provided with credit facilities for such purpose. This gives them ownership. They are encouraged to make suggestions for the better conduct of the business. They are requested to apply their inventive ability in the various mechanical operations. Through trade-unions and shop committees they have a large share in the determination of wages and conditions of labor.... This gives them management. Thus industrial democracy is being gradually developed.

Ideas of this kind were being bandied about by some economists and sociologists, who were deemed "advanced," if not radical. Secretary of Commerce Hoover presented a version of this concept later on. After World War II, New York Stock Exchange (NYSE) Chairman Keith Funston gave it another rendering as "People's Capitalism," a weapon in the struggle against communism. This, however, was not Coolidge's approach. Rather, he asked his audience to consider that "people are not created for the benefit of industry, but industry is created for the benefit of people." Coolidge espoused these ideas while in the Massachusetts legislature, and he echoed them in Washington. In this respect, at least, he was not turning more conservative. It hardly was the kind of sentiment expected from the man who was supposed to have believed that the business of America was business.

Eight days later Coolidge was in San Francisco to deliver before the American Bar Association a speech dealing with "The Limitations of Law," in which he told the assembled attorneys, many of whom doubtless worked in the corporate sector, "The spirit of reform is altogether encouraging. The organized effort and insistent desire for an equitable distribution of the rewards of industry, for a wider justice, for a more consistent righteousness in human affairs, is one of the most stimulating and hopeful signs of the present era." He praised progressive efforts to bring government closer to the people. "The outcome of this doctrine has been the adoption of the direct primary, the direct election of the United States senators, the curtailment of the powers of the Speaker of the House, and a constant agitation for breaking down the authority of decisions of the courts."

His political philosophy came through in other speeches as well. In one before an Amherst Alumni Dinner shortly after the 1920 election, he spoke out, as he often did, on the relationship between the desire for wealth and the need for civilization. The former is acceptable, he seemed to say, so long as it furthers the latter:

> We believe in maintaining modern civilization for the
> protection and support of free governments, and the
> development of our economic welfare. We claim they are

sound and minister in the best way to human welfare.
The great test of an institution is its ability to perpetuate
itself. It seems fairly plain that whether or not these
institutions can survive without the aid of higher
education, without it they haven't a chance. We justify
the greater and greater accumulation of capital because
we believe that therefrom flows the support of all
science, art, learning, and the charities which minister to
the humanities of life, all carrying their beneficent effect
to the people as a whole. Unless this is measurably true
our system of civilization ought to stand condemned. It
is to be condemned, anyway, unless it possesses the
ability to perpetuate itself.

In the process of delivering these speeches Coolidge not only
introduced himself to politicians in all sections, but also received a
tutorial on the complexities of the nation. This reinforced the
impressions he received from dealing with senators and other officials in Washington. He took his role as understudy seriously, and his
experiences as vice president provided Coolidge with a depth of
understanding that would have been missing had he received the
1920 presidential nomination and been elected. In this, as in many
other areas, Coolidge was fortunate.

Dining out, presiding over the Senate, attending cabinet meetings, dedications, and other miscellaneous activities—all of this still
left time on Coolidge's hands, and he despised leisure. So he read a
lot, especially newspapers, perused official documents, studied legislation, and in the process became well informed regarding the business of government. He was at his desk even when Congress was not
in session, but this does not mean he was wired into what was happening in Washington. Coolidge lacked access to the movers and
shakers of the city. True enough, he spoke with them, but they did
not confide in the vice president. He also wrote for magazines, which
gave him an outlet, enabled him to organize his thinking, and provided the Coolidges with additional funds—and throughout his life,
Coolidge would save all he could. If Harding had ever truly meant to
use Coolidge as some kind of unofficial assistant and confidant, he

soon dropped the idea. So Coolidge often sat in his office, alone but not lonely. He enjoyed looking out the window and thinking.

As Coolidge sat on the sidelines, the Harding administration veered from political and diplomatic accomplishments to scandal-ridden distraction. Among the most important of Harding's achievements was in helping to heal the demoralized and divided country he had inherited from Wilson. Peace treaties were signed with the Central Powers, and Harding supported Borah's call for a conference to limit naval forces. The resulting Washington Naval Conference convened on November 12, 1921. In his address to the delegates, Secretary Hughes asked for the wholesale scrapping of capital ships—battle-ships and cruisers—and a halt to their construction. One observer noted that Hughes proposed to sink more British ships than its enemies had ever done. It ended with an agreement to scrap approximately 40 percent of the capital ships then sailing or in the process of being built. The western powers then pledged not to expand further into China, to maintain the Open Door Policy there, and to continue the status quo in the Pacific.

The Red Scare ended, and Harding did what he could to ease the remaining fear and suspicion. He surprised the country by pardoning twenty-four prisoners who had violated the wartime espionage laws. One of these was Eugene V. Debs, whom Harding invited to the White House. "Well, I have heard so damned much about you," he said to the surprised Socialist leader, shaking his hand and leading him into the White House. When Debs emerged he told reporters, "Mr. Harding appears to me to be a kind gentleman. We understand each other perfectly."

Other than that, Harding did not veer far from the agenda he had established in his address to Congress. In his first two years in office Harding signed a restrictive immigration law, approved an act to expand the merchant marine, and another creating the Bureau of the Budget, to which he named General Charles G. Dawes the first director. The Veterans Bureau was created; a series of acts was passed designed to alleviate stress on farmers; and Harding vetoed a measure to provide veterans with large bonuses. He supported Secretary of the Treasury Mellon's plan for tax reduction, but opposition from farm and other interests was too strong to overcome, and little was done in the 1921 bill. He favored a treaty with Colombia designed to heal the rift between that country and the United States resulting from Roosevelt's support of the Panamanian Revolution—the United States would pay Colombia $25 million and apologize.

Harding supported and helped pass an emergency tariff that increased rates substantially on agricultural goods to protect American farmers. Then he worked for and lobbied successfully for the permanent Fordney–McCumber Tariff of 1922, which retained the high tariffs on agricultural products. The tariff issue would be an important matter for the rest of his administration and into the Coolidge and Hoover administrations. The party consistently favored protectionism for workers, businessmen, and farmers. Later the Republican presidents would be charged with being advocates of business and opponents of the farmer. All three presidents attempted to set the record straight on this matter, usually unsuccessfully.

During the campaign Harding had talked about the desirability of an "association of nations"; nothing more was heard of this, but the Republicans in the Senate—who were astonished at Harding's independence—rejected his recommendation that the United States join the World Court. There were other indications that Harding wanted to be more than a puppet of the bosses. In 1922 he urged U.S. Steel CEO Elbert Gary, an old friend, to change the twelve-hour workday and seven-day workweek at his company to eight hours and six days. Gary rejected the appeal, but Harding persisted, pushing other industries, as well. In the end Gary bowed, and the reform went into effect in 1923. As several Harding biographers have pointed out, Harding grew in his time in office.

When Harding came to office, the nation was in the midst of its post–World War I recession and stock market slump. As it turned out, the recession was short, but it was deep, and of course Americans had no idea how long it would last. Little wonder that Wilson was so unpopular with the general public. Economic fears now compounded the disillusion with the war. In 1919–1920 there were more than thirty thousand bankruptcies, almost half-a-million farm foreclosures, and five million unemployed workers. On June 12, when

Harding–Coolidge were nominated, the Dow-Jones Industrial Average closed at 78.93. On Election Day in November, it was at 85.23, primarily because Wall Street expected that Harding's election would be good for business.

In January 1921, as Harding organized his administration, the unemployment rate stood at 20 percent. The GNP, which had reached a record peak of $88.9 billion in 1920, dropped to $74 billion in 1921. The recovery began in late 1921, although this was not recognized for several months.

In this period in which governmental actions to alleviate economic distress were all but nonexistent, the Harding policies had next to nothing to do with the recovery, and Harding did not take credit for it. Wages fell, prices declined, and in time the consumers returned and business investment picked up. He did something that was new in American history, however. In September 1921 Harding called a Conference on Unemployment, to be headed by Hoover, "to consider relief for four or five million unemployed resulting from the business slump of 1921." Out of this came plans for what to do if and when the country underwent another economic calamity.

The Republicans lost ground in the 1922 congressional elections, which was not too surprising for an off-year election, but retained control of both houses of Congress. Among the departed were Porter McCumber in the Senate and Joseph Fordney in the House— the men who gave their names to the tariff would not return. Lodge won, but at the age of seventy-two, with the League issue out of the way, he was a spent force, and would die in 1924. Knox and Penrose died within months of one another in 1921, and this too left a leadership gap.

The fact that the Republicans retained Congress masked one of the most important political developments of the decade: the emergence of a cohesive farm bloc in the Senate, along with the victory of farmer representatives in the House and midwestern states' races. The depression and the distress in the midwestern farms were largely responsible for the emergence of this group. Actually, the bloc first appeared in 1921, with a meeting of twelve midwestern farm state senators called by Senator William Kenyon of Iowa, and others soon joined. A similar bloc assembled in the House but wasn't as well organized or as effective. The bloc transcended party lines, functioning as a party within the parties, or even as a legislative third party on issues relating to farmers. The bloc formed alliances with others as well. The elections of 1922 swept a number of members of this contingent into office. As these generally progressive politicians replaced more moderate and conservative members of Congress, they all but guaranteed that farm legislation would be on the front burner for as long as the bloc existed—and President Coolidge would certainly deal with this powerful group.

Many historians, and particularly those who consider Harding an abject failure, believe his administration was beholden to the large economic interests. They point to the influence peddling that took place under his watch, but they have overblown the case against Harding. Recall that fat cat donors supported Wood and even Lowden in the campaign for the Republican nomination, while Harding contributors were far smaller fry. Certainly, Harding–Coolidge supporters were not divorced from economic forces, but businessmen supported the Republican ticket for a variety of historic and economic reasons and would have supported *any* Republican to the right of Hiram Johnson.

One of the issues that Harding's critics cite as a sign that he was beholden to big business was the matter of Muscle Shoals, an industrial complex on the Tennessee River, built during the war to extract nitrogen from the air by means of the cyanamide process. The cost of the facility, which comprised two large plants and the partially completed Wilson Dam, was in excess of $100 million. Other dams in the area were in the planning stage when the war ended. During the Wilson administration a special House committee investigated the situation and recommended abandoning the facility. Accordingly, the House refused to authorize additional appropriations for Muscle Shoals, and the government decided to sell it to private interests. This was not unusual; sales of surpluses and properties the government no longer needed occurred after both world wars.

A group of progressive senators, headed by George Norris of Nebraska, had visions of the people of the region receiving inexpensive power from the Wilson and other dams, and so they wanted the government to keep Muscle Shoals. Given the political atmosphere of the time—Harding had been elected on a platform calling for cutbacks in government—it was unlikely that Congress would approve and the president would sign a measure putting Washington in the power business. Nonetheless, on April 10, 1922, Norris introduced a bill for a government facility, "for the purpose, first, of supplying explosives in time of war, and, second, fertilizer in time of peace." Excess power, he said, could be sold to states, counties, and municipalities in the area.

When Harding took office, Secretary of War John Weeks had asked for bids for the complex, and the highest came from industrialist Henry Ford on July 8, 1921. Ford offered to pay $5 million and pledged to sell nitrate fertilizer to farmers in the region for a profit of 8 percent, lower than the traditional margin. Many groups encouraged Ford, including the American Farm Bureau, the American Federation of Labor, the Grange, and prominent farm newspapers. A majority of the congressmen and senators from the region supported the sale, while opponents were progressives from other parts of the country, such as Governor Gifford Pinchot of Pennsylvania. The National Fertilizer Association, whose members would have had to compete with Ford if the offer were accepted, asserted the scrap value of the plants would be more than $8 million, so the Ford offer was far too low. Nonetheless, the House Military Affairs Committee approved of the offer as a chance to cut back on unneeded expenses.

True enough, Ford's offer was far below the costs incurred by the government; he was trying to get in on a good deal. But government surpluses usually sold for pennies on the dollar, and Ford's bid was, after all, the highest offer. Nevertheless, with Norris leading the charge, a senatorial committee rejected the Ford offer by a vote of 9 to 7. The issue remained, and would reappear during the Coolidge administration. The attempted sale of Muscle Shoals was not, however, a Harding toss-off to big business.

By then Harding must have realized that his hope of relying upon the "best brains" wouldn't do. He had learned to trust and rely upon some cabinet members—Mellon, Hughes, and Hoover in particular—

but there were differences of opinion with others. More important, two members of the cabinet and other members of the administration were involved with corrupt practices.

While some individuals in the Harding administration were dishonorable, the president himself, except for one questionable transaction, was not. When he sold his newspaper, the *Marion Star*, for $550,000 to two newspapermen, Louis Brush and Roy Moore, charges of bribery were brought against the two. Brush and Moore, however, argued the newspaper was worth that amount because Harding had agreed to write for it after he left the White House. They won the case, and received $100,000 in damages.

The serious corruption in the Harding administration involved Secretary of the Interior Albert Fall, Secretary of the Navy Edwin Denby, and Director of the Veterans Administration Charles Forbes, and all evidence indicates the president was shocked to learn what they were doing. Fall and Denby were looting the government in what came to be known as the "Teapot Dome Affair," which involved questionable leasing practices at the naval petroleum reserve; Forbes looted the Veterans Bureau.

The first hint of trouble came on February 1, 1923, when Charles Cramer, counsel for the Veterans Bureau, resigned abruptly. By itself this wasn't considered unusual, but then the White House announced a reorganization of the Bureau, and this was surprising. The unraveling of the "Harding Scandals" had begun.

On February 12 the Senate ordered an investigation of the Veterans Bureau, and three days later Charles Forbes resigned his post; he couldn't account for hundreds of millions of dollars of supplies lost or stolen. It was clear he was selling government supplies and pocketing the proceeds. On learning of this Harding summoned Forbes to the White House and demanded his resignation, but allowed him to leave the country.

Fall resigned "for personal reasons," and took a well-paid position with the Harry Sinclair oil interests, which he was later found guilty of improperly assisting. On March 14, Cramer, who was afterward revealed to have been involved with Forbes in irregularities in the awarding of hospital sites, shot himself in the head. Harding confronted Jess Smith, one of Harry Daugherty's assistants, with evidence of peddling influence, whereupon Smith committed suicide on May 29. Daugherty was charged with corrupt practices, and was the subject of an impeachment attempt by the Senate in 1922; he was exonerated, but clouds of corruption remained over his head.

Rumors of additional malfeasance, perhaps involving the president himself, swirled around Washington in this period. According to some, Coolidge could not have helped but know of them. Yet there is no evidence Harding had sought his advice regarding any of this, or had informed Coolidge of his suspicions. This was the situation in June 1923, as the Hardings and their party prepared to set out for what he called the "Voyage of Understanding," a tour of the United States, including Alaska. On their return to Washington, they would presumably deal with the developing scandals.

Through all of this Coolidge remained in the background. He had family problems. His father-in-law, Andrew Goodhue, died on April 25 after a short illness, and the Coolidges attended the funeral. While not as close to Goodhue as he was to members of his own family, Coolidge continued to be deeply affected by the deaths of those close to him.

At this time, Coolidge had to contemplate that he might soon be obliged to retire from politics. In early July Coolidge attended a political conference in Woodstock, Massachusetts, where he conferred with Governor Cox, who raised the matter of Coolidge's future. Would it make good political sense to prepare for a run against David Walsh for his Senate seat in 1924? Having experienced life in the Senate, Coolidge wasn't interested. "No, if I don't run for vice president again, I won't run for anything."

It was reasonable. While he had been a political power in Massachusetts, Coolidge was now a cipher in Washington, where he lacked a constituency or even associates. He would lunch in the Senate restaurant, usually by himself, and senators seldom approached him to talk or invited him to join a group at another table. This treatment of a vice president by members of his own party surprised freshman Republican Congressman James Sinclair of North Dakota. Sinclair spoke of this unusual situation with his fellow North Dakotan, freshman Republican Senator Edwin Ladd, with whom he was having lunch. Glancing at Coolidge, who was munching away in a corner by himself, facing the wall, Sinclair asked, "Is this how you treat your presiding officer?" "Nobody has anything to do with him," replied Ladd. "After this, of course, he is through."

Ladd held the by-then general belief that Coolidge would be dropped from the ticket. One of Harding's close advisors, advertising man Albert Lasker, said he would support the reelection bid only if the president pledged to support Hiram Johnson for the presidential nomination in 1928. A Harding biographer, Francis Russell, asserted that in 1923, shortly before Harding's death, Kansas Senator Charles Curtis lobbied the president to replace Coolidge. According to Russell, the president responded, "We are not worried about that little fellow in Massachusetts. Charlie Dawes is the man!"

It didn't happen. Ladd died in 1925, by which time Calvin Coolidge was not only still around, but was president, and Charles Dawes was his vice president.

9

·····················

President

When I became president it was perfectly apparent that the key by which the way could be opened to national progress was constructive economy. Only by the use of that policy could the high rates of taxation, which were retarding our development and prosperity, be diminished, and the enormous burden of our public debt be reduced.

The Autobiography of Calvin Coolidge

THE COOLIDGES WERE NO LONGER in Washington when the Harding party left Washington's Union Station on June 20 for St. Louis, the first destination on what was planned as a two-month speaking and fact-finding tour. After Congress recessed on March 3, the Coolidges set out for a few days' vacation in Virginia, and then went to their Northampton home, where Coolidge read, attended to correspondence, visited old friends, and delivered some speeches. Toward the end of the month they packed for a stay with John Coolidge, who had indicated he could use the vice president's help with some household repairs. The Coolidge boys found work in the area, and so in late July Coolidge was in Plymouth Notch, at his father's home, taking care of chores, while the president was in Alaska, making speeches, seeing the sights, and doubtless considering what to do about the unraveling scandals that threatened his administration. Harding was asleep when his ship, heading to Washington State, struck another in the fog. One of his aides ran to the presidential cabin and found Harding there, his head in his hands. The president asked what had happened and was told of the collision. "I hope the boat sinks," he replied.

Harding and his party reached Seattle on July 27. The president was weary and troubled, and reporters wrote of how tired he appeared. His voice was hoarse, his face pallid. There was some thought he might be suffering from ptomaine poisoning. When he arrived in San Francisco two days later, he was met by a heart specialist and a wheelchair. Harding disdained the wheelchair, walking instead to the waiting limousine, which took him to the Palace Hotel. He developed a fever the next day, but soon recovered. Then his situation worsened. He died there on Friday, August 2, at 7:32 PM. While there was some disagreement as to the cause of death, it was given as apoplexy.

What happened next in Plymouth Notch turned out to be the most dramatic moment of the forthcoming Coolidge administration, a near-perfect way for the nation to be introduced to its new president.

August 2 was to have been Coolidge's last day vacationing in Plymouth Notch. On August 1, Coolidge was photographed attending to a diseased maple. He climbed a bench, hatchet in hand, and chipped away at a cavity in the tree so it could be cemented. The vice president was in a three-piece business suit, minus the jacket. Grace Coolidge was raking some leaves. The picture appeared in the next day's newspapers.

Only a small detail of newspapermen had been sent to cover the vice president, taking photos of Coolidge in his shirt sleeves, pitching hay, and performing other tasks. Coolidge obligingly permitted photographers to take as many pictures as they wanted; they particularly enjoyed taking pictures of Coolidge wearing a blue woolen frock his father and grandfather had worn when doing chores. He wrote of this in his *Autobiography*:

> When I went to visit the old home in later years I liked
> to wear the one he [his grandfather] left, with some fine
> calfskin boots about two inches too large for me, which
> were made for him when he went to the Vermont
> legislature about 1858. When news pictures began to be

taken of me there, I found that among the public this
was generally supposed to be a makeup costume, which
it was not, so I have been obliged to forego the comfort
of wearing it. In public life it is sometimes necessary in
order to appear really natural to be actually artificial.

That night the Coolidges retired early, so as to be fresh the next
morning.

A Harding secretary sent a telegram to Washington to inform officials of the death. It took several hours to get through. The message
was relayed to White River Junction, Vermont, then to Bridgewater,
eight miles from Plymouth. In Coolidge's hometown there was no
telegraph station and only one telephone, at the general store.

Wilfred Perkins, the Bridgewater telegrapher, tried to telephone
the store, but no one answered, presumably because the proprietor
was sleeping. Perkins made two copies of the message, and rushed
outside. He roused a stenographer, Erwin Geisser, the vice president's
chauffeur Joseph McInerney, and newspaperman William Crawford,
who was at a boardinghouse in Bridgewater. Together they set out in
the vice presidential limousine to Plymouth Notch.

Other newspapermen at the Ludlow Hotel received the news,
and all of them hastened to the Notch. The Crawford party arrived
first, and McInerney knocked on the door. John Coolidge awoke,
lit a kerosene lamp, and went to see who was there at that time of
night. They told him the news, and John Coolidge called up to his
son on the second floor. The vice president came to the top of the
stairs. As he recalled in his *Autobiography*, he noticed that his
father's voice trembled.

> As the only times I had ever observed that before were
> when death had visited our family, I knew that
> something of the gravest nature had occurred. His
> emotion was partly due to the knowledge that a man
> whom he had met and liked was gone, partly to the
> feeling that must possess all of our citizens when the life
> of their president is taken from them. But he must have
> been moved also by the thought of the many sacrifices

he had made to place me where I was, the twenty-five
mile drives in storms and in zero weather over our
mountain roads to carry me to the academy and all the
tenderness and care he had lavished upon me in the
thirty-eight years since the death of my mother in the
hope that I might sometime rise to a position of
importance, which he now saw realized.

According to Senator George Pepper of Pennsylvania, whose
source was presidential portrait artist Charles Hopkinson,
Coolidge's first thought on learning of Harding's death was: "I
believe I can swing it."

Coolidge and his wife returned to the bedroom. They washed,
dressed, and knelt by the bed to pray. Then they went downstairs,
where Coolidge dictated a message of sympathy to Mrs. Harding.
The house was now crowded with reporters and others.

Coolidge received a telegram from Attorney General Daugherty
urging him to take the oath of office immediately. He went across the
street to the general store and telephoned Secretary of State Hughes,
who informed him the oath could be administered by a notary.
Coolidge told Hughes his father was a notary, and the secretary
replied, "Fine." Coolidge returned home, and in the downstairs sitting room John Coolidge, using the family Bible, swore his son in
as president. The time was 2:47 AM.

It was a small room, fourteen by seventeen feet, with an eight-foot
ceiling. It held a worn carpet, a wood stove, a rocking chair, and was
lit by an oil lamp. Paintings and drawings of the scene appeared in
virtually all the nation's newspapers, and were replicated and sold
in the hundreds of thousands. Some reporters noted that this was the
only time a president had taken the oath in his home (or to be precise, his father's home). It still is. In addition to the Coolidges, there
were their sons, Geisser, McInerney, Congressman Porter Dale, and
his associate, L.L. Lane, and Crawford.* It wasn't Abraham Lincoln's

---

* Dale was campaigning for reelection, and heard the news of
Harding's death from a newspaperman. He rushed to Plymouth Notch
to inform Coolidge of what had happened, but arrived after the others.

log cabin, but nothing in John Coolidge's small home—with its faded furniture, and its lack of electricity, indoor plumbing, a telephone, and central heating—would have surprised Lincoln.

This dramatic ceremony was yet another instance of the uncanny good political fortune Coolidge experienced throughout his career. Had Harding died on August 3 rather than August 2, Coolidge would have been at the Currier mansion, and probably would have taken the oath from a judge in a huge ballroom. Newspapermen seeking symbols surely would have made a commotion about that. As it was, they played up the humble John Coolidge residence. Americans were deeply impressed by the way the transfer of power had occurred.

After the swearing in the Coolidges returned to their rooms and went back to sleep. They were up again at 6:00 AM. Before taking leave of his father, Coolidge noticed that a stone step to the front door had been knocked over. "Better have that fixed," he said, and went into the waiting limousine. It had not gone far when Coolidge ordered it stopped. He got out of the car, walked to the family cemetery, went to his mother's grave, and stood silently by it for a short time.

> When I started for Washington that morning I turned aside from the main road to make a short devotional visit to the grave of my mother. It had been a comfort to me during my boyhood when I was troubled to be near her last resting place, even in the dead of night. Some way, that morning, she seemed very near to me.

Because Coolidge had such a close relationship with his family, this was undoubtedly a sincere and genuine gesture, but it did add greatly to the humble, devoted image the new president was presenting to the country. In this period virtually all Americans liked what they were learning about him. As the months that followed brought out more and more details of the Harding scandals, his successor remained untouched.

The funeral train arrived in Washington on August 7, and Harding lay in state in the Capitol. The name of Lincoln continued to be heard incessantly during the week between the death and the burial, and afterward as well. Harding and Coolidge were both being compared to Lincoln, and for good reason. Harding was genuinely loved, and even those who lampooned him seemed to bear him some measure of affection. Prior to his elevation to the presidency, Coolidge was known for the Boston police strike and those jokes and stories about Silent Cal. The swearing in immediately changed all of this—at least for a while.

All presidents come to office with a reservoir of good will, especially those who arrive as a result of the death of the incumbent. Coolidge was no exception. What was unusual in his case was that he continued to retain this good will throughout his life. Other vice presidents who succeeded on the deaths of their predecessors did not fare as well. Andrew Johnson was impeached, Lyndon Johnson was driven from office, and Harry Truman's popularity declined sharply soon after succeeding Franklin D. Roosevelt.

In the introduction to his perceptive *Coolidge and the Historians*, Thomas Silver wrote:

> Think back upon a decade of upheaval in American history. The country's youngest president, having succeeded a conservative Republican and having sounded a clarion call to the progressive forces in the country, is now gone forever from the presidency. An activist Democratic president skillfully shepherds legislation through Congress, but wolfish war follows close upon the heels of domestic reform. Radical protests against the system, and a few bombings, ignite national hysteria. The president retires in bitterness, soon to die. His Republican successor at first holds forth the hope of restoring the national composure; but he is replaced by his vice president after a truncated term marred by economic dislocation and executive scandal unprecedented in American history.

Of course, Silver is referring here to the line of presidents from William McKinley to Theodore Roosevelt to Wilson and on to Harding, but he knows the reader will be thinking of Eisenhower–

Kennedy–Johnson–Nixon. He might have added that the next persons in line, Coolidge and Ford, could not have achieved the presidency except in the ways they did.

The mechanical aspects of the presidential transition were familiar enough; McKinley had died within the memory of many in Washington, and those in government knew the drill. Mrs. Harding was invited to remain in the White House as long as she desired, and in fact the Coolidges did not move into the White House until four days after she had left. Coolidge issued a proclamation of national mourning, and the Coolidges went to Marion for the funeral, which took place on August 10. Before then, however, Coolidge took the oath a second time, since Daugherty worried about the legitimacy of having a state official swearing in a national figure. This was done without the public learning of it; Coolidge realized it would take the edge off the drama of that scene in Plymouth Notch.

The nature of the presidency in 1923 was different from what it is today, or even as it evolved under Herbert Hoover and Franklin D. Roosevelt. Coolidge was the last president to spend hours standing in the White House lobby greeting and shaking hands with casual visitors on their tours. He was the last president to have only one secretary and no other aides. Coolidge still didn't know how to drive an automobile. He didn't have a telephone on his desk; there was one in a little booth outside his office, but he never used it. He explained to Bruce Barton, "The president should not talk on the telephone. In the first place, you can't be sure it is private, and, besides, it isn't in keeping with the dignity of the office."

In his first few weeks in office the American people learned more about Coolidge. Of course there had already been stories about him, some apocryphal, others true, and many a blend of the two. During this period the public learned that on the living room wall of Coolidge's Northampton, Massachusetts, home was a sampler that read:

> A wise old owl lived in an oak
> The more he saw, the less he spoke,
> The less he spoke the more he heard,
> Why can't we be like that old bird?

How had the public learned of the poem? Through Coolidge. His image was no accident. Rather, he carefully cultivated it from the moment he entered politics. In his own quiet way, he was a media virtuoso. Coolidge was, quite simply, the master of the self-made myth. He knew his limitations and strengths better than did most of our presidents. His public persona was different from any the country—or even Massachusetts—was accustomed to. In February 1920, when he was being talked of as a presidential possibility, a journalist had written of him:

> If Coolidge shakes hands, the shake is brief, businesslike; he has none of that conversational small change with which the majority of us endeavor to give value to our casual meetings; he can sit unperturbed in the midst of silence and company; he tells no stories, cracks no jokes; he seldom laughs. Warmth, geniality, good fellowship, all seem alien qualities. And yet he is regarded as the best "vote-getter" in Massachusetts. Old railbirds about the State House in Boston will tell you: "Cal Coolidge has upset all our ideas of how to succeed in politics."

Cartoonists during the 1920s often portrayed Coolidge as a dour, disgruntled soul who, as Alice Roosevelt Longworth supposedly said, looked as though "he was weaned on a sour pickle." The Coolidge archives have many pictures of him laughing heartily, but the press rarely used these; newspapers seemed to prefer the photographs in which he looked blandly and blankly out on the world. Of course, that was the image the president had deliberately fixed on reporters who covered him. Yet he possessed a fine, wry, sense of humor, marked by understatement, introduced when the listener least expected it, and delivered with that Vermont twang and solemn face and demeanor.

William Allen White, who interviewed Coolidge in 1924 for a series of articles in *Collier's Weekly*, recalled that Coolidge told him, "A lot of people in Plymouth can't understand how I got to be president, least of all my father." He then added, "Now a lot of those people remember some interesting things that never happened." To this, White observed, "I noticed that President Coolidge never grinned after his jokes to punctuate them. This misled people. They sometimes thought his remarks were dumb. Whatever may be said of Calvin Coolidge, he was not dumb. And many a dumb remark of his afterwards recounted merely reflects the dullness of the narrator."

That was the way some rural Vermonters cracked jokes; they could appreciate the Coolidge wit, while outsiders sometimes had trouble fathoming it. The humor was rarely displayed publicly, in part because when it was, many of his listeners, unattuned to it, would be puzzled rather than delighted. Coolidge understood this. "Whenever I do indulge my sense of humor, it always gets me into trouble," he said plaintively. So he often remained silent.

There was another, more plausible reason for the silence. Coolidge did not suffer fools gladly, wanted to save time, and he found silence was the best way to accomplish this. Once he was quite talkative in a meeting with Bernard Baruch, and after a while Coolidge asked why the financier was smiling. Baruch replied, "Mr. President, you are so different from what people say you are. Your smile indicates both amusement at that and interest—and I hope, friendliness." Coolidge seemed genuinely pleased at this, so Baruch added, "Everybody said you never say anything." "Well, Baruch," Coolidge replied, "many times I say only 'yes' or 'no' to people. Even that is too much. It winds them up for twenty minutes more."

While in the Coolidge cabinet, Secretary of Commerce Hoover had the same experience. After Hoover's election to the presidency in 1928, Coolidge gave him some advice: "You have to stand every day three or four hours of visitors. Nine-tenths of them want something they ought not have. If you keep dead-still they will run down in three or four minutes. If you even cough or smile they will start up all over again."

In 1933, when the country had supposedly soured on Coolidge and all he represented, a friendly book appeared entitled *Coolidge Wit and Wisdom: 125 Short Stories about "Cal."* Most of the Coolidge stories that survive do indeed deal with his sense of humor. It was said that at one of his well-known breakfasts for politicians, the president poured his coffee and cream into his saucer. Seeing this, some of his guests did the same, and waited for Coolidge to start slurping it up. Instead, he bent down and placed the saucer on the floor for his dog.

Once he invited White House Secret Service agent Edmund Starling to a late night snack. They went to the butler's pantry, and the president sliced the bread and cheese for sandwiches. "I'll bet no other president ever made cheese sandwiches for you," he said to Starling, who quite properly replied, "No indeed, it is a great honor." Coolidge then added glumly, "And I have to furnish the cheese, too." Starling didn't know whether the president was joking.

Will Rogers, the leading humorist of the time, appreciated Coolidge wit, and wrote:

> Mr. Coolidge had more subtle humor than almost any
> public man I ever met. I have often said I would like to
> have been hidden in his desk somewhere and just heard
> the little sly "digs" that he pulled on various people that
> never got 'em at all. I bet he wasted more humor on
> folks than almost anybody.

Rogers noted that Coolidge was the master at short quips. Coolidge's humor was not of the kind that causes belly laughs. Rather, it was light and often appeared mean to those who did not understand it. There was that famous tale about his wife asking about the preacher's sermon on a Sunday morning. "What did he talk about?" she wanted to know. "Sin," was the concise reply. When asked to expand upon this, Coolidge said, "He's against it." When he heard the story, Coolidge looked ahead blankly and remarked, "It would be better if it were true." But the joke itself indicates the teller understood Coolidge rhetoric—short, to the point, and epigrammatic. Moreover, it illustrates the affection in which the tellers of such stories held Coolidge; he was not the butt of stories, but rather the protagonist.

The dry wit was a Coolidge family trait. In 1920, when Calvin was considered a presidential possibility, his father, John, was asked about his son. He replied with a straight face, "It always seemed to be that Calvin could get more sap out of a maple tree than any of the other boys around here." To those who couldn't understand what

John Coolidge meant by that, Calvin's similarly oblique statements would be incomprehensible. Calvin Coolidge's younger son, also named Calvin, flashed the family wit while he was working as a laborer in the Hatfield, Massachusetts, tobacco fields. Calvin mentioned who he was, to which one of the boys said, "Gee, if the president was my father, I wouldn't be working here." Calvin replied, "You would, if your father were my father."

Coolidge took steps in those early days in the White House geared to ensure himself the nomination of a political party that hadn't wanted him as vice president in 1920. He joined a church, the First Congregational, whose pastor was an Amherst man whom Coolidge liked. He met with the press, telling the reporters he intended to continue Harding's practice of twice weekly press conferences. Coolidge was good with the press. "I want you to know the executive offices will be open as far as possible, so that you may get any information your readers will be interested to have. This is your government. You can be very helpful in the administration of it." He was as good as his word. Coolidge was to hold 520 press conferences, an average of nearly 8 a month, and according to Sheldon Stern of the John F. Kennedy Library, he delivered more speeches than any of his predecessors. For the press conferences, he adhered to the format Harding had used. All questions were written and gone through by his secretary beforehand. Then Coolidge would answer those he wished to, and discard the others. No direct quotations would be allowed; instead, the reporter could attribute the statement to a "White House spokesman."

Coolidge handled reporters with skill, tact, and imagination, and they genuinely liked him. He certainly knew how to massage reporters' egos. In his *Autobiography,* Coolidge noted, "One of my most pleasant memories will be the friendly relations which I always had with the representatives of the press in Washington. I shall always remember that at the conclusion of the first regular conference I held with them at the White House office they broke into hearty applause." And things got even better. In a 1926 press conference, he told the Washington press corps, which contained fewer than twenty reporters at the time, "I wish to take this opportunity to express my amazement at the constant correctness of my views as you report them to the country. It is very seldom that any error creeps in. I don't know how that could be done."

The press not only was courteous to and respectful of Coolidge— that was to have been expected of their attitudes toward all presidents in this period—but most of the reporters genuinely liked him. Frank Kent, who was highly critical of Coolidge, wrote in the *Nation*, one of the leading anti-Coolidge publications, of this in the March 16, 1927, edition, when Coolidge had been dealing with the Washington press for almost four years:

> Since Mr. Coolidge entered the White House he has had more solid press support than any other president. Frequently he has through the spokesman expressed his appreciation. It would be strange indeed if he did not feel it.

One of the reporters, Lyle Wilson, later wrote, "Calvin Coolidge was the contriver of the most persistent and transparent political hoax of twentieth century America," referring to the press conferences. "The president would be completely relaxed. I always had the impression he had not peeked at the questions before we arrived. The briefings and skull sessions which preceded the Eisenhower and Kennedy press conferences were not for Mr. Coolidge."

Coolidge summoned House Speaker Gillett and Senate Whip Charles Curtis, who did most of the work for Republican leader Lodge, and asked for recommendations for a private secretary. According to one account, Coolidge told them, "I recognize that a large part of the work of the presidency is political. I want a secretary who understands that phase of the work. I ask you to recommend to me a man who knows the House and Senate and their membership. Particularly, he must know the House, for I know something about the Senate myself."

They helped him select C. Bascom Slemp, a fifty-three-year-old political veteran, who at the age of eleven had served as a page in the Virginia House of Delegates, obtaining the post at the behest of his father, a member of the legislature who later went on to the U.S. House of Representatives. Slemp filled his father's post on his death, and served in the House for eleven years, ending in early 1923. Slemp was considered a master political manipulator who knew his way around the Capitol. He was a private man who spoke sparingly, whose personality would fit in well with that of Coolidge. Clinton Gilbert, a veteran Washington correspondent, described Slemp as having "a slim, rather elegant-looking figure, his movements are cat-like, his fingers slender and rather deft."

The new president was well aware of the need to win the respect and support of the congressional Republicans, and this was one of Slemp's most important assignments. His selection was the first clear indication that Coolidge intended to contest for the nomination in 1924.

Some familiar faces were on hand to lend assistance. Harding had his "Ohio Gang." Coolidge brought with him a group of Massachusetts confidants. Frank Stearns was there, of course. Coolidge called on him for company and to take care of delicate errands. He thought better with Stearns in the room. There were times Coolidge would call him to his office and the two men would simply look out the window in silence. Once, after an hour or so of this, without a comment from either man, Stearns rose to leave, and Coolidge said, "Stay a while longer."

Dwight Morrow, now a partner at J.P. Morgan, had known Coolidge since they were classmates at Amherst. He remained a close friend. William Butler, who had been Murray Crane's right-hand man, now worked with Coolidge. Butler was on the Republican National Committee. With Coolidge's support he became chairman in 1924. When Henry Cabot Lodge died in November that year, Butler took his place in the Senate. Coolidge remained intimate with Gillett. These four constituted the "Massachusetts Gang." Senator Weeks of Massachusetts, who had never been close with Coolidge, was not included in the inner circle, and of course, even before his death, Senator Lodge and Coolidge were at odds with one another. Aside from the "gang," Coolidge had few friends in Washington.

Coolidge retained Harding's cabinet, but by the end of his presidency all but four members had been replaced. The last to go was

Hoover, who resigned to run for president in 1928. Coolidge respected but disliked Hoover, whom he called the "Wonder Boy," because he always seemed to want to change things. Coolidge said of Hoover, "That man has given me nothing but advice, and all of it bad." When Hoover persisted in warning against some problem or other, Coolidge said, "Mr. Hoover, if you see ten troubles coming down the road, you can be sure that nine will run into the ditch before they reach you and you have to battle with only one of them." In recounting this story, Hoover added that he agreed, but "when the tenth trouble reached him he was wholly unprepared, and it had by that time acquired such momentum that it spelled disaster." Hoover's replacement was William Whiting, a Massachusetts paper manufacturer who had never held political office—but who had graduated from Amherst in 1886, one year after Coolidge, and Coolidge tended to favor Amherst men in his appointments.

Treasury Secretary Mellon was Coolidge's most trusted advisor in the cabinet. After their first meeting on Coolidge's becoming president—a meeting that centered on financial issues—Mellon said, "Mr. President, I neglected to tell you that I had come to resign," to which Coolidge replied, "Forget it."

Coolidge had a somewhat unusual style. He delegated a great deal of authority, and once told Bruce Barton, "The president shouldn't do too much, and he shouldn't *know* too much." It was a sentiment he often repeated, leading some to believe him lazy and uncaring, which was not the case; Coolidge worked harder than most presidents of his time. He explained himself this way:

> The president can't resign. If a member of the cabinet
> makes a mistake and destroys his standing with the
> country, he can get out, or the president can ask him to
> get out. But if he has involved the president in the
> mistake, the president has to stay there to the end of his
> term, and to that extent the people's faith in their
> government has been diminished. So I constantly said to
> my cabinet: "There are many things you gentlemen must
> not tell me. If you blunder, you can leave, or I can invite

you to leave. But if you draw me into all your
department decisions and something goes wrong, I must
stay here. And by involving me you have lowered the
faith of the people in their government."

One can only wonder whether presidents in the 1970s and afterward have considered this matter.

In his first weeks and even months in office, Coolidge did little that differed from the Harding agenda. Coolidge was a careful president. In his *Autobiography* he wrote, "The words of the president have an enormous weight and ought not to be used indiscriminately." He was as good as his word, adding to his reputation as Silent Cal.

Bruce Barton wrote in the *American Review of Reviews* that the best way to understand the new president would be to read his speeches in *Have Faith in Massachusetts*. "They will find in it evidence of all the qualities which have been touched upon in this brief article—his straight thinking, his courage, his familiar knowledge of history, his utter freedom from pretense."

Coolidge was the last president to compose almost all of his speeches. True, some of them were polished by assistants, and others, until 1925, were the handiwork of speechwriters, the most important of whom was a newspaperman, Judson Welliver. According to Fuess, "President Coolidge took notes on yellow paper, dictated his speech, revised it then in longhand, and then had the final clean copy made." Grace Coolidge later recalled:

Up to the time that he became president, Mr. Coolidge
wrote his speeches on sheets of foolscap paper in pencil,
going over them again and again, changing a word here,
transposing and rewriting with infinite pains. When he
had finished a speech, it was given to his secretary to be
typewritten. None was ever wholly satisfactory to him at
the time. Afterwards, he would read one and say, "That
was a pretty good speech, after all."

When he became president, he began dictating his
speeches to his stenographer, a quiet young man of
inexhaustible patience, devoted to his chief.

Mrs. Coolidge went on to cite an exception to this practice. While governor of Massachusetts, Coolidge delivered a speech that dealt with composers and musical compositions, subjects about which he knew next to nothing. "When he joined us at the conclusion of the ceremony, I burst into laughter in which he quietly joined, a little shamefacedly, as I asked him where he obtained all that information. He did not commit himself."

When one of his devoted admirers collected Coolidge's speeches into a volume entitled *Have Faith in Massachusetts*, to be used in an attempt to win the 1920 GOP presidential nomination, Coolidge refused to permit this speech to be included. It wouldn't have been right to have done so.

A writer in the *Outlook* thought, "Few, if any, public men of national reputation in our history have been so little known as Calvin Coolidge is and yet so much trusted." Before he became president, the American people outside of Massachusetts knew him only for his actions in the police strike, but this would now change. Scores of magazine and newspaper articles sketched his upbringing and career, and some speculated about his possible agenda and political philosophy.

In 1923 the *Literary Digest* discerned the theme of the new administration:

> Monroe had his era of "good feeling"; Jackson, as one
> of our editors recalls, his shibboleth of "local self-
> government"; we associate "Union" with Lincoln, the
> "square deal" and the "strenuous life" with Roosevelt,
> the "New Freedom" and "making the world safe for
> democracy" with Wilson; and, as Harding was
> consecrated to the restoration of "normalcy," so the
> correspondents tell us, President Coolidge is pledged to
> the preservation of "stability."

Coolidge supposedly told reporters that he stood for "stability, confidence, and reassurance." He added that his administration did not intend to "surrender to every emotional movement seeking remedies for economic conditions by legislation." The *New York*

Times took this to mean that Coolidge wanted to assure the business community that it could make plans without worrying about sudden shifts from Washington; the *New York World* thought Coolidge would not alter tariff rates unless absolutely necessary, and would not "rush to the front with proposals to Congress that would tend to undermine stability." This, reflected the *Philadelphia Inquirer*, "is the kind of assurance that will be appreciated." The *Philadelphia Public Ledger* called the policy of stability "good hard sense."

> This country has come to a considerable degree of "normalcy." What it needs now is a stabilization of its favorable situation and confidence that this will continue. Wages are very high and unemployment is negligible. Labor is, indeed, very well off. Business is good and industry is humming. The farm hysteria is hardly as vocal now as it was thirty days ago. Outside the wheat states, the farmer is going along very well. He had ample credit—too much in fact, according to his best friends. The all-around condition of the country is sound and warrants much optimism. Far-reaching changes, such as are constantly sought by the political dare-devil doctors, are the last thing this country needs.

In large part, the country had calmed down from the turbulent postwar period and was growing economically. Many of the heated debates of that time had also either ended or muted. Given his temperament and inclination, Coolidge was a near-perfect person to preside over a period of stability. Once again, he was fortunate in coming to office when he did.

The *Syracuse* [N.Y.] *Post-Standard* observed that Coolidge "has made less change in the policy and personnel of the administration bequeathed to him than any vice president succeeding to the presidency before him." A Washington correspondent reported, "the new president [has] assured the people that he does not contemplate any changes in the policy of his predecessor, and that honest folk can sleep o' nights."

Of course, not all mainstream newspapers applauded the situation and the policy of stability. The Democratic *New York World* warned that "in time of change no policy is so unstable as stability." The *Knoxville Sentinel*, also Democratic, observed that "the maliciously minded are now saying that 'stability' is another way of passing the word to 'stand pat.'" But this was rather mild criticism.

Throughout this transitional period Coolidge enjoyed widespread support in the press. The only harsh criticism of Coolidge came from the doctrinaire fringes. The *New York Call*, a socialist newspaper, called Coolidge "probably the man of smallest caliber who has ever been made president of the United States." The reaction of the *Nation*, which rarely had anything good to say about a Republican, was typical of those who felt dismay at the thought of a Coolidge presidency, and should be viewed against a special backdrop. Editor Oswald Garrison Villard had a particular distaste for Coolidge, and wrote of him in the August 1 edition, just before Harding's death:

> Take that midget statesman, Calvin Coolidge, vice
> president of the United States, for instance. Every honest
> Boston journalist knows the inwardness of the police
> strike and how little, if any, credit Mr. Coolidge deserves
> for his part in it. I happened to be sitting among the
> Massachusetts journalists at the Chicago convention
> when Mr. Coolidge was nominated as vice president.
> Their astonishment and their disgust were amusing to
> watch. Returning later to the Congress Hotel I found
> two of the most influential editors in New England in
> excited conversation about Mr. Coolidge's nomination.
> Never have I heard more vigorous profanity; each
> sought to outdo the other in his epithets. "Never," said
> the elder, "in years of political experience have I met a
> man in public life so despicable, so picayune, so false to
> his friends as Cal."

Now that he was president the magazine ran an article entitled: "Calvin Coolidge: Made by a Myth":

> And now the presidency sinks low indeed. We doubt if
> ever before it has fallen into the hands of a man so cold,

so narrow, so reactionary, so uninspiring, and so unenlightened, or one who has done less to earn it, than Calvin Coolidge.... Every reactionary may today rejoice; in Calvin Coolidge he realizes his ideal, and every liberal may be correspondingly downcast.

But there were no reservations regarding Grace Coolidge. In this period, when the families of vice presidents were not particularly well known, she was an exception, at least in Washington. As mentioned, she was quite different from her husband. Grace Coolidge exuded warmth, was vivacious and talkative, and had a hearty, conventional sense of humor. Moreover, she was an attractive woman, and her looks and dazzling smile only added to her popularity. As was customary, she told the press that her job was to stay at home and raise the two Coolidge sons, but when Coolidge was vice president she urged him to attend plays, musicals, and other diversions. Occasionally she let it be known she wanted even more. In a 1921 interview she told a reporter:

Everyone talks of the restlessness of women since the war, of their dissatisfaction to return to the old kinds of life. Of course they are restless. Soon there will not be an intelligent woman who is content to do nothing but live a social life. I should think Washington would be an excellent place to begin the change.

Grace Coolidge was not a closet feminist, but she was quite outspoken. After Coolidge's death, she indicated that he never asked her thoughts on public matters, and that he had a low opinion of her education. She was able to laugh this off. Grace Coolidge was quite confident in her own abilities, and willing to take an independent course, which her husband approved. She was the first president's wife to smoke cigarettes, and that was fine with him—or at least, he said nothing about it. Coolidge was known as a penurious man, but there was one area in which he didn't mind spending money: his wife's clothes. There was never any doubt that their marriage was very happy indeed.

Political reporters had to make do with speculation until Congress reconvened on December 6 and received Coolidge's message. This meant that Coolidge had four months to prepare himself for command before having to joust with the legislature, which included many who considered him not only an accidental president, but an accidental nominee. In this period Coolidge would have to become the master of the Harding policies and political strategies, and ponder programs of his own. He had to learn more about foreign policy. France had recently sent its army into the Ruhr because Germany had defaulted on its reparations payments. The debate on whether or not the United States should enter the World Court continued, and the League question would not die. It was generally agreed that the Washington Naval Conference was a success, and there was pressure for another such meeting to continue the cutbacks. America's relations with Mexico had been poor since that country's revolution in 1911, and the United States did not have diplomatic representation in that country. Likewise, there was no official contact with the Soviet Union. While none of these issues required immediate attention, they would have to be addressed in time.

The domestic situation was another matter. A good deal of what was happening in government occurred without much in the way of input from either Harding or Coolidge. Both men believed in delegating powers, Harding because he felt some in his cabinet were smarter and better informed than he, Coolidge because this was very much in his nature. For example, in 1922 Secretary of Commerce Hoover had called a Radio Conference, and for the rest of the Harding administration and into the Coolidge years would help define this important industry, without input from either president.

Such was the situation when Coolidge addressed Congress on December 6, 1923. The speech was well received; according to the newspaper reports, it was interrupted many times by applause from both Democrats and Republicans. This was to have been expected; such a reaction was by way of greeting the new president and assuring him of Congress's good will. The address contained a long list of requests, most of them familiar as part of the Harding program. Coolidge favored immigration restriction. The railroads, which were in shabby shape due to negligence during the war, needed assistance; Coolidge thought "consolidation appears to be the only feasible method for the maintenance of an adequate system of transportation," and he supported rate increases. He also called for greater government spending for highways. Coolidge endorsed the efforts of a Senate committee seeking to develop a new reforestation program. And he asked for legislation to abolish the rights of states and municipalities to issue tax-exempt securities, arguing that new investment funneled into these securities could be better employed in the private sector.

Because of a major coal strike in Pennsylvania in September, the president asked for power to appoint commissions "to aid conciliation and voluntary arbitration." Coolidge wanted to continue the program of governmental reorganization Harding had initiated, and he wanted reforms in the civil service, diplomatic corps, and the Justice Department. He also supported American membership in the World Court, increased military and naval appropriations, and greater federal efforts in Prohibition enforcement. Coolidge opposed American entry into the League, the proposed veteran's bonus, and suggestions that foreign debts be canceled. "The current debt and interest due from foreign governments, exclusive of the British debt of $4.6 billion, is about $7.2 billion. I do not favor canceling this debt, but I see no objection to adjusting it in accordance with the principle adopted for the British debt."* He rejected recognition of the Soviet Union, and opposed tariff revision.

On many occasions, sometimes when it was politically imprudent, Coolidge spoke out for the rights of those who were then called "negroes." Of course, in this period, most black Americans were Republicans, while the white South was solidly Democrat. But few

---

* Recall that Coolidge supported a veterans' bonus while governor and indicated an interest in the League. In June 1923 the United States and the United Kingdom signed the Debt Refunding Agreement, which provided that the UK pay its debt in semi-annual installments over a period of sixty-two years, with an interest rate of 3.3 percent.

presidents were as outspoken on the need to protect the civil rights of black Americans as Calvin Coolidge:

> Numbered among our population are some twelve million colored people. Under our Constitution their rights are just as sacred as those of any other citizen. It is both a public and private duty to protect those rights. The Congress ought to exercise all its powers of prevention and punishment against the hideous crime of lynching, of which the negroes are by no means the sole sufferers, but for which they furnish a majority of the victims.

Coolidge took note of the migration of blacks to the North, and recommended a commission consisting of both blacks and whites "to formulate a better policy for mutual understanding and confidence." He asked for an appropriation of "about half a million dollars" for Howard University "to help contribute to the education of five hundred colored doctors needed each year."

Coolidge came out firmly against various programs for crop support. He said, "No complicated scheme of relief, no plan for government fixing of prices, no resort to the public Treasury will be of any permanent value in establishing agriculture. Simple and direct methods put into operation by the farmer himself are the only real sources for restoration." He urged farmers to organize, as had labor, and then voluntarily cut back on acreage in order to lower production, which would boost prices. This kind of statement was necessary because by then the farm bloc had come together in support of the McNary–Haugen Bill, which was to be introduced the following month and would become one of the central battlegrounds of political debate for the next four years.

The key recommendation of Coolidge's address, as far as many newspapers were concerned, was his call for a tax cut. The president wanted a 25 percent across-the-board decrease from the high wartime rates, and in addition he would reduce the surtax rates to begin at $10,000 rather than $6,000. To make up for some of the cuts, he would alter the capital gains tax to bring in more revenue, change deductions for interest charges, and increase the estate taxes, all of which would hit the wealthy harder than the middle class and poor taxpayers.

The federal income tax had only been instituted in 1913. The following year it produced $28 million, almost all of it coming from taxes on the very wealthy. Fewer than 360,000 of 99 million Americans paid income taxes that year. This was by design, as the progressives who pushed for an income tax saw it as a redistributionist measure to take the rough edges off capitalism and help the poor.

At the time, there were no large governmental spending programs. Federal expenditures in 1913 came to $715 million, having risen from $690 million the previous year. In 1914 they would go to $726 million, and in 1915, $746 million. Meanwhile, government revenues actually declined, falling from $714 million in 1913 to $683 million in 1914.

This situation changed in 1917, when Congress passed and President Wilson signed a temporary war tax measure, broadening the tax base. It also added a surtax on taxpayers with incomes of more than $6,000 (approximately $60,000 today). The additional taxes were progressive, rising to 25 percent on incomes of more than $100,000. That year 3.5 million returns were filed, bringing in $691 million, and the figure rose to $1.1 billion the following year, when the war ended. Despite peace, the tax remained in place, fetching $1.3 billion in 1919 and more than $1 billion in 1920. That election year, both parties called for an end to the wartime taxes, and tax reform was a popular issue. Wilson's Secretary of the Treasury David Houston called for their abolition and the reduction of surtaxes in a message to Congress that year. The top bracket was 70 percent, he observed. "We are confronted with a condition, not a theory. The fact is that such rates cannot be successfully collected." Candidate Harding agreed. Indeed, outside of some progressives, there seemed political unanimity on the subject.

Consider that Americans of the period hadn't any experience with income taxes prior to 1914, and those who paid them hardly could have welcomed the change. Moreover, bear in mind that what today would pass for poor and middle class Americans didn't pay any income taxes. In 1924 a two-parent family with two children and an income of $3,200 (approximately $32,000 in current dollars) paid no tax at all, but note also that the total tax bite increased for some Americans in this period. In some states the sales tax, the gasoline tax, and other taxes rose in the 1920s, and so offset the decreases in income taxes. The matter of taxation will be addressed in detail later in this book, since it was central to the Coolidge philosophy and program.

Many Americans did not have to wait for their newspapers to arrive to know what the president had said in his address to Congress. His was the first State of the Union to be broadcast. The press response to Coolidge's State of the Union address was generally favorable. The *New York World* said, "Mr. Coolidge has worked out an able message." The *New York Tribune* added, "There is an unmistakable American flavor to President Coolidge's first message to Congress." The *St. Louis Globe Democrat* thought, "The outstanding feature of the message is its sound, practical common sense." And the *Philadelphia Public Ledger* asserted, "The nation now knows exactly what President Coolidge thinks. He has given it a map of his mind and the country will approve the course he has charted." The *Cincinnati Enquirer* wrote:

> No one can read the message of President Coolidge without appreciating how fully he is in sympathy and accord with every vital policy of the Harding administration. Comprehensive in scope, frank and clear in all suggestions and recommendations, dealing plainly with the most controversial issues, it is a message to all the people as well as to the Congress. In this respect it may be regarded as a Coolidge platform for 1924.

The next day brought reports that, as expected, leading Democratic legislators opposed various parts of the program. They took note of its reception, and couldn't help but recognize that Coolidge could be a formidable figure in 1924.

Coolidge had opened his speech with a tribute to Harding, and his actions since taking office indicated a willingness to be associated with his agenda and appointments. Congress adjourned after the president's speech out of respect to Harding's memory, but first passed a bill providing Mrs. Harding with a $5,000 pension and franking privileges. Then, on the next evening, at the annual Gridiron Dinner, riding the crest of his popularity, Coolidge announced his candidacy for the presidency in 1924. This, too, was greeted with acclaim by the press. None of the major newspapers mentioned that by so doing, he would discourage potential rivals, but some noted that it would be difficult to deny him the nomination.

The State of the Union message may have surprised some long time Coolidge watchers. It was not cautious, but quite ambitious. If Coolidge drew his inspiration from the Harding agenda he also indicated that he wanted to be an agent of change.

Coolidge returned time and again to the need for cutting taxes. In a speech before the National Republican Club in New York on February 12, 1924, Coolidge emphasized:

> If we had a tax whereby on the first working day the government took 5 percent of your wages, on the second day 10 percent, on the third day 20 percent, on the fourth day 30 percent, on the fifth day 50 percent, and on the sixth day 60 percent, how many of you would continue to work on the last two days of the week? It is the same with capital. Surplus income will go into tax-exempt securities. It will refuse to take the risk incidental to embarking in business. This will raise the rate which established businesses will have to pay for new capital, and result in a marked increase in the cost of living.

But as much as he wanted to be a tax-cutter, that could only be achieved by reaching compromise legislation with Congress. Congress passed and Coolidge reluctantly signed the Simmons–Longworth Bill, which reduced the surtax to a top rate of 40 percent. In return, the estate tax was increased, and a gift tax was added. It wasn't what he had in mind—Coolidge wanted to slash rates to their prewar level—but it was the best he could get.

Coolidge knew he was regarded with suspicion by progressives like La Follette and by Republicans who would have preferred a different candidate to lead the party. Coolidge tried to do something about this, telling La Follette he would always be welcome at the White House for consultations and hoped for his support. In November he wrote to every Republican senator asking for recommendations for appointments. When Congress reconvened he regularly had legislators to breakfasts, although some who attended complained that he said so little. As much as he could, Coolidge reached out for support, friendship, and assistance. Indeed, the Coolidges did much more entertaining in the White House than the Hardings, and for that matter, any previous president, probably due in part because Harding had managed to push through Congress a measure providing his successors with an entertainment allowance. It did no good.

If Mark Sullivan, considered one of the most astute Washington correspondents, knew anything of machinations to displace Coolidge, it did not appear in his columns. Writing in November, after Coolidge had been in office three months, he said that "the presence of Congress in Washington will reveal one of Mr. Coolidge's traits as an individual, namely the degree to which he has the inclination—and the capacity—to impress himself on Congress as its leader."

> There is evidence that Coolidge has been aware of the importance of the meeting with Congress as a dividing point in his presidency. During the four months preceding the event he has made it obviously a definite policy to refrain from public speaking and from appearing at any of the immense number of functions to which he has been invited. He has refrained also from any important declarations of policy and from any revealing of Coolidge's purposes with respect to public questions.

There was one exception to this practice. Harding had scheduled a meeting with the nation's governors to discuss Prohibition enforcement, and in keeping with his pledge to carry out the Harding agenda, Coolidge attended. Pennsylvania's Governor Gifford Pinchot, a passionate supporter of Prohibition, felt that Coolidge's stated willingness to enforce the Volstead Act according to the letter of the law was not strong enough, and a sign that he secretly opposed the measure. Pinchot and others also knew that Coolidge had represented brewery interests in Northampton, and that he had their support when he ran for mayor in 1909. Pinchot voiced his disappointment, which resulted in prohibitionist meetings and a call for Pinchot to challenge Coolidge for the 1924 presidential nomination. Failing in this, they urged him to consider a run for the presidency on a Prohibitionist ticket. If something as slight as this could result in a challenge, Coolidge must have thought, what might a confrontation with Congress prompt?

Coolidge had clashed with Pinchot before. In 1921 the United Mine Workers union in Pennsylvania had signed a contract with the operators which neither side liked, and there had been a strike the following year in which half a million miners left the pits, not to return until September. At the time Coolidge took office, discussions were being conducted between the operators and the union, which was headed by John L. Lewis. Pinchot and representatives of the United States Coal Commission had attempted mediation, with no success. Pinchot urged the operators to raise wages (then $4.20–$5.60 a day) and permit a checkoff of union dues. The operators wouldn't budge on either matter.

Coolidge met with Daugherty to find out whether he had any responsibility in this situation, and was told he could do nothing until there was an actual strike. According to Senator George Pepper of Pennsylvania, Coolidge summoned his temporary secretary, George Christian, and said, "Mr. Christian, it is about time for many people to begin to come to the White House to discuss different phases of the coal strike. Whenever anybody comes, if his special problem concerns the state, refer him to the governor of Pennsylvania. If his problem has a national phase, refer him to the United States Coal Commission. In no event bring him to me."

Pinchot contacted the president on August 15, asking for his intercession, but Coolidge refused to act. It might have seemed a larger version of the police strike, and Coolidge was only following the pattern set down on that occasion, but the situation in the coal matter was not remotely like that in Boston in 1919. Pinchot not only was a more astute politician than Mayor Peters, but also had a constituency aching for a confrontation. The progressive Republicans had threatened to bolt the 1920 convention. A party split might easily occur were Coolidge to anger Pinchot sufficiently.

On August 23 Pinchot again telephoned Coolidge to inform him that wildcat walkouts had already begun, and that he was prepared to act in the situation if nothing was forthcoming from the White House. Coolidge invited him to Washington, where the two men, together with Coal Commissioner John Hays Hammond, discussed the situation. Although later accounts differ, it seems Coolidge proposed to order an investigation of conditions at the mines and, if necessary, provide mediation services. In any event, Pinchot left Washington with the title of Special Coal Strike Mediator, believing he had the president's support to act on his own. Then a White House press release implied that he was doing so in cooperation with federal officials. Pinchot would have known of charges that Coolidge had attempted to snatch credit for action in the police strike from Curtis, and might have concluded this was happening in the coal walkouts.

The strike began on September 1, when Lewis called out 150,000 miners. Pinchot did attempt mediation, and on September 7 the two sides agreed to a 10 percent wage increase, a checkoff, and an eight-hour workday. The settlement was ratified on September 17. Coolidge publicly praised Pinchot and did what he could to mollify the fiery governor, but this wasn't enough to turn the trick, and Pinchot started to explore the possibility of a run for the presidency in 1924.

Most newspapers believed Coolidge would have little trouble obtaining the Republican presidential nomination. How could he possibly be cast aside? The *Columbus Dispatch* tried to imagine a scenario in which this might happen.

> One would be such a rising of the more radical element
> in the Republican Party as would take control of it

wholly out of the hands of the Coolidge supporters, even at the risk of a split fatal to the party's chances in the election. The other would be such a failure in the administration of President Coolidge as would make it impossible to hold the party together in his support.

This did not take into account the matter of scandal. On October 22, a month and a half before Congress was due to reconvene, the Senate Committee on Public Lands met to investigate the naval reserves oil leases at Elk Hill and Teapot Dome.

The naval reserves at Elk Hill had been established in 1912, and the one at Teapot Dome three years later. At the time the navy had been converting the fleet from coal to oil, and it was feared that the supply of oil would be too small to meet future needs. Thus, the need for the reserves was deemed pressing.

In the spring of 1922 a Wyoming citizen wrote to his senator, John Kendrick, complaining that some of the Teapot Dome reserves had been secretly leased by Interior Secretary Fall to the Mammoth Oil Company, which was controlled by Harry Sinclair, an important contributor to the Republican Party. Fall had convinced Harding to transfer control of the land from the Navy Department to the Interior Department. He testified that he had leased Teapot Dome to the Sinclair Oil Company, in return for a royalty and the construction of a pipeline to Kansas City. He also leased the Elk Hill, California, reserve to the Pan-American Petroleum and Transportation Company, headed by an old friend, Edward Doheny, in return for a royalty and construction of storage tanks. Secretary Fall explained that the oil was being drained, quite legally, by wells on adjoining lands. As a result, the reserves would be depleted in a few years. By leasing the land, Fall argued, the government received revenues that would otherwise be lost. Senator La Follette doubted this and called for an investigation.

By right of seniority, La Follette should have chaired the investigation, but he was busy with other matters, so the chairmanship fell to conservative Republican Reed Smoot, who had been friendly with Harding. But La Follette trusted the investigating committee because it included Democrat Thomas Walsh of Montana.

Walsh was a colorful character. He was born in Wisconsin on the eve of the Civil War, spent a year at the University of Wisconsin, whereupon he took and passed the bar examination, and he and his brother set off for the Dakota Territory to set up his practice. One day, according to an oft-told story, he and his brother came to a river. Walsh's brother gazed at it for a while, and said, "Tom, isn't that river flowing north?" "Yes," said Walsh. After a moment of silence, his brother remarked, "Tom, let's go on. I don't feel right about a place where the rivers run north and Irishmen vote the Republican ticket."

In 1890 Walsh moved to Montana, where he entered local politics. He won election to the Senate in 1912, where he soon became known for his fiery temper, capacity for hard work, intelligence, integrity—and his exaggerated long black handlebar mustache. By 1923 the mustache had turned to gray, and Walsh had earned a reputation for his maverick stances and independence.

At first the committee could find no wrongdoing. Secretary Fall testified that he had received no compensation from Sinclair or Doheny. Secretary of the Navy Denby said he had no idea why the transfer of the lands had taken place. Then Walsh called in experts who contradicted Fall, testifying that there would have been little loss through drainage. Doheny was called to the stand, and said he thought there were at least 250 million barrels in the reserve. "I would say that we will be in bad luck if we do not get $100 million profit."

While this was happening Walsh learned that Fall, who had not been a wealthy man in 1921, had been purchasing land and made improvements on his properties, which along with other expenditures came to more than $175,000. How did he come by such a sum? Pleading illness, Fall sent the committee a letter in which he said he had obtained $100,000 from Edward McLean, a prosperous friend. This seemed plausible, since McLean was known to have an open purse for those close to him. McLean promptly verified this, but when Walsh asked for canceled checks, McLean replied he gave Fall cash, which seemed odd. Under pressure, McLean admitted he had not made the loan. Fall now acknowledged he had not taken money from McLean, but received it from another person. Who was that person? Fall refused to say.

In the midst of the Teapot Dome and Elk Hill investigations, Director of the Veterans Administration Charles Forbes agreed to testify before another congressional committee. He tried to exonerate himself, but failed to do so, and was bound over for trial for conspiracy to defraud the government.

On January 3, 1924, Democratic Senator Thad Caraway of Arkansas introduced a measure to ask the president to cancel Sinclair's lease on the grounds that it had been obtained through bribery. On January 23, Caraway, who spoke often on the matter, called Fall a "traitor," and implied others were involved in the affair.

On January 24 Doheny appeared before the committee, stating that on November 30, 1921, he had made a loan of $100,000 to Fall. Doheny said it wasn't a major transaction, "no more than $25 or $50 perhaps to the ordinary individual." It was in cash, contained in a satchel. Clearly, it was a bribe. Further evidence was introduced indicating that Sinclair had lent Fall another "$25,000 or $50,000." Sinclair had also presented Fall with some blooded cattle and prize hogs.

When the full story was known, the country learned that Fall had taken more than $400,000 in bribes and payoffs. Secretary Fall had miscalculated badly by not taking the full measure of Senator Walsh. Had Fall said immediately that he had received a loan from his old comrade, and had Doheny verified it, the matter might have been dropped. As it was, the Fall–Doheny connection was to form the foundation for the Teapot Dome scandal.

Under further questioning, Doheny testified that Fall was not the only government official with whom he had dealings. He declared that he himself was a Democrat and as such had attended the 1920 convention as a delegate. He was an important contributor to both the Democratic and the Republican Parties, and several Wilson administration figures had been on his payroll. He proceeded to tick off the names of four cabinet members, including William Gibbs McAdoo, the leading contender for the 1924 presidential nomination. McAdoo had been retained as his attorney for $25,000 a year during the Wilson administration.* Later it came out that he was also to receive a $900,000 contingency fee. "I hired them for their influence," said Doheny, and the meaning was unmistakable.

---

* Recall that McAdoo was Wilson's son-in-law as well as secretary of the treasury and a front-runner for the 1920 Democratic nomination.

The *New Republic* wanted to know more about this:

> Just what Mr. Doheny hoped to get in return remains to
> be explained, but it looks as if it might have something
> not unlike personal political influence. If this is true, Mr.
> McAdoo was converting his former public positions...
> into a source of enormous private profit.

As Teapot Dome attracted more attention, rumors flew that others in the cabinet had been involved in the matter. Some thought that Coolidge, who sat in on cabinet meetings, not only knew what was going on and did nothing about it, but may have been involved himself. Hearing such talk, Coolidge started to move, but cautiously. He dispatched a representative of the Justice Department to observe the committee hearings "on account of certain rumors which came to me," but that was all he intended to do for the moment. At the January 25 press conference he addressed the Caraway allegations:

> I don't recall that the proposal to make a lease of the oil
> lands was ever discussed in the cabinet, before I became
> president. I don't say that it wasn't. But I don't recall. I
> think I should have recalled, had it been discussed at any
> length or referred to.

To another question Coolidge said that he intended to protect the interests of the country and see to it that wrongdoers were properly punished. He added, "You can't start a criminal action on mere rumor." When the Senate called for Denby's resignation, Coolidge refused to comment.

The inclusion of Democrats in the developing scandal did not blunt aggressive Democrats and progressive Republicans from furthering the investigation. On Sunday, January 26, Walsh told the Public Lands Committee that he intended to submit a resolution giving the president the authority to cancel the oil leases and appoint an independent special counsel to investigate the entire affair. This would force Coolidge to act, and at the same time prevent him from putting the matter in the hands of Harry Daugherty, who by now was suspected of being heavily involved in all of these affairs. Daugherty was a prime Democratic and progressive Republican target.

The president was in a delicate position. Nothing he did would mollify progressive Republicans and the Democrats. Moreover, if he moved swiftly and decisively, he would anger Republican conservatives. If he attempted to slow the investigations, he might pacify some conservative Republicans, but it would also stir rumors that he was trying to hide something. If, however, the corruption proved bipartisan, as Doheny suggested it was, and he took an important role in the investigations, Coolidge could win popular support.

At the time, Coolidge was on the presidential yacht *Mayflower* conferring with Butler and several other advisors. He returned to the White House and consulted further with members of the Justice Department. Then he dictated a statement that was released to the press. After promising to prosecute any criminal acts, he outlined his plan:

> I feel the public is entitled to know that in the conduct
> of such actions no one is shielded for any party,
> political, or other reasons. As I understand, men are
> involved who belong to both political parties, and
> having been advised by the Department of Justice that it
> is in accord with former precedents, I propose to employ
> special counsel of high rank, drawn from both political
> parties, to bring such actions for the enforcement of
> the law.

Thus, Coolidge, not Walsh, would take the credit for the next move.

Secretary Fall appeared before the investigating committee on February 2. He pleaded the Fifth Amendment and refused to testify. Meanwhile, House Majority Leader Nicholas Longworth noted that Wilson's navy secretary, Josephus Daniels, had also removed land from the public domain and sold it to private interests.

Coolidge next did something that would become quite familiar in Washington half a century later: he searched for special counsels to investigate the matters. On January 29 he named former Attorney

General Thomas Gregory, a Democrat, and Silas Strawn, a Republican, but both men's names had to be withdrawn because of Gregory's prior connections with Doheny, while Strawn was rejected by the Public Lands Commission. At that point George Pepper suggested that Coolidge consider Owen Roberts, a distinguished Philadelphia lawyer. At Coolidge's request, Roberts came to the White House and Coolidge interviewed him. It went well; "I don't see any reason why I shouldn't appoint this man," the president said, and he did. To balance things, the second counsel was to be former Democratic Ohio Senator Atlee Pomerane. Both men were confirmed, and set to work. With this, the matter was taken out of Walsh's hands, and by so acting Coolidge did much to defuse Teapot Dome as a credible issue in the 1924 election. Quickly most of the leases were declared invalid, and the two counsels moved to liquidate the private holdings.

With this done, Democratic Senator Joseph Robinson of Arkansas called for Denby's resignation on the grounds of misconduct. His resolution passed, as ten Republicans joined the united Senate Democrats. After consulting with Borah, to whom he had become close, Coolidge sent the Senate a statement that such a resolution was not binding on him. "I do not propose to sacrifice any innocent man for my own welfare, nor do I propose to retain in office any unfit man for my own welfare." Denby resigned a week later. In his letter accepting the resignation, Coolidge said, "You will go with the knowledge that your honesty and integrity have not been impugned." By the time all of the evidence was in, the verdict was that Denby had been inept and foolish, but he was not venal or involved with illegal activities.

Fall's physicians stated he was too ill to appear before the committee again. Sinclair followed Fall's lead by pleading the Fifth Amendment and refusing to testify. The committee's agenda appeared to have run out. The malefactors had been caught, and now the matter should have gone to the courts. But the committee wanted to inquire about Harry Daugherty, who owned a small amount of Sinclair Oil stock.

The full force of the Senate Democrats' focus was on Daugherty. Almost from the start of the Coolidge administration, Borah had recommended that Coolidge rid himself of the attorney general. Daugherty was aware that the Old Guard regarded him as a shady character. When the Teapot Dome and Elk Hill scandals broke, questions were raised as to whether Daugherty had provided Denby and Fall with legal opinions. There were no written opinions on file, and Daugherty denied under oath that he had been asked about the transfers. Were there unwritten opinions? Daugherty said there was no precedent for such practices, and he hadn't initiated one, but there was a connection to Sinclair, who had made a major contribution to the 1920 campaign and was friendly with Daugherty. The attorney general did help enforce the leases, but that was his job. There was talk, too, that he had grown wealthy while in government, but none of this was proven, and it never became the basis of legal action against him.

Daugherty must also have reflected that while he had been able to count on Harding's support due to his role at the convention and their friendship, he had no such relationship with Coolidge, who was a completely different kind of person. Harding might place friendship over ethics, but not the austere Coolidge. There were other signs of their cool relationship. At one point Coolidge indicated to Daugherty he might place him in charge of the investigation, but then turned to Roberts and Pomerane.

Even so, Coolidge stood by Daugherty. Raymond Robins, a veteran Republican, told Coolidge that he believed getting rid of Daugherty would be a popular move. The president responded:

> I will not so remove the attorney general, for two
> reasons. First, it is a sound rule that when the president
> dies in office, it is the duty of his successor for the
> remainder of that term to maintain the counselors and
> policies of the deceased president. Second, I ask you if
> there is any man in the cabinet for whom—were he still
> living—President Harding would more surely demand
> his day in court, would more surely *not* dismiss because
> of popular clamor than the man who was his closest
> personal and political friend? I am satisfied that you are
> right, the people would be pleased, the party would be

helped, my campaign would be advanced, by the
summary removal of Mr. Daugherty. We shall have to
bear that burden. Regarding my being afraid to dismiss
Mr. Daugherty, I can assure you that if the attorney
general does any act I regard as wrong while I am
president, he will be removed.

The Daugherty affair was to be one of the earliest tests of the
Coolidge mettle.

Coolidge remained steadfast in early 1924. On the evening of
February 18 Borah urged the president to ask for Daugherty's resignation. While they were talking, Daugherty entered the room, as
arranged by Coolidge. He wanted to witness a verbal trial by com-
bat between the two to clarify his own thinking.

The next day Democratic Senator Burton Wheeler of Montana
introduced a resolution calling for an investigation of the Justice
Department, charging that it had been Daugherty's duty to prosecute
Fall, Denby, Sinclair, Doheny, and Forbes and had failed to do so.
Much of this was sheer innuendo. Wheeler, who was Walsh's first
term stablemate, was young, brash, and ambitious, and he utilized
the kinds of words that had been heard during the Red Scare.
According to him:

Recently when the oil scandal first developed it appears
the attorney general's name was mixed in it. It
appeared, if you please, that he was a friend of Ned
McLean. Everybody knows that he was a friend of
Doheny. Everybody knows that these three men met in
the apartment of the attorney general from time to
time. Everybody knows that Jess Smith, who was
brought from the state of Ohio and had an office in the
Department of Justice, and who was not on the
payroll, was accepting cases that arose in the
Department of Justice.

Coolidge conferred with Lodge, Borah, Pepper, Hughes, and
Hoover, all of whom wanted Daugherty out of the cabinet. Coolidge

clearly was troubled on this score. Just what was it that Daugherty had done to merit dismissal? This wasn't akin to the case of Fall, who clearly was a transgressor. Even Denby appeared more culpable.

Daugherty's memoir, *Inside the Harding Tragedy*, is of little help in the matter. It is a bitter, slanted, and self-serving document, yet it is difficult to escape the conclusion that there was much smoke and little fire in the Daugherty situation, and also that the real target was Coolidge himself. The president clearly was very popular with the public, although the GOP professional politicians did not care for him, and they were willing to cooperate with the Democrats if there was a way. It would be their excuse to find another nominee.

Thus it was with some trepidation that Slemp appeared as a witness on February 25. The committee questioned Slemp about telegrams he had sent and received in this period, and Caraway suggested that there was something sinister in that some of them had been coded. When Lodge rose to defend Coolidge and attack the Democrats who were attempting to smear him, some Democrats replied that Lodge, who had vilified Wilson mercilessly, was the last person to talk about such matters. In the end, the attacks backfired. Nothing was introduced that remotely tied Coolidge to the scandals, and he emerged stronger than ever.

On February 29 the Democrats sponsored Senate Resolution 180, asking Coolidge to direct the Secretary of the Treasury to turn over to the Public Lands Committee the income tax records of Doheny, Fall, and Sinclair. Coolidge refused to do so, stating this would be a violation of the Revenue Act of 1921.

The next assault came from Senator Wheeler of Montana, who charged Daugherty with criminal activities. Daugherty countered by charging Wheeler was a "leader of the International Workers of the World" and had once been indicted on bribery charges. Wheeler called two chief witnesses: Roxie Smith, Jess Smith's widow, who hated Daugherty, and Gaston Means, a former Treasury Department employee, who later boasted he had been accused of every crime in the book and convicted of none. In July 1924, however, Means's luck ran out. He was convicted of accepting bribes in a Prohibition-related charge, and was sentenced to two years in prison and a $10,000 fine. Means achieved some notoriety later by charging that

Harding had been murdered. Little material came out of the hearings, but in the process of the investigation Daugherty refused the committee access to some Justice Department files, and refused to testify. The committee turned up innuendoes, charges, and circumstantial evidence, but nothing that merited an indictment.

Nevertheless, the president by then had decided that Daugherty had to go. Borah was twisting the screws, threatening to ask for Daugherty's impeachment. Coolidge had already decided on a replacement, an old friend from Amherst, Harlan Fiske Stone, the former dean of Columbia Law School and a distinguished jurist. Stone had been recommended to Coolidge by Congressman Bertrand Snell, another Amherst man. To replace Denby, Borah suggested Curtis Wilbur, an Annapolis graduate who was serving as chief justice of the California Supreme Court. Both nominations were deemed outstanding, quite a change from Fall and Denby, or even Daugherty.

In the end, Coolidge prevailed upon Chief Justice William Howard Taft, with whom he had formed a strong relationship, to urge Daugherty to resign. But Daugherty would not give in without a fight. When learning on February 27 that Coolidge intended to ask for his resignation, he wrote to the president, arguing that he had "as much at stake as you have and you must do me the justice of assuring yourself on that point."

The refusal to turn over the Justice Department files provided Coolidge with the excuse to ask for his resignation on March 27. In his letter, Coolidge said:

> I am not questioning your fairness or integrity. I am
> merely reciting the fact that you are placed in two
> positions, one your personal interest, the other your office
> of attorney general, which may be in conflict. How can I
> satisfy a request for action in matters of this nature on the
> grounds that you, as attorney general, advise against it,
> when you are the individual against whom the inquiry is
> directed necessarily have a personal interest in it?

Daugherty's reply was immediate and forceful:

Your suggestion that an attack upon a cabinet officer disqualifies him from further official service is a dangerous doctrine. Mr. President, all the pretended charges against me are false. But, whether true or false, if a member of the cabinet is to be incapacitated or disqualified by the preferment of charges against him, no matter how malicious and groundless, and he is compelled to give up his responsible position and sacrifice his honor for the time being because of such attacks, no man in any official position is safe, and the most honorable, upright, and efficient public servants could be swept from office and stable government by clamor.

Nevertheless, Daugherty resigned the next day. The press approved. The *St. Louis Globe-Democrat*, an administration newspaper, wrote, "It is with regret and relief that we view the resignation—regret that it was forced by unfair and outrageous methods, relief that the government has been relieved of an embarrassment that was a great burden."

Daugherty intended to resume his law practice in Columbus, Ohio, but he couldn't escape censure. With the Republican convention about to begin, the Senate condemned the former attorney general by a vote of 70 to 2. From Columbus, Daugherty said that Wheeler was a dupe of the communists, and that the files he refused to surrender contained "abundant proof of the plans, purposes, and hellish designs of the Communist International."

Harlan Stone was appointed attorney general on April 2, and had no difficulty being confirmed. By then the country had wearied of the Harding scandals. The Wheeler hearings continued, but the committee was unable to demonstrate additional scandals or sensational revelations. Then, on April 8, Wheeler himself was indicted on a charge of unlawfully receiving a retainer from businessmen trying to obtain prospecting permits from Secretary Fall. The senator denied the allegations, and in time would be exonerated, but the tide of public opinion had turned against the committee. News of the hearings disappeared from the front pages and soon disappeared altogether. By late May, some sessions had not a single onlooker. By June, when the hearings ended, there were no indicted individuals besides Fall, Sinclair, and Doheny.

Coolidge emerged unscathed, and even treated the events with his trademark wit. Senator Wheeler later wrote of how he and Senator Walsh went to see the president about obtaining his support for a road in Montana:

> So when we went to the White House to discuss the matter, Coolidge didn't pay much attention to Walsh as he talked earnestly about the merits of a new road. The president gazed thoughtfully out the window into the rose garden. When Walsh finished, all Coolidge said, in his extra-dry manner, was: "Well, I don't want to see any scandal about it."

Of all Coolidge's actions during the trying period, his abandonment of Daugherty should have been the most bothersome. True, in two trials in 1927 and 1928 involving the American Metal Company, Daugherty appeared guilty of wrongdoing and possibly criminal action. It now appears he was intimately connected with bootleggers, and was on the take, but in 1924 nothing had been proved. In any case, the lack of an indictment by itself was no reason to retain a cabinet member who had become a liability. An election was coming up, and Coolidge was sweeping away the embarrassments before the convention. The generation that remembered the Red Scare might have reflected on the simple unfairness of the surrender. A generation that recalls the witch hunts of the late 1940s and early 1950s should do so as well. It was not one of Coolidge's finest moments.

Furthermore, it would not help him politically. The party leaders in the Senate may have wanted Coolidge to dispose of Daugherty, but not because they wanted to assist him to win election in his own right. Rather, they were thinking of congressional, state, and local races that might be lost had this not been done. Half a year after assuming the presidency, Coolidge still was extremely popular in the countryside, but not in Washington, where he remained the man the party leaders didn't want for second place in 1920 and were dubious about for 1924. This was a recipe for electoral success but political failure. It showed in the way Congress treated his legislative proposals. In his first State of the Union message, Coolidge had asked for more than thirty pieces of legislation. Only one of them, the Rogers Bill reorganizing the diplomatic service, was enacted as he wished. On the other hand, the Insurance Plan, known as the Soldier's Bonus Bill, passed both houses, was vetoed by Coolidge, and then passed over his veto, giving veterans a twenty-year paid-up insurance policy, for a cost to the government of $2 billion.

There was a solid majority in both parties for immigration restriction, and a bill—strongly supported by organized labor—to reduce immigration from 350,000 annually to 150,000 and to create a border patrol passed without much trouble. Coolidge signed the bill, but with some reluctance, because it singled out Japanese nationals as people who should be excluded from coming to America. In his State of the Union message he said:

> I regret the impossibility of severing from it the exclusion provision, which, in the light of existing law, affects especially the Japanese. I gladly recognize that the enactment of this provision does not imply any change in our sentiment of admiration and cordial friendship for the Japanese people, a sentiment which has had and will continue to have abundant manifestation. The bill rather expresses the determination of the Congress to exercise its prerogatives in defining by legislation the control of immigration instead of leaving it to international arrangements.

This did nothing to ease the situation. A less studied president might have vetoed the measure, but that was not the Coolidge style. Relations with the Japanese deteriorated. It was another step on the road to war.

Coolidge clearly had no real control over the Republican Congress. The *Kansas City Star*, generally considered independent, wrote about the poor Republican record in Congress, and wondered "how those Republican senators and representatives who have opposed the Coolidge policies and have voted to override his vetoes can say anything for the party candidate without condemning themselves." Other newspapers remarked that it wasn't only the progressives and the farm bloc that opposed Coolidge. An independent newspaper, the *Milwaukee Journal*, put the matter bluntly: "To the blindest of partisans it should now be evident that President Coolidge has no control over his party." The paper noted, "The captains on his staff listen to his commands and then do as they please." It resembled a war, thought the *St. Joseph News-Press*: "The GOP must take sides one way or another—either with the president and against Congress, or with Congress and against the president. There is no half-way ground." The Democratic *New York Post* ran a column with Coolidge quotes on legislation to one side and the Republican congressional action in opposition on the other.

Yet most of the newspapers—Republican, Democratic, and independent—also agreed that the public was behind Coolidge. Polls showed that Coolidge enjoyed support from all parts of the nation. The independent *St. Louis Globe-Democrat* wrote:

> The people are sick of congressional inefficiency and
> turmoil, they are sick of the lack of cohesion and
> purpose, they are sick of the Senate's usurpation of the
> control of foreign affairs, sick of the domination by
> blocs and cliques, sick of its mistakes and its failures;
> and whether they elect a Republican or Democrat to the
> presidency they are going to demand that there be a
> leadership in the White House, and that that leadership
> shall have the support of the majority in Congress, so
> that constructive legislation can be deliberately and
> wisely planned and carried through, and that the
> administration of government be placed again upon
> the basis contemplated by the Constitution.

Coolidge, of course, was not that sort of leader. He lacked the stomach for daring battles that marked the administrations of Theodore Roosevelt and Woodrow Wilson. The Massachusetts politician who in his "Have Faith in Massachusetts" speech had recommended, "Don't hurry to legislate. Give administration a chance to catch up with legislation," had for a brief instant been superseded by the president who made those requests in the State of the Union speech. Which was the true Coolidge? For the remainder of his presidency, the former proved itself to be the dominant style of Calvin Coolidge.

10

....

In His Own Right

With the exception of the occasion of my notification, I did not attend any partisan meetings or make any purely political speeches during the campaign. I spoke several times at the dedication of a monument, the observance of the anniversary of an historic event, at a meeting of some commercial body, or before some religious gathering. The campaign was magnificently managed by William M. Butler and as it progressed the final result became more and more apparent.

The Autobiography of Calvin Coolidge

COOLIDGE CONCENTRATED MORE on domestic than on foreign problems while president—not because he was an isolationist, but because he knew there was little he could do about affairs in Europe and Asia, and there were positive things he might accomplish in the United States. The two domestic proposals Coolidge had hoped Congress would approve were the sale of government facilities at Muscle Shoals to private interests, and tax reform, both of which he had inherited from Harding. The one he wanted defeated was the McNary–Haugen bill, which dealt with farm surpluses. It was the measure of America's unclouded vista that such matters, important only to local and special interests, could be priorities to the president of the United States.

In March 1924 the House approved the sale of the Muscle Shoals complex to Henry Ford by a vote of 227 to 142. A series of hear-

ings before the Senate Agriculture Committee followed. Chairman
George Norris opposed the sale, and the Agriculture Committee
voted against the Ford offer. In disgust, the industrialist withdrew his
bid, and no other bidder appeared—Ford's offer was apparently not
too low, as Norris and his supporters had argued.

The Muscle Shoals situation distressed Coolidge more than most
of his legislative defeats, and he said, "If anything were needed to
demonstrate the almost utter incapacity of the national government
to deal with an industrial and commercial property, it has been provided by this experience."

In time Muscle Shoals would develop along the lines Norris had
wanted, but only when approved by a different kind of president
with a different approach in startlingly different times—when
President Franklin D. Roosevelt instituted the Tennessee Valley
Authority during his first Hundred Days. But this was not the kind
of project a president of the Harding–Coolidge stripe could have
been expected to accept.

For the short run, the affair intensified progressive Republican
opposition to Coolidge, and made a challenge to his nomination or
a third party candidacy more likely, but Coolidge's stance in the matter helped him dispose of a potential rival in the upcoming presidential race. For a while there had been talk of a Henry Ford
candidacy in 1924. The *Wall Street Journal* even ran an editorial asking, "Why Not Ford For President?" Ford, a Democrat, appealed
to certain segments of the population. Farmers appreciated his distrust of urban America, his production of the Model T, and his
pledge to provide inexpensive fertilizers had he taken over at Muscle
Shoals. His anti-Semitic and anti-Catholic proclivities, combined
with more than a touch of xenophobia, appealed to Klan members.
Nevertheless, Ford appreciated Coolidge's support of the Muscle
Shoals sale, and in December 1923 he endorsed the president: "I
would never for a moment think of running against Calvin Coolidge
for president on any ticket whatever."

Throughout his presidency Coolidge would oppose several versions of the McNary–Haugen bill. This measure had its origins in
agricultural despair following World War I. High food prices had
encouraged farmers to expand their holdings and invest in machin-

ery. Wheat acreage rose from forty-eight million acres to more than seventy-five million between 1914 and 1919. Iowa farmland that sold for $82 an acre in 1910 went for $200 in 1920. Then, as a result of the European recovery, American farm exports slumped from $4.1 billion in 1919 to $1.9 billion in 1922. Commodity prices collapsed in the face of oversupply, with corn and wheat leading the way. Land prices declined sharply, especially in the Midwest. There was some recovery after 1922, but the circumstances in the nation's agricultural heartland remained serious, and farmers there called for government assistance.

The situation was more complicated than it appeared. According to the Department of Agriculture, using 1910–1914 as a base of 100, farm income, which was 259.7 in 1919 and fell to 96.8 in 1921, rose to a decade high of 171.2 in 1924. By this measure, the farmers, in the aggregate, were better off in the mid-1920s than they had been before the war. Even so, they were not as well off as nonfarmers, whose incomes were at 184.1 in 1924. Nor was there a mass exodus from the farms, as might have been expected if conditions had been as dire as portrayed. However, the agricultural sector was shrinking. In 1921 the farm population was 31.8 million; in 1924 it was 30.1 million; and in 1929, 30.2 million. Since the total population was expanding, the percentage of Americans on farms declined. In 1880 three out of every four Americans lived in rural areas; by 1930 it was less than one out of every two.

Part of the reason for these anomalies results from the use of aggregates in presenting the farm picture. There was a world of difference between the truck farmers in the Northeast, the cotton and tobacco farmers in the South and Southwest, the wheat and corn farmers of the Midwest, and the citrus growers of Florida and California. Their agendas were as different as their crops. Also, because of the increased productivity of farmers resulting from mechanization, the use of superior fertilizers, and improved management, the country didn't require as many farmers as before. Even so, those farmers who were suffering wanted help, and rallied behind the McNary–Haugen bill.

McNary–Haugen was a plan whereby farmers would sell their surpluses to the government, which would then market them abroad. In 1924 agricultural surpluses included wheat, corn, cotton, wool, cattle, sheep, swine, and flour. Since McNary–Haugen would remove excess agricultural goods from the domestic market, domestic prices would rise and benefit the farmers. Foreign competition would be kept out by high tariffs. The government would sell the surplus at world prices, and the losses would be made up through an "equalization fee" charged to the farmers who produced that particular crop.

It was a contentious measure. Midwestern farmers, especially in wheat, strongly supported McNary–Haugen, and expressed themselves through the farm bloc in the Senate. However, cotton farmers in the South and West and the more diversified eastern farmers tended to oppose the measure, as did fruit farmers.

Coolidge believed that raising agricultural prices would encourage farmers to increase their production, which would require more subsidies, and the process would be repeated. As an alternative, he favored cooperative marketing arrangements made without government intervention. His opposition to McNary–Haugen hardened the antagonism of the progressives and the farm bloc.

The bill was introduced in the House during the next session and defeated on June 3 on a sectional vote, 155 to 233, with the Midwest in favor and the South and East opposed. But the matter did not die; it was to be an important issue for the rest of the decade.

After his well-received address to Congress and subsequent announcement of his candidacy, there was little doubt Coolidge would receive the Republican nomination. Coolidge, like Roosevelt before him, would successfully defy the tradition that presidents who succeed on the death of predecessors have no chance of receiving the nomination on their own. By then, too, Slemp was working effectively behind the scenes to assure Coolidge's success. Slemp managed to alter a rule adopted in 1920 reducing the number of delegates from Mississippi, South Carolina, and Georgia, states all safely for Coolidge, and restored their old strengths. He called in favors throughout the country, not an onerous task, since Coolidge was quite popular in his own right. While Slemp was winning solid southern support, Butler was taking care of matters in the Northeast.

Outgoing National Committee Chairman John Adams scouted the Midwest and Far West, while Chief Justice William Howard Taft wrote letters to his large circle of friends and admirers on Coolidge's behalf. Coolidge was in control of the situation and was willing to use his power to advance his interests. Johnson and Lowden had wanted the convention to be held in Chicago, the former for its progressive tradition, the latter because it was in Illinois. At Coolidge's behest, the national committee selected Cleveland as the host city.

One by one potential rivals dropped aside. Only Lowden remained as a possible threat. The former governor experienced renewed approval after the bruising 1920 convention. By the summer of 1924 he was being urged to run for the governorship or the Senate. After Harding's death several prominent Republicans, among them former Speaker Joe Cannon, offered to endorse him publicly, and Lowden confided to a friend that it was "very likely" he would challenge Coolidge. Aware of this, Coolidge offered Lowden the ambassadorship to the United Kingdom, which would get him into the administration and out of the country. Lowden rejected the offer.

For a while Lowden thought the Harding scandals might damage Coolidge, but when the president emerged unscathed, Lowden gave up on the idea of a run. Governor Pinchot, once an almost certain challenger, also backed down. Hiram Johnson, who believed he had been cheated of the nomination in 1920, remained in the field, but he was a long shot. La Follette was there once again, but he knew he didn't stand a chance in the GOP, and so he prepared to revive the Progressive Party and make the run as its candidate. Thus, in early 1924, Coolidge knew he would obtain the nomination without serious opposition. "We cannot now see that anything can prevent my nomination on the first ballot at the Republican Convention, but one never knows what will happen in politics."

Only Johnson remained to contest Coolidge. Johnson's name was entered in the primaries, and in March he defeated Coolidge by a slim margin in North Dakota. The biggest challenge would come in California, Johnson's home state, and there the Coolidge machine swung into action early. Hoover was deputized to take charge of the campaign, and won support for his progressive stances and conservative statements. Coolidge won the primary and ended Johnson's bid for the nomination.

Johnson could not have had much hope given the nation's condition, which was quite agreeable. The 1921 GNP had been a depressed $69.9 billion; for 1923 it came to $85.1 billion, and would go on to $93.1 billion in 1924. This worked out to a growth rate of 9 percent from 1921 to 1924, much of it due to the shabby condition of the economy in 1921. In this same span the consumer price index fell from 53.6 to 51.2, and the unemployment rate from 11.7 percent to 5 percent. There had been a budget surplus of $291 million in 1920, which rose to $509 million in 1921, $736 million in 1922, declined slightly to $712 million in 1923, and rose to $963 million in 1924.

In 1923 a record 3.6 million automobiles were sold; 3.2 million were sold the following year. Radio sales skyrocketed; 2.7 million households had receivers in 1924, more than twice as many as in 1923. Statistics for refrigerators, washing machines, vacuum cleaners, and clothing were taking off. In the aggregate, Americans had never been so well off, and the prospects for the future were pleasing. There were some soft spots in the economy, to be sure—coal mining, textiles, some farm products, among others—but for the rest, prosperity was the rule.

Coolidge, who continued to work in the White House and did not attend the convention, signed the 1924 Revenue Act as the Republicans gathered. It was not the bill he had preferred, as a coalition of progressive Republicans and Democrats had hacked away at the Mellon proposals. In its final form the measure cut taxes for all levels of income. Missing were those tax increases on the wealthy he had asked for, and the decrease in the surcharge was less than what he had wanted. The estate tax was increased, and a new gift tax was to go into effect. Thus, the measure that reached his desk was not what Coolidge had wanted, and he said so in his message. "A correction of its defects may be left to the next session of Congress," he said. "I trust a bill less political and more economic may be passed at that time. To that end I shall bend all my energies." In this fashion, Coolidge indicated that he would consider his election a sign of public approval for his stand on taxes, and expected the congressional Republicans to do the same. Yet the Republican Congress, just before adjourning, had defied a Republican president certain of renomination on this key issue, clearly illustrating Coolidge's standing within his own party.

In another instance, Coolidge vetoed the Bursum pension bill, which would have increased the pensions of soldiers who had served in the Civil, Indian, and Spanish–American Wars, and of their dependents. His veto was upheld. Just before Congress adjourned, he vetoed a measure to increase the salaries of postal employees, which would have added $69 million annually to government expenses. In his message Coolidge observed that the Post Office workers had had three wage increases since 1919, and that they were already better paid than the average government worker. He noted that in 1923 the salaries for postal clerks were $1,750, a 110 percent increase over the 1918 figure. Coolidge favored making the Post Office Department self-supporting and independent of federal largesse—an idea that would not come to fruition for another six decades.

After Coolidge had been nominated, Judson Welliver, the presidential assistant who had become a well-regarded journalist, wrote that such policies put Coolidge at odds with his party, but endeared him to the voting public:

> Individuals might disagree with some of his vetoes, might disapprove of some of the measures he advocated, might favor policies he opposed. But all that was unimportant compared to the fact that he was constantly demonstrating a calm, simple, unhesitating courage in his convictions. Moreover, his convictions seemed to coincide with a decidedly preponderant public opinion.
>
> To have won his nomination in such a time of turmoil; to have gained so remarkable a testimony of public confidence at the very time when it might have seemed that all the fates were in a conspiracy against him—this is the big, impressive achievement of President Coolidge. Whatever may be the standing of his party,

it has been made as plain as anything in politics can be,
that he holds the confidence of the masses of his party.
He has won that confidence in a time so brief, and in the
face of difficulties so great, as to make the
accomplishment unique in our politics.

Although Coolidge had no serious opposition for the presidential nomination, the vice presidential contest was wide open. Coolidge had earlier announced that he would not interfere, and allowed the delegates to select his running mate. The leading prospects were Lowden and Charles Dawes, the director of the Budget Bureau. There was some talk of Johnson, Borah, and a handful of others, but this was not taken too seriously. Ordinarily these candidates would be dismissed outright, but memories of 1920 dictated that one of them might sway the convention.

There were two sticky, emotional issues in 1924. One was Prohibition, for which Coolidge had a simple response: Congress had passed the Volstead Act, and he would support it. But he also said, "Any law that inspires disrespect for other laws—the good laws—is a bad law." In his own oblique manner, Coolidge made his meaning quite clear.

Prohibition continued to breed lawlessness; in 1923 the Justice Department complained that it "has been called upon to prosecute a member of the judiciary, prominent members of the American bar, high officials of federal and state governments. The sordid story of assassination, bribery, and corruption has been found in the very sanctums where the law was presumed to be sacred." In response, Coolidge convened a meeting of the nation's governors for October 20 to consider the matter of enforcing the Volstead Act.

With this in mind, brewer Adolph Busch, a leader of the moderate anti-Prohibitionists, wrote to the new president, stating:

Mr. President, we have always stood for law
enforcement and real temperance. We recognize that
we labor under the disadvantage of having our
motives misunderstood, but we hope that you will at
least give us some credit for our interest in good

citizenship and genuine temperance.... An unpopular statutory control of individual habits can never be substituted for voluntary temperance, individual self-restraint and reasonable statutory regulation. The law should be written in terms of temperance and reasonable regulation; then the evils of the present system would disappear.

Coolidge never indicated what he thought of this position. He replied with a noncommittal "Thank you," and let it go at that.

Under Prohibition, scores of organizations formed to demand outright repeal of the Eighteenth Amendment or its modification. The Association Against the Prohibition Amendment, the Moderation League, and the Constitutional Liberty League were three of the more prominent. The American Federation of Labor was also in favor of a drastic overhaul of the law. All had lobbying groups in Washington. So did the forces favoring Prohibition, but they also had a political party. On the day before the GOP convention, the Prohibition Party held its convention in Columbus, Ohio, and nominated H.P. Faris for the presidency, and a woman, Maria Brehm, for the vice presidency.

The second thorny issue was the Ku Klux Klan, which posed more of a problem for the Democrats than for the Republicans, but it still had to be addressed in Cleveland. Unlike the earlier Klan, this one contained Republicans as well as Democrats. The Klan had been reorganized by Colonel William Simmons of Atlanta in 1915. The organization was more than just anti-black, anti-Catholic, and anti-Semitic; the Klan offered a broad program aimed at "uniting native-born white Christians for concerted action in the preservation of American institutions and the supremacy of the white race." It conducted a crusade against foreign-born citizens of all religions, and was strongly pro-farmer, pro–poor Americans, and anti–Wall Street. The Klan program, which was clearly articulated and forcefully presented, demanded "100 percent Americanism," and had broad appeal.

This new Klan was more northern and midwestern than the post–Civil War organization had been—some major centers of activity were Oregon, Maine, Kansas, California, Texas, and Long Island,

New York. At its height the Klan had some four million members and was a potent national political force. Texas Klansman Earle Mayfield was a U.S. Senator, as was Samuel Ralston of Indiana, and the governors of Georgia, Alabama, California, and Oregon had won their seats with Klan support.

Both sides were prepared for a struggle. R.B. Creagar, a GOP national committeeman from Texas, was in Cleveland to work for an anti-Klan plank in the platform, which read, "We condemn any or all secret organizations founded on racial or religious intolerance, and oppose all secret political societies as being against the spirit of the American people." Imperial Wizard Hiram Evans arrived in Cleveland to work against this condemnation.

Coolidge said nothing directly regarding the Klan, but he was not morally neutral on the issue of race. Harding and Coolidge, presidents generally considered conservative, had much better records on this issue than the progressive Woodrow Wilson. Coolidge spoke out on the subject obliquely but unmistakably. On June 6 he delivered the commencement address at Washington's all-black Howard University—in itself an unusual move for the time. In his speech Coolidge touched on themes of interest to his audience. He spoke of the progress of American blacks, contrasting this with the lack of progress in Africa, indicating that one of the tasks for the graduates would be to assist in the modernization of that continent. Coolidge noted that at the time of Emancipation, there were four million black Americans—twelve thousand of whom owned their own homes, twenty thousand their farms—and the aggregate wealth of the race was growing rapidly.

> In a little over half a century since [Emancipation] the number of business enterprises operated by colored people has grown to nearly 80,000, while the wealth of the negro community has grown to nearly $1,100,000,000. And these figures convey a most inadequate suggestion of the material progress. The 2,000 business enterprises that were in the hands of colored people immediately following Emancipation, were almost without exception small and rudimentary.

More than 80 percent of all American negroes are now able to read and write; when they achieved their freedom not 10 percent were literate. There are nearly 2,000,000 negro pupils in the public schools; well-nigh 40,000 negro teachers are listed, more than 3,000 following their profession in normal schools and colleges. The list of educational institutions devoting themselves to the race includes 50 colleges, 13 colleges for women, 26 theological schools, a standard school of law, and two high grade institutions of medicine.

In the context of 1924, these statements constituted a liberal attitude toward black America. But to underline his thoughts, Coolidge talked about contributions during the war. "The propaganda of prejudice and hatred which sought to keep the colored men from supporting the national cause completely failed. The black man showed himself the same kind of citizen, moved by the same kind of patriotism, as the white man." Coolidge's position on this issue was clear; what concrete measures he initiated was another matter.

The Republican Convention opened on June 10 in a celebratory mood. It was, as expected, quite placid and totally unlike the 1920 convention, which had been marked by uncertainty and drama.

From the first the convention was Coolidge-controlled insofar as operations and agenda were concerned, with William Butler, the new national chairman, carrying out his wishes. At this convention Henry Cabot Lodge was nothing more than a delegate, a sign that a new era had arrived. For the first time in a quarter of a century—except for 1912, when he had not been present—Lodge would not serve on any committee. Nor would he head the Massachusetts delegation; that position would to go to Governor Channing Cox, a staunch Coolidge man. Butler wouldn't even provide Lodge with a decent hotel room. At one point in the proceedings some of the delegates started to boo him, and others picked up on it. It was a sad end for the proud old man, who would die four months later.

Lodge was not the only prominent figure of the 1920 convention who either was relegated to minor status or had died since then. As mentioned, Crane had died in October 1920, before the election. Philander Knox died in October 1921, and Penrose on the last day of that year. Frank Brandegee died days before Lodge, and Chauncey De Pew went in April 1928; neither man attended the Cleveland convention. Nor did La Follette, Borah, Pinchot, and former Speaker Joe Cannon, who would die in November 1926. Had they been there, these men would have had only secondary roles.

There were still bosses within the party, but none had the power or influence of Penrose and others in 1920. Regionalism was fading in the 1920s, and, with the arrival of radio, communication between candidates and the public would be far easier and more effective in the future. Indeed, the GOP convention of 1924 was the first to be carried over the airwaves. Back room deals were still struck, but not by the powerful brokers of the past.

Early in the convention Butler attempted to provide women delegates with equal representation on the National Committee, not unusual since both major parties were wooing female voters. After a bitter and acrimonious debate Butler won his point, but in defiance of his wishes, the Old Guard representatives managed to elect Paul Howard, chief counsel for Daugherty during the investigations, as chairman of the Rules Committee. Butler also learned that the progressive Republicans would be watching the vice presidential situation to gauge Coolidge's attitude toward them, in preparation for a possible bolt. Butler could not quell the opposition felt by some of the Old Guard and those progressive Republicans. Coolidge hoped they would not defect if, as expected, La Follette ran as an independent.

The *New York Times* suggested a short platform: "Coolidge, that's all," but in the end the Platform Committee produced a long document, which the *Times* thought was "not only verbose but labored," as are most platforms. It began with a tribute to Warren Harding, and then went on to catalogue the sorry state of the nation in 1921 and compare it with the prosperity America enjoyed in the summer of 1924. As expected, the Republicans took credit for all of this:

> We believe that the achievement of the Republican
> administration in reducing taxation by $1,250,000,000
> per annum; reducing of the public debt by

$2,432,000,000; installing a budget system; reducing the public expenditures from $5,500,000,000 per annum to approximately $3,400,000,000 per annum, thus reducing the ordinary expenditures of the government to substantially a pre-war basis, and the complete restoration of the public credit; the payment or refunding of $7,500,000,000 of public obligations without disturbance of credit or industry—all during the short period of three years—presents a record unsurpassed in the history of public finance.

Much of this, of course, occurred during the Harding years. The Republicans were implying that the way to keep prosperity was to keep Coolidge in the White House.

The rest of the platform was also an echo of 1920. The Republicans came out for a protective tariff and membership in the World Court, and congratulated themselves for improving relations with Mexico. While opposing McNary–Haugen, they favored higher tariffs on agricultural products, lower freight rates, and especially cooperative marketing, which had become Coolidge's standard response to farmers' demands for aid. The party also favored an amendment prohibiting child labor, which had been discussed since before World War I. The Republicans defended the immigration laws, and called for improvements in highways and assistance to commercial aviation. There was no mention either of Prohibition or race relations. The closest the GOP came to dealing with the Klan was a bland statement to the effect that "the Republican Party reaffirms its unyielding devotion to the Constitution and to the guarantees of civil, political, and religious liberty contained therein."

The opening of the convention was front-page news, but the public's attention was being diverted by the Leopold–Loeb murder case in Chicago. From Washington, La Follette called for railroad and farm legislation, as well as government control of Muscle Shoals— a warm-up for and preview of his near certain presidential bid on a third party ticket.

There were some light moments. On Thursday, June 12, the last survivor of the 1860 convention was presented and cheered, and a quartet from Plymouth sang some songs. Seventy-three-year-old Representative Theodore Burton of Iowa delivered a well-received keynote address containing a tribute to Harding. Former Congressman Frank Mondell of Colorado was named permanent chairman, and Marion Burton, president of the University of Michigan and a Coolidge friend who had been president of Smith College, nominated Coolidge, whom he characterized as "the virile man—the staunch American—the real human being—Calvin Coolidge!" Then came the usual seconding speeches. There were no further nominating speeches, so the roll call began. All the states gave Coolidge their votes except for Wisconsin, which cast twenty-eight for La Follette, and North Dakota, which gave La Follette six votes and Johnson ten. Then a South Dakota delegate moved the vote be made unanimous, and there were protests from the La Follette and Johnson people. The chairman announced, "With the exception of a very few voices the nomination of Calvin Coolidge for president of the United States is made unanimous." That was it.

Throughout the day rumors regarding the vice presidential choice were hatched and heard regularly. The names ranged from James Harbord, CEO of Radio Corporation of America and a war hero, to Herbert Hoover, Dawes, Borah, Lowden, William Kenyon of Iowa, and many more. Lowden had earlier disavowed any desire for the nomination, and Borah now did the same. It was no secret that Borah and the others considered themselves better qualified than Coolidge for the presidency. (A story holds that Coolidge, through an intermediary, approached Borah to ask him to join the ticket in 1924. "At which end?" Borah wanted to know.)

Then Butler sent out feelers to Kenyon, which became one of the convention's stranger episodes. Kenyon, a Republican from Iowa, had entered the Senate in 1911, and immediately became identified with the party's progressive wing. He supported Taft in 1912 and was considered a regular. Kenyon was outspoken in favor of trade unions, and he opposed entry into World War I but supported Wilson after the United States became a belligerent. In 1920 he had led the investigation into Republican campaign spending, and he attended the convention that year pledged to Hiram Johnson. Kenyon was a leading member of the farm bloc and one of its most effective organizers. Harding had offered him a federal judgeship to rid himself of this highly capable opponent. Since he had always wanted a judicial career, Kenyon accepted. One of his earliest decisions was in *United States* v. *Mammoth Oil*, in which he canceled the Teapot Dome leases and criticized the Harding administration. In 1924 he supported Coolidge for the nomination and urged Borah to accept the vice presidential designation.

Despite Kenyon's record, a Coolidge–Kenyon ticket would not have been hypocritical on the part of either man. Kenyon had always been a party loyalist, which would have made him acceptable to Coolidge. Besides, while vice president, Coolidge had become friendly with Kenyon, and later twice invited him to join his cabinet. Republican progressives would have applauded a Kenyon nomination, since it would be a sign to progressive voters that Coolidge was leaning in their direction and would thus be enough to convince them to remain in the party.

Butler might have thought that if Kenyon would accept a judgeship that removed him from a leadership position against Harding, he might accept a vice presidential nomination that would placate progressives. Trouble had already developed. The New York Republicans had split, with Senator James Wadsworth, an Old Guard stalwart who headed the delegation, urging Butler to select a conservative, while the progressives wanted Kenyon. When Butler's intentions became clear, the word went out that progressives would protest publicly unless Coolidge personally asked them to name Kenyon, which the president refused to do. The Wisconsin delegation then all but announced its intention to walk out and join La Follette. Other midwestern delegations were split on the issue. Butler had to do something to placate this group. In any case, Kenyon was not interested in the nomination, so Butler looked elsewhere.

Bascom Slemp was at the convention, and he was appalled at Butler's approach and strategy. Slemp favored a conservative regular, believing that the progressive voters would go for La Follette no matter who was in the second place on the GOP ticket, and that having a progressive on the ticket might lead moderate Republicans to vote for a Democrat or stay home. Butler persisted, and purportedly put out a feeler to the seventy-three-year-old Burton. When that fizzled,

Butler considered Hoover, again to please the progressive element, although he should have known that Coolidge would not accept the secretary of commerce.

What did these potential candidates have in common? All had roots in the Midwest. Coolidge, the New Englander, wanted the same combination as the party had in 1920, and that meant going to Harding country for the vice presidency. But at least equally important was Butler's attempt to keep the party united in the face of the La Follette challenge.

Butler's maneuvers continued as the vice presidential nominations were being made. Kenyon, Lowden, Senator James Watson of Indiana, Dawes, Senator Charles Curtis of Kansas, and Burton were placed in nomination. Lowden was ahead on the first ballot, and behind him in order were Kenyon and Burton. That Burton received so many votes was an indication of the convention's desire to honor him but also of an awareness that it was all over anyway. Lowden was the clear favorite.

Lowden was nominated on the second ballot. By then Coolidge had written Lowden a letter of congratulations, which was not sent, since Lowden's representative immediately announced his intention to decline the honor. With this, Butler recommended Hoover, but the convention turned instead to Dawes, with Hoover running a distant second.

Why Dawes? According to Dawes biographer Bascom Timmons, before Lowden announced his refusal, he spoke with Mark Woods of Lincoln, Nebraska. Woods had approached Dawes and suggested he support General John J. Pershing, only to learn that he favored Lowden. A political amateur, Woods didn't know what to do next, so he went to see another Dawes friend, the venerable William Jennings Bryan, who was covering the convention for a press syndicate, and who was quite friendly with both Pershing and Dawes. Bryan thought nominating Pershing would be difficult, since even the Nebraska delegation was split, with most for Kenyon. But one of the delegates, A.W. Jefferis, hoped to get the GOP senatorial nomination, and Woods convinced him to nominate Dawes— Jefferis wanted to be heard over the radio in Nebraska and win instant fame.

After Lowden's nomination, Woods approached some of those who had voted for him and won their support for Dawes in case Lowden declined (no candidate had refused the nomination since well before the Civil War). Then, when the rejection letter was read to the convention, the delegates went for Dawes, who received 682½ third ballot votes to Hoover's 234½. The candidate swiftly accepted.

Dawes was fifty-nine years old in 1924, seven years older than Coolidge. Throughout his life, Dawes was a maverick, hard to pin down or place in any category. The progressives considered him conservative, the conservatives, progressive. In reality, he was an independent who loved contention and entered many battles he must have known were unwinnable.

Dawes, a talented executive with an ability to get things done, had bounced back after being wiped out financially in the panic of 1893. He served as comptroller of the currency under McKinley, but he resigned in 1901 to run—unsuccessfully, as it turned out—for a Senate seat. From then on he stayed on the political periphery, working in banking and finance. During World War I, Dawes volunteered and served as head of the General Purchasing Board, which made him responsible for provisioning the army—and gave him control of vast amounts of money. Before the war ended, Dawes was promoted to brigadier general, and he became the military member of the United States Liquidation Commission, responsible for disposing of American supplies in France.

Dawes made his mark on the national consciousness in February 1920, when he was called to testify before the House Committee on War Expenditures. Eager to demonstrate Democratic malfeasance, the Republican-led committee probed deeply into matters of waste and corruption, going so far as to question the integrity of some of the witnesses. "Just how much thievery was there under the Democratic administration during the war?" asked Representative Frank Mondell, who became presiding officer at the 1924 convention. By the time he appeared before the committee, Dawes, who had a short fuse anyway, was quite upset. "Is it not true that excessive prices were paid for some articles?" he was asked. Dawes exploded. "When Congress declared war, did it expect us to beat Germany at

20 percent discount?" he wanted to know. "Sure we paid high prices. Men were standing at the front to be shot at. We had to give them food and ammunition. We didn't stop to dicker. Why, man alive! We had a war to win! It was a man's job!"

For the next seven hours Dawes answered similar questions with shouts, near insults, and suggestions that the committee members didn't understand the demands of war and were simpletons. "Is it not true that excessive prices were paid for mules?" "Helen Maria!" Dawes shouted, "I would have paid horse prices for sheep, if the sheep could have pulled artillery to the front!" That day Dawes was not a Republican, but an executive defending his policies and actions by slashing out with scathing wit and righteous indignation at members of his own party.

When it was all over Dawes was front-page news. The "Helen Maria" was supposed to be an exclamation well-known in Nebraska, but the newspapers had it as "Hell and Maria"—from then on he was known as "Hell and Maria Charlie Dawes." While respected, he was almost immediately seen as a colorful eccentric, capable of making wild statements, down to smoking a strange pipe whose stem came out of the top rather than the bottom of the bowl.

Dawes did not seem like a politician, but rather a man of integrity and principle—qualities the public thought should mark their vice president. And he was certainly a man of many parts. Americans learned Dawes played the piano and flute, and composed music. One of his pieces, written at one sitting in 1911, was called "Melody in A Major." It became a popular concert piece soon after. Words were added, and the song, "Let Me Dream," was played often in the early 1920s. Then, in 1951, new lyrics were added, and what resulted was "It's All in the Game," one of the most popular songs of that year.

During the 1920 presidential campaign Harding had been attracted by an article Dawes had written entitled "How a President Can Save a Billion Dollars." After the election the new president-elect asked Dawes to serve as his secretary of the treasury. Dawes was not interested, but he convinced Harding to make him the first director of the budget. His effective work heading the Bureau of the Budget was one of the reasons Harding was able to turn in a surplus, which continued into the Coolidge years. It was the combination of the Harding–Coolidge tax cuts and the Dawes economy programs that enabled the government to show a large surplus in each year of the Harding–Coolidge presidency. Due in large part to the savings Dawes had generated, government spending declined from $5 billion in 1921 to $2.9 billion in 1924, the year he left office to run for the vice presidency.

In 1923 Dawes was asked to join the Committee of Experts of the Allied Reparations Committee, designed to rescue the German economy. Out of his work came the Dawes Plan, which stabilized the German currency on a gold basis, established the Reichsbank, revamped the tax structure, restructured the railroads, and authorized the issuance of railroad and industrial bonds to generate income to pay part of the reparations. Germany was granted a one-year moratorium on reparations payments, a cut of 80 percent in future annual payments, and a $200 million loan from the United Kingdom, France, and the United States. The Dawes Plan was hailed throughout Europe, and earned him additional fame in America, and for this he was to share the 1925 Nobel Peace Prize.

With this background, Dawes joined the Coolidge ticket, and he proved to be the right man for it. Once again, the Coolidge luck prevailed. The Coolidge–Dawes team, campaigning on a platform calling for lower taxes and government efficiency, had a good record in both areas. Where Coolidge was reticent and disliked campaigning, Dawes was made for the stump. Coolidge was an accidental president and Dawes an unexpected nominee, but it was a near-perfect ticket for the times. The Republicans had reason to celebrate when the convention adjourned.

On August 14 Coolidge formally accepted the nomination, and unsurprisingly lauded his party's accomplishments. From the start he spoke not of the Coolidge accomplishments, but of those of the Harding–Coolidge administration. "Perhaps in no peace-time period have there been more remarkable and constructive accomplishments than since March 1921."

Coolidge outlined what amounted to his personal stance on the issues. He paraphrased many sections of the platform, but added two of his own. "There should be no favorites and no outcasts; no race or religious prejudices in government. America opposes special privileges for any body and favors equal opportunity for every body." Then, to underline the thought, in another section he said: "As a plain matter of expediency the white man cannot be protected and as a plain matter of right and justice is justice for everybody." But Coolidge did not follow up with action.

He then stated his own credo in succinct, unmistakable but unremarkable terms:

> Many principles exist which I have tried to represent and propose to support. I believe in the American Constitution. I favor the American system of individual enterprise, and I am opposed to any general extension of government ownership and control. I believe not only in advocating economy in public expenditure, but in its practical application and actual accomplishment. I believe in a reduction and reform of taxation, and shall continue my efforts in that direction. I am in favor of protection. I favor the Permanent Court and further limitation of armaments. I am opposed to aggressive war. I shall avoid involving ourselves in the political controversies of Europe, but I shall do what I can to encourage American citizens and resources to assist in restoring Europe with the sympathetic support of our government. I want agriculture and industry on a sound basis of prosperity and equality. I shall continue to strive for the economic, moral, and spiritual welfare of my country.

A week after the Republicans adjourned in Cleveland, the Farmer–Labor Party met in St. Paul and nominated Duncan MacDonald for the presidency and William Bouck for the vice presidency. This regional party drew little attention; the Farmer–Laborites did not come out for La Follette as Republicans feared.

Republican hopes were given their greatest boost when the Democratic Party proceeded to commit political suicide at its New

York convention, which opened on June 24 in the midst of a heat wave and lasted until July 10. Like the Republicans, the Democrats had strong positions on agriculture, taxes, and the other economic issues, but the GOP had been able to finesse the Prohibition and Klan issues, while the Democrats were divided on both—and more.

During the primary season the odds-on favorite was McAdoo, who had been a front-runner four years earlier. No one in the party could claim a closer relationship with Wilsonian progressivism, which, if La Follette made a run, might appeal to liberal Republicans disgruntled with Coolidge yet not prepared to bolt their party for the seemingly radical La Follette. Like the other Democrats, however, McAdoo was tainted by the two issues. Though he did not seek Klan support, he had it. He was also a dry, which hurt him with the urban minority groups, the key to the Democratic vote in the eastern and midwestern cities.

McAdoo, however, had an impressive organization, and was expected to do well in the primaries, where his major opponent was Senator Oscar Underwood of Alabama. Underwood, who had entered Congress in 1895 and was the Democratic floor leader, also claimed progressive credentials, and was strongly in favor of the League of Nations. He was pro-business, unusual for politicians from his region. Underwood supported low tariffs because he believed the higher ones favored northern and midwestern business, and low tariffs would lead to business expansion and industrialization in the South. Privately Underwood deplored racism, believing it was one of the prime reasons for the poverty of southern whites. But he had opposed women's suffrage and Prohibition, at a time when the country voted dry and drank wet.

In the background was Governor Al Smith of New York, who represented a new kind of urban reformism. Smith seemed uninterested in the prewar progressive campaigns, concentrating instead on the rights of labor, environmental issues, and wages and unemployment insurance. He did not enter the primaries, conceding the Midwest, South, and Far West to McAdoo, who would have to battle favorite sons there and so earn their enmity. For the Smith supporters, who included Franklin D. Roosevelt, the real battleground would be the convention itself. All knew the key to the Smith campaign was the cities, and the candidacy would revolve around the issues of the Klan, Prohibition (Smith was a wet), and especially the candidate's Catholic religion.

McAdoo entered the Madison Square Garden Convention with an impressive delegate count, having done well in the primaries and winning support in state houses. But the Democratic Party still had the two-thirds rule, and McAdoo was far from that level. Alliances were needed, but none was possible with Smith. Perhaps there was some way to win the Underwood delegates.

Senator Walsh was the chairman, with the unenviable task of ruling this fractious convention. Since the platform committee was not ready to make its report, attention turned to the nominations. McAdoo's hope of an alliance was shattered when on the first day Forney Johnson nominated Underwood, noted that in 1856 the party had condemned the anti-Catholic Know-Nothings, and suggested that the 1924 Democrats do the same with the Klan.

This brought the issue to the fore, and fistfights broke out; the eastern delegates clashed with the southerners, and the Midwest was divided. The convention never recovered, and the whole country learned what was happening from live radio coverage.

The high point of the nominations was Franklin Roosevelt's speech praising Al Smith as "the Happy Warrior." Although the McAdoo delegates did not receive the speech well, it marked Roosevelt's return to the national scene after his bout with polio.

The convention entertained a motion to condemn the Klan, but it failed to pass by a single vote, showing how divided the delegates were. William Jennings Bryan, attending his last convention, tried to push through a compromise resolution condemning violence, but the delegates rejected it. The McAdoo people spoke of Smith's religion and his opposition to Prohibition; the Smith delegates screamed "Oil! Oil! Oil!" in reference to McAdoo's connections with Teapot Dome. The balloting began, with McAdoo ahead, with 431 votes to Smith's 241, and Underwood's 42, trailed by six other nominees, and continued on, seemingly endlessly. By the fiftieth ballot some delegates talked of adjourning without a candidate. The party seemed doomed to the kind of irreconcilable differences that had destroyed the Whig Party before the Civil War.

The Smith forces outnumbered the McAdoo element in the galleries, and hooted down the McAdoo people, who demanded the convention relocate to neutral ground, perhaps Kansas City. Others wanted the convention closed to the media, and particularly to radio reports—the whole country had been able to listen to the Democratic squabbling.

Meanwhile, Coolidge worked away at the White House. By then he knew that La Follette would become a candidate, but also that he would gain more votes from the shambles the Democrats were making of their convention than he would lose to La Follette. The political outlook was bright.

Then Coolidge was crushed in a wholly unexpected fashion. His sixteen-year-old son, Calvin, Jr., stubbed his toe while playing tennis. He developed a blister on one of his toes which soon became infected. The doctor thought the situation serious, that blood poisoning might have set in. Coolidge dropped everything to tend to his son. Edmund Starling recalled that the president moved in a semi-trance. He caught a small rabbit in the White House garden because he knew his son loved animals, and he brought it to the boy's room, hoping it would cheer him. Coolidge dined with Dawes on July 2. Dawes, whose twenty-one-year-old son had drowned in 1912, was thinking about him that evening:

> While I did not realize that there was anything serious
> about Calvin's illness I think the president must have
> sensed it from the first. He seemed to lose all interest in
> the conversation and the dinner soon ended. I was to
> leave that night to continue my talks with [Owen]
> Young and [Dwight] Morrow in New York on the
> preparations for putting the Reparations plan into effect.
> As I passed the door of Calvin's room I chanced to look
> in. He seemed to be in great distress. The president was
> bending over the bed. I think I have never witnessed
> such a look of agony and despair that was on the
> president's face. From that moment I felt a closeness to

Coolidge I never felt before, and have never lost. I had gone through the same great sorrow that he faced.

On July 4 Coolidge wrote to his father about the situation. "The toe looks all right but the poison has spread all over his system." Young Coolidge was taken to Walter Reed Hospital, where he died on July 7. Newspaperman John Lambert, who was there, later wrote of the president's reaction.

"I am sorry," I said to him. "Calvin was a good boy."
He turned slowly until the back of his chair was against the desk. He faced the wide and beautiful expanse of the south lawn. Beyond it he could see the green eminence which the Washington Monument surmounts. He spoke slowly.
"You know," he said, "I sit here thinking about it, and I just can't believe it has happened." His voice trembled. He repeated, "I can't believe it has happened."

According to Lambert, "His eyes were moist. Tears filled them. They ran down his cheeks. He was not the president of the United States. He was the father, overcome by grief and love for his boy. He wept unafraid, unashamed. The brief moments seemed to bear the age of years."

Coolidge stalked the White House in the days that followed young Calvin's death, or sat at his desk gazing out the window. He received the undertaker's bill on July 9, but ignored it for three months, quite out of character for a person who always met his obligations promptly. Grace Coolidge later said that he had "lost his zest for living." He told one visitor, "When I look out that window, I always see my boy playing tennis on that court out there," and asked another, "How are your boys? One of my boys has gone." To a friend whose son also died young, Coolidge inscribed a book: "To my friend, in recollection of his son, and my son, who by the grace of God have the privilege of being boys throughout eternity."

Coolidge's devotion to his sons was complete. In 1935 Edward Brown, the longtime Coolidge family physician, recalled how

Coolidge reacted when Calvin, Jr., had to have an operation for empyema—a deposit of pus—when he was six years old, a serious operation at the time; it was 1915, when Coolidge was a state senator. Coolidge questioned Brown about the possibility of retaining the services of specialists. "I am a poor man," he said, "but I could command considerable money if you need it." Dr. Brown wrote:

> He let no one know how deeply worried he was. I doubt
> if even Mrs. Coolidge knew. I remember that just after
> the operation it had come time for him and his boy,
> John, to leave the hospital. Mrs. Coolidge was permitted
> to remain. I happened to glance out the window, and
> there below in the street, standing quite still, with John's
> hand in his, was Mr. Coolidge, looking up fixedly at his
> boy's room. It was a forlorn and touching picture. I
> think in that moment I knew him best.

After the election, wrote Colonel Starling, something quite typical of Coolidge in this period occurred:

> Very early one morning when I came to the White
> House I saw a small boy standing at the fence, his face
> pressed against the iron railings. I asked him what he
> was doing up so early. He looked up at me, his eyes
> large and round and sad. "I thought I might see the
> president," he said. "I heard that he gets up early and
> takes a walk. I wanted to tell him how sorry I am that
> his little boy died." "Come with me, I'll take you to the
> president," I said. He took my hand and we walked into
> the grounds. In a few minutes the president came out
> and I presented the boy to him. The youngster was
> overwhelmed with awe and could not deliver his
> message, so I did it for him. The president had a difficult
> time controlling his emotions. When the lad had gone
> and we were walking through Lafayette Park, he said to
> me: "Colonel, whenever a boy wants to see me, always
> bring him in. Never turn one away or make him wait."

The death of Calvin, Jr., was most certainly a watershed event in Coolidge's life. Imagine how his father, John Coolidge, felt. He, too, had seen one of his two children die at a young age. Now the same thing had happened to his surviving child. Less than two years later, John Coolidge died, and the president took this quite hard, as well. Mrs. Coolidge also suffered after young Calvin's death, but she said and wrote little at the time. Four years later she published a poem dealing with her son.

"The Open Door"
by
Grace Coolidge

> You, my son,
> Have shown me God.
> Your kiss upon my cheek
> Has made me feel the gentle touch
> Of Him who leads us on.
> The memory of your smile, when young
> Reveals His face,
> As mellowing years come on apace.
> And when you went before,
> You left the gate of Heaven ajar
> That I might glimpse,
> Approaching from afar,
> The glories of His grace.
> Hold, son, my hand,
> Guide me along the path,
> That, coming,
> I may stumble not
> Nor roam,
> Nor fail to show the way
> Which leads us—Home.

Meanwhile, in New York, where the Democratic balloting droned on, reports of the death reached Walsh, who graveled the convention to order. "News has been reached of the death of Calvin Coolidge, Jr., son of the president of the United States." For once the convention was stilled. The session was adjourned, and a little after midnight the delegates went out of Madison Square Garden into the sweltering evening heat.

Smith passed McAdoo on the eighty-sixth ballot but was halted. The count on the hundredth ballot was virtually unchanged from the dozen earlier ones. At that point James Cox, the 1920 presidential nominee, suggested John W. Davis of West Virginia as a compromise candidate. Although he had served briefly in the House of Representatives, Davis was better known as a Wall Street lawyer, solicitor general during the Wilson administration, and ambassador to the United Kingdom. Davis had been mentioned as a possible nominee in 1920, and in 1924 was his state's favorite son candidate. Some of the McAdoo delegates, weary, hot, and tired of paying New York rates for their hotel rooms and meals, drifted into the Davis camp. Then the Smith people followed, with Roosevelt announcing the switch. Davis received the nomination on the 103rd ballot, after 3 AM.

The convention now turned to the matter of the vice presidential nomination. There was a groundswell of support for Walsh, who had conducted the convention in a fair, impartial, and dignified fashion, and who was recognized for his work during the Harding scandals. But Walsh would have nothing to do with it. There was some talk of Smith, but a compromise was unrealistic given how contentious the balloting had been. In the end the convention selected Nebraska Governor Charles W. Bryan, the round-faced younger brother of William Jennings Bryan, an odd looking man with a bald head and a decorative white mustache—a westerner, a progressive Democrat, and a dry.

Davis was an intelligent, thoughtful, handsome, well-spoken attorney, who was known as "the lawyer's lawyer." While not exactly politically experienced, he was no novice. But many thought Davis, like James Buchanan in 1856, had been named because he had nothing to do with the controversies of the time—he had been out of the country as ambassador to the United Kingdom. As for Bryan, he added nothing to the ticket. As the Democrats packed to leave, they knew their only hope was for the La Follette candidacy to split the Republican vote to give them a narrow victory or throw the election into the House of Representatives.

La Follette, sixty-nine years old in 1924, had been chasing after the presidency for close to three decades. Unlike Roosevelt in 1912, he was not going to form a political party; he did not want to place progressive Democrats and Republicans in a tight spot, having to choose between joining the new party and almost certain defeat, or remaining in their own parties and alienating progressive supporters. Then, too, if the election were thrown into the House, La Follette wanted to count on their support. Instead, he relied upon the Conference for Progressive Political Action (CPPA), formed in 1922 by labor and farm groups, Socialists, Farmer–Laborites, a scattering of old Populists, and other progressive individuals and organizations who came together in convention. Seeing in La Follette a way to hitch itself to a possible winner, the Socialist Party decided not to nominate a candidate, but instead supported La Follette.

At their convention that July the delegates adopted a platform written by La Follette's son, which called for aid to the farmers, stronger regulation of railroads, the abolition of injunctions in labor disputes, a constitutional amendment permitting Congress to override court decisions, the direct election of federal judges, and government operation of Muscle Shoals. There was no mention of Prohibition, the Klan, or foreign affairs.

La Follette offered the vice presidential nomination to Justice Louis Brandeis, who wasn't tempted, after which he selected Senator Burton Wheeler, who had won notoriety with his investigation of the Justice Department. At this convention, completely dominated by La Follette, there was much talk of "taking government from the bosses," and the need for popular control of the parties. The platform was short and to the point. "The great issue," La Follette asserted, was "the control of government and industry by private monopoly."

Coolidge's campaign was both unusual and dull. Americans had been, and still are, accustomed to campaigns in which the presidential candidate occupies center stage, talks about the issues, and criticizes his opponents. Coolidge would have none of this. As in the

Massachusetts elections, he didn't mention his opponents by name. Indeed, he didn't deliver traditional campaign speeches, limiting himself instead to the kinds of addresses he had been giving as vice president and president. He spoke on such topics as "Education: The Cornerstone of Self-Government," "What It Means to Be a Boy Scout," "The High Place of Labor," "Ordered Liberty and World Peace," "Authority and Religious Liberty," "Good Sportsmanship," and, just before the election, "The Duties of Citizenship," in which he mentioned the right to vote.

He did the same in his several radio addresses, the first president to use the new medium effectively. It was Coolidge, and not Franklin D. Roosevelt, who truly was the first president of the radio age. Harding had used radio, but he had a resonant voice, as did most politicians of the time, and employed it as an organ, geared to reach those in the back rows of a large hall. Harding boomed into the microphone as though addressing a throng directly. So would Hoover and others of that generation. Coolidge had a small, reedy voice, which, together with precise New England pronunciation, was a drawback on the stump, but advantageous on radio. When Coolidge left office, a representative of the National Broadcasting Company presented him with the microphone over which he delivered his sixteen radio addresses in five years. A *New York Times* reporter, covering one event, wrote of Coolidge and the radio: "the president was quick to see its possibilities in aiding him to reach the people and readily adapted himself to the new science. Because of his naturally good radio voice and quiet demeanor, the task of the broadcasters in presenting him has been a pleasant one." More at ease than most politicians of the time, Coolidge, even with his twang, sounded almost conversational and professional on the radio, and he knew it. In a conversation with Congressman James Watson of Indiana, he remarked:

> I am very fortunate that I came in with the radio. I can't make an engaging, rousing, or oratorical speech to a crowd as you can, and so all I can do is stand up and talk to them in a matter-of-fact way about the issues of the campaign; but I have a good radio voice, and now I

can get my messages across to them without acquainting
them with my lack of oratorical ability or without
making any rhetorical display in their presence.

And then, said Watson, he laughed heartily. Coolidge was always
a man who knew his strengths and weaknesses, and played to the
former. In a 1927 poll rating radio personalities, Coolidge came in
fourth, behind John McCormack, Walter Damrosch, and Madame
Schumann-Heink (all musicians), but ahead of Will Rogers, who was
in seventh place. One scholar calculated that during his presidency,
Coolidge spoke, on the average, 8,688 words per month over the
radio. Coolidge even appeared in a film, a "talkie" that antedated
the famous *Jazz Singer*.

The country had never seen anything like Coolidge's refusal to
campaign in a political campaign. The closest to it had been
McKinley's "front porch" campaign of 1896, which was literally
conducted from the front porch, from which he addressed delegations. But McKinley had at least dealt with political issues, and
Coolidge did not even do that.

One reason for Coolidge's lack of activity must have been the
death of his son, which haunted him for the rest of his life. "When
he went," he wrote in his *Autobiography*, "the power and glory of
the presidency went with him.... I don't know why such a price was
exacted for occupying the White House." He remarked, "My own
participation [in the election campaign] was delayed by the death of
my son Calvin, which occurred on the seventh of July. He was a boy
of much promise, proficient in his studies, with a scholarly mind, who
had just turned sixteen. He had a remarkable insight into things."

Coolidge remained grief-stricken and aloof during the electoral
season, but Dawes took up the slack. He delivered more than a hundred speeches in four months and traveled 1,500 miles. He was a
dynamo. As Robert Murray put it, "His delivery was electric. It was
said that he was the only man in the world who when he spoke could
keep both feet and both arms in the air at once."

Before leaving on his tour, Dawes received a letter of instruction
and advice from Coolidge: "The more simple you can keep it, the
better they will like it." He suggested Dawes "keep as much as you

can to an expression of general principles, rather than attempting to go into particular details of legislation," and closed with, "Whenever you go anywhere, take Mrs. Dawes along."

If he intended to take this advice, it didn't show in his speeches. Dawes hammered away at two themes, one for the La Follette candidacy, the other for the Democrats. La Follette, in his estimation, was the agent of "red radicalism." Dawes also spoke out forcefully against the Klan on August 23, in an area in Maine in which the organization was strong. But he stopped talking about the Klan when informed it would hurt the ticket.

John Davis took a different tack. The man who had always been ahead of his party on this issue (but who in 1954 would oppose integration in *Brown* v. *Board of Education*) was scheduled to speak out against the Klan on August 21. The night before a Klan representative offered to help deliver the South in return for silence. Davis read the Kleagle's letter, tore it up, and the next day attacked the Klan in no uncertain terms: "If any organization, no matter what it chooses to be called, whether it be KKK or any other name, raises the standard of racial and religious prejudices, or attempts to make racial origins or religious beliefs the test of fitness for public office, it does violence to the spirit of American institutions and must be condemned by all who believe as I do in American ideals."

Despite his exertions, Davis was almost the forgotten man in this election. He was a fine speaker, and some of his speeches were well crafted and thought out. But he hadn't a chance; in fact, Davis hadn't even a strategy. Coolidge had the conservatives, and La Follette the old progressives, while Davis was in the middle. Should he attempt to win progressives or conservatives? Should he write off the East and concentrate on the Midwest, or let La Follette draw off Coolidge votes in the Midwest and go for an eastern strategy? Should he attack La Follette, or Coolidge? Or both? Davis and his managers were unable to find answers. He grew frustrated at his own inability to draw Coolidge into taking stands on the issues. Many years later he said, "I did my best... to make Coolidge say something. I was running out of anything to talk about. What I wanted was for Coolidge to say something. I didn't care what it was, just so I had someone to debate with.

He never opened his mouth." In one of his speeches, Davis put it this way:

> If scandals break out in the government, the way to treat them is—silence.
>
> If petted industries make exorbitant profits under an extortionate tariff, the answer is—silence.
>
> If the League of Nations... invites us into conference on questions of worldwide importance, the answer is—silence.
>
> If race and religious prejudices threaten our domestic harmony, the answer is—silence.

But Coolidge did respond, though as was his wont, obliquely: "I don't recall any candidate for president that ever injured himself very much by not talking."

La Follette's speeches, for their part, were rambling and strangely out of date, and toward the end, shrill and filled with malice and bitterness. He knew this was his last hurrah. La Follette's supporters comprised an interesting mix of old progressives and young students, along with labor leaders—he was endorsed by the AFL—and assorted radicals.

Republicans spoke of the peace and prosperity under Coolidge, contrasting that with the war and depression they had inherited from Wilson in 1921. The Democrats spoke of the scandals and government of, for, and by big business. In this contest the Republicans had by far the better issues, as well as a popular incumbent. On October 23 Coolidge wrote his father, saying, "The outlook appears to be promising, but as I have often told you elections are very uncertain. I hope this is the last time that I shall ever have to be a candidate for office." This was three years before he made his famous public statement on the subject.

The Coolidge people were not above attempting to frighten the undecided into voting for their man. One slogan that has come down as symbolizing the campaign was "Keep Cool with Coolidge," but another summed it up better for that generation of Americans: "Coolidge or Chaos." In a typical article on the subject, "The Paramount Issue: Coolidge or Chaos" in the *North American Review* of September 1924, the writer drew a somber scenario, in which the election was thrown into the House of Representatives due to the inability of any candidate to obtain a majority of the electoral votes. In his fantasy, no candidate would be able to obtain a majority of the state votes either. At the same time, the Senate—where the vote would not be by states, but individuals—would vote for the vice president. Assuming the Farmer–Laborites there voted for Bryan, along with several of the Republicans in the farm bloc, Bryan would become vice president on March 4, 1925, and in the absence of a president, would succeed to that office. The article concluded, "Neither Davis nor La Follette can, at any time, win a majority of votes in the Electoral College. It is doubtful if Coolidge could obtain a clear majority now or next week. Looking to November, then, the Paramount Issue is: Coolidge or Chaos."

Whether this imagery swayed anyone is doubtful. The final *Literary Digest* poll indicated that Coolidge would receive 56.6 percent of the popular vote, Davis, 21.2 percent, and La Follette, 21.3 percent.

On November 4, in his last press conference before the election, Coolidge tried to sum up his campaign:

> I don't know that there is any comment that I can make
> on the election or the campaign that isn't perfectly
> obvious to all of you. I have conducted a campaign that
> I think will not leave me anything to be sorry for,
> whether I am elected or not. I don't know of anything in
> the conduct of the campaign that I have been responsible
> for which I shall have to make any apology.

Coolidge received 15,718,211 votes; Davis, 8,395,283; and La Follette, 4,831,470. In the Electoral College Coolidge earned 382 votes; Davis, 136; and La Follette, 13. The *Literary Digest* poll had been fairly accurate; Coolidge had 54 percent of the popular vote; Davis, 28.8 percent; and La Follette, 16.5 percent. It was the largest Republican plurality in history, a smashing victory, but Harding's 1920 achievement was in some ways more impressive. In that election Harding had 60 percent of the popular vote, and he received 400,000 more votes than Coolidge did. But, of course, Harding had been in what essentially was a two-man race, while Coolidge had to face two major opponents.

Voter turnout was very low; 51 percent of those eligible cast ballots, slightly more than the 49 percent of 1920. Later analysis indicated that only 35 percent of qualified women voted in 1924. As in earlier elections, there were definite regional patterns. Davis carried the states of the former Confederacy, plus Oklahoma and the large northern cities. His popular vote was 800,000 fewer than Cox's 1920 total.

La Follette won his home state of Wisconsin and came in second in eleven other states. He didn't do as well with farmers and laborers as anticipated, but scored strongly with intellectuals. It also appeared that fears of La Follette, combined with the certain knowledge Davis couldn't win, led many moderate and conservative voters to cast their ballots for Coolidge. Of all six candidates, it seemed Coolidge had the greatest appeal to voters, while Bryan was the weakest.

The new Senate was narrowly Republican, with 50 Republicans, 40 Democrats, 1 Farmer–Laborite, and 5 La Follette Republicans. The GOP had a wider margin in the House—232 Republicans, 183 Democrats, 2 Farmer–Laborites, 2 Socialists, and 15 La Follette Republicans. Nonetheless, Coolidge could not count on Congress to support some of his programs. Despite his achievement, there was no indication Coolidge's coattails had carried many Republicans to victory.

This election dented the Klan's reputation for determining winners and losers. Al Smith won the governorship of New York, and Walsh won in Montana; both men had been targeted for defeat. In Texas, "Ma" Ferguson, the wife of former Governor "Farmer Jim" Ferguson, won easily on an anti-Klan platform. Moreover, Prohibition did not seem to have played much of a role in the election.

Coolidge received the news of his victory without surprise, and later made a brief, standard statement of gratitude:

> I can only express my thanks to all those who have
> contributed to this result and plainly acknowledge that it
> has been brought to pass through the works of a Divine

Providence, of which I am but one instrument. Such
powers as I have I dedicate to the service of all my
country and all my countrymen.

What had it all meant? William Allen White, whose feelings
regarding Coolidge were mixed but whose opinions were usually
shrewd and always honest, wrote his analysis in his 1938 biography:

No Republican ever came to the White House, except
possibly Theodore Roosevelt, who was elected in his
own right with fewer strings on him. Calvin Coolidge
had remade the Republican Party in his own image. He
was an organization man but the organization of the
party owed more to him than he owed to it. He was a
natural ally of organized capital, those vast
amalgamations of wealth which controlled the banks
and so had suzerainty over major commodity industries
of the land. But there again Calvin Coolidge was free.
He had befriended the bankers and their industrial
lieges. They had done little for him. No scandal
surrounded the campaign fund of 1924. It was an
inexpensive Republican campaign. The president for the
most part stayed in the White House and paid his own
way when he went out to make the few speeches which
graced the campaign.

Yet White was not quite correct. The new Senate would have the
likes of Hiram Johnson, Borah, James Watson of Indiana, Arthur
Capper of Kansas, Norris, La Follette, and Lenroot, all Republicans—at least nominally—who were quite independent. The election had changed nothing as far as they were concerned. La Follette
even talked of a foray into the 1926 congressional and state elections, but this wasn't taken too seriously, and soon after the CPPA
voted itself out of existence, even though the progressives remained
defiant.

A more forceful president might have whipped some of them into
line. The Coolidge of 1923 had at least made a try, ineffectual

though it had been. In 1925 Coolidge could have claimed a mandate for his program and policies, which was what Roosevelt had done after his victory in 1904. But the man who was still grieving over the death of his son, who was clearly weary of politics, was not likely to do so.

After Calvin, Jr.'s, death the president stopped being a workaholic. He delegated responsibility, where earlier he had been on top of most matters. He was listless, and Grace Coolidge later noted he complained of asthma and had troubles with his digestion. He feared a heart attack, and had two electrocardiograms a day, and often took his own pulse at his desk. All this as he had become president in his own right, achieving the pinnacle of success and power.

11

·····················

Domestic Affairs

Many occasions arise in the Congress when party lines are very
properly disregarded, but if there is to be a reasonable
government proceeding in accordance with the express mandate
of the people, and not merely at the whim of those who happen
to be victorious at the polls, on all the larger and important
issues there must be party solidarity. It is the business of the
president as party leader to do the best he can to see that the
declared party platform purposes are translated into legislative
and administrative action. Oftentimes I secured support from
those without my party and had opposition from those within
my party, in attempting to keep my platform pledges.

The Autobiography of Calvin Coolidge

ON DECEMBER 3, 1924, a month after his smashing electoral victory, Coolidge had a clerk read his annual State of the Union message
to the Special Session of the outgoing Congress. It was quite different
from that first message, which he had delivered in person. Gone was
the long list of legislative requests, as well as the lobbying Coolidge
had engaged in for them. Some attributed this apathy to the letdown
after the campaign, others to Coolidge's belief that his task was to
administer what Congress legislated, and not to attempt to lead it in
one direction or another. But his campaign had not been onerous,
and he had provided legislative leadership in Massachusetts and during his first year in office as president. After he left the White House
those close to him ascribed this lassitude to continued brooding over

the death of his son, and took literally what he said in his *Autobiography* regarding how he felt about the office afterward. In 1924 Coolidge had pressed for action; in 1925 he did not.

In his address Coolidge asked for the further development of internal waterways, the sale of Muscle Shoals, government assistance in the consolidation of the railroads, and judicial and prison reforms. He wanted further cutbacks in military procurement, favored another disarmament conference, and opposed suggestions that the United States forgive the World War I debts. He also condemned lynching, and asked that black Americans receive full civil rights—without going into specifics. The matter that received most of Coolidge's attention was taxes:

> The country is now feeling the direct stimulus which
> came from the passage of the last revenue bill, and under
> the assurance of a reasonable system of taxation there is
> every prospect of an era of prosperity of unprecedented
> proportions. But it would be idle to expect any such
> results unless business can continue free from excess
> profits taxation and be accorded a system of surtaxes at
> rates which have for their object not the punishment of
> success or the discouragement of business, but the
> production of the greatest amount of revenue from large
> incomes. I am convinced that the larger incomes of the
> country would actually yield more revenue to the
> government if the basis of taxation were scientifically
> revised downward.

He returned to this theme in his Inaugural Address on March 4, 1925, the first to be broadcast:

> I want the people of America to be able to work less for
> the government and more for themselves. I want them to
> have the rewards of their own industry. That is the chief
> meaning of freedom. Until we can re-establish a
> condition under which the earnings of the people can be

kept by the people, we are bound to suffer a very
distinct curtailment of our liberty.

The State of the Union and the Inaugural Address contained the
essence of Coolidge's thought, which would be on display for the
remainder of his administration. At the time and afterward his critics continued to assert that he advocated more tax cuts in order to
reward the wealthy individuals he admired. Lower taxes did benefit wealthy individuals, of course, but they also helped the middle
class. As Coolidge would observe in his 1927 State of the Union
address, "Exemptions have been increased until 115,000,000 people make out but 2,500,000 individual taxable returns." It was
equally untrue that Coolidge geared his programs to provide most
of the relief for the wealthy. Secretary of the Treasury Mellon quite
correctly observed in 1924 that only 2.5 percent of the cuts in his
original program would have gone to taxpayers with incomes of
more than $100,000, while 70 percent went to those with incomes
below $10,000.

In 1927, 56 percent of Americans had incomes between $3,000
and $25,000, which—in this period of $30 monthly rentals for two-
bedroom apartments in New York City and nickel subway rides and
hot dogs—meant middle class. Some 70 percent of income taxes that
year came from those with incomes of more than $50,000—the
upper classes. Americans with incomes below $3,000 paid less than
1 percent of total income taxes collected.

However, Coolidge was not a "supply sider" as Arthur Laffer and
his disciples were to be in the 1980s. He meant for the tax cuts to
be paid for mainly by reductions in government spending. "While I
am exceedingly interested in having tax reduction," he said at his
October 11, 1927, press conference, "as I say, it can only be brought
about as a result of economy, and therefore it seems to me that the
Chamber of Commerce and all others that are interested in tax
reduction ought to be first of all bending their energies to see that
no unwise expenditures are authorized by the government, and that
every possible effort is put forth to keep our expenditures down, and
pay off our debt, so that we can have tax reduction."

More important to Coolidge than alleviating the plight of the wealthy was the minimization of government activities. In his view, government was largely unproductive; true progress and prosperity were generated by the private sector, which included farmers as well as businessmen, laborers as well as managers. Government-induced prosperity, such as during World War I, was artificial and unsustainable, a chimera purchased at the cost of increased debt—which would have to be repaid. In his 1924 acceptance speech, Coolidge said, "I am not disturbed about the effect on a few thousand people with large incomes because they have to pay high surtaxes. What concerns me is the indirect effect on the rest of the people. Let us always remember the poor."

While this juxtaposition may have jarred some, to those who knew Coolidge's basic philosophy and accepted it the meaning was clear and obvious. The money not taken from the wealthy would be invested in the economy, to provide products, services, and a higher standard of living. Put another way: only a few of those who worked for government created wealth, while those who worked in factories and offices made the country more prosperous by producing goods and services and purchasing them with their decent wages. "We require a national defense, but it must be limited. We need public improvements, but they must be gradual," he told a business audience in 1924. "We have to make some capital investments, but they must be certain to give fair returns. Every dollar expended must be made in the light of all our natural resources, and all our national needs." He went on:

> One of the rights which the freeman has always guarded
> with most jealous care is that of enjoying the rewards of
> his own industry. Realizing the power to tax is the
> power to destroy, and that the power to take a certain
> amount of property or of income is only another way of
> saying that for a certain proportion of his time a citizen
> must work for the government, the authority to impose
> a tax upon the people must be carefully guarded.... It
> condemns the citizen to servitude.

Yet Coolidge was not an absolutist about government spending. Above all, government existed to assure peace and law, without which economic activity would be crippled. In short, those who assert Coolidge was a believer in classical *laissez faire* are wrong. As he stated:

> It would be difficult, if not impossible, to estimate the contribution which government makes to business. It is notorious that where the government is bad, business is bad. The mere fundamental precepts of the administration of justice, the providing of order and security, are priceless. The prime element of the value of all property is the knowledge that its peaceful enjoyment will be publicly defended.

In between the State of the Union message and the Inaugural Address the president delivered a speech in which he uttered the words to which detractors habitually refer when they discuss Calvin Coolidge: "the chief business of the American people is business." On January 17, 1925, Coolidge spoke before the American Society of Newspaper Editors, the talk entitled "The Press Under a Free Government." Although Coolidge delivered scores of such addresses before special interest groups, this one was better reasoned than most of his talks. In the middle of the speech, the president said:

> There does not seem to be cause for alarm in the dual relationship of the press to the public, whereby it is on one side a purveyor of information and opinion and on the other side a purely business enterprise. Rather, it is probable that a press which maintains an intimate touch with the business currents of the nation, is likely to be more reliable than it would be if it were a stranger to these influences. After all, *the chief business of the American people is business*. They are profoundly concerned with producing, buying, selling, investing, and prospering in the world. I am strongly of the opinion that

the great majority of people will always find these are moving impulses of our life [emphasis added].

The next day's *New York Times* headlined the speech: "Coolidge Declares Press Must Foster America's Idealism." Subheads added: "In Address to Editors, He Warns Them Against the Evils of Propaganda," and, "Financially Strong Journalism, He Says, is Not Likely to Betray the Nation." In the second paragraph the *Times* reporter wrote, "President Coolidge declared that the cause of liberty was dependent upon the freedom of the press, saying that under a system of free government it was highly important that the people could be correctly enlightened."

There was no mention in the newspaper story about "the chief business of the American people...."

Indeed, Coolidge's speech actually praised idealism and criticized materialism:

It is only those who do not understand our people, who believe our national life is entirely absorbed by material motives. We make no concealment of the fact that we want wealth, but there are many other things we want much more. We want peace and honor, and that charity which is so strong an element of all civilization. The chief ideal of the American people is idealism. I cannot repeat too often that America is a nation of idealists. That is the only motive to which they ever give any strong and lasting reaction. No newspaper can be a success which fails to appeal to that element of our national life. It is in this direction that the public press can lend its strongest support to our government. I could not truly criticize the vast importance of the counting room, but my ultimate faith I would place in the high idealism of the editorial room of American newspapers.

So in the end Coolidge appears to be saying that, while he knows newspapers are businesses and want to show profits, he has confidence such matters will not sway reporters and editors.

Coolidge often struck a similar note in other of his speeches. On July 5 of the following year, speaking in Philadelphia at the celebration of the 150th anniversary of the Declaration of Independence, he said:

> We live in an age of science and of abounding accumulation of material things. These did not create our Declaration. Our Declaration created them. The things of the spirit come first. Unless we cling to that, all our material prosperity, overwhelming though it may appear, will turn to a barren sceptre in our grasp.

On June 11, 1928, in a speech dealing with the budget, Coolidge put it this way: "Prosperity is only an instrument to be used, not a deity to be worshiped."

Still, the phrase, "the chief business of America is business," (most of the time the word "chief" is dropped, making it sound even more pro-business) remains the one scholars, textbook writers, and journalists fall back on to characterize the man and the age.

Those who believe that Coolidge was pro-business occasionally point to his actions during the great Mississippi flood of 1927. During this period Congress mounted major efforts for flood control, which Coolidge supported feebly. In the spring of 1927 there were severe rainstorms in the Mississippi Valley, inundating 4 million acres and causing property losses of more than $300 million. In Baton Rouge, Louisiana, the Mississippi crested at forty-seven feet, a record that has not been surpassed. Business activity ground to a halt. There were also floods in New England, though of lesser severity. As many as 1.5 million people were homeless, at a time when the population was 120 million.

Hoover was placed in charge of relief efforts, and governors in New England and the Midwest called upon the federal government for assistance. For months Coolidge resisted, holding that the states were responsible for dealing with such matters. Then, in his December 1927 message to Congress, he did ask for flood control legislation, but with much of the burden borne by property owners, and more in the form of loans than in outright grants. As pressures for additional funding developed, however, Coolidge relented, and in February 1928 he supported a $180 million program with more of the money to come from the government. His congressional critics, especially those from affected areas, said this was inadequate, since damages amounted to close to $1.4 billion.

Under the terms of a measure introduced by Democratic Congressman Marvin Jones of Texas, the federal government would not only assume responsibility for this flood control, but would also provide future assistance in calamities of this nature. Coolidge initially fought this measure, not only because it would cripple his financial program, but also on the principle that the government should not back programs assisting one segment of the population at the expense of others. The logic that ruled in McNary–Haugen applied here as well. During his April 10 press conference, he said:

> The flood control legislation is getting into a very unfortunate situation. I was afraid it would, when it became apparent that there was great reluctance on the part of Congress to have any local contribution. Of course, as soon as that policy is adopted, then it becomes a bestowal of favors on certain localities and naturally if one locality is to be favored, all the other localities in the United States think they ought to come in under the same plan and have their floods taken care of. The bill, of course, is an entire reversal of the policy that has been pursued up to the present time, which was that of helping the locality. This undertakes to have the United States go in and assume the entire burden....
>
> It leaves the United States government also to pay all the major costs of maintenance, which it has never done before. It almost seems to me as though the protection of the people and the property in the lower Mississippi that need protection has been somewhat lost sight of and it has become a scramble to take care of the railroads and the banks and the individuals that might have invested in levee bonds, and the great lumber

concerns that own many thousands of acres in that
locality, with wonderful prospects for contractors.

Coolidge thus indicated that a prime reason he opposed the measure was that he wanted to withhold assistance not from individuals,
but from business interests that would profit from such aid.

Congress ignored Coolidge, and in April approved a $1.4 billion
flood control measure, with all the money to come from the federal
government. The final legislation, agreed upon in May, had a price
tag of $500 million, and placed responsibility for future flood con-
trol in the hands of the Army Corps of Engineers. While often
ignored or downplayed in discussions of the Coolidge administration, the flood control measure marked an important step in the
expansion of government responsibilities and obligations, which
Coolidge hadn't wanted to take. It set into motion a major program
of river and harbor improvements that continued into the Hoover
and Roosevelt administrations.

In other areas, the president supported merchant marine expansion, and, while criticizing naval expenditures, he increased those for
the Army Air Corps. He also accepted public works projects.
Secretary Hoover was an ardent believer in the expansion of hydro
power in the West, in particular the development of the Colorado
River basin, and as early as 1922 he set to work on an enterprise that
would culminate in the construction of the Hoover Dam. Coolidge
did not voice any objection to this plan and permitted Hoover,
together with Interior Secretary Hubert Work, to go ahead.

Coolidge was a triumphant if morose figure in this period. The progressives continued to view him as a tool of business, the farm bloc
as the enemy of rural America, and the intellectuals as the personi-
fication of Babbitry. But those who belittled Coolidge did not
explore the record itself, especially that of the Justice Department.
Under Coolidge the government initiated more than seventy
antitrust suits, more than under any of his predecessors, but admit-
tedly most of them were minor. When National Cash Register was
found guilty of price fixing, it was fined $2,000, but on appeal it was
reduced to $50. Rumor had it that Coolidge advanced Attorney

General Harlan Fiske Stone to the Supreme Court was because Stone was about to initiate an antitrust action opposed by the president, against Aluminum Corporation of America, a key Mellon holding. Some progressives, however, protested that as attorney general Stone had been less than energetic in prosecuting his predecessor, Daugherty, even though he fired William Burns, the chief of the Bureau of Investigation, who was suspected of having conspired with Daugherty to block the Teapot Dome matter. Stone was nonetheless confirmed by a large majority.

In the three most important antitrust cases—against Standard Oil of Indiana, the cement manufacturers, and the maple flooring interests—the government lost on appeal. Coolidge named William E. Humphrey, a lawyer for the lumber industry, to the Federal Trade Commission (FTC). During the Coolidge years, with individuals like Humphrey on board, the FTC did little.

Coolidge's critics also might have charged him with being ineffectual and timid and with ignoring important issues. The president spoke out on the abstract issue of the patriotism of black Americans and immigrants, but he refused to go beyond that. In an October 1924 speech on "Toleration and Liberalism," Coolidge told an Omaha audience:

> Well-nigh all the races, religions, and nationalities of the world were represented in the armed forces of this nation, as they were in the body of the population. No man's patriotism was impugned or service questioned because of his racial origin, his political opinion, or his religious convictions. Immigrants and the sons of immigrants from the central European countries fought side by side with those who descended from the countries which were our allies; with the sons of equatorial Africa; and with the Red men of our own aboriginal population; all of them equally proud of the name American.

But he wouldn't take the next step—confronting the bigots by discussing specifics, not philosophy. Nor would he denounce the Klan directly, as had the other major candidates. During the 1924 campaign, the *Brooklyn Eagle*, which backed the Democratic ticket, chided Coolidge on this point:

> With candidate Davis and candidate La Follette out
> flatly and squarely against the hooded night riders of the
> anti-negro and anti-Jew and anti-Catholic Ku Klux
> Klan, candidate Calvin Coolidge, Puritan of the
> Puritans, coming of the stock from which the old Know-
> Nothings were chiefly recruited, seems to imagine that
> without denouncing the Klan he can avoid loss of votes
> by saying nice things about the classes that are the
> victims of the Klan's hostility.

True, but as noted, he did not campaign in 1924 and said next to nothing about the other issues. He forcefully opposed suggestions that Charles Roberts, a black dentist from Harlem whom the GOP nominated for a House seat, be asked to step down. In his letter on the subject Coolidge said:

> During the war, 500,000 colored men and boys were
> called up under the draft, not one of whom sought to
> evade it. They took their places wherever assigned in
> defense of the nation of which they are just as truly
> citizens as any others. The suggestion of denying any
> measure of their full political rights to such a great
> group of our population as the colored people is one
> which, however it might be received in some other
> quarters, could not possibly be permitted by one who
> feels a responsibility for living up to the traditions and
> maintaining the principles of the Republican Party.

How far would he go with this belief? Attorney General John Sargent wrote:

> From time to time the president was much troubled by
> the insistent discrimination by white employees against

the colored people employed by the department—such, for instance, as insistence that they would not work in the same room, at the same kind of work. On one occasion some outburst on the subject that had occurred was brought up by a cabinet office. After a general discussion the president said:

"Well, I don't know what you can do, or how you will solve the question, but to me it seems a terrible thing for persons of intelligence, of education, of real character—as we know many colored people are—to be deprived of a chance to work because they happen to be born with a different colored skin. I think you ought to find a way to give them an even chance."

This may not seem much by the standards of our time, and there is no record of Coolidge having taken action to change the situation. But presidents from the beginning of the century to the end of World War II made disparaging statements or indicated insensitivity on race, and there is no evidence that Coolidge thought or said anything inconsistent with his belief in a colorblind society.

His stance on the immigration law was quite similar. Although Coolidge opposed the law's Japanese exclusion, he would not veto it. In effect, the charge that Coolidge was a tool of business cannot be convincingly demonstrated, but his timidity—his unwillingness to take political risks—can be seen time and again throughout his life.

Likewise, his lack of boldness stands out in his refusal to capitalize on his personal victory in 1924 in respect to Congress that year. After the election, the congressional Republicans were in a muddle. The regular Republicans in 1925 were as intent as the regulars in 1913 had been to punish the progressive defectors, but with a difference: in 1913 the GOP did not have control of Congress, but in 1925 they did. In 1913, moreover, Roosevelt had formed a political party, but La Follette had refused to do so. The congressional regulars sought vengeance, which was merely symbolic, even though conciliatory gestures might have worked wonders.

Their chief target was La Follette, who was quite ill and not likely to last out the year. La Follette, Smith Brookhart of Iowa, and Lynn

Frazer and Edwin Ladd of North Dakota were read out of the party on November 28, and when Congress convened, stripped of their seniority on committees. It was symbolic because it didn't change matters much in the Senate, but it was foolhardy because it assured that these four, together with Henrik Shipstead, the Farmer–Laborite from Minnesota, and the rest of the bipartisan farm bloc, would retaliate by harassing the administration.

Coolidge could have avoided this had he worked more energetically with the leadership. Speaker Gillett had been elected to the Senate and had been replaced by Nicholas Longworth, the silky and subtle native of Cincinnati, who soon proved more effective than his predecessor. By then Lodge had died, and was followed as Republican leader by Charles Curtis of Kansas, who was prepared to work with and for the president. While lacking Lodge's skills and reputation, Curtis had many friends among the regulars. Had Coolidge given the word to Longworth and Curtis that he wanted to win back the dissidents, he might have had an easier time with the outcasts, but he didn't.

Vice President Dawes was also a problem. During his swearing in he harangued the Senate on the filibuster and other issues, pointing at individual senators as he shouted and pounded on the lectern. Senator Harry Ashurst, the droll Arizonan, remarked, "It was the most acrobatic, gymnastic speech I have ever heard in the Senate," while James Reed of Missouri dryly commented that "his melody of voice, grace of gesture, and majesty of appearance were excelled only by his modesty." Dawes meant to be forceful, but like other newcomers who arrived with their own ideas on how the Senate should be run, he met with instant opposition from all quarters, and soon proved an embarrassment as well. That day he took the first step toward becoming a joke.

Coolidge developed further problems with the Senate when he named Stone to the Supreme Court. For his replacement as attorney general, Coolidge selected Charles Warren of Michigan, who had been ambassador to Japan and Mexico, and had worked assiduously for Coolidge at the 1924 convention. He had also been an attorney for and later president of Michigan Sugar, said to be a member of the "Sugar Trust," which had been cited by the Federal Trade Commission for illegally marketing sugar. Warren was, moreover, an imperious and irritating person. His nomination arrived at a time when the progressives who had been expelled from their positions were still smarting and seeking to retaliate. Ironically, Franklin Lane, Wilson's progressive secretary of the interior, had stated after Harding's 1920 electoral victory that Warren would be his choice for attorney general.

After the Judiciary Committee favorably reported the nomination, Democrats Reed and Walsh led the attack against Warren, and other Democrats soon joined in. Few Republicans voiced their support for the nominee, in part because initially Curtis felt he had sufficient votes to put him over, and besides, presidents had traditionally been permitted to select their cabinets. In fact, no cabinet appointment had been denied since 1868.

On March 9, 1925, the debate continued. Dawes had no idea what was happening. As far as he could see, the debate would drone on for hours or even days. He asked Senators Curtis and Joseph Robinson of Arkansas, the majority and minority leaders, whether there would be a vote that day, and they replied that six senators wanted to speak, making a vote impossible. So Dawes beckoned for a replacement as presiding officer, and set off for his apartment in the Willard Hotel to take a nap—at which point five of those senators who had wished to speak withdrew.

Seeing his support melting rapidly, Curtis called for a vote. Word was sent to Dawes, who dressed quickly, went downstairs, and took a cab to the Capitol. But before he could get there the vote was taken, and resulted in a 40-40 tie. Senator Lee Overman, a North Carolina Democrat who had voted for Warren, now switched his vote, making it 41 to 39. The nomination was defeated. Had Dawes been there, he could have cast the deciding ballot in Warren's favor.

The president was irate that the Senate Republicans had been unwilling to support him and that the Democrats had defied tradition. Dawes's gaffe was also troublesome, as were rumors that he deliberately missed the vote because the one vote against him for the vice presidential nomination had come from Warren. Nevertheless, Coolidge should have realized Warren was a poor nominee, certain to be attacked given that his activities at Michigan Sugar were suspect and perhaps subject to Justice Department inspection.

Meeting with the president, Curtis informed him that Warren had no chance of being confirmed, and recommended that he select a substitute. Uncharacteristically, Coolidge dug in his heels on what he should have recognized was an embarrassing, losing cause. He sent the nomination back to the Senate, but by then there was little support for Warren. On March 18 the nomination was again defeated, this time by a margin of 46 to 39. Coolidge might have made a recess appointment, but Warren had had enough, and asked for his name to be withdrawn.

Coolidge now turned to an old friend, John Garibaldi Sargent, a fellow Black River Academy graduate, who had been attorney general of Vermont, and the nomination had no trouble getting through the Senate. But Coolidge didn't forget; he retaliated against some of the senators who had opposed Warren by withholding patronage, but inconsistently, giving off false signals.

The president and Warren were not the only losers in this episode. Dawes, who early on had been considered a possible presidential nominee for 1928, had become the butt of gags. Someone placed a sign at the Willard's entrance: "Dawes Slept Here." In another instance, shortly after the vote, Dawes was escorting a friend around the Capitol and went to the Supreme Court, where a particularly boring case was being heard. Justice Van Devanter was nodding, and Justice Holmes was having difficulty keeping his eyes open. Chief Justice Taft, who noticed Dawes, sent him a note: "Come up here. This is a good place to sleep." Then again, when Dawes formed an organization of conservative businessmen he foolishly called "The Minutemen," a reporter commented, "Minute Man was two minutes late." He was no longer presidential timber.

Warren wasn't the only Coolidge nominee rejected by the senators. In 1925 Coolidge selected Wallace McCamant for a recess appointment as a federal appeals judge. McCamant was unquestionably qualified for the position, but he probably wouldn't have been selected had he not nominated Coolidge for the vice presidency in 1920, setting him on the road to the White House. The following year the Judiciary Committee approved the nomination, but Hiram Johnson asked for it to be sent back for reconsideration— McCamant had opposed Johnson's presidential nomination in 1920. It was a gratuitous slap in the president's face, a striking indication of how little control he had over his congressional party.

The change from Stone to Sargent as attorney general was one of several switches in the administration during this period. Secretary of Agriculture Henry C. Wallace died on October 25, whereupon Coolidge offered the post to farm bloc leader Arthur Capper of Kansas, who was critical of McNary–Haugen. As Coolidge had expected, Capper rejected the offer, but the president sought his advice on another nominee. Capper supported William Jardine, a Kansas educator, who had no trouble being confirmed with Capper's strong support.

Slemp, who had lost his contest with Butler at the convention, submitted his resignation in January, and was replaced by Everett Sanders. Sanders may have lacked Slemp's political astuteness, but a president who had already decided not to seek reelection no longer had any real use for that.

Secretary of State Hughes resigned in March 1925. Once again Coolidge asked for recommendations, and Hughes suggested Frank Kellogg. Kellogg had had a long career, making his mark as one of Roosevelt's trust-busting attorneys, and although he bolted the GOP to support Roosevelt in 1912, he returned to be elected senator from Minnesota. Kellogg had become more conservative as he grew older. At the time he was ambassador to the Court of St. James, and at the age of sixty-eight prepared to retire. But Coolidge convinced him to accept the post, and Kellogg was easily confirmed.

On December 8, 1925, Coolidge again had the clerk read his State of the Union message, to the first session of the new Sixty-ninth Congress. And again, he wrote of the need for economy and reduced taxes. There were the usual references to agricultural policy, Muscle Shoals, and the need to reorganize government. But in this message Coolidge asked for very little specific legislation. It was as though he knew Congress would shoot down his requests. In any case, why should there be additional legislation? Coolidge reported that "it is exceedingly gratifying to report that the general condition is one of progress and prosperity," which indeed was the case. "Here and there are comparatively small and apparently temporary difficulties needing adjustment and improved administrative methods, such as are always to be expected, but in the fundamentals of government and business the results demonstrate that we are going in the right direction."

Coolidge's budget message, sent down the following day, was similar in that he asked for little. Again, the theme was, "If it isn't broken, don't fix it."

At this time John Coolidge fell ill. He had been a semi-invalid for several months, and the president knew the end was near. Coolidge pleaded with his father to come to the White House to live, but John Coolidge would not leave Plymouth. On January 1, 1926, Coolidge wrote to his father:

> It is a bright day for the New Year, but rather cold. I wish you were here where you could have every care and everything made easy for you, but I know you feel more content at home. Of course we wish we could be with you. I suppose I am the most powerful man in the world, but great power does not mean much except great limitations. I cannot have any freedom even to go and come. I am only in the clutch of forces that are greater than I am. Thousands are waiting to shake my hand to-day.

Clearly the presidency had become a burden for Calvin Coolidge.

> It is forty-one years since mother lay ill in the same room where you are now. Great changes have come to us, but I do not think we are any happier, and I am afraid not much better. Every one tells me how cheerful you are. I can well understand that you may be. So many loved ones are waiting for you, so many loved ones are daily hoping you are comfortable and are anxious to know about you.

The president had a direct telephone line installed between the White House and the Coolidge home in Plymouth, and he spoke to his father every day, until John Coolidge died on March 18, 1926. The next morning several newspapers noted that this was the first time a president's father had died while his son was in office. The Coolidges traveled to Vermont for the funeral, and then returned to Washington.

The month before John Coolidge's death Coolidge got the one piece of legislation he very much wanted that session: another tax cut. The Revenue Act of 1926 had been introduced as a bill the previous year and was reintroduced in the new Congress. The debate was fierce, and once again pitted Secretary Mellon against the progressives, this time with Norris, chairman of the Agricultural Committee, in the lead. At one point in the debate Norris observed that under the proposed measure, "Mr. Mellon himself gets a larger personal reduction than the aggregate of practically all the taxpayers in the state of Nebraska." If Mellon responded, it went unrecorded, but, as historian Thomas Silver noted a generation later, in 1924 Mellon had paid more taxes than all the people of that state.

The act as finally reported was largely what Coolidge had wanted—it would cut taxes while at the same time enabling him to lower the national debt. It repealed the gift tax, halved estate taxes, and lowered rates down the line. The rate on the first $7,500 of income was 1.5 percent, with an exemption of $1,500 for a single taxpayer and $3,500 for married ones. Approximately one-third of those who paid taxes in 1925 would be off the rolls. A married person with an income of $7,500 paid less than $70 in federal income taxes under the new rule. But contrary to Coolidge's wishes, the corporate tax rate was increased. The measure was passed in February by a vote of 58 to 19 in the Senate and 390 to 25 in the House. Coolidge congratulated the legislature, and pledged further reductions as budgetary considerations permitted.

That year Coolidge had to face another round in the continuing battle over McNary–Haugen. Although conditions on the midwestern farms were improving—wheat rose from an average price of $1.11 a bushel in 1923 to $1.67 in 1925—the farmers were still debt-ridden. In a discussion with agriculture expert R.A. Cooper,

Coolidge remarked, "Well, farmers never have made money." All he could offer was his plan that farmers cooperate to limit production and thus raise prices. This, and tariffs to keep foreign crops from American shores, were his palliatives for the problem. "I don't believe we can do much about it," he told Cooper. "But of course we will have to seem to be doing something; do the best you can without much hope." On another occasion he related a tale to illustrate his view:

> At every cabinet meeting for a year or so back, Secretary Henry Wallace used to be grumbling and complaining about the price of corn and was always wanting the government to do something about it. Then corn took a rise. The government didn't do it. I noticed that Wallace had shut up on the price of corn.

On other occasions Coolidge noted that population shifts from the countryside to the cities had accelerated. He had seen this in Vermont, and now it was taking place throughout the nation. "The life of the farmer has its compensations but it has always been one of hardship," he remarked.

None of this was particularly assuring to the midwestern farmers, who continued to press their representatives to push for McNary–Haugen. The bill was introduced in early 1926, along with several moderate programs Coolidge espoused. Mellon came out against McNary–Haugen, writing to congressmen saying that in his view the measure would cause inflation, increase production while decreasing consumption, and thus lead to a depression. "If the bill were to become law it would present the unusual spectacle of the American consuming public paying a bonus to the producers of five major agricultural products."

Coolidge threw his support behind a substitute measure, the Curtis–Crisp bill, which provided for the creation of a Federal Farm Board, with $250 million to lend to farm cooperatives to keep perishable crops off the market in times of surplus. In the end neither McNary–Haugen nor Curtis–Crisp passed, but the Division of Cooperative Marketing was created in the Agriculture Department and provided with a token sum of $250,000 to encourage farm cooperatives.

Although this session of Congress passed almost one thousand measures, all but a few were minor. Coolidge had asked for little, and that was what he got. Other than the Revenue Act, Congress didn't pass a major bill. Surveying the scene, Walter Lippmann wrote in May:

> The politicians in Washington do not like Mr. Coolidge very much, for they thrive on issues, and he destroys their business. But the people like him, not only because they like the present prosperity, and because at the moment they like political do-nothingism, but because they trust and like the plainness and nearness of Calvin Coolidge himself. This is one of the most interesting conjectures of our age.

On the day Coolidge left office, Lippmann wrote, "Surely no one will write of those years since August 1923, that an aggressive president altered the destiny of the Republic. Yet it is an important fact that no one will write of those same years that the Republic wished its destiny to be altered."

Claude Fuess, who wrote the closest we have to an official Coolidge biography, came to pretty much the same conclusion in his 1940 book. In analyzing Coolidge's smashing victory in the 1924 presidential election, he inquired into the reasons. Quoting Theodore Roosevelt's 1912 statement, he wrote, "The country ought not take me unless it is in a heroic mood." To which Fuess added, "In 1924, the United States was not looking for either heroism or romanticism. What it wanted was plain ordinary common sense. Calvin Coolidge had character—and in the long run character outlasts what is temporarily spectacular."

In the autumn of 1926 the Republicans campaigned on the Coolidge record, or it would be more precise to say, the strong economy, the tax cuts, and the budget surpluses. The country was doing quite well, for the economic boom that followed the postwar depression had gathered steam and power. But this time Coolidge attempted to take some credit for it. "Our present state of prosperity has been greatly promoted by three important causes," he said, "one of which is economy, resulting in reduction and reform in national taxation. Another is the elimination of many kinds of waste. The third is the general raising of the standards of efficiency."

If the Republicans wanted Coolidge's coattails, he did not give them gladly. As in 1924, he did little campaigning. GOP National Chairman Butler was too busy with his own campaign to spare time for other races. Since Butler was in trouble, running for the Senate seat against the popular David Walsh, and Massachusetts Governor Alvan Fuller was plagued by fallout from the Sacco–Vanzetti murder case, Coolidge agreed at the last minute to campaign for them. In Massachusetts the party indicated that votes for Butler and Fuller were votes of confidence in Coolidge. Fuller won reelection, but Butler lost, which the Democrats claimed implausibly was a repudiation of Coolidge.

Historically the party in power loses seats in off-year elections, and 1926 was no exception. The Sixty-ninth House had 247 Republicans, 183 Democrats, and 4 members of other parties; the Seventieth Congress had 237 Republicans, 195 Democrats, and 3 minor party members. In the Senate the Republicans went from 56 members to 49, the Democrats rose from 39 to 46, with one Farmer–Labor member. On the surface it appeared the Republicans once more controlled both houses, but, as is often the case with opposition parties, the Democrats were united, while the Republicans were still split by memories of the La Follette insurgency and the strengthening of the farm bloc. On many issues an anti-administration majority ruled in the Senate, and the margin in the House was sufficiently slim to cause Coolidge problems. Further tax cuts were possible, but so was passage of the McNary–Haugen bill.

Coolidge's fourth annual message to Congress, sent up to Capitol Hill on December 7, 1926, was much like the previous one. It opened with the familiar optimistic analysis of the state of the Union. "I find it impossible to characterize it other than one of general peace and prosperity." He again called for tax cuts, and noted that the high tariff had brought in record revenues that in a measure made up for previous reductions. In the longest section Coolidge noted that his administration had been responsible for several measures to assist agriculture, indicating his continued opposition to McNary–Haugen. He also called for passage of a measure, largely designed by Hoover, to regulate radio. And he favored strengthening the national banks, but he was vague about what he wanted done, which implied his support of the Pepper–McFadden Act authorizing branch banking by national banks. Finally, Coolidge hit out at government directives, calling for a reduction in "government bureaus which seek to regulate and control the business activities of the people."

As was his custom, Coolidge ended with a peroration right out of his early mentor, Garman.

> America is not and must not be a country without
> ideals. They are useless if they are only visionary; they
> are only valuable if they are practical. A nation can not
> dwell constantly on the mountain tops. It has to be
> replenished, and sustained through the ceaseless toil of
> the less inspiring valleys. But its face ought always to be
> turned upward, its vision ought to be fixed on high.

The Pepper–McFadden Bill passed, which Coolidge gladly signed, as he did the radio legislation he had requested.

Coolidge had not presented a legislative agenda. From the beginning his most important task that session, other than taxes, appeared to be to prevent passage of McNary–Haugen. The new Congress was more inclined toward it than the old had been, and it had new allies. From the outside there was Lowden, a recent convert, and within the administration Vice President Dawes had come over to the cause. Senator Curtis was weakening, and within the cabinet his only strong supporter was Mellon. A revised McNary–Haugen Bill was introduced soon after Coolidge's address, passed the House easily, and the Senate by a smaller margin, but Coolidge promptly vetoed it.

Unlike most of his vetoes, this one was surprisingly forceful and closely reasoned. Carefully and precisely, Coolidge picked it apart.

He noted that the measure discriminated against farmers who did not concentrate on the favored crops; those who did would be aided "at the expense of the farmer who has toiled for years to build up a constructive farming enterprise to include a variety of crops and livestock that shall, so far as possible, be safe, and keep the soil, the farmer's chief asset, fertile and productive." Coolidge asserted that the middlemen would be the real beneficiaries. "It seems almost incredible that the producers of hogs, corn, wheat, rice, tobacco, and cotton should be offered a scheme of legislative relief in which the only persons who are guaranteed a profit are the exporters, packers, millers, cotton spinners, and other processors." As for the Federal Farm Board, which was to administer the law, "A board of twelve men are [*sic*] granted almost unlimited control of the agricultural industry and can not only fix the price which the producers of five commodities shall receive for their goods, but can also fix the price which the consumers of the country shall pay for these commodities." In his view, "the effect of this plan will be continually to stimulate American production and to pile up increasing surpluses beyond the world demand."

Coolidge hit hard at the idea of special relief for one segment of the population at the expense of others. "This so-called equalization fee is not a tax for purposes of revenue in the accepted sense. It is a tax for the special benefit of particular groups." This, arguably, was precisely the intent and effect of the tariff that Coolidge supported. The tariff, of course, protected farmers as well as businessmen and industrial workers, but still, each item on the list protected one or another special interest. Throughout, however, Coolidge stressed that one of the major reasons for tariffs was to raise revenues, and he justified his stance on this point. In his annual address Coolidge had noted with satisfaction that receipts exceeded $615 million in 1926.

The bill returned to Congress, which was unable to overturn the veto. As before, its supporters worked diligently to overcome congressional objections and win new converts. Another version was passed in 1928, and again Coolidge vetoed in unusually strong language; "It embodies a formidable array of perils for agriculture which are all the more menacing because of their being obscured in a maze of ponderously futile bureaucratic paraphernalia. In fact, in spite of the inclusion in this measure of some constructive steps proposed by the administration, it renews most of the more vicious devices which appeared in the bill that was vetoed last year."

Coolidge offered a "detailed analysis" of his objections to the measure, including (1) its attempted price-fixing fallacy; (2) the tax characteristics of the equalization fee; (3) the widespread bureaucracy it would set up; (4) how it would encourage profiteering and wasteful distribution by middlemen; (5) its stimulation of overproduction; and (6) its aid to our foreign agricultural competitors.

In his conclusion, Coolidge complained that "this taxation or fee would not be for the purposes of revenue in the accepted sense but would simply yield a subsidy for the special benefit of particular groups of processors and exporters.... It would be difficult to conceive of a more flagrant case of the employment of all of the coercive powers of the government for the profit of a small number of specially privileged groups." He spoke of a "bureaucracy gone mad" and a "preposterous economic and commercial fallacy."

Had Coolidge unleashed this flash of temperament in the cause of other items on his original agenda, his legislative record might have been more productive. The question remains: Why was Coolidge so heated in his denunciation of McNary–Haugen? He felt strongly about the importance of tax cuts, but his messages on that subject were calculated, almost bloodless. Not so with government assistance to farmers.

These two positions are the centerpiece of Coolidge economics—and are at the very core of his philosophy. The president believed that lower taxes and reduced government spending would result in a freer, more democratic society. He hoped to return the country to a version of what it had been before passage of the Income Tax Amendment, a time of small—and primarily local—government. Thus, he considered McNary–Haugen even more threatening to freedom than the existing tax structure. To Coolidge, McNary–Haugen was a radical change in the relation between government and the people, between economics and government. Coolidge believed these two elements should be separated: Government should remain out of the economy, and businessmen should not interfere with the proper functions of government. He articulated this thought, at the foundation of his philosophy, in several of his presidential speeches. In "Government and Business," a speech delivered before the New York Chamber of Commerce on November 19, 1925, he said:

> New York is an imperial city, but it is not a seat of government. The empire over which it rules is not political, but commercial. The great cities of the ancient world were the seats of both government and industrial power. The Middle Ages furnished a few exceptions. The great capitals of former times were not only seats of government but they actually governed. In the modern world government is inclined to be merely a tenant of the city. Political life and industrial life flow side by side, but practically separated from each other. When we contemplate the enormous power, autocratic and uncontrolled, which would have been created by joining the authority of government with the influence of business, we can better appreciate the wisdom of the fathers in their wise dispensation which made Washington the political center of the country and left New York to develop into its business center. They wrought mightily for freedom.

Coolidge believed that the wedding of government and business would lead to socialism, communism, or fascism, and would certainly alter the nature of American life. Yet Coolidge saw no difficulties in government aid to commercial aviation, grants for road building, or the protective tariff, once known as "Mother of the Trusts." It was a common enough thought of the time, shared by moderate Democrats and Republicans alike. Herbert Hoover certainly believed this; writing in his *Memoirs* about Secretary of Agriculture Henry C. Wallace, who supported McNary–Haugen, Hoover said, "My colleague, the secretary of agriculture, was in truth a fascist, but did not know it, when he proposed his price- and distribution-fixing legislation in the McNary–Haugen bill."

Supporters of McNary–Haugen were not so much throwbacks to the progressives or populists as antecedents to the New Dealers. They believed, quite simply, that the government had a responsibility for the economy—in Coolidge's terms, that Washington and New York had to come together, under Washington's aegis. If agricultural recovery depended on direct government intervention, so be it.

But the times were against the McNary–Haugen advocates. This, as well as deep flaws in the program and divisions among farmers as to the measure's desirability, lost them their fight. The attempt to override the veto failed in the Senate by a vote of 50 to 31. The idea, however, did not die; it would be reintroduced during the Hoover administration, and again fail. Agricultural reform dependent on government input would not be realized until the Great Depression and the New Deal—when the times were strikingly different, and farmers were united in its support.

Congress adjourned for the spring and summer on March 3, 1927, and the country's interests turned to other matters. This was the summer that Babe Ruth hit his 60 home runs, and the Yankees took the American League pennant by winning 110 games and losing 44, for a winning percentage of .714, a level as yet unsurpassed. In September Gene Tunney defeated Jack Dempsey in a fight noted for "the long count." It was also the year of *The Jazz Singer*, generally credited with being the first feature sound film.

The greatest sensation of the time was Charles A. Lindbergh's May 20–21 flight from Roosevelt Field on Long Island to Paris. It would be difficult to find a more striking contrast than Coolidge and Lindbergh—one embodying the ethos of a vanished America, the other the world of the future. Yet these two were not so dissimilar. Both men were shy and diffident, believers in individualism, and considered pure and clean in a world that was becoming more corrupt. Coolidge, however, was the real thing. The modest, self-effacing Lindbergh was as prepared to cash in on his exploits as any modern hero. He permitted his name to be used, for around $6,000 a pop. ("I was able to carry very few things in my *Spirit of St. Louis*, but I took special care not to forget my Waterman pen.") After Coolidge left the White House, a cosmetics company approached him, offering a large sum to get Grace Coolidge to endorse its product; Mr. Coolidge turned the company down—his wife simply didn't use that product.

Coolidge arranged for Lindbergh's return on the cruiser USS *Memphis*, and a flotilla of destroyers, two army airships, and forty airplanes greeted the ship and escorted it into New York harbor. There Lindbergh met cabinet members and other dignitaries, and was treated to the biggest parade in the city's history to that time. Lindbergh and his mother then went to Washington to stay with the Coolidges at the temporary White House (the official residence was undergoing repairs), and at a dinner Dwight Morrow introduced the aviator to his daughter, Anne—who later became Mrs. Charles Lindbergh. Songs were written about him, babies named after him, and a dance was titled in his honor. On Wall Street the aircraft stocks soared, with Wright Aeronautical leading the way, rising 500 percent. The Dow-Jones Industrials closed over 200 by year's end, a new record. The country forgot McNary–Haugen, arguments for and against tax cuts, and all else in an outburst of national pride and affection for the young man. In the "feel good" atmosphere of the time, some of the glory was reflected on Coolidge. It was, for many in retrospect, the high noon of the decade.

In his December 6, 1927, annual message, which opened with, "It is gratifying to report that for the fourth consecutive year the state of the union in general is good," Coolidge reviewed his previous tax reductions. In the face of an economic slowdown, he asked for changes that were "mainly for the purpose of removing inequalities." In many ways it was a repeat of the 1926 report—he wanted to sell Muscle Shoals, opposed large scale naval expansion, and wanted more attention paid the merchant marine. As for agriculture, he wanted funds to help create marketing cooperatives, but without governmental input.

> This is not a proposal to lend more money to the farmer, who is already fairly well financed, but to lend money temporarily to experimental marketing associations which will no doubt ultimately be financed by the regularly established banks, as were the temporary

operations of the War Finance Corporation. Cooperative marketing especially would be provided with means of buying or building physical properties.

Coolidge again had kind words to say about the negro and alluded to the lynchings in the South. "The Congress should enact any legislation it can under the Constitution to provide for its elimination." But he would go no further, and did not press for such a bill. To the negro he now added the American Indian, and spoke of the time "when the Indians may become self-sustaining." But here, too, he took no action.

On May 8, 1928, Coolidge had complained to reporters about the costs of some of the programs Congress had passed, even those of which he approved.

> I am a good deal disturbed at the number of proposals that are being made for the expenditure of money. The number and the amount is becoming appalling. Practically none of these bills have reached me yet, and it may be that the Congress won't pass all of them. Of course, there is this flood bill. It is impossible to estimate what that will cost. If it is carried out as suggested, I think $500,000,000 would probably be the minimum. Nobody knows what the maximum might be. There is this farm bill calling for $400,000,000. The Boulder Dam bill. I think the lowest estimates on that are $125,000,000. Other estimates run to $250,000,000. There is a pension bill, running $15,000,000 or $20,000,000. The salary bill, the so-called Welch bill, of about $18,000,000. The Muscle Shoals bill, which I think was reported to me would cost perhaps $75,000,000. I think that is rather excessive. That is only a part of them. I don't know just what will happen to the Treasury if we try to put all those proposals into effect.

At the time Coolidge was devoting more time and energy to the relatively minor tax reduction measure than any other. It was as though this was the capstone of his tax program. Congress was compliant, and a few days later passed much of the Coolidge program. The corporate tax was reduced, and graduations in the individual tax rates made less progressive. But Congress denied Coolidge the elimination of the estate tax. He signed the measure into law anyway, reflecting that his work on the matter at least was completed. In July the president crowed that the surplus for the fiscal year came in at $398 million. It was the conclusion of a very good session as far as he was concerned.

12

....

Foreign Relations

The presidency is primarily an executive office. It is placed at
the apex of our system of government. It is a place of last resort
to which all questions are brought that others have not been
able to answer. The ideal way for it to function is to assign to
the various positions men of sufficient ability so that they can
solve all the problems that arise under their jurisdiction.

The Autobiography of Calvin Coolidge

WHEN HE ARRIVED IN OFFICE, Coolidge had almost no interest
in foreign relations and left matters in this sphere to his secretaries of
state and the diplomats. Former Secretary of State Elihu Root—a
leading Republican foreign policy expert whom Coolidge called on
for assistance—once remarked, the president "did not have an inter-
nationalist hair in his head." This was not so, for as will be seen,
Coolidge had a clear concept of America's role in the world, and
the ways the president could contribute toward it.

Still, Coolidge arrived in the presidency without experience in foreign affairs, although his library included works on America's pos-
sessions and the tariff. He came to office with less preparation to
handle matters of foreign policy than any of his presidential predecessors in the twentieth century, except McKinley. Harding had been
on the Foreign Relations Committee; Wilson knew Europe from his
many prior visits there; Taft had been secretary of war, had been
abroad, and had been prominent in the creation of the Panama

Canal; and Theodore Roosevelt had traveled extensively in Europe, had served as assistant secretary of the navy, and had led the "Rough Riders" in the Spanish–American War.

In this period an ignorance of foreign affairs was not considered a drawback. While the World War and the Spanish–American War had widened the vista for literate Americans, few had been overseas, and public interest remained centered on American problems. Lack of experience hadn't troubled earlier presidents, who tended to rely on foreign policy specialists for information and advice, and that was a practice that suited Calvin Coolidge.

Several threads ran through the fabric of Coolidge's foreign policy, but they tended to be dominated by business considerations. Coolidge believed the wartime debts owed the United States by the Allies had to be paid. Still, he was willing to make concessions regarding interest rates and terms. His reasoning was that if foreigners didn't pay their debts, someone—and that meant the American people—would have to do so. Coolidge could not accept this notion. "Every dollar that we have advanced to these countries they have promised to repay with interest," he told a gathering during Memorial Day in 1926. "Our National Treasury is not in the banking business. We did not make these loans as a banking enterprise."

In response to a suggestion that the United States might forgive the foreign debt, Coolidge was supposed to have said, "They hired the money, didn't they?" In fact, he never said that, though he might have thought that. Mrs. Coolidge once remarked that it sounded like her husband. What he did say, however, was, "Unless money that is borrowed is repaid, credit cannot be secured in time of necessity." In other words, deadbeats have low credit ratings.

One way to help foreign countries pay the debt would have been to lower the tariff to encourage imports. Indeed, some bankers, like J.P. Morgan and other Wall Streeters, favored tariff reduction, at least on a temporary basis, until Europe recovered. But tariff reductions were opposed by manufacturers, farmers, and workers and would have flown in the face of long-time Republican policies. Coolidge's deeply felt dedication to protecting American workers from foreign competition, and his desire for tariff revenues to help lower the debt—they contributed more than

$3.8 billion during his administration—combined to make a high tariff sacrosanct.

Coolidge was prepared, however, to take steps to help the Europeans repay their debt. Harding had eased the payment burden for the United Kingdom through renegotiation of terms. Coolidge did the same for Italy, France, and Belgium, and was even more generous. He also supported the Dawes Plan, which provided loans so the Germans could pay their reparations to the United Kingdom and France. Thus, a curious triangular system was established: the United States government and its private investors loaned money to Germany, which paid reparations to the UK and France, whereupon these countries then paid portions of their debts to the United States, where this money was used to help reduce the national debt.

Moreover, Coolidge did want the State and Commerce Departments to expand American foreign trade and investment. With State Department approval, New York investment bank Dillon Read led the way, providing $160 million in investment for German industry during the 1920s. In 1928 Dillon Read banker Ferdinand Eberstadt noted:

> We have the iron, coal, and steel industry, the United
> Steel Works, which is approximately the size of
> Bethlehem Steel, and second only to the United States
> Steel Corporation…. In the electrical industry we took
> the Siemens, which recognizes as a rival only the United
> States General Electric…. In the banking field, we
> selected the Disconto and Deutsche Banks. Now, what
> do they correspond to in the United States? The
> Disconto and the Deutsche Banks correspond to the
> First National and the National City.

Dillon Read's entry into Germany was made possible through an arrangement with J.P. Morgan & Company and done with the State Department's blessings. When it came time for the United States to ante up its share of the $200 million Dawes Plan loan, the government approached Morgan and persuaded the company to assemble a syndicate for the purpose of selling the securities to American investors. This was the way Washington and Wall Street cooperated in such matters. American investors plunged into foreign markets as never before—to their ultimate sorrow.

Coolidge himself was not an isolationist, although he had been raised on Washington's Farewell Address and the Monroe Doctrine. But he also had witnessed the Spanish–American War, the Caribbean diplomacy of Roosevelt and Taft, and Wilson's Mexican foray and World War I. All of these events influenced him. He supported a version of dollar diplomacy for Latin America, but at the same time worked to improve relations with nations in the region, especially Mexico. He worked energetically for arms reduction, not only because he wanted to avoid war, but also because this would enable him to cut back on military spending, and so provide larger surpluses which would lower the national debt. But when this failed, Coolidge supported increased military spending, especially for army aviation.

Coolidge continued the policy of supporting the expansion of American big business throughout the globe that had existed under Wilson and continued under Harding, and he endorsed legislation favorable to American commercial interests. The Merchant Marine Act of 1920, passed in the waning days of the Wilson administration, provided for preferential railroad rates for goods exported or imported on American vessels, lower customs on such goods, and low rates on loans used for the construction of ships in American yards. Several of these provisions, such as the preferential rates, were not applied since Wilson and Harding considered them violations of international treaties.

This changed with the passage of the Jones–White Act of 1928, which affirmed the principles stated in the 1920 legislation, and also provided for a $250 million construction funds for ships built in American yards. It was an indication of Coolidge's interest in such matters. Support of the merchant marine and foreign trade were often mentioned in Coolidge's speeches and messages to Congress. In his first annual message, Coolidge said, "The entire well being of our country is dependent upon transportation by sea and land." The following year he called for joint Canadian–American cooperation on the construction of a St. Lawrence waterway to open the Midwest to European commerce. In his third message he asserted, "The maintenance of a merchant marine is of the utmost importance for national defense and the service of commerce." Coolidge spoke of the need for attention for "merchant ships as an auxiliary of the navy." In his final message, in 1928, he proudly noted, "We have established American flag lines in foreign trade where they had never before existed as a means of promoting commerce and as a naval auxiliary." Coolidge did what he could to create a beneficial atmosphere domestically for business, which he considered the generator of American wealth and progress. He also believed that fostering international commerce was part of this policy. In the 1928 message he asserted:

> It is desirable that the government continue its helpful attitude toward American business. The activities of the Department of Commerce have contributed largely to the present satisfactory position in our international trade, which has reached $9,000,000,000 annually. There should be no slackening of effort in that direction. It is also important that the department's assistance to domestic commerce be continued. There is probably no way in which the government can aid sound economic progress more effectively than by cooperating with our business man to reduce wastes in distribution.

Much of this runs contrary to the image of isolationist America during the 1920s, a nation that wanted to retreat behind the two oceans that had provided so much security throughout the nation's history, turning in disillusionment and disgust from foreign entanglements after the war. Coolidge may have wanted the United States to remain aloof from Europe politically and concentrate its attention on the western hemisphere, but economically he was inclined toward internationalism. While Coolidge rarely discussed this in public, others in the administration did so. One of the clearest summaries of the forces that animated Coolidge foreign policy came in a speech by Secretary of the Navy Curtis Wilbur before the Connecticut Chamber of Commerce on May 7, 1925:

Americans have over twenty million tons of merchant
shipping to carry the commerce of the world, worth
$3 billion. We have loans and property abroad,
exclusive of government loans, of over $10 billion. If we
add to this the volume of exports and imports for a
single year—almost $10 billion—we have an amount
almost equal to the entire property of the United States
in 1868 and if we add to this the $8 billion due us from
foreign governments, we have a total of $31 billion,
being about the total wealth of the nation in 1878....
These vast amounts must be considered when we talk
about defending the flag.... We fought not because
Germany invaded or threatened to invade America but
because she struck at our commerce on the North Sea
and denied to our citizens on the high seas the
protection of our flag.... To defend America we must be
prepared to defend its interests and our flag in every
corner of the globe.... An American child crying on the
banks of the Yangtze a thousand miles from the coast
can summon the ships of the American navy up that
river to protect it from unjust assault.

The reference to the Yangtze was not pulled out of the air. At the
time Wilbur spoke, there appeared a chance that this would happen, though intervention in Mexico seemed more probable.

Mexican–American relations had been quite rocky during the
decade prior to Coolidge's accession to the presidency, and he
inherited a thoroughly bad situation, with ill-will on both sides.
Complicating the matter was the matter of Mexican petroleum,
which at the time was being developed largely by American and
British companies.

In 1914 General Alvaro Obregon captured Mexico City, and
installed Venustiano Carranza as president, replacing Victoriano
Huerta. At first President Wilson withheld recognition. One reason
was his belief that the United States should not recognize governments that came to power in this fashion, but in addition there

appeared some danger Carranza might nationalize American interests in Mexico, especially petroleum, as permitted under terms of the country's constitution. When in 1915 Carranza failed to nationalize the holdings, and indicated any move in this direction would be made in such ways as to compensate holders, the United States and other countries recognized his regime. The improved relations were short-lived. Border raids by Mexican forces under the command of Pancho Villa prompted an American incursion into Mexico in 1916.

The following year German Foreign Minister Arthur Zimmerman instructed the German minister in Mexico to propose an alliance in case the United States entered the World War. Zimmerman suggested Germany would assist Mexico in regaining the "lost provinces" of Texas, New Mexico, and Arizona, and he also urged Mexico to help persuade Japan to join the alliance. The note was intercepted by the British and turned over to Wilson, and was a precipitant in the American decision to enter the war. While Mexico hadn't accepted the offer, or even appeared to have considered it, Wilson was increasingly wary of the Carranza government.

Then, in 1918, when the United States was involved in the war, Carranza announced that petroleum was an inalienable national resource, and a tax was levied on oil lands and contracts made prior to 1917. Titles to such properties were to be transformed into concessions, and this masked confiscation prompted American and British protests and an awareness that Carranza's word was not worth much.

This was a serious matter. In 1919 Secretary of State Robert Lansing, quoting "the best technical authorities," had declared the "peak of petroleum production in the United States will be practically exhausted within a measurable period." A year later, the U.S. Geological Survey said that the country had twelve years' petroleum reserves and that new discoveries were diminishing. In the last year of the Harding administration, Secretaries Hughes and Hoover recommended supporting American petroleum companies, who were becoming more involved in Latin America, and obtaining concessions before the Europeans took most of them. When he became president, Coolidge organized an Oil Conservation Board to look into the matter. At the time the fear of running out of domestic petroleum that had sparked the Teapot Dome affair intensified interest in Mexico, which at the time was one of the world's leading petroleum producing countries. Just as in the post–World War II period American government by necessity had to be concerned regarding who controlled the Middle East, so it had the same kind of interest in the nature of the Mexican government in the 1920s. American actions in Mexico have to be interpreted in the light of this situation.

In September 1920 Obregon was elected president in what was generally considered an honest election, and he announced he would continue the Carranza policy regarding petroleum. Harding refused to recognize the new government. When he became president, Coolidge was besieged by representatives of former American interests there seeking American intervention to restore their rights, which he rejected. Coolidge extended recognition on August 31, in his first significant act in the foreign field.

In return for recognition, Obregon agreed to a settlement asked for by Wall Street banks, whereby petroleum export taxes would be used to pay off American holders of Mexican bonds. At the time some expropriated oil companies were providing arms for those rebelling against the Mexican government. Coolidge put an end to this practice, and allowed Obregon to purchase American weapons, and even permitted Mexican troops to enter the United States in pursuit of dissidents. Coolidge justified this in a speech before the National Republican Club on February 12, 1924:

> A situation has arisen in Mexico which has caused some
> solicitude. We recognize that the people of that country
> have a perfect right to set up and pull down
> governments without any interference from us, so long
> as there is no interference with the lawful rights of our
> government and our citizens within their territory. We
> do not harbor the slightest desire to dictate to them in
> the smallest degree. We have every wish to be friendly
> and helpful. After a long period of shifting and what
> appeared to us to be unsubstantial governments in that
> country, we recently reached the opinion that President

Obregon has established a government which is stable
and effective, and disposed to observe international
obligations. We therefore recognized it.

If one reads between the lines—or reads even the lines themselves,
for that matter—it appears clear that Coolidge was concerned as
much with protecting American business's interests in Mexico as
with any other consideration.

When disorder arose there, President Obregon sought
the purchase of a small amount of arms and munitions
from our government for the purpose of insuring his
own domestic tranquility. We had either to refuse or to
comply. To refuse would have appeared to be equivalent
to deciding that a friendly government, which we had
recognized, ought not to be permitted to protect itself.
Stated in another way, it would mean that we had
decided that it ought to be overthrown, and that the
very agency which we had held out as able to protect the
interests of our citizens within its borders ought not to
be permitted to have the means to make such protection
effective. My decision ran in a counter direction.

The Mexican situation proved an anomaly. America's economic foreign policy would not be generated in the White House, but rather in
the Commerce Department, to a lesser degree in the State Department,
and on Wall Street and in the nation's corporate headquarters.

Plutarco Calles was elected president in 1925 and additional
American property was seized. Secretary of State Kellogg protested,
but in December nationalization began. Some of the companies
involved appealed to Washington for assistance. Coolidge and
Kellogg wanted to protect American citizens and their property, but
there was also the matter of petroleum supplies. Kellogg was
obsessed with the thought that the USSR was behind the Mexican
moves, which he took as one of the first steps toward the sovietiza-
tion of Latin America. He was not alone in thinking this was so. To
Americans of this period, nationalization meant Bolshevism. In addi-

tion there was a religious factor to consider. Calles had come into conflict with the Catholic Church, which resisted his nationalization efforts. In response Calles ordered the seizure of Church property, and foreign monks, nuns, and priests were deported and others were forced to flee or go underground. Prominent leaders of the Catholic Church in Mexico protested these actions, and American Catholics and others demanded Coolidge act to protect them. When in January 1927 former Soviet leader Leon Trotsky selected Mexico as his country of exile, it appeared he did so because he felt that country was hospitable to his ideas. Kellogg took this as another sign of Soviet penetration in the Americans. In testimony before the Senate Foreign Relations Committee shortly after Trotsky arrived in Mexico, he said:

> The Bolshevist leaders have had very definite ideas with respect to the role which Mexico and Latin America are to play in their program of world revolution. They have set up as one of their fundamental tasks the destruction of what they term American imperialism as a necessary prerequisite to the successful development of the international movement in the New World. Thus Latin America and Mexico are conceived as a base for activity against the United States.

Coolidge was besieged by demands that he intervene in some forceful manner. He faced a firestorm of criticism in this period, but he remained calm, and did what he could to put the American people in the same frame of mind while his diplomats attempted to work out a solution to the problem. Coolidge saw nothing to be gained from an armed conflict with Mexico. To Henry Stoddard, editor of the *New York Evening Mail* who believed in American action against Mexico, he said:

> Now look at the other side of the picture. Here we are the most powerful nation in the world. At this moment we have special representatives in Europe as well as all our diplomats urging reduction of armaments and

preaching peace. The world of today would harshly
condemn us if, despite our attitude, we should go to war
with a neighbor nation not nearly our equal. What do
you suppose people in years to come would say?
Powerful United States crushing powerless Mexico!
Don't you think it better for us to find another way to
handle the situation?

Fearing the situation might escalate into war, Calles asked
Coolidge to dispatch a special, personal representative to Mexico
City for talks to ease the tensions. Frank Stearns and Secretary
Kellogg thought Dwight Morrow, Coolidge's old friend and a J.P.
Morgan banker, would be the ideal person for the task. Coolidge
made the offer, but Morrow was reluctant to take the assignment.
In the end he relented, and in October left for Mexico. Coolidge told
him, "My only instructions are to keep us out of war." That
Morrow, with Coolidge's complete confidence, managed to pull this
off was one of the major foreign policy successes of the Coolidge
administration. What was important in the Mexican situation was as
much what didn't happen as what did. During the Coolidge years the
United States did not go to war with Mexico, and so avoided a
potential disaster, a 1920s version of the Vietnam conflict.

It was a typical Coolidge move. Find the right man, tell him what
has to be done, and then step aside. Morrow accomplished much
in bringing the two countries closer together. He helped negotiate
compromises between the Church and Calles, and managed to satisfy the businessmen and government officials. He even arranged for
Charles Lindbergh to fly to Mexico City, and when Lindbergh and
Anne Morrow fell in love and married, it only added to the luster of
the mission. Other celebrities on "good will missions" followed,
including Will Rogers.

It took both sides to come to this kind of understanding. The
Mexican president realized that he had gone too far in his reforms
and his anti-Church crusade. He was losing popularity with the
Mexican people, and wanted to move closer to that country's political center. In November 1927 the Mexican Supreme Court declared
unconstitutional two articles of the law regarding petroleum con-

cessions, and this was seen as a favorable sign to the concessionaires. The following month the Mexican Congress enacted a measure to provide for compensation for foreigners. This was followed in 1928 by the Calles–Morrow Agreement, which allowed American firms to retain property acquired prior to 1917, in effect returning to the early Obregon position. By the time Morrow returned to the United States in 1930, Mexican–American relations were in better shape than at any time in the century. Morrow was given a good deal of credit for this accomplishment. There was talk of him as a possible vice presidential running mate for Herbert Hoover in 1928, and Morrow became Coolidge's and Kellogg's candidate for Hoover's secretary of state.

Even so, the petroleum companies did not make large new investments in Mexico, but instead turned elsewhere. In 1924 total American investments in Mexican petroleum production was $250 million; by 1929, the figure had dropped to $206 million. In the same period American petroleum companies increased their investment in South American petroleum from $220 million to $444.5 million, with the largest increases coming in Venezuela and Colombia. In addition, American petroleum companies made their initial forays into the Middle East and boosted stakes in the Dutch East Indies.

It is worth noting that the American companies' decision not to make large commitments in Mexico was provident. When Lazaro Cardenes became Mexico's president in 1934, he returned to the policy of confiscation and anti-Church activities. In 1938 the government seized American and British petroleum properties valued at close to half a billion dollars, which the Roosevelt administration handled with far less success than Coolidge obtained in the late 1920s.

The other trouble spot in Latin America was Nicaragua, which had been occupied by American marines since 1912. This was a sensitive matter, due to Nicaragua's proximity to the Panama Canal. Coolidge withdrew almost all the marines in 1925, asserting matters had been set in order. Once the Americans left, civil strife returned, and by 1926 there were clashes between rival claimants to the presidency.

The United States backed Adolfo Diaz, who had been chosen by the Nicaraguan Congress, while Mexico supported Juan Sacasa, who was rumored to have Soviet connections. Aided by Mexican arms, the Sacasa forces, commanded by Jose Moncada, won several victories, prompting Coolidge to send the marines back to Nicaragua in May, where they remained for two months. He also dispatched former Secretary of War Henry Stimson to the area to attempt to bring about a settlement. Within a few months Stimson managed to win the approval of both sides to a compromise that enabled Diaz to remain in office with opposition participation. By then, too, Mexico stopped sending in arms as a result of the new arrangement with Washington. As part of the agreement there was to be an election in 1928, which resulted in Moncada's election. But Augustino Sandino refused to lay down his arms, obliging Coolidge to keep the marines there, and they were there when he left office in 1929. Coolidge was involved in several other, minor matters in Latin America, and on the whole this was a successful part of his presidency.

That short trip to Havana in 1928 to attend the Sixth International Conference of American States—the only time Coolidge ever left American shores—indicated the concern he had in creating an atmosphere of harmony with the other American nations. After Coolidge delivered the opening address, in which he attempted to be conciliatory, El Salvador's delegate, backed by Argentina and Mexico, sharply attacked the United States, criticizing the belief that any nation had the right to interfere in the internal affairs of other nations. The resolution offered by the delegate failed to pass, but the obvious anger demonstrated by the Latin Americans prompted Kellogg to seek a new policy that would be more acceptable.

The State Department's chief legal advisor, J. Reuben Clark, drew up a memorandum for Kellogg in which he argued against the Roosevelt Corollary—TR's "amendment" to the Monroe Doctrine asserting that the United States could exercise an international police power if provoked. The Monroe Doctrine, Clark noted, was aimed at Europe, not American nations. The Clark Memorandum was not considered an official statement of American foreign policy, and it wasn't even released until 1930, after Coolidge had left the White House, but its tone did mark a change of direction for the United States, which was continued by his successors.*

Troubles in China did lead to an American initiative in that part of the world, and for a while it appeared Navy Secretary Wilbur's statement regarding American ships on the Yangtze might eventuate. That country was in the midst of civil war, and the European powers, including the USSR, were backing one side or the other, with the western Europeans hoping to broaden their influence in the country. Coolidge adopted the classic American position of standing for the Open Door. There was a marine garrison of some four thousand troops in Shanghai, and the navy had a flotilla in the waters off that city to enforce American rights, but not, as it turned out, to take action. Secretary Kellogg, always aware of the Soviet presence, reported to Coolidge in 1924:

> I feel that the critical conditions in China require some
> action to allay the public agitation. I am quite aware
> that this anti-foreign sentiment is due partly to
> Bolshevik activities and propaganda, but there is no use
> disguising the fact that there had been growing for some
> time in China a nationalistic movement resentful of
> foreign control.

At the Washington Naval Conference the Chinese had been promised tariff revisions and a reconsideration of extraterritorial rights, and Coolidge supported both programs, while at the same time warning that foreign lives and property had to be guaranteed. Treaty revision had begun when, in late 1926, rebel forces threatened to close the vital road that connected Peking to the sea. With

---

* Coolidge's voyage to Havana was unusual, given the notion that American politicians had no need to venture abroad. Borah, who succeeded Lodge as chairman of the Foreign Relations Committee and was in this position at the outbreak of World War II, had never set foot out of the United States—a mystic had predicted he would die at sea, and Borah was afraid of water travel.

Coolidge's approval, Acting Secretary of State Joseph Grew warned the rebels of an American naval blockade. From then on his major objective in China was to keep American troops off the mainland—he had no intention of having an American military presence in China while several thousand marines were in Nicaragua. In 1928 he extended diplomatic recognition to the Nationalist government, but the civil wars continued long after Coolidge had left the presidency.

Throughout it all, Coolidge was silent on China. This was of a piece with his approach to the presidential role in foreign policy.

> The presidency is primarily an executive office. It is placed at the apex of our system of government. It is a place of last resort to which all questions are brought that others have not been able to answer. The ideal way for it to function is to assign to the various positions men of sufficient ability so that they can solve all the problems that arise under their jurisdiction. If there is a troublesome situation in Nicaragua, a General McCoy can manage it. If we have differences with Mexico, a Morrow can compose them. If there is unrest in the Philippines, a Stimson can quiet them. About a dozen able, courageous, reliable, and experienced men in the House and Senate can reduce the problem of legislation almost to a vanishing point.

Coolidge's twin desires to prevent wars and save money motivated his energetic attempts to convene a follow-up to the Washington Naval Conference to limit naval construction. The Washington Conference had addressed the matter of capital ships, but had done nothing for those in other categories, such as destroyers and submarines. Coolidge hoped a second conference, to convene in Geneva, would address these matters. In 1924 Congress had authorized the construction of eight new cruisers, which would have cut into those Coolidge budget surpluses. Soon after, the League of Nations voted to establish a Preparatory Commission for the Disarmament Conference, and Coolidge urged American participation as an alternative to the construction program. As late as December 1925, in his annual message to Congress, Coolidge believed "that it is the reduction of armies rather than navies, that is of the first importance to the world at the present time." A year later he changed his tune. "We have recently expressed our willingness at Geneva to enter into treaties for the limitation of all types of warships according to the ratio adopted at the Washington Conference," he said in his message. "This offer is still pending."

The army was quite small in the 1920s—it had fewer than 135,000 men under arms in 1927. The navy was even smaller in terms of personnel, with 95,000 men. But the army's equipment was crude and inexpensive, while the navy's was sophisticated and costly. One of Coolidge's most critical budget requirements was to place limits on an expansion of the navy, which was necessary if he was to continue to pay off the national debt—hence his desire for another naval conference.

The Coolidge call for a conference was accepted by the United Kingdom and Japan, but France and Italy held back—they sent only observers to the conference. British fears of losing primacy on the high seas and Japan's ambitions in Asia were problems, but so were France and Italy, who harbored hopes of great power status and who were unhappy with the results of the Washington Conference. These problems doomed the conference, which opened on June 20, 1927, to failure. The Geneva Conference also opened a bitter dialogue between the United States and the United Kingdom that poisoned relations between the two countries for the remainder of the Coolidge administration.

That December, after the failure at Geneva, Coolidge asked Congress for an increase in naval appropriations, the first shot in a nine-year, billion-dollar naval program. Congress authorized the construction of fifteen large cruisers as permitted under terms of the Washington Conference agreement. This set off an arms race—between the United States and the United Kingdom—that Coolidge had hoped could be avoided.

There remained one more method by which Coolidge might assure peace and lower military spending. In mid-decade most

European countries evinced interest in pacts to ensure against another war. At Locarno in 1925, the German and French governments pledged to respect the Rhine frontier between the two countries. This led to other treaties worked out by delegates from France, Germany, Belgium, the United Kingdom, Italy, Poland, and Czechoslovakia. The first three nations agreed to respect their boundaries and never go to war against one another again except in self-defense. The United Kingdom and Italy were to be the guarantors of this agreement. Germany pledged to settle all disagreements with the other countries by peaceful means. The Locarno Agreements were hailed as a clear demonstration that wars in Europe were no longer possible.

In the spring of 1927, as Kellogg prepared for the Geneva Conference, Columbia University Professor James Shotwell called upon French Foreign Minister Aristide Briand with a proposal to build upon the Locarno Agreements and create a multilateral pact to outlaw war, based upon the 1924 Geneva Protocol for the Pacific Settlement of International Disputes. At the time Briand was more concerned with a Franco–American pact to be introduced on the tenth anniversary of America's entry into the war, April 6, 1927. Briand delivered a speech on this subject on that date, an unusual way to call for a diplomatic discussion. Shotwell, attorney Salmon Levinson, and others drafted a document in which war was condemned as an instrument of national policy and government pledged to settle all disputes in an amicable fashion. The draft was published and elicited widespread interest. At the time, Kellogg's hands were full, having to deal with Mexico, Nicaragua, and China. France's refusal to attend the Geneva Conference did nothing to improve relations with the United States.

Borah had been talking about similar ideas for much of the decade, and had become further energized by the Locarno Agreements. He thought a multilateral pact along these lines was a more effective way to keep the peace than was the League of Nations. He wanted to go further—not only to outlaw war but to make it part of international law. Borah persuaded Kellogg to grant Levinson a hearing, and he agreed, but Levinson was unable to convince the secretary of the merits of such a treaty. Borah now took his case to the public, delivering several speeches on the subject, which were well received. Meanwhile Kellogg attempted to convince Coolidge that separate arbitration treaties with various countries were a more sensible approach. The secretary and the senator clashed over this matter in December hearings before Borah's Foreign Relations Committee, at a time when public opinion was swinging toward the Borah approach.

Coolidge was also coming around, and accordingly, Kellogg sent two messages to Briand shortly before the end of the year, one proposing a renewal of an existing treaty between France and the United States, the other containing a suggestion that the French bilateral concept be replaced by a multilateral approach. At first Briand would not be swayed, but by March he accepted in principle the American position. The following month he suggested that the two countries approach the United Kingdom, Germany, Italy, and Japan to discover whether they had any interest in such an agreement.

Briand went ahead and made the contacts, even though there clearly remained differences between him and Kellogg on the final form of such an arrangement. In early May the by-then enthusiastic Briand wrote to Kellogg, suggesting that such a treaty would be "the greatest accomplishment of my administration or of any administration lately," and talking of the possibility of a Nobel Peace Prize for those involved in achieving acceptance of the proposed pact. Briand, who had shared the award with Gustav Streseman in 1925, might have dreamed about being the first person to win the award twice.

Toward the end of the summer it appeared that fifteen countries that had been involved in the negotiations were prepared to sign the treaty, the ceremony to take place in Paris, but there remained some seemingly minor problems to be worked out. Kellogg said he would not attend unless his counterparts in the other countries did so as well. He excluded the Japanese foreign minister, however, on the grounds that the distances were too long and the expenses would be onerous. The Italian foreign minister tried to beg off, but in the end opted to come.

Borah organized support for the pact skillfully. The fact that the classic isolationist favored it certainly helped. Coolidge lobbied for the measure, inviting doubtful senators to the White House for consultation. Dawes helped where he could, noting the finer points of the pact, but also warning that a rejection would be a slap in the face for the president, especially poignant since this was to be the last request he would be making of the Senate. Supporters of the pact noted that it had to be seen in the light of the large-scale American military buildup; Dawes claimed that the two measures were "the declared and unified policy of the United States."

Coolidge, who had been lukewarm about the pact when the idea was first broached, now was a supporter. In his annual message of December 4, 1928—his final annual message—he wrote warmly of the pact:

> One of the most important treaties ever laid before the Senate of the United States will be that which the fifteen nations recently signed at Paris, and to which forty-four other nations have declared their intention to adhere, renouncing war as a national policy and agreeing to resort only to peaceful means for the adjustment of international differences. It is the most solemn declaration against war, the most positive adherence to peace, that it is possible for sovereign nations to make. It does not supersede our inalienable sovereign right and duty of national defense or undertake to commit us before the event to any mode of action which the Congress might decide to be wise if ever the treaty should be broken.

This section of the address was followed by one in which Coolidge discussed the costs of national defense, which he characterized as "stupendous." The bill came to $668 million, which was $118 million more than it had been in 1924. "We have reached the limit of what we ought to expend for that purpose." He went on to say that America's foreign interests had to be protected: "Our largest foreign interests are in the British Empire, France, and Italy." This wasn't so, and represents the underside of American foreign concerns during the Coolidge years.

On January 15, 1929, the Kellogg–Briand Pact was ratified by the Senate by a vote of 85 to 1. Ultimately 62 nations signed. Coolidge signed the measure in a White House ceremony on January 17. Briand did not receive his second Nobel Prize; it was awarded to Kellogg alone.

It became fashionable during the 1930s and with the coming of World War II in 1939 to deride the pact and consider it a foolish chimera drawn up by timid men. Given the horrors of World War I, it is difficult to consider it ill-advised or those who drew it up and signed it craven. Rather, it was idealistic and perhaps utopian. The men of 1928 believed in international law. The cynicism that existed toward the concept had not yet become manifest. That would come later.

Developments in Mexico, Nicaragua, and China were front page news during the Coolidge years, as was the Geneva Conference and the Kellogg–Briand Pact, but they did not excite national debate. Foreign policy was not as important to Coolidge—or to most of the country—as were domestic affairs. But under his watch America remained at peace, and trade and foreign investment rose to new heights, with American business rushing to take advantage of the new opportunities in a global economy in which the European powers, still shattered by World War I, were in retreat.

13

· · · · · · · · · · · · · · · · · · ·

The Last Year

There were others who constantly demanded that I should state that if nominated I would refuse to accept. Such a statement would not be in accordance with my conception of the requirements of the presidential office. I never stated or formulated in my own mind what I should do under such circumstances, but I was determined not to have that contingency arise.

I therefore sent the secretary to the president, Everett Sanders, a man of great ability and discretion, to Kansas City with instructions to notify several of the leaders of state delegations not to vote for me. Had I not done so, I am told, I should have been nominated.

The Autobiography of Calvin Coolidge

WRITING IN FEBRUARY 1927, Walter Lippmann addressed the matter of "The Causes of Political Indifference To-Day." In his view, old political and economic differences had been eliminated by prosperity.

During the last four years the actual prosperity of the people, combined with the greater enlightenment of the industrial leaders, has removed from politics all serious economic causes of agitation. There has been no pressing reason for an alignment of "haves" and of "have nots," and no reader of history needs to be told that when

you remove economic discontent you remove what is
certainly the greatest cause, if it is not the mainspring, of
political activity. Politics carried on for justice, for liberty,
for prestige, is never more than the affair of a minority.
For the great majority of men political ideals are almost
always based upon and inspired by some kind of
economic necessity and ambition.

Other observers were not as sanguine as Lippmann. To them the
American economy was dangerously unstable and liable to collapse.
This was a period when several Austrian economists, among them
Ludwig von Mises and Frederick Hayek, were arguing that artifi-
cially low interest rates were setting up the world economy for a major
blowoff. During the Great Depression these critics and other like-
minded individuals were featured in the press and public discussions
as having accurately predicted the disaster, while bankers, stock market manipulators, and the Republican presidents of the 1920s, including Coolidge, came to be blamed for the bad times. Couldn't they have
realized the weaknesses in the system and done something to correct
them? The answer was "no" to both. Because of this, the nature of
Coolidge's response to the economy is one of those features of his life
and administration that requires attention and analysis.

William Z. Ripley, a well-known Harvard economist, was one of
the American economists who in the Coolidge years sounded warnings about the economy, and, later, critics of the Washington leadership would invariably quote his statements. In Ripley's view,
American business was replete with unsound practices. To him, the
leaders of American industry, especially the railroaders and their
banker allies, were robber barons whose baleful influence and power
were harming the American people. Their powers would have to be
curtailed, their practices reformed.

At a time when academics were largely anonymous, Ripley
became a fairly well-known figure. He ultimately earned a meeting
with President Coolidge because he had written an article—which he
later turned into a book—that came to Coolidge's attention. This
encounter became a touchstone for historians of the period, a sym-

bol of the Coolidge approach to what, in retrospect, was the greatest economic tragedy in American history, the Great Depression.

In a January 1926 *Atlantic Monthly* article entitled "From Main Street to Wall Street," Ripley argued that lax state incorporation laws and the growth of holding companies, especially in public utilities, were concentrating power in Wall Street. He was also concerned about the use of no-par capital stock, which to him indicated frivolous financing, and about the nonvoting stock some companies had begun to issue. Moreover, Ripley demonstrated how some companies' financial reports—in those pre–Securities and Exchange Commission days, financial statements were not monitored—did not reflect the true situation of the corporations; some companies didn't even issue reports. He also bemoaned the lack of responsibility taken by shareholders, many of whom didn't even bother to vote; he saw the separation of ownership and management as a fundamental problem facing the nation. Although Ripley's attitude appears strange to today's investors, who don't want the responsibilities of overseeing a company, he lived through an era that witnessed the great merger and incorporation wave that started to transform the face of American business—small, local companies disappeared into regional and national giants.

Although Ripley and his followers yearned for the time when a company's assets were physical—like railroad cars, buildings, and machinery—there was a larger contingent, including some eminent academics, who believed the nation had entered a "new era" in which the old verities were no longer valid. They argued that intangibles such as trademarks, brand names, and labor forces were starting to count for more than they had in the late nineteenth century. Lippmann, for instance, suggested there was a "New Capitalism" abroad in the land, led by a new breed of businessman. He said, "There is no doubt that the large corporations are now under the control of a very different kind of man than they were when Roosevelt and Bryan and La Follette were on the warpath." He continued:

> The new executive has learned a great deal that his
> predecessor would have thought was tommyrot. His
> attitude toward labor, toward the public, toward his

customers and his stockholders is different. His behavior
is different. His manner is different. His press agents are
different. I am far from thinking he is perfect now, but I
am certain that he is vastly more enlightened and that he
will take ever more trouble to please. He is no doubt as
powerful as he ever was, but his bearing is less autocratic.
He does not arouse the old antagonism, the old bitter-end
fury, the old feeling that he has to be clubbed into a sense
of public responsibility. He will listen to an argument
where formerly he was deaf to an agitation.

Lippmann spoke for those who challenged the pessimism of
Ripley, stating, "Whatever may be the intrinsic good and evil of such
things as the wide distribution of securities, however questionable
may be some of the practices to which Professor Ripley has called
attention, the net result of the new attitude on the part of capital
has been to create a new attitude on the part of the public."

Ripley's writings had attracted the attention of Judson Welliver,
a former Coolidge assistant who had become editor of the *Washington Herald*. Many years later, during the Great Depression, Welliver
told William Allen White how the president came to be aware of
Ripley. He said he went to see Coolidge about what he, Welliver, had
read, and also spoke of his fears that speculation had gotten out of
hand on Wall Street. "Well, Mr. Welliver," Coolidge began, "even if
you and Professor Ripley are right about it, what is there I can do?
The New York Stock Exchange is an affair of the state of New York,
not of the federal government. I don't think I have any authority to
interfere with its operations."

The trouble with this recollection is that at the time Welliver was
no longer on the White House staff, having left on November 1,
1925. And Coolidge was not in the habit of holding casual conver-
sations with newspapermen, even former associates—although it
could have happened.

"But Mr. President," Welliver continued, "whether through the
Federal Trade Commission, the Federal Reserve Board, or any other
agency, you have legal authority, you are the president and have a
measure of moral authority that would be effective. President

Roosevelt and President Wilson many times invoked this moral authority, and made it effective." Welliver suggested that Coolidge invite Ripley to the White House: "This gesture of interest in him, at this time, will be all the hint the stock market boys will need." Coolidge agreed to do so.

Coolidge knew Ripley from his days as Massachusetts governor, and had even consulted with him on economic matters. In addition, he had discussed Ripley's 1926 article at several of his press conferences. On August 27, 1926, for example, he spoke of Ripley's criticism of nonvoting stock, and about state "blue sky" laws that controlled the issuance of equities. "So I assume," Coolidge had said, "that what Professor Ripley is discussing is the question of corporate financing and the management of its business and the opportunity of the ordinary investor to get accurate information in relation to his investment." All of which, he told reporters, was clearly within the purview of the states, not the federal government.

According to Welliver, Coolidge greeted Ripley, and the two men sat and talked for hours, with Ripley doing most of the talking, and Coolidge smoking and listening. Although Coolidge had to break for an appointment, he asked the professor to return in the afternoon, and at that time Ripley spoke of the dangers in the economy, of how speculation was triggering a massive bull market. Later he would tell Welliver about the "prestidigitation, double-shuffling, honey-fugling, hornswoggling, and skulduggery" being practiced.

In a letter to White eight years later, Ripley wrote that Coolidge leaned back in his chair and asked, "Well, Mr. Ripley, is there anything we can do down here?" "No, it's a state matter," Ripley replied. Coolidge had been right—nothing could be done at the presidential or even the federal level. Besides, few at the time agreed with Ripley's forebodings. As we have seen, this was a period of peace, prosperity, and business expansion.

Nevertheless, when the meeting took place—probably in early 1927—the boom on Wall Street was not too heady, prices were not abnormally high. The postwar depression ended, and business was expanding. Earlier in the decade, trading volume had grown, jumping from 261 million shares in 1922 to 452 million in 1925. But then activity leveled off.

Though prices continued to rise, the figures were not outlandish. As measured by the Dow-Jones averages, the market had gone nowhere in 1926—the Industrials started out at 156.66 and ended at 157.20, while the Rails rose from 112.93 to 120.86. In the January–March 1927 period, during which Ripley probably visited Coolidge, the Industrials traded between 155.20 and 160.08, not a particularly lively market. There had certainly been an upward move until that time, but it was hardly wild; in January 1920, even as the country was experiencing postwar economic problems, the Industrials had traded above 100, and the Rails were in the mid-70s. True, trading was 50 percent higher seven years later, but this was a period of economic growth and high corporate earnings. So it is puzzling that Welliver and Ripley thought prices were high.

As it turned out, their warnings were ill-timed. The real boom didn't hit until a year or so later; in April 1928 the Dow Industrials was over 200. This suggests that the alarms were being rung in the early stages of a major bull market. The Industrials would top out in September 1929 at 381.17, more than doubling since the early 1927 warning.

Welliver and Ripley didn't know at the time that the market was about to soar; and Coolidge did not know there would be a crash a year-and-a-half later. This is not to say that Coolidge refrained from acting because he thought that the market was healthy, or that, if it were in trouble, the federal government had no duty to interfere. He only gave off signals and made some comments, but, as usual, he made no definitive statement revealing what he truly thought of the situation.

Both he and Ripley were correct in believing that regulation of the New York securities markets was a state matter. But in 1927–1928, Governor Al Smith did nothing about the situation on Wall Street, perhaps because he did not believe it dangerous. Nor did Governor Franklin D. Roosevelt, who was sworn into office only nine months before the Great Crash.

Coolidge's inaction did not reflect a lack of concern for the economy and the market. In fact, inviting Ripley to the White House and listening to him for hours showed he was concerned. But what could he do? Even Ripley had little by way of agenda to offer, and he did not think the situation critical. At the end of his *Atlantic Monthly* article, he wrote:

> I would not conclude with the advocacy of any
> particular plan. The first duty is to face the fact that
> there is something the matter. For a remedy I am groping
> as yet like a child in the dark. I am conscious that things
> are not right. The house is not falling down—no fear of
> that! But there are queer noises about, as of rats in the
> wall or borers in the timbers. I believe that the trouble
> has to do with the dissociation of ownership of property
> from responsibility for the manner in which it shall be
> put to use.

In short, Ripley was not calling for government intervention. Rather, he appealed to shareholders themselves, and he sought ways to energize these people to take command of business—what some today might call "shareholder capitalism."

Critics of Coolidge often doubt whether he understood what was happening on Wall Street. He was not, of course, an economist. Only two presidents—Ronald Reagan and George Bush—have majored in economics in college, and both had probably forgotten whatever they learned by the time they arrived at the White House. Most presidents learn on the job, which is what Coolidge did. He held to his core principles, and never veered from them.

But Coolidge knew much more about the economy and Wall Street than most realize. The evidence for this, as with so much regarding Coolidge, comes from letters to his father.

On January 21, 1897, the twenty-five-year-old Coolidge wrote to his father about the prospects for a new street railroad:

> Mr. Hammond has gone today to look it over, he has
> had the matter in mind for several years. If the road is
> made the Northampton Company will lease it for
> twenty years and guarantee 5 percent dividend. This

stock is not taxable in this state. It will rise above par.... I do not feel that I can advise you at all in a matter of this kind. I only thought you might like to consider it. Should you desire to examine it further, I should be pleased to keep you informed as it progresses or declines.

In a letter of September 30, 1897, Coolidge sent his father information regarding the Northampton & Amherst Street Railway, a new company. "It seems to me that the enclosed promises to be a good investment. Street ways around here have always paid well and the stock has risen above par."

This was a period when fortunes were made in trolley car lines by the so-called "traction magnates," which included Nelson Aldrich of Providence, Peter A.B. Widener and William L. Elkins of Philadelphia, and Charles T. Yerkes of Chicago. Recommending such stocks at that time was like suggesting the purchase of shares in software companies today. Then again, this was a period when prudent investors purchased and held railroad bonds, not stocks. His recommendations were somewhat racy for the time. Coolidge recognized this. In a letter postmarked October 4, 1897, he told his father, "Now of course I do not believe in speculation any more than you do. I think I am more timid in making investments than you are—and on which I do not believe I should dare to make and on which I presume the returns are 'small' enough to please even you."

Coolidge also seemed to understand some of the dynamics of an international economy. In a February 26, 1898, letter to his father, he wrote, "There is considerable chance of a war with Spain and a more remote war involving all of Europe which no one can tell the end. These conditions will very probably cause Govt. Bonds to fall in price."

Not many of these letters survive. There were two in 1908, when Coolidge was a member of the Massachusetts House of Representatives. In one he referred to the quarterly dividend of the Union Pacific Railroad, a stock he earlier had recommended John Coolidge purchase. Then, a letter of May 26, which sounds like market letters of the 1920s, offered an analysis of several stocks:

Good securities in railroads sell in good times on about
a 4 percent basis. U.P. has not paid 10 percent for two
years, yet it sold at 195. Penn has been to 180,
Anaconda to 75. There is every human probability that
in the course of a year they will go higher than they are
now. Copper is only 13 cents now; last year it was 26.
I do not know where you could put money with any
better prospect of a fair return on a safe investment than
leave it in these securities for the present. There will
come a time when it is best to sell and take 3½ percent in
a safe bank. That will be when times are good like they
were last year in the winter. It is very likely these will
drop off 10 or 15 percent—not points—but there is the
same likelihood they will thereafter go higher than they
are now. It usually takes two years or more for business
to recover. No one can tell when it is best or worst. This
is all I know or anybody else about the *general* market.
You use *your own judgment,* if you think the nation
won't get any more prosperous than it is now, *sell.*

Apparently the Coolidge of 1927–1928 had the same interests
and concepts as the Coolidge of twenty years earlier; he was moni-
toring the markets and had some idea of what was happening. In any
event, at the time of the Coolidge–Ripley meeting neither the economy nor the markets appeared a major concern. Indeed, no consequential problems were present or on the horizon.

After Charles Lindbergh's visit to the temporary White House, the
Coolidges departed for their vacation in the Black Hills of South
Dakota, arriving there on June 15. Washington was closed down
for the summer, but Republican Party Chairman Butler was busy
preparing for Coolidge's renomination in 1928. The president would
not go unchallenged, for Columbia University President Nicholas
Murray Butler, a perennial hopeful, had indicated he would enter the
contest. And some progressive Republicans were talking about backing Hoover, but the commerce secretary wasn't making a move.
Instead, Hoover was making another of his many reputations by

leading the fight against the Mississippi River flood, but he could not translate the popularity earned along the Mississippi into support at the convention.

There were several major news stories that year. The biggest revolved around the speculation regarding whether Nicola Sacco and Bartolomeo Vanzetti would be executed for their crimes. There was the Florida land boom, one of the largest speculative bubbles in the history of real estate, which was deflated in the aftermath of a hurricane in September 1926, but in the summer of 1927 speculators did not yet fully realize it, and Florida land prices were rising once more. The Geneva Conference on Naval Reduction opened, but Coolidge had nothing to say on the matter. Baseball, not politics, interested the American people. Somewhere in between was the stock market. Industrial stocks were trading in a narrow range, but the Rails were moving higher, close to an all-time record.

In late July Coolidge told his secretary, Everett Sanders, "Now—I am not going to run for president. If I should serve as president again, I should serve almost ten years, which is too long for a president in this country." After recovering from his surprise, Sanders remarked, "I think the people will be disappointed." Coolidge said nothing, but handed Sanders a slip of paper on which he had written, "I do not choose to run for president in nineteen twenty-eight." Sanders asked, "You feel sure that you have reached a definite decision about the matter?" Coolidge said he did, to which Sanders replied, "Well, since there is no occasion for speaking now, I do not see why there should be any hurry about making the announcement."

Ever since Coolidge made the announcement, historians and journalists have debated the meaning of these words. At the time many believed Coolidge wanted to be drafted for another term. Why did he use the phrase, "I do not choose"? What if the people chose to have him in office for another four years? But others noted that in Vermont, "I do not chose" signifies refusal—the speaker has decided not to do something. So it was not so equivocal as it may have at first seemed.

August 2 marked the fourth anniversary of Coolidge's accession to the presidency, but to most that was not a particularly notable date. Coolidge was scheduled to have a press conference that morning. He remarked to his wife after breakfast, "I have been president four years today." Just before 9:00 AM, he set out with his host, Senator Arthur Capper, to face the reporters. Coolidge indicated to Sanders that he wanted to make the announcement then, but Sanders encouraged him to wait until noon: "I think it would be well if you made it at twelve o'clock instead of nine o'clock. There is a three-hour difference in time between Rapid City and New York, and if the announcement is made at twelve o'clock, it will come after three there, and the stock market will be closed. News of this kind is sure to affect the stock market. It is always best to have the news break at a time when the effect can be digested while the stock market is closed." Coolidge agreed.

Coolidge started off the press conference by saying, "If the conference will return at 12:00 I may have a further statement to make." One of the reporters seems to have asked what Coolidge considered the most important contributions he had made during his White House years, providing the president with a chance to sum up the accomplishments of his administration. It was another of the rare times Coolidge appeared to take credit for the economic prosperity—perhaps because he considered that a form of political valedictory was expected on such occasions:

> It is rather difficult for me to pick out one thing above another to designate what is called here the chief accomplishments of the four years of my administration. The country has been at peace during that time. It hasn't had any marked commercial or financial depression. Some parts of it naturally have been better off than other parts, some people better off than other people, but on the whole it has been a time of a fair degree of prosperity. Wages have been slightly increasing. There has been no time that there has been any marked lack of employment. There have been certain industries like the textile industry and the boot and shoe industry in certain localities like New England, which have not been running on full time. But generally speaking, there has

been employment for everyone who wished
employment. There has been a very marked time of
peace in the industrial world. There have been some
strikes. When I first came into office there was a strike
in the hard coal fields and another strike I think in the
same line a couple or three years later, but those
differences have been adjusted without any great conflict
or any great suffering on the part of the industries or the
public, so that there has been rather a time of marked
peace in industry as between employer and employees.
There has been considerable legislation which you know
about, and which I do not need to recount. There have
been great accomplishments in the finances of the
national government, a large reduction in the national
debt, considerable reduction in taxes.

At 11:00 AM Coolidge summoned Sanders, picked up a pencil,
and wrote the message again. He handed it to the secretary and said,
"Take this, and about ten minutes before twelve call in Mr. Geisser
[his stenographer], have him run off a number of these lines on legal-
sized paper, five or six on a sheet, with carbons enough to supply
the newspapermen, and some to spare. Then bring the sheets to me
uncut." When it was done, Coolidge cut the papers into slips. He
said, "I am going to hand these out myself; I am going to give them
to the newspapermen, without comment, from this side of the desk.
I want you to stand at the door and not permit anyone to leave until
each of them has a slip, so that they may have an even chance."

The reporters received the slips from a clearly amused president,
and as expected they rushed from the press conference to the tele-
phones. Afterward Senator Capper saw Mrs. Coolidge and remarked,
"That was quite a surprise the president gave us this morning." Mrs.
Coolidge, who had suspected something like this, said, "Isn't that just
like the man! He never gave me the slightest intimation of his intention. I had no idea!"

The effect on the securities markets was as Sanders expected. The
Dow Industrials closed at 185.55 on August 2, on a trading volume

of 2.6 million shares. The following day's trading ended at 183.56, with 2.7 million shares traded, making it the busiest session of the year to that date. Since there had been a rally late in the session, the interday index had been lower. The market continued to fall, hitting 177.13, and then went on to new highs.

The reason for the rally, according to some analysts, was that the public realized that prosperity did not rest on the shoulders of one man. Others, however, thought investors had concluded that Coolidge would still accept a draft in 1928. Then, too, he stated he would not run specifically in *1928*. Did this mean he would be willing to return to the political wars in 1932? Upon such slender reeds Coolidge supporters hung their hopes.

Why did Coolidge decide not to run in 1928? In his *Autobiography* he sent mixed signals: "But irrespective of the third-term policy, the presidential office is of such a nature that it is difficult to conceive how one man can successfully serve the country for a term of more than eight years." He then added, "While I am in favor of continuing the long-established custom of the country in relation to a third term for a president, yet I do not think that the practice applies to one who has succeeded to part of the term as vice president. Others might argue that it does, but I doubt if the country would so consider it."

Some two-term presidents had hungered for a third term, among them Wilson, and, if he is indeed considered a two-term president, Theodore Roosevelt as well. Coolidge had a different temperament. For one thing, while self-assured, he was more modest than most presidents. And for another, he recognized the dangers of self-deception the office could engender:

> It is difficult for men in high office to avoid the malady
> of self-delusion. They are always surrounded by
> worshipers. They are constantly, and for the most part
> sincerely, assured of their greatness. They live in an
> artificial atmosphere of adulation and exaltation which
> sooner or later impairs their judgment. They are in grave
> danger of becoming careless and arrogant.

I had never wished to run in 1928 and had determined
to make a public announcement at a sufficiently early
date so that the party would have ample time to choose
someone else. An appropriate occasion for that
announcement seemed to be the fourth anniversary of my
taking office. The reasons I can give may not appear very
convincing, but I am confident my decision was correct.

A typical Coolidge statement: apparently straightforward, but it
doesn't really answer the question. Historians and journalists, then
and now, have put forth other explanations. In 1938 General
Sherwood Cheney, a White House military aide, said that his physician had warned Coolidge that he had a heart condition, and this,
perhaps, prompted his decision. But his personal physician, Dr.
Edward Brown, writing in 1935, denied it. Coolidge suffered from
minor digestive problems, he said, adding, "Indigestion is occasionally mistaken for heart trouble, but I do not believe this was true in
his case. About two months before his death I had examined him.
There were no heart symptoms at that time." Edmund Starling
offered a more plausible answer:

The novelty of being president had worn off; the glory of
it had gone with [young] Calvin's death; there was no
great national crisis which demanded a continuation of his
leadership. From now on the office was more a burden
than anything else. The steady grind of work was wearing
him down, and the duties of the First Lady, plus Washington's weather, were weakening Mrs. Coolidge's health.

Mrs. Coolidge offered another explanation after her husband's
death that later on became the subject of much discussion.

In a conversation with a former member of his cabinet a
short time before he left Washington, that gentleman
expressed his conviction that the president's decision not
to run again had been a wise one; that, not to mention
other reasons, he felt the country would undergo the

most serious economic and financial convulsion which
had occurred since 1875; that the president would carry
a heavy burden and one which no man should be asked
to bear who had passed through two successful terms.

To this, the president replied in terse colloquial style, "It is a pretty
good idea to get out when they still want you."

Writing in 1935, Mrs. Coolidge offered this insight into Coolidge's thoughts at the time. In another discussion with a cabinet
member, he said:

I know how to save money. All my training has been in
that direction. The country is in a sound financial
position. Perhaps the time has come when we ought to
spend money. I do not feel that I am qualified to do it.

A friend recalled her replying to the question of why he was leaving office, "Poppa says there's a depression coming."

There is scant evidence for this. His public statements of this time
were invariably optimistic. As for private statements, these were
always aired years after the fact, and of doubtful provenance. For
example, according to White House Secretary Edward Clark, writing
in 1935, Coolidge had been worried for a long time about the possibility of economic troubles. In 1927, after naming Dwight Morrow his
special envoy to Mexico—shortly before announcing his decision not
to run for another term—Clark recalled him praising Morrow as the
kind of person who should be in power in the event of a financial crisis. Clark asked, "Do you expect some sort of financial crisis?" "I do
not attempt to predict anything," Coolidge replied, "but people do
not seem to see that while we in this country are increasing production
enormously, other countries are closing their doors more and more
against our products. Our foreign outlets are constantly diminishing."
Coolidge named the USSR, an independent India, and China as future
powers and potential danger spots: "Competition is increasing
tremendously. We shall have to meet it in every field."

Finally, what remained to be done? On the domestic scene he had
his tax cuts and had blocked McNary–Haugen. The Kellogg–Briand

Pact was generally applauded. Nicaragua and Mexico were problems, but hardly major ones. Europe was at peace, and the national economies seemed healthy enough. On a more personal level, what did he have to prove and whom did he have to impress? His father had died, and Coolidge had made him proud of his accomplishments. Those fellow students at Black River Academy and Amherst now knew that the person they thought would not amount to much had done pretty well. The novelty of the presidency might have interested him initially, but that was gone, too. In other words, he saw no reason to remain, and so he intended to leave office.

Hoover went to the White House in September 1927 to speak with Coolidge about the nomination. On this occasion and two others he said he would support a Coolidge candidacy, but, were the president not to run, he wanted to enter the lists. Coolidge replied in his usual cryptic fashion, but in the end Hoover believed the president would not be a candidate. Still, Hoover made one last try the following May 1928. At the time Hoover had pledges from four hundred delegates, close to half the total. He told Coolidge that, though by law most had to vote for him on the first ballot, he still thought the president could win the nomination on that ballot, and that he would be pleased to continue serving under Coolidge. Hoover later recalled that Coolidge was skeptical about the figure, but said, "If you have four hundred delegates, you better keep them." Hoover added, "I could get no more out of him."

Hoover, Senator Charles Curtis of Kansas, and Senator F.B. Willis of Ohio announced their candidacies. Senators Norris and James Watson of Indiana were interested. And there was some support for Senator Guy Goff of West Virginia. Lowden, too, remained a possibility, and his old friend, Vice President Dawes, supported him, but Lowden would be sixty-nine years old by the next inauguration day.

Late that year several Washington insiders opined that Coolidge might consider a Hoover candidacy as a run by a protégé, but might change his mind about his own candidacy if it appeared Lowden, Dawes, or some other hopeful who supported McNary–Haugen had a chance to be nominated. In any case, as 1927 drew to a close, Coolidge hadn't budged on his refusal to make the race. Even so, in January 1928 Senator Robert La Follette, Jr., who had taken his father's place, introduced a resolution declaring that failure to observe the two-term tradition would constitute a precedent "unwise, unpatriotic, and fraught with peril to our free institutions." It was a transparent effort to block a draft Coolidge movement, but at the same time so bland as to be meaningless. Nonetheless it passed by a vote of 56 to 26; the senatorial Republicans were still not Coolidge devotees.

As always, the economic scene was mixed. There was a slowdown in 1927; corporate earnings fell to $5.5 billion from the previous year's $6.9 billion, but dividends rose, a sign that businesses were confident and that the corporations were not in need of funds for expansion of physical plant.

Today, business news is featured in newspapers and on television and radio, but this was not the case in the 1920s. Few outside the professional circles understood the impact of the growing financial relationship of America to Europe, Wall Street to Lombard Street, and their unanticipated consequences. One development, in retrospect, might have been the beginning of a problem that brought on the economic disaster of 1929. At the time, however, it was perceived only as an attempt to resurrect the prewar glory of the British Empire.

In 1925 the UK chancellor of the exchequer, Winston Churchill, resumed the convertibility of sterling at its prewar rate of $4.86 a pound. This made the pound far too dear, raised the costs of the UK's exports, lowered those for imports, and resulted in an outflow of gold, much of it to the United States. Individuals in other countries were sending their gold to America for the best reasons: their economies appeared sluggish, while the American economy was strong. This money flowed out of their markets and economies, and much of it was used to purchase American government securities, which offered attractive yields. But if this continued for long, the European recoveries might abort, bringing down the triangular system of the Dawes Plan, in which American loans to Germany helped pay reparations to the UK and France, who then repaid their loans to the United States.

If this situation had been allowed to persist, it would have surely created serious international problems, as it may have forced

European nations from the gold standard. Benjamin Strong and Secretary Mellon both saw the situation as dire. Strong, who headed the New York Federal Reserve Bank, had inherited some of J.P. Morgan's aura. Not only was Strong trusted in American banking circles, but he had an international reputation, as well, and worked smoothly with his European counterparts.

In 1927 the two Americans conferred with their counterparts at the Bank of England, the Reichsbank, and the Bank of France. The Europeans urged the United States to lower its interest rates in order to make American securities less attractive to European investors. This would also encourage borrowing in the United States, and so stimulate the economy there. They believed a booming American economy was the engine that drove the European economies. Lower interest rates would also encourage borrowing by speculators who would then use the money to purchase American stocks, but at the time this was not considered too important a matter.

This situation prompted the New York Federal Reserve Bank to reduce the rediscount rate from 4 percent to 3½ percent in August 1927. However, this was not unexpected; the Fed had kept the rate between 4 percent and 3½ percent since 1922, and investors were learning to expect stimulation in declining markets, and dampening when recovery appeared. In addition, in the second half of the year the Fed purchased close to half a billion dollars in open market operations, thus increasing the money supply. So all looked well. The Fed, originated in part to perform the stabilizing effects once provided by J.P. Morgan, seemed to be the friend of business and the investors.

Additional support came from the brokers' loan money market. Nowadays, Wall Street looks to such money indicators as the discount and prime rates, money supply, and open market operations, but not so in the late 1920s. The key rate then was the brokers' loan rate. In this period the purchaser typically would put up only a portion of the funds required for the purchase of stocks and borrow the rest at competitive bank rates, a practice known as "buying on margin." Solid customers could borrow 90 percent of the price, putting up the purchased stock as collateral, while others might borrow 75 percent.

In the 1920s one of the key distinctions between investors and speculators was that the former paid cash and held their securities, while the latter bought on margin and sold when they had profits or were "called out"—that is, when the stocks fell to the point at which no margin remained. If the stock declined to that point, the customer might be asked to provide "more margin," which might be borrowed from the broker with additional collateral. The increase in the money supply, combined with the growing financing by corporations, meant that more funds were available for brokers' loans. The low rates and ease of obtaining money fueled the stock market and led it into new high ground. Speculators continued to borrow when rates increased, because by then they were convinced there were fortunes to be had.

Given his earlier knowledge of the securities markets, Coolidge might have concluded there were dangers ahead, but then, anyone who knows investments well realizes that this is ever the case. Nonetheless, he did what he could to maintain confidence in business, and by extension, indicate the situation was not hazardous. In early 1927 Coolidge predicted—accurately, as it turned out—that the year would be "one of continued healthy business activity and prosperity." When asked to comment on the Fed's rate cut, Coolidge, wary as always, noted that the central bank was an independent agency: "A great many times a question seems to be very complicated and almost insoluble." Coolidge indicated that he would not interfere with the Fed on the matter of policy. Strong was universally trusted; Coolidge certainly could not have been blamed for letting him take charge.

Just before New Year's Day, 1928, Francis Jones, director general of the Employment Bureau of the Department of Labor, predicted that industry and business would reach "new high levels in 1928," based on reports from the department's field offices. "Contrary to precedents established in former presidential election years, when the business world stood by awaiting results before charting their programs, the opposite is true at this time," said Jones. "The pessimists and doubting Thomases and the iconoclasts will be obliged to revise their opinions with respect to the nation's industrial future." He continued:

> All signs point to the biggest year in the history of the
> automobile industry. Iron and steel point to market
> increases over 1927. Indications are that building
> construction will compare favorably with the previous
> year. The position of agriculture shows improvement.
> Railroads will undoubtedly enjoy normal business. Owing
> to the increased introduction of labor-saving machinery,
> considerable labor will be displaced, but the volume of
> business is expected to register a new high level.

Congressman William Oldfield, an Arkansas Democrat, demurred. He noted that there had been more than 48,000 bankruptcies in 1927, and freight car loadings, an important economic indicator at the time, showed 1,000,000 fewer loadings than in 1926. During the Harding–Coolidge years there had been approximately 3,000 bank failures, with more than $1 billion in liabilities, and more than 125,000 commercial failures, with liabilities of $3 billion. "It is very much to be hoped that Secretary of the Treasury Mellon's prediction that business will be better during 1928, than it has been during 1927, will come true. Certainly there is room for improvement." But, as Jones predicted, the country would have another good year in 1928.

In early January 1928, the NYSE announced that brokers' loans had increased sharply, standing at $4.4 billion, a billion dollar increase for 1927. The market, already skittish, now showed signs of correcting. Moody's Investment Service said that it thought stock prices had "over-discounted anticipated progress," but Professor Irving Fisher of Yale, one of the nation's premier economists, was bullish. The market opinions in early 1928 were as they usually are except during periods of great optimism or deep pessimism—which is to say, divided.

Coolidge was asked at his January 7 press conference what he thought about the level of brokers' loans, and again he was cautious. On balance, he seemed untroubled:

> I am not familiar enough with the exact workings and
> practice of the Federal Reserve System so that comments

that I might make relative to the amount of brokers' loans would not be of very much value. I do know in a general way that the amount of securities in this country has increased very largely in recent years. The number of different securities that are dealt in on the stock exchange are very much larger than they were previously. The deposits in the banks also are larger. And those two things together would necessarily be a reason for doing more business of the kind that is transacted by brokers and would naturally result in a larger sum of money being used for that purpose. Now, whether the amount at the present time is disproportionate to the resources of the country I am in no position to judge accurately, but so far as indicated by an inquiry that I have made of the Treasury Department and so on. I haven't had any indications that the amount was large enough to cause particularly unfavorable comment.

Industrialist and stock market figure William C. Durant seconded the thought. "Why all this hue and cry about the bank loans to brokers?" he wanted to know, and added:

The function of a bank is to receive and loan money. The banks, due to the wonderful prosperity of the country, have accumulated enormous deposits, and will continue to do so. These deposits must be loaned. Where or to whom could the banks loan $3,000,000,000 to better advantage or more safety than to brokers or individuals, secured by choice collateral of their own selection? In the ordinary course of business, I am of the opinion that brokers' loans, or "Street loans," so called, will within the next twelve months exceed $5,000,000,000.

The *New York Times*'s headline the next day, Saturday, was: "Coolidge's Optimism Gives Stocks a Lift." Volume that half-day session was 1.7 million shares, the second heaviest for a Saturday in history. The Dow, which had slid from its 1927 closing of 202.40 to 199.61 on the day before the press conference, now rose above 200 again, but before the session was over, had given up much of its gain on profit taking.

Coolidge's statement surprised the *Times*, who added, "Old-timers in Wall Street tried without much success yesterday to recall any precedent for Mr. Coolidge's remark on brokers' loans, quoted in the morning newspaper dispatches. None of them could remember an instance in which the country's chief executive had made a public declaration on a controversy of just that character."

According to William Allen White's Coolidge biography, H. Parker Willis, Coolidge's cousin and the editor of the *New York Journal of Commerce*, doubted that the president truly believed that the level of brokers' loans was reasonable. A few days after that statement the two men had discussed the financial situation at some length. Willis told White later on that Coolidge said, "If I were to give my own personal opinion about it, I should say that any loan made for gambling in stocks was an 'excessive loan.'" Willis replied that he wished Coolidge had said that, and Coolidge wanted to know why. "Simply because I think it would have had a tremendous effect in repressing an unwholesome speculation, with which, I now see, you have no sympathy." Coolidge thought this over and said:

> Well, I regard myself as representative of the government
> and not as an individual. When technical matters come
> up I feel called upon to refer them to the proper
> department of the government which has some
> information about them and then, unless there is some
> good reason, I use this information about them as a
> basis for whatever I have to say; but that does not
> prevent me from thinking what I please as an individual.

The market then dropped below 200, and remained there with brief interludes until mid-March, whereupon prices resumed their upward move.

After the Great Depression was a reality, some charged that Coolidge and Mellon, realizing in 1928 that the economy would enter into a major slump, put out optimistic broadsides throughout the last years of the Coolidge administration, hoping to delay the falloff until after he left office. "The process was simple," wrote an anonymous author in 1931. "It was prosperity by political proclamation. If the stock ticker showed a slump at Monday closing or Tuesday opening, Mr. Coolidge invariably devoted his Tuesday noon press conference to bullish statements. 'Don't sell America short,' was their tenor. If the market's fluctuations necessitated it, he did it again on Friday afternoon."

The records of the press conferences indicated no such pattern, and this scenario doesn't explain why Mellon remained in the cabinet after Coolidge left, but by then this conclusion had become standard lore. White, who was critical of Coolidge during this period, wrote in his biography, "Bullish statements by Coolidge and Mellon in 1928 were infrequent. Their previous remarks, in conjunction with other favorable factors, had given rise to an upward move on the stock market which, with few setbacks, rolled on and on, gathering momentum and increasing in size to the end, which was still a year away."

There were several market corrections in 1928 and 1929, during which respected analysts and commentators said the bull market was ending, only to be contradicted by the rising market. When the Dow fell below 200 on January 28, 1928, and remained there during February and into March, some analysts once again concluded that the bull market was finished. "The public is not likely to change its bearish state of mind until about the time when money becomes so plethoric as to lead the banks to encourage credit expansion," wrote *Moody's*. Some brokerages started running ads like, "Will You Overstay the Bull Market?" and "Is the Process of Deflation Under Way?" But, by the end of March, the Dow was at 213.35, and the mood was optimistic once again.

At his April 24, 1928, press conference, Coolidge commented on the rise in the rediscount rate to 4½ percent, a signal the central bank thought required some dampening of Wall Street's exuberance: "No information has come to me concerning the increase in rediscount rates except that which I have seen in the press. That is a matter entirely for the Federal Reserve Board, a matter that I wouldn't happen to know anything about." If Coolidge was being completely honest here, the statement is bothersome. Of course, Coolidge believed strongly in the separation of state and federal governments and the executive and legislative branches. But to say he had no knowledge of what was going on at the Fed, and to imply he had no interest, was one of the most serious errors of judgment he made while president.

By the time the Republican convention opened in Kansas City on June 12, the Dow had fallen from a mid-May high of 220 to 202.01. That day, volume was more than five million, and the ticker was two hours late at times. Certainly this seemed an end to the market rise and the beginning of bad times for Wall Street. Was this finally the beginning of the bear market?

In short, no one could tell. It was a period in which, for every William Ripley, there were a dozen experts who foresaw a vista of uninterrupted economic growth. The unprecedented market developments led commentators to change their minds continually; after the crash, analyst Roger Babson was lauded for having "predicted" the market collapse in September 1929, but just a year earlier he had predicted "continued prosperity for 1929."

Meanwhile, pressures on Coolidge to make a run for the presidency, or at the very least agree to accept a draft, intensified.

Hoover was far and away favored for the nomination. Several senators opposed him, frustrated first with Coolidge and now with Hoover, since they wanted neither man. Yet Coolidge was mentioned in many orations in the days that followed. Ralph Cole, a delegate from Ohio, said that his first choice had been his state's Senator Frank Willis, who had died in March. His second choice was Lowden, who had withdrawn. "I wish now to choose my third candidate.... My really first choice and the first choice of America in the beginning of this campaign."

With this there were cries of "Coolidge! Coolidge!" Cole then continued:

> Some delegates in this convention have the power of
> reading the human mind. My candidate is a Republican.

This is a Republican convention. We have adopted today
a Republican platform. We must nominate a Republican
for president of the United States. My candidate cast his
first vote in 1896 for Ohio's illustrious son, William
McKinley, the great champion of protection. He did not
fail to vote in that campaign.* He next followed the
leadership of that great American of his day and
generation, Theodore Roosevelt. But he did not forget to
vote. He did not forget his name when he came to vote.
My candidate voted the ticket in 1916…. My candidate
was chosen vice president in 1920, elected president in
1924—an exalted specimen of American manhood,
better than wealth, better than all power, better than all
position, to have the courage, character, and conscience
of Calvin Coolidge, my candidate.

For an instant it appeared that Cole might have reprised the
McCamant role of 1920, and that the convention might stampede to
Coolidge. But Senator George Moses, chairman of the convention,
went ahead and called the role of the states followed by seconding
speeches and the balloting. Hoover was nominated on the first ballot. Then the Republicans went home to await the acceptance speech
and, after Labor Day, the beginning of the campaign.

Coolidge did not say much during this time, but Hoover came
for a visit and the traditional laying on of hands. When posing for a
picture together, a photographer asked Coolidge to say something to
Hoover, to which Coolidge replied, "Let him talk. He's going to be
president." In September he told reporters, "This time the only thing
I was a candidate for was retirement and apparently I am going to be
successful in that."

The Democrats gathered in Houston on June 26, and in a relatively quiet convention nominated Al Smith. He represented just
about everything southern Democrats, an important segment of the

---

* This refers to the fact that Hoover had been out of the country during much of that period and did not vote in the elections.

party, opposed, while Hoover had been a national figure, and largely admired, for more than a decade. In image, he combined the old-fashioned virtues of Coolidge with the new technology of the 1920s, embodied by men like Lindbergh.

In 1928 both parties nominated candidates who truly were new political types. Many seemed to have sensed this, because the Democrats clearly were divided on Smith, just as few Republicans at the Kansas City GOP Convention seemed enthusiastic for Hoover. For all his singularity, Coolidge belonged to the era of Harding, Wilson, and Taft. Hoover, who had been an engineer and business-man before entering government service, became the only major party candidate, excluding military men, to be elected president in his first political campaign. For his part, Smith's record as New York's governor was one of concern with urban America, and not a restatement of Wilsonian Progressivism. Still, both Hoover and Smith were in some ways heirs of the progressives, since both men's policies had their roots in turn-of-the-century reform.

It was a lively campaign. Hoover ran on the Coolidge record. "We in America today are nearer the final triumph over poverty than ever before in the history of any land," he told one audience that August, and he often repeated the thought. Smith spoke of the need for reform and indicated that, if he were elected, the govern-ment would play a more active role in the economy than it had under Harding and Coolidge.

Coolidge remained in seclusion during the campaign, but he did deliver some speeches supporting Hoover. In September he spoke to a crowd in Bennington, Vermont, from the back of a train. It was a short talk, seemingly extemporaneous. The next day's newspapers reprinted the talk, and remarked on the beauty of one section:

> Vermont is a state I love. I could not look upon the
> peaks of Ascutney, Killington, Mansfield, and Equinox,
> without being moved in a way that no other scene could
> move me. It was here that I first saw the light of day;
> here I received my bride, here my dead lie, pillowed on
> the loving breast of our everlasting hills. I love Vermont
> because of her hills and valleys, her scenery and

invigorating climate, but most of all because of her indomitable people. They are a race of pioneers who have almost beggared themselves to serve others. If the spirit of liberty should vanish in other parts of the union and support of our institutions should languish, it could all be replenished from the generous store held by the people of this brave little state of Vermont.

This did not seem to be typical Coolidge, but after his death it came out that he wrote poetry, which few had known. This segment of the speech had been carefully prepared, but delivered so as to make it appear a sudden inspiration. It was all part of that image-making.

After the election was over, conventional wisdom claimed that Smith demonstrated that a Catholic could not hope to become president. Smith might have believed this. He later remarked, "I guess it isn't time yet when a man can say his beads in the White House." More recent scholarship demonstrates that the religious issue was not that great. Although he lost, Smith received fifteen million popular votes, more than Davis and La Follette's combined votes in 1924, and almost as much as Coolidge's total that year.

No Democrat could have hoped to win in 1928. The reason was not religion, but "Coolidge Prosperity." Undeniably, some Americans voted against Smith who might have voted for a Protestant candidate, but then again, many Catholics voted for him who would not have voted for a Protestant, indicated by the sharp jump in voter participation that year. In 1924, 48.9 percent of qualified voters went to the polls, a modern low; in 1928, 56.9 percent voted, the highest level since 1916. Many have attributed this jump in voting to Catholic women, who had not voted in large numbers in 1920 and 1924 but turned out for Smith in 1928.

Had Coolidge run he probably would have won the 1928 election handily—by an even larger margin than Hoover's.

In June, a week after the Hoover nomination, the Dow went below 200 before recovering for a small gain. Activity was intense, with over four million shares trading on some sessions with the ticker running late. But then, as before, the market recovered, and by

Labor Day, the Dow was over 240. The demand for brokers' loans increased, with the interest rate at times coming close to 20 percent. Even so, speculators plunged into the market, figuring that if a stock doubled in a year, that kind of interest was perfectly acceptable. Corporations, realizing that such returns were more than they could make in their own businesses, started to go into brokers' loans with their surpluses. For instance, Electric Bond & Share placed $156 million, and Bethlehem Steel about the same. William Durant's January prediction that by year's end there would be $5 billion in brokers' loans had been too timid—the figure was more than $6.4 billion. Also, large pools headed by one or another speculator had formed. So, when RCA, Chrysler, General Motors, National City Bank, or some other favorite rose or fell 20 to 40 points in a session, one or another pool manager was quite often responsible.

On December 4 Coolidge sent his final annual message to the Capitol. He went over the by-then-familiar litany—the reduction of the debt, the surpluses, the situation in agriculture, and Muscle Shoals. Coolidge noted that since 1922 wages had risen by 12.9 percent, and that in some industries, they had increased by as much as 38 percent. "As the rise in living costs in this period is negligible, these figures represent real wage increases." In his conclusion, Coolidge struck themes that reflected his general view of the nation and that had marked his public statements since he had been a Massachusetts legislator:

> The country is in the midst of an era of prosperity more
> extensive and of peace more permanent than it has ever
> before experienced. But, having reached this position,
> we should not fail to comprehend that it can easily be
> lost. It needs more effort for its support than the less
> exalted places of the world. We shall not be permitted to
> take our ease, but shall continue to be required to spend
> our days in unremitting toil. The actions of the
> government must command the confidence of the
> country. Without this, our prosperity would be lost.
> We must extend to other countries the largest measure

of generosity, moderation, and patience. In addition to dealing justly, we can well afford to walk humbly.

The end of government is to keep open the opportunity for a more abundant life. Peace and prosperity are not finalities; they are only methods. It is too easy under their influence for a nation to become selfish and degenerate. This test has come to the United States. Our country has been provided with the resources with which it can enlarge its intellectual, moral, and spiritual life. The issue is in the hands of its people. Our faith in man and God is the justification for the belief in our continuing success.

14

....

Retirement

It was therefore my privilege, after seeing my administration so
strongly endorsed by the country, to retire voluntarily from the
greatest experience that can come to mortal man. In that way, I
believed I could best serve the people who have honored me and
the country which I love.

Last paragraph in *The Autobiography of Calvin Coolidge*

AFTER THE ELECTION, President-elect Hoover traveled to
Washington to meet with Coolidge and make a request. There were
four months between Election Day and the inauguration. Hoover
planned to spend a month and a half of that time on a tour of Latin
America, and asked Coolidge to place a battleship at his disposal
for the trip. He recorded Coolidge's response in his *Memoirs: The
Cabinet and the Presidency*:

> He suggested I take a cruiser—"it would not cost so
> much." However, since battleships as well as cruisers
> always must keep steam up and their crews aboard, that
> did not worry me much. I wanted room enough to take
> Mrs. Hoover, whose California upbringing enabled her
> to speak considerable Spanish. Also I wanted a
> diplomatic staff and representatives of the press, so as
> not only to evidence great interest in these countries but
> to educate the American people a little on our neighbors

to the south. Finally, Mr. Coolidge put the battleship *Maryland* at my disposal; and the battleship *Utah* met us in Montevideo and brought us home.

In early December Coolidge prepared his final budget message, taking a day off to go quail shooting in Staunton, Virginia. He wore a ten-gallon hat and a white shirt and yellow tie underneath a bright green mackinaw, and posed for the photographers with his usual dead-pan face. Coolidge, who was not a sportsman, took many shots, but the quail had little to fear: he didn't hit one.

Coolidge dispatched his final annual message to Congress on December 4. The confident document revealed the optimism felt by Coolidge and the nation as a whole:

> No Congress of the United States ever assembled, on surveying the state of the Union, has met with a more pleasing prospect than that which appears at the present time. In the domestic field there is tranquility and contentment, harmonious relations between management and wage earner, freedom from industrial strife, and the highest record of years of prosperity. In the foreign field there is peace, the good will that comes from mutual understanding, and the knowledge that the problems which a short time ago appeared so ominous are yielding to the touch of mutual friendship.

In his budget address, read to Congress the following day, December 5, Coolidge said there would be a smaller than hoped for surplus for 1929, due to the increased cost of government, especially in the area of national defense. Estimated receipts for 1929 were \$3.831 billion and expenditures, \$3.794 billion. Therefore, he did not ask for another tax cut.

In the message, Coolidge noted that in 1928, 54 percent of receipts had been derived from income taxes, against 42 percent in 1923. Coolidge had often asserted the tax cuts would boost income tax collections, and on the basis of these figures, he was correct. As indicated, Coolidge believed that lower taxes would stimulate the economy and lead to greater employment and higher wages, which would translate into higher tax revenues.

The budget caused no major discussions, and two days later the newspapers turned to Coolidge's suggestion of a summer White House in the mountains near the city, perhaps in Maryland. Coolidge spoke of the stifling heat of the summer in the city, and how it was deleterious to the First Family's health. Congressmen deserted Washington in late spring and returned in the fall for that reason. Work at the government's offices fell off, and the pace of activity, always slow compared to New York or Chicago, became positively languid. But the president had to remain in Washington, and worked as hard in August as he did in March. In this suggestion, as with so much in his administration, Coolidge was repeating a proposal first made during the Harding years.

Toward the end of his administration, Coolidge's supporters applauded and his opponents criticized him for having helped bring the country back to where it had been before the war. But Coolidge had not, of course, done this; annual government expenditures had more than quadrupled since the last prewar year—in 1916 government spending amounted to only $716 million; by 1928, the amount was up to $3.1 billion. Many argued that he had reversed the trend toward big government, but, despite his philosophical opposition to federal growth, Coolidge was prepared to expend funds for programs even Wilson, Taft, and Roosevelt had largely rejected. For example, he endorsed Mellon's program to construct federal buildings in Washington, which in time transformed the capital from a dusty backwater to a major American city. Mellon told Coolidge that while the program would be costly—he spoke in terms of $250 million—it would be less expensive for the federal government to own its buildings than to lease space from private interests. This program, and others like it, had to be justified to Coolidge on these grounds.

This approach was the key to understanding Coolidge's actions and reactions to expenditures. His goal was to hold the line on spending, and if possible roll it back, while at the same time reducing taxes, for he expected that this would result in greater personal freedom, continued prosperity, and a more moral population. To a large degree Coolidge succeeded in realizing the first two objectives during his administration. In 1923 total federal expenditures were $3.1 billion, and they were $3.0 billion in 1928. In these two years, despite the tax cuts, budget receipts were the same—$3.9 billion. The national debt fell from $22.3 billion to $17.6 billion. Even as the number of federal employees rose slightly during his tenure—537,000 in 1923 versus 561,000 in 1928—the number in Washington fell from 70,000 to 65,000; much of the increase was isolated to the growth in the Post Office Department.

Coolidge felt himself an anachronism even in the pre–New Deal Hoover administration, as he was a relic of a pre–World War I America in which state and local government had preeminence. In most ways, he was not comfortable with the increasing federalization of government. Indeed, Reagan, who so admired the Coolidge philosophy of reduced taxes and small government, actually did not cut spending, and he ran deficits that would have been unimaginable to Coolidge.

In the days leading up to Christmas 1928, the Coolidges were guests at several farewell dinner parties. In that season it was traditional for cabinet officers, in the order of seniority, to give parties, but the Coolidges' imminent departure made them special that year. Secretary of State Kellogg was first, followed by Secretary of the Treasury Mellon, who basked in a popularity second only to that of Coolidge. Rumor had it that in putting together his cabinet, Hoover intended to ask him to remain in office, not surprising for the man who was being hailed as the greatest Treasury chief since Alexander Hamilton.

The economy seemed in fine shape, and in November Wall Street celebrated with a rally, the Dow rising from 255.23 on November 1 to 293.38 on November 30.

On December 4, 1928, as Coolidge's optimistic State of the Union address was being read to Congress, the Dow ended the day at 291.30, only four points from its all time high. But there had been a selloff in the morning which was troublesome. Brokers' loans were more than $5 billion, and interest rates on them more than 10 percent, a sign of overheating. There were also signs that investment pools were taking certain favored stocks "in hand"— that is, the market was rigged. For instance, RCA, one of the favorites for both bull and bear pools, closed at 407½, down 7½ points, but that day traded within a range of 47½ points.

Prices collapsed on December 6, the Dow closing at 279.79, for a loss of almost 4 percent in market value, as brokers' loans reached 12 percent, the highest in eight years. Volume was 5.4 million shares, and the selling started with the opening bell and continued through the session. The Dow fell to 271.05 the following day, and to 257.33 on December 8, which was a half-day Saturday session. In three days, then, stocks declined 33 points, or 11 percent, which would translate by early 1998 standards to a more than 900 point selloff. The talk on Wall Street was that now that Coolidge was leaving office, he would take the Coolidge luck with him.

The market, however, recovered the next session, Monday, December 10, closing up by more than six points. Of the actions that day, the *New York Times* said, "After Saturday's convulsive reaction, the interest of the whole financial community was focused on the opening of the Stock Market yesterday. Large crowds were gathered wherever there was a ticker."

After the recovery, brokers' loans fell to 7½ percent. The short panic was over, and stocks advanced irregularly for the rest of the month. On the last trading session of 1928, the market celebrated with a 4.9 million share day, with the Dow ending at a record 300.00.

The economic news cheered the bulls. Adjusted for inflation, the GNP grew 49 percent from 1921 to 1928, the Harding–Coolidge years, the highest growth on record. By comparison, the growth from 1961 to 1968 was 38 percent, and that from 1982 to 1989, 29 percent. Family disposable income rose during the Coolidge years, when the unemployment rate averaged only 3.3 percent. Business prospered, and so did a great many ordinary Americans.

And, of course, the stock market performed well in Coolidge's presidency. Critics point out that the crash came just half a year after Coolidge left office, and they argue that he should have foreseen the economic calamity. Yet historians have allowed their advantage of hindsight to color their assessment of the market leading up to the Great Crash of October 1929. As H. Stuart Hughes wrote, the historian "cannot give the full sense of events as reality in the process of becoming—*because he knows the outcome*. By no literary device or trick of false innocence can he recapture his historical virginity; it is idle for him to pretend to an unsophistication of judgement which fools nobody."

As has been noted, after the crash, many pointed to seers like Roger Babson who had come close to calling it correctly, but Babson had at another time predicted sustained economic prosperity. And many, many more "seers" had been mistaken. During bull markets there are those who warn of impending disaster, and in bear markets those who talk of a market rise.

The front page news of early 1929 was of Britain's ailing King George V, whose sons were rushing to his bedside from faraway lands, but the business pages focused on RCA's $116 million purchase of the Victor Talking Machine Company, which came just weeks after the company acquired Keith–Albee–Orpheum and renamed it Radio–Keith–Orpheum, or RKO. RCA's stock would hit a high of 420 in 1928, with a price-to-earnings ratio of better than 26. This was considered giddy, even for those times, but the news was so good that RCA seemed destined for even higher levels.

The December selloff and recovery were not unusual. There had been several such "corrections" during the 1920s, and there would be more to come. Stocks declined from 307.01 on January 2, 1929, to 296.98 on January 8, and then recovered to end the month at 317.51. As Coolidge prepared to leave office, investors, speculators, and others interested in the stock market were accustomed to such corrections and took them in stride. Why not? Didn't stocks always come back?

Anyone familiar with the markets of the late 1990s would have been at home in the markets of 1928–1929. David Sarnoff of RCA and Alfred Sloan of General Motors were for that period what Bill Gates of Microsoft and Andrew Grove of Intel are for the late 1990s; media and autos dominated the late 1920s as software and microprocessors dominated 1997. The economic outlook in 1929—and in 1998—was unclouded, with impressive statistics reported for growth, inflation, and employment.

The stock markets in both periods were monitored carefully, and the bulls were delighted with the message—in September 1924 the Dow was just above the 100 level; in March 1929 the market closed above 300. The Dow had tripled over a five-year period. It was a staggering performance, one which would have impressed investors of early 1998.

Who could explain this unprecedented situation? Not since accurate records had been kept had the market soared as it did in this period. Stock market analysts found nothing in American history to compare to the Giant Bull Market. Wall Street analyst Thomas Shotwell resorted to comparing the situation to a similar period in European history—at the end of the Napoleonic Wars, no less. According to the "Financial and Economic Review of 1928," published in the widely read *1929 World Telegram Almanac and Book of Facts*, Shotwell argued that the sustained economic growth France and England experienced after the Napoleonic Wars offered the only situation comparable to the American boom in the 1920s. Shotwell stated that "the whole mystery of the present rise in stocks disappears" since "exactly the same thing happened in France and England after" the Battle of Waterloo in 1815. Those countries came out of a major war with a great deal of wealth, and with the war over the nations could focus their attention on a prospering economy. In Shotwell's scheme, World War I served as the catalyst for the boom of the late 1920s, just as the Napoleonic Wars caused stocks to skyrocket for decades in the nineteenth century.

Shotwell's argument was indeed a stretch, but his far-reaching indicated how difficult it was to explain the phenomenon of the bull market, especially for those who thought it would last indefinitely. And Shotwell's central conclusion was optimistic: "The market is following natural laws of economics, and there is no reason why both prosperity and the market should not continue for years at this high level or even higher."

Fortunately, the markets of the mid-1990s offer today's readers a more plausible comparison. In the two years from March 1995 to March 1997, the Dow rose from the 4000 level to 7000—approximately 70 percent in a two-year span. At an annualized rate this performance is not very different from the 1924–1929 expansion. Did that mean that the market was preparing for a crash? Or, to duplicate the 1920s experience, would it have to rise to around 16000 before the calamity hit? Or even higher, because the market continued to rise irregularly to September 1929, when it peaked at 382.02.

In December 1996 Federal Reserve Chairman Alan Greenspan asked openly whether there was too much speculation on Wall Street, "irrational exuberance" causing a "bubble." The next day the market declined sharply, but then recovered. Some criticized Greenspan for having caused the dip, while others praised him for sounding the warning. But the market set new records throughout January 1997, reaching a high of 7085 on March 11 and then declining 10 percent by April 14—the traditional level to be labeled a bear market correction—before moving upward once more.

The analysts of 1997 had chimed in before the upswing. The bears sounded their warnings. For instance, on March 28, 1997, Carlton Lutts wrote, "We are now in a bear market. We have no idea of how long this market decline will last. Right now, it's smart to be out of the market to a large degree." Robert Prechter, articulating the opinion of a number of economists, agreed: "Long term, the market is rolling over from bull to bear." But the bulls were active, too. Curtis Hesler wrote, "I believe we could eventually see the Dow make it to the 8000 level this year," and Donald Rowe went even further: "The sales and profits of American corporations have been improving relentlessly, quarter after quarter. Dow 7600 in 1997 and Dow 10000 by the year 2000 are not unreasonable targets for the U.S. stock market." As it happened, the Dow crossed the 8000 level in July—so the bears had been wrong, and the bulls too timid.

In late July Greenspan told the House Banking Committee, "The recent performance of the economy, characterized by strong growth and low inflation, has been exceptional—and better than most anticipated."

Clearly, economic predictions in 1997—and even comments from the Federal Reserve chairman—were all over the map, just as they had been in 1929. In the summer of 1997, there was no way to make predictions with any confidence. Likewise, there was no way of making an accurate forecast in the summer of 1929, when the outlook

appeared more encouraging than it would at any time in the future—
save perhaps the spring of 1998.

Did Coolidge offer optimistic statements in 1928? Certainly, but
Clinton did the same in 1997, celebrating "the strongest economy
in American history." If the market declines sharply sometime in
the Clinton administration and we enter a recession, what will the
historians' view of Clinton become? Despite his critics' assertions,
Coolidge had no way of foreseeing the crash. If there was *any* cloud
in the sky before the Great Crash, it came in October 1928 with the
death of Benjamin Strong, which in 1998 would be akin to the death
of Alan Greenspan. Strong's successor at the New York Fed, George
Harrison, seemed content to continue his easy money policies, but
Harrison lacked Strong's credibility on Wall Street, which proved a
problem when difficulties arose.

Coolidge delivered a speech on Washington's birthday that caused
some talk, for in it he referred to Washington's Farewell Address,
noting that it was Jefferson, not Washington, who coined the phrase
"entangling alliances." He suggested that Washington had warned
against alliances in which two countries banded together against
other nations; "It had no reference to an association of nations in
an attempt to recognize their common interests and discharge their
common obligations." Many took this as an endorsement of the
League of Nations. Curiously, this section was omitted from the
version dispatched to Europe. But the revelation caused only fleeting
concern, since Coolidge would be out of office shortly.

In early March, Washington prepared to bid farewell to the
Coolidges and greet the Hoovers. Flags were raised on many buildings, and the sanitation workers were busily cleaning the streets.
Union Station was packed, as special trains arrived filled with cele-
brators eager for the festivities. At the White House Coolidge
worked long into the night, signing bills and taking care of other
last-minute details. His work during the day had been interrupted by
visits of well-wishers, and he spared the time to greet visitors personally at the White House front door.

In New York, theater owners reported record attendance. More
than three dozen shows were playing in the district, including vehi-

cles starring Ethel Barrymore, Eddie Cantor, Edward G. Robinson, Beatrice Lillie, and the Marx Brothers. Motion picture theaters advertised "sound pictures," better known as "talkies." *The Broadway Melody*, called an "All-Talking, Singing, Dancing, Sensation," was playing to standing room only crowds, and other popular films were *My Man* starring Fannie Brice, *Wolf Song* with Gary Cooper, *The Iron Mask* with Douglas Fairbanks, and fittingly, *The Wolf of Wall Street* starring George Bancroft. Radio fare was largely music and talks, and many stations carried the Wall Street closing prices.

By 1929 automobiles jammed the roads, spurring a major construction boom. The Ford Model A, introduced in 1927, had been greeted enthusiastically, but the talk of the industry was of Walter Chrysler, who had come from almost nowhere to construct the third largest company in the industry. In early 1929 Chrysler described the rise of the automobile: "As I visualized its future, it far outran railway development, which had reached its zenith." Auto sales for February reached an all-time high for that month. But soon after came a familiar warning; the Federal Oil Conservation Board announced that there was a danger the country would run out of petroleum in the foreseeable future because of the mania for automobiles. Steel production was at capacity.

Overall, Wall Street was moving along nicely. New issue offerings set a February record of $688 million; dividends that month also set a record. Gold exports were rising, indicating Europe's growing confidence in the future there. But on February 2 the Fed complained that banks were using their money to finance speculation on Wall Street, prompting a selloff. In its 1928 Annual Report, released in late February, the Fed warned against the level of member bank borrowings, and in response the Dallas branch raised its rediscount rate to 5 percent.

Mixed signals or not, the outlook on Wall Street was optimistic, as prices rose in what was called "the inaugural market" by some and "the Hoover market" by others. At its annual meeting RCA announced a five-for-one stock split. In discussing radio's impact on the 1928 election, President James Harbord said, "So clearly and completely were the issues of the campaign laid before the electorate that the possibility is visualized of future presidential campaigns being shortened to perhaps a month, thus minimizing the demoralization and interruption of business hitherto characteristic of the quadrennial campaigns."

In March 1929 some airline passengers were able to view in-flight films for the first time. That same month "automatic traffic controls"—or traffic lights—were introduced in New York. Among the clichés of the time were "What will they think of next" and "new and improved." The present was satisfying, the future promising, the outlook unclouded. This was supposed to be the Coolidge legacy.

Coolidge bade farewell to the press on February 28. He said he wanted to be remembered as an administrator who was not "constantly harassing business" and finding panaceas for government. Two years later, in one of his articles, he phrased it another way: "I would like to be known as a former president who tried to mind his own business."

Nevertheless, the newspapers credited his policies with causing the greatest economic expansion in history.

On Friday, March 1, Coolidge arose at 6:30 AM. After surveying the decorations for the inaugural, he went to the office and signed nearly two hundred measures. Then he stood at the front door and shook hands with 553 visitors. Saturday was quiet, and on Sunday the *New York Times* offered its assessment of the business scene:

> On the evening of the inauguration all is quite well in business as a general thing. The credit situation is the one cloud and it has grown somewhat darker with the further outburst of security speculation. So far rising money rates, caused by the siphoning of funds into the stock market, appeared to have affected only building operations, which for the month just closed ran some 15 per cent under the same month last year. The Conference of Statisticians in Industry points out in its latest report, however, that since building and automobile manufacture have gone ahead so largely as a result of credit expansion their prospects may depend largely upon the trend in credit.

Unsurprisingly, the press was kind to the departing president. In its editorial, the *Times* wrote of his "distinctive personality" and called him "one of the shrewdest politicians who ever came to direct the destinies of this nation," and concluded:

> The best remains to be said. It is of the deep impress made by President COOLIDGE'S rugged integrity. This was like a rock in 1924. While the country was left shuddering and ashamed by the revelations of corruption under President HARDING, it turned with relief and confidence to the unchallenged simplicity and purity of the life which, both official and private, was going on in the White House. Mr. COOLIDGE had such a shield in his demonstrated character that political arrows fell from it blunted and broken. And how greatly he was helped in all this by the charm and unaffected kindness of the First Lady in the White House is needless to say, for the whole nation has been a gratified witness of it. The two now return to their Massachusetts home, not amid wild acclaim, but with solid and enduring evidence of public affection and gratitude.

But he had always had his opponents in the media. The *Nation* summed up its case against him on March 6:

> Mr. Coolidge retires amid the acclaim of those whom he has served. To the business men who wanted a moratorium on reform and newfangled ideas and wished to get the government out of business he has been a godsend. For others it is possibly too early to appraise his work, but it has certain outstanding characteristics. The Coolidge administration has been distinguished. It has been distinguished, first, by its complacent attitude toward shocking corruption in high office; second, by its complete surrender of the regulatory powers of the government to the interests to be regulated; third, by the mediocrity or downright shabbiness of the men

appointed to high administrative and judicial posts;
fourth, by its hypocritical and despotic treatment of our
small Latin-American neighbors; and fifth, by the policy
whereby it was resolved that the period of greatest
national prosperity was the proper time to inaugurate
the practice of starving all productive public enterprise.
Curiously enough, the things for which Mr. Coolidge
will be longest remembered—the Kellogg Treaty and the
appointment of Dwight W. Morrow as ambassador to
Mexico—were in a sense accidental, notably the pact.
Mr. Kellogg, who proposed the treaty, did not realize its
significance and wanted to drop it when France and
England made their reservations. It is doubtful if even
today Mr. Coolidge realizes what it is all about.
Otherwise, it is hard to understand why he has stood for
the fifteen-cruiser bill. Vision, courage, the knowledge
how to serve the masses and the desire to aid them, a
realization of a new and better world—these, and much
else, have been denied him.

Sherwin Lawrence Cook, a Massachusetts politician and journalist, tried to rank Coolidge among the other presidents. Cook,
who had at times been critical of President Coolidge, wrote:

Coolidge is not among the great American presidents.
Neither is he among the presidential failures. You may
put a few, three or four, into the first class. You may put
Grant, Harding, Buchanan, Tyler, and Pierce into the
third class. Between these two groups stand the great
bulk of our presidents, leaving out of the reckoning the
first Harrison, Taylor, and Garfield, who died too soon
for estimates. This long line were able, honorable,
generally useful men. The serviceable Coolidge does not
lead the group. He had neither the great qualities of
Hayes, the deep intellect of Harrison, nor the tact of Van
Buren. On the other hand, both in purpose and ability,
he transcends a Polk or a Fillmore.

On inauguration day, March 4, Coolidge arose at 7:00 AM, and after breakfast went to his office. On the way he saw Ike Hoover, the White House chief usher. "Good morning, Mr. Hoover," he said. "How's the weather?" "Rather uncertain; looks as though it might rain," said Hoover. "Well, I hope not," replied Coolidge. "But it always has rained on my moving days." Then he went to his desk and signed more bills. Herbert Hoover was driven to the White House and arrived at 10:30. Then he and Coolidge went to the ceremonies. Hoover was smiling, and Coolidge, as usual, had a blank look on his face.

After the inaugural speech the Coolidges slipped away to take the train to Northampton. At Union Station he made a brief statement: "Good-bye. I have had a very enjoyable time in Washington." Coolidge later wrote, "Although I was in excellent health and felt greatly relieved from governmental responsibilities, of course I found I was both physically and mentally considerably exhausted." In his *Autobiography* Coolidge added, "We draw our presidents from the people. It is a wholesome thing for them to return to the people. I came from them. I wish to be one of them again." And so the Coolidges returned to the two-family house on Massasoit Street, where the rent had been boosted to $36 since he left for Washington.

Claude Fuess and others have estimated that when Coolidge left office he had $400,000 in assets, a great deal of money for the times. Coolidge had no need financially to seek employment or return to his law practice, but he had worked hard all his life, and he wouldn't change now.

Many rumors regarding Coolidge's post-presidential work surfaced during the last weeks in the White House. At various times he was supposed to become president of the American Petroleum Institute, president of a Vermont insurance company, and a spokesman for Merrill Lynch. There was some vague talk about a connection with American Telephone & Telegraph. One story had it that Hoover would name him to the Supreme Court when the next vacancy occurred. Another had him running for a Senate seat. On November 24, 1928, the *New York Times* reported, "President Coolidge had not even made a tentative decision as to what occupation he will follow when, on his retirement from the White House, he returns to Northampton, after more than twenty years of holding office." Coolidge found all of this troublesome. "You cannot realize how much I long for peace and privacy," he wrote to Henry Stoddard, who was with the *New York Sun.*

On the day after he left office Coolidge revealed he had signed contracts to write articles for three magazines—a series of autobiographical pieces for *Cosmopolitan,* an installment article on "Promoting Peace" for the *Ladies Home Journal,* and two articles on the "human interest" side of the presidency for the *American Magazine.* He received $15,000 for the *Ladies Home Journal* article and $30,000 for the two *American Magazine* articles. In addition, the *Encyclopedia Americana* offered him $25,000 a year and $1 a word for whatever he chose to write. And he apparently received an advance of $65,000 for his autobiography, which he completed in April. The book, published in November, was short, and was fleshed out with two articles published earlier.

Some complain that his *Autobiography* is opaque and masks his thoughts, because the book does not delve in much detail into Coolidge's activities while president. Surprisingly, the narrative section ends after he was elected in his own right in 1924. (Try to imagine a Lyndon Johnson autobiography that concluded with his election in 1964, and had nothing about the other four of his five years in office.) Yet there is more about the man and his philosophy in its mere 247 pages than in presidential memoirs three times as long. This is because it is not really an autobiography, but more by way of being a memoir, in which Coolidge looks back on his life and career and reflects on what it all meant. Moreover, the *Autobiography* displays a literary grace that is lacking in most such books by former presidents.

Either Coolidge had devoted a good deal of time to writing during that last year in office or was remarkably industrious and dedicated to his craft after leaving Washington. That kind of production is difficult even for today's professional freelancers, armed with their computers, while Coolidge composed with pen and ink. In all, Coolidge received more than $110,000 for his writings in 1929.

The articles were graceful and spare, not particularly revealing, and unmistakably Coolidge. As always, he was businesslike about his work. Rising at 8:00 AM, after breakfast he would have his chauffeur drive him to the office he shared with his old partner, Ralph Hemenway, where his secretary would have sorted his mail. After going through the letters, he would write, and then return home for lunch, after which it was back to the office for more writing.

Coolidge joined the board of the New York Life Insurance Company, and received $50 for each of the monthly meetings. With Al Smith and Julius Rosenwald, he served as co-administrator of the estate of an inventor, Conrad Hubert, who wished to endow charitable institutions. Smith, who became close to Coolidge during the next few months, told how a representative of one charity said to him during his presentation, "By the way, Governor, you know So-and-So—he's deeply interested in the home. You know him well—you play poker with him." Without looking up and with his characteristic dead-pan expression, Coolidge said, "Is that why he needs the money?" Later on he took on the job of president of the American Antiquarian Society, which gave him great pleasure.

Coolidge didn't comment on the stock market, which was as mercurial as ever. Prices declined in March, rallied into April, but bottomed out at Dow 291.82 on May 27. Then, in early June it boomed again, rising to 380.33 by August. It peaked at 382.02 during trading on September 5. In less than three-and-a-half months, the market had risen more than 30 percent. What's more, within less than two years the market had close to doubled.

Consider what might have gone through the minds of those who sold their stock anywhere along the way, especially during the corrections.

The crash came the following month. It would take more than twenty-five years for the average to reach that September 5 peak again.

It later came out that after leaving office Coolidge was on the list of "preferred" J.P. Morgan customers who were able to purchase shares at lower prices than could the general public. But J.P. Morgan was bipartisan in offering this privilege—others included on the roster were Democrats William Gibbs McAdoo and Newton D. Baker. Coolidge never revealed his own financial position before, during, and after the October 1929 crash, but he clearly was not so deeply into the market that he suffered. He must have been fairly secure financially even after the crash, since he traveled extensively in the winter of 1929–1930—to St. Petersburg, Florida; to California, where they met stars like Douglas Fairbanks and Mary Pickford and publisher William Randolph Hearst; and to Arizona to participate in the opening of the Roosevelt Dam.

Coolidge was busy with his regular schedule when the market collapsed. In his biography, William Allen White imagines him as morose, unhappy, and weary, and probably so, though he never let on to the public. His world was fading, to be sure, and once again deaths had to be faced. Coolidge's mother-in-law died soon after he left the White House, followed by Guy Currier and Dwight Morrow in 1931. He hadn't been particularly close to Currier, but Morrow had been his friend since Amherst, and he probably took it quite hard.

In January 1930 it was announced that Coolidge would write a history of the United States to be placed on a tablet near the site of the Mount Rushmore National Memorial. Only five hundred words long, the history was "expected to endure for 5,000 centuries." The story inspired a cartoonist for *Liberty* magazine to draw a troubled Coolidge, pencil in hand, staring at a page, with the caption: "Calvin Coolidge, commissioned to write the history of the United States in 500 words, feels the pangs of creation as he tried to think up 425 words of padding." But the project never developed, in part because sculptor Gutson Borglum wanted to edit Coolidge's words.

Coolidge continued to be a popular commodity. In the summer of 1930, the United Press approached him about writing a regular column of 1,500 words, for publication in American and foreign newspapers, for which he would be paid $1,000 an article. Doubleday, Doran offered him $50,000 a year for a monthly article in its magazine, *World's Work*. And Ralph Pulitzer, publisher of the *New York World* and the *St. Louis Post-Dispatch*, offered a minimum of $104,000 for weekly articles on topics of his choosing. Other newspapers made similar offers. Coolidge finally accepted an offer from Ralph Waldo of the McClure Newspaper Syndicate, to write a daily column of 150 to 200 words. Coolidge received $3,000 a week as an advance against sales, plus 60 percent net. The New York outlet was the *Herald Tribune*, the leading Republican newspaper in the country. Approximately sixty newspapers subscribed for the column, entitled "Calvin Coolidge Says." His first essay appeared on July 1, 1930, and he wrote the column for a year, earning $203,045. In contrast, his presidential salary had been only $75,000, plus $25,000 for travel, and the use of the White House and the presidential yacht, *Mayflower*.

The pieces, which Coolidge scholar Edward Lathem collected and published in 1972, show that Coolidge was not a natural journalist. Writing a daily column was perhaps too much for him, since some of the columns, especially toward the end, were inconsequential and bland. Or perhaps Coolidge was worn out and incapable by then of expressing himself as he had as governor and president. Yet the *Autobiography*, written only a short time earlier, is vintage Coolidge. The reader can judge for himself or herself from the following column, written on December 12.

> Three or four years ago there began considerable discussion of the practice of installment sales. While the system was by no means new, it was then being expanded into new fields with extraordinary rapidity and assumed such large proportions that it aroused considerable alarm. Some thought it might be undermining our whole credit structure. No definite and separate figures were obtainable as to the extent to which banks were involved and this raised the question of what funds were tied up in it. The developments of the past few months have demonstrated that there was nothing unsound in the movement. The percentage of losses has been insignificant. Probably of all commercial credits this form stands well toward the top in satisfactory results. Because installments have been paid, most of the fear of it as a breeder of extravagance has been dispelled. Probably conducted, it is no more subject to that criticism than the open account.
>
> But the great lesson is the honesty and integrity of the people. The consuming public pay their debts. It is another powerful demonstration of the justification of faith and confidence in each other.

As it became more evident that the country was sliding into bad economic times, Coolidge wrote a few words about proper public policy:

> Some confusion appears to exist in the public mind as to the proper function of the national government in the relief of distress, whether caused by disaster or unemployment.
>
> Strictly construed, the national government has no such duties. It acts purely as a volunteer. President Cleveland was much opposed to such measures. When the disaster is very great, federal aid has sometimes been extended.
>
> In case of unemployment, relief is entirely the province of the local government which has agencies and appropriations for that purpose. We have no few if any municipalities and certainly no state that cannot take care of all their unemployed.
>
> Every government should spend its own money. Otherwise the appropriating agency has no control over the disbursing agency and no check on extravagances.
>
> What the Congress properly is attempting is not direct relief for unemployed but indirect relief by a general stimulation of business by the expenditure of money on public works. The law properly can specify the purposes for which such money is to be spent. No doubt the federal executive departments already in existence are the most available agencies for the administration of such national appropriation.

And so it went.

The combination of Coolidge's new wealth—added to the old—and the need for privacy and more room led the family to move from Massasoit Street. In the spring of 1930, the Coolidges purchased a twelve-room house called "the Beeches" on Munroe Street, one of the better sections of Northampton, with nine wooded acres, a tennis court, and a swimming pool.

There was one slight hitch in Coolidge's personal affairs in this time. In the autumn of 1931 Coolidge delivered a radio address for New York Life Insurance, prepared by the public relations department, in which he warned policyholders against agents who might try to convince them to change their policies in order to obtain another commission. It was an innocent enough talk, hardly contentious, but an agent, Lewis Tebbetts, sued Coolidge and New York Life for $100,000 each, asserting they had slandered innocent agents. But nothing much came of it: Tebbetts agreed to settle out of court for $2,500, and Coolidge sent Tebbetts a letter saying he had not intended to offend him or any other agent.

Coolidge remained well-liked in the early years of the Great Depression. During the summer of 1932 there was even talk of a Coolidge nomination for the presidency, but it was nostalgia more than anything else. Coolidge clearly had no intention to run for any office. Those who yearned for a return to the Arcadian days of 1928 couldn't help wanting to believe that with him back in the White House, it would be possible to turn back the clock. He even received letters criticizing him for not running in 1928, from people who thought there would have been no depression if he had been in the White House. In 1936, with Coolidge in his grave, the Republicans nominated Alf Landon for the presidency, calling the rather bland but honest Landon the "Kansas Coolidge." This hardly would have been so unless there was a large reservoir of good will for "Silent Cal."

Despite Coolidge's continued popularity, Hoover apparently never consulted Coolidge during his administration, and Coolidge did not offer advice to Hoover. Richard Waldo, Coolidge's editor at McClure, wrote, "But he was a very lonely man. The failure of his successor to consult with him at all, and the consciousness that close contact of political friends with him would not be well received at the White House, made for a certain disturbance of mind...."

In the fall of 1932 Coolidge wrote three articles supporting Hoover's reelection. The Depression, he said, was due to matters beyond Hoover's control. "In the late winter of 1930 there were many indications of a business revival," he wrote in the September 10, 1932, issue of the *Saturday Evening Post*. "About this time there came a worldwide crash in agricultural products. As the season advanced, a large part of the country found itself suffering from a lack of rainfall, which extended over a wide area reaching from the Atlantic seaboard to the Rocky Mountains." Then the USSR dumped agricultural products on the world market, followed by banking crises in central Europe, then the rest of Europe, and eventually the United States.

Coolidge presented a situation that was beyond the capacity of government to resolve. "When men in public office have to meet a crisis which they themselves did not in any way create, the measure of credit or blame which should attach to such officeholders is not the intensity of the crisis, nor the danger or damage that results from it, but the manner in which they may meet it and the remedies which they apply to it." He approved of Hoover's relief efforts, which went beyond any attempted by previous administrations in similar circumstances. This was surprising: the president who had called for minimal government was supporting aggressive governmental programs to alleviate distress.

True, Coolidge also called for a balanced budget, lower costs of government, and a sharp reduction in military spending, but the key element was his support for governmental intervention to ease suffering. He did not, moreover, advocate piecemeal approaches, but rather wide and broad strategies and tactics:

> When a person is suffering from hunger, the common-sense method of relief is to put food into the stomach, whence it is sent to all parts of the body. Under the method of relief that is proposed for the body politic by the critics, instead of providing food in this way to nourish the hands and feet, I suppose that the needle would be used to inject nourishment into the fingers and toes. Under such a treatment the whole body would soon perish and the fingers and toes would become useless. The policy of the president has been to place nourishment in the digestive organs of society in order that through the natural distribution of the channels

already in existence the whole body would be
strengthened and able to function in the usual way.

Many have considered Coolidge indifferent to human suffering
and unwilling to use government powers to alleviate it, but he
demonstrated that he was far from immune to the calamity.

Coolidge was asked to campaign for Hoover, but was not certain
he should. Writing to Everett Sanders, who was the new Republican
party chairman and wanted Coolidge on the stump, he said:

> You know I should be glad to do anything I can to help.
> My throat, you will remember, always bothers me, and
> it is in such shape that I do not think I could do much of
> anything in the way of speaking. Just at present I am
> having some trouble with my breathing again. I am
> going to Vermont tomorrow for an indefinite stay, where
> I can be out of doors, and think I shall be all right when
> I get a little exercise.

Coolidge did deliver an address on radio from Madison Square
Garden in New York on October 11. He began with, "When I was
in Washington..." and the crowd roared with laughter. But according
to an associate, Congressman John Tilson, "he had not meant
to say anything funny, and was in fact displeased over it." He delivered
another radio address in Hoover's behalf on the night prior to
the election. It did no good. Franklin Delano Roosevelt swamped
Hoover.

On December 14, 1932, Coolidge traveled to New York for the
New York Life meeting. There he and his secretary, Harry Ross,
met with newsman Henry Stoddard. Not surprisingly, they reminisced
and reflected on how the world had changed, during which
Coolidge demonstrated a remarkable clarity of political thought.
The following year, after discussions with Ross, Everett Sanders set
down what Coolidge had said:

> I have been out of touch so long with political activities
> that I feel I no longer fit in with these times. Great

changes can come in four years. These socialistic notions of government are not of my day. When I was in office, tax reduction, tariff stability, and economy were the things to which I gave attention. We succeeded on those lines. It has always seemed to me that common sense is the real solvent for the nation's problems at all times—common sense and hard work. When I read of these newfangled things that are now so popular I realize that my time in public affairs is past. I wouldn't know how to handle them if I were called upon to do so.

That is why I am through with public life forever. I shall never again hold public office. I shall always do my part to help elect Republican candidates, for I am a party man, but in no other way shall I have anything to do with political matters.

Coolidge then turned to talk that the Republicans wished to nominate him in 1936. "That cannot be. There is no way I can decline something not yet offered, but I am embarrassed by the discussion of my name." And he continued:

We are in a new era to which I do not belong, and it would not be possible for me to adjust to it.

These new ideas call for new men to develop them. That task is not for men who believe in the only kind of government I knew anything about. We cannot put everything up to the government without overburdening it. However, I do not care to be criticizing those in power. I've never been much good attacking men in public office. If they succeed, the criticism fails; if they fail, the people find it out as quickly as you can tell them.

By "socialistic notions of government" Coolidge was not referring to the New Deal, which had not yet come to power. He was talking about the activities of his successor, Herbert Hoover.

While Coolidge and Stoddard spoke in his rooms at the Vanderbilt Hotel, elsewhere in the city the future New Dealers were conferring on the changes they planned to bring to Washington in little more than three months. They intended to alter the relationship of government to the people, to initiate a more activist administration than Hoover's, who himself had been far more vigorous in applying federal power than Coolidge had been. Nevertheless, Coolidge, while not sharing their vision, seemed to understand the way the world was changing at least as well as they did. Toward the ends of their lives men such as Woodrow Wilson, Robert La Follette, Hiram Johnson, and even Theodore Roosevelt were men of the past, but they still hoped to propagate the visions of their youth. Coolidge, who was soon to die, understood that his times were over; he had no place in the new world. Hoover soon left the White House, and for the rest of his long life would relive the period from 1914 to 1933, arguing and rearguing the past. The Republican Party of the 1930s would do the same, and, although Republicans nominated fairly progressive candidates during the next two decades, the heart of the party would belong to men who remembered Coolidge fondly.

In a December 21 letter to his former secretary, Ted Clark, Coolidge said, "The fact is I feel worn out," but he then added, "No one can tell these days what a short time or three or four years may bring forth, but, of course, I know my work is done."

On New Year's Day, 1933, Charles Andrews, who had entered Amherst with Coolidge in 1891 and had gone on to become treasurer of the college, made a call on the Coolidges at the Beeches. Andrews wanted to know how the former president felt. Coolidge said:

> I am very comfortable because I am not doing anything
> of any account; but a real effort to accomplish anything
> goes hard with me. I am too old for my years. I suppose
> the carrying of responsibilities as I have done takes its
> toll. I'm afraid I'm all burned out. But I am very
> comfortable.

After a while the talk turned to public affairs, and Coolidge returned to themes he had struck in his conversation with Stoddard:

> In other periods of depression it has always been
> possible to see some things which were solid and upon
> which you could base hope, but as I look about, I now
> see nothing to give ground for hope—nothing of man.
> But there is still religion, which is the same yesterday,
> today, and forever. That continues as a solid basis for
> hope and courage.

That was all he could offer.

Andrews thought Coolidge looked tired. Grace Coolidge later remarked that he was easily fatigued and walked slowly. In December he had seen his physician, and he took his pulse more often than before.

On Wednesday, January 4, 1933, Coolidge left the office earlier than usual, and told Harry Ross, "I have an idea that we might stop going down to the office each day and do our work up here. Then we can go out and walk in the open air whenever we choose."

The following day he arose early after a bout of indigestion, and after breakfast went to the office and read some newspapers. The larger newspapers carried a story about President-elect Roosevelt's forthcoming trip to Muscle Shoals; Senator Norris and others, including Chairman Frank Walsh of the New York State Power Authority, would accompany FDR. The trip was a clear sign that the incoming president intended to follow Norris's suggestion that the government retain Muscle Shoals and use it as the basis for regional development. The government would do just that with the Tennessee Valley Authority. That morning, Coolidge would have realized his efforts to privatize Muscle Shoals had failed. Another news story dealt with Roosevelt's intention to ask for a tax increase, which he felt was necessary in order to balance the budget. Under the plan, married taxpayers with no children earning $2,500, who previously had not paid taxes, would be assessed $30, and it went up from there, until those earning $1 million would go from $571,100 to $610,980. Coolidge cherished balanced budgets, but this tax increase went against everything he stood for.

Many newspapers carried news that the American Association for the Advancement of Science had awarded a prize of $1,000 to Henry

Eyring of Princeton University, for his pioneering work on quantum mechanics and subatomic physics. During his post-presidential years Coolidge advocated teaching Latin and Greek in colleges, and in general maintaining the kind of curriculum he had experienced at Amherst. Now he was reading of the dawn of the atomic age. That day the papers also reported that Yale Law School would drastically revise its curriculum; students would have complete freedom from formal courses in their first two years of study. Calvin Coolidge's world was indeed fading.

At 10:00 AM Coolidge called for Ross, and said he wanted to return home. Grace Coolidge was about to leave, and the president asked whether she wanted the car. "No," she replied, "it's such a fine day I think I'll walk." Coolidge and Ross entered the house, and after a while Coolidge went to the kitchen for a glass of water. He walked outside and spoke to the gardener for a moment, and then went upstairs. Coolidge took off his jacket and vest and prepared to shave. Then he keeled over and fell to the floor. He was dead, at the age of sixty-one.

The news spread over the front pages of the next day's newspapers. President Hoover declared a thirty-day mourning period. Congress adjourned. Newspaper reporters contacted many prominent people for their reactions, and unsurprisingly, virtually all had kind words for Coolidge. Chief Justice Charles Evans Hughes called the loss "irreparable." Secretary of State Henry Stimson was "shocked and grieved." Senator Hiram Johnson, who rarely had anything positive to say of the president, said, "His passing will be a matter of exceeding regret to all Americans, and the whole country will sorrow." Reporters contacted even Jim Lucey, Coolidge's shoemaker acquaintance from Northampton, who said, "I'm sorry. I'm sorry. He was the best friend I ever had." Gifford Pinchot, his old political foe, told a reporter, "The loss that millions feel so deeply is not merely the loss of an ex-president, it is not merely the loss of America's first private citizen, it is the loss of Calvin Coolidge the man," and he went on to praise "his simplicity, his homely wisdom, his quiet personal courage—these are the things for which he will be best remembered." Then he added, "As president he typified an era. That era is passing or has passed. Coolidge will be remembered as its symbol. And his passing is the symbol of its passing also."

The newspaper editorials chimed in, but were understandably more circumspect. "Few presidents have had a more individual quality of speech, of manner, of thought," wrote the *New York Herald Tribune*. The *Atlanta Constitution* offered, "He was a unique figure in the annals of American public life, possessing public confidence in his sincerity and uprightness of character." The *New Orleans Times-Picayune* wrote: "Calvin Coolidge's stature as president will grow with the years." The verdict of the *Pittsburgh Post-Gazette* was: "Probably no other president, not even Theodore Roosevelt, was as personally popular with all classes of his fellow citizens as was Calvin Coolidge." The *Los Angeles Times* wrote: "It is too early to anticipate the verdict of history upon either Coolidge or the Coolidge administration, but it does seem probable the future will regard him as a man who was wiser than his generation." And the *Portland Oregonian* echoed many editorials in saying, "History will record that Coolidge was just the kind of president that his time called for."

The *Nation*, which was even more critical of Coolidge than Pinchot had been, did not permit death to soften its disapproval. In its editorial, it said, "Calvin Coolidge succeeded in pleasing the great masses of his fellow citizens and yet never comprehended, or was able to comprehend, the deeper meaning of the economic surge on which he was borne forward like a chip on the crest of a wave." To The *Nation*, he was a cipher: "He dealt with the issues only when they were forced upon him, left no constructive suggestions to cure our ills, and made no contribution whatever to the science of government." But, it conceded, "the Coolidge myth persisted to the end." Editor Oswald Garrison Villard, who wrote venomously of Coolidge throughout the years he was a public figure, added a separate article of his own:

> The "masters of America"—as Woodrow Wilson called
> them—the great heads of the corporations which
> dominate our social, business, and political life, found in
> him just the complaisant national figurehead they so

eagerly desired. He had been utterly silent in the face of
the corruption of the Harding cabinet, in which, by
invitation, he sat; he never talked, as did Mr. Wilson,
about our being "in the midst of a revolution" against
the great capitalists. Nor did he denounce any of the big
businessmen as "malefactors of great wealth," as did
Theodore Roosevelt; and there was no chance under him
of such shocking scandals as disgraced the Harding
regime. So as the tide of prosperity rose higher and
higher, it became "Coolidge Prosperity," as if he had
created it by some wave of a magic wand. And when he
capped the climax, just before the expiration of his
presidency, by prostituting the White House as it has
never been prostituted before by his statement of
January 7, 1928, encouraging the maddest, wildest
speculation in the world's history, the spokesmen of
finance and big business called him blest.

During the years he was in the White House, Mencken, who had
few good words to say about democracy and the average person,
saw in Coolidge a man who had a knack of appealing to "the
boobs." "He will be ranked among the vacuums," Mencken wrote
in 1927. "It would be difficult to imagine a more obscure and unim-
portant man." He noted Coolidge's passivity: "It seems incredible
that one with such towering opportunities in this world should use
them so ill." But in his less bombastic moments, Mencken acknowledged that Coolidge was one of the shrewder statesmen of the period
and a master politician. He ultimately conceded that perhaps he
really didn't understand Coolidge, and in this he was in good company. "There is something deeply mysterious about such a man." In
his obituary of him, Mencken, who was not the type to speak well of
the dead, wrote:

We suffer most when the White House bursts with ideas.
With a World Saver [Wilson] preceding him (I count out
Harding as a mere hallucination) and a Wonder Boy
[Hoover] following him he begins to seem, in retrospect,

an extremely comfortable and even praiseworthy citizen. His failings are forgotten; the country remembers only the grateful fact that he let it alone. Well, there are worse epitaphs for a statesman. If the day ever comes when Jefferson's warnings are heeded at last, and we reduce government to its simplest terms, it may very well happen that Cal's bones now resting inconspicuously in the Vermont granite will come to be revered as those of a man who really did the nation some service.

That day cannons fired off throughout the nation, Coolidge's last forty-eight gun salute. All the flags were at half mast. Trains and automobiles were already arriving in Northampton for the funeral. President and Mrs. Hoover were there, as were Vice President and Mrs. Curtis. Chief Justice Hughes and Associate Justice Stone came. The governors of nearby states arrived, along with a large delegation from the Massachusetts legislature. The Congregational Church was crowded, and many more stood outside. It was a dreary day, with a cold drizzle.

The body lay in state for an hour, and those present filed past the coffin. Among the pall bearers were Frank Stearns, William Butler, and former Governor Trumbull of Connecticut, whose daughter had married John Coolidge. The procession then traveled the one hundred miles north to the cemetery in Plymouth Notch in which all the Coolidges, including the president's parents and son, were buried. In his description of the day, playwright Clarence Day wrote:

> Across the road, in a rocky field, the men and women of the village had gathered. They were not the kind of people to intrude or crowd nearer, and they kept complete silence. The young minister said a few words as the coffin was lowered. A sudden storm of hail pelted down.
>
> The widow, who had tried to smile that morning coming out of the church, could no longer hold back her tears.
>
> The cars left. The bent-shouldered sexton signaled to his helpers. They filled in the grave. Four country

militiamen took up their positions on guard. Snow fell that night on the hillside and the slopes of Salt Ash Mountain.

The headstone that now marks the quiet spot bears no inscription but the name, Calvin Coolidge, the dates, and the president's seal.

* * *

In the months that followed scores of prominent individuals chimed in with their reactions to Coolidge's death and assessments of his accomplishments as president. They ranged from the adulatory to the unpleasant, from the eloquent to the clumsy. Al Smith offered one of the clearest and fairest assessments of the man:

> I had a great liking and respect for him. Beneath a chilly, reserved, and dignified exterior, he was keen, kindly and entirely free from conceit, pompousness, and political hokum. We are often told politics in a republic produced only demagogues. Calvin Coolidge was a most successful and popular politician, but he had nothing of the demagogue in him.

Coolidge was not a great president, thought Smith, but rather belonged

> ...in the class of presidents who were distinguished for character more than for heroic achievements. His great task was to restore the dignity and prestige of the presidency when it had reached the lowest ebb in our history, and to afford in a time of extravagance and waste, a shining public example of the simple and honest virtues which came down to him from his New England ancestors. These are no small achievements, and history will not forget them.
>
> Calvin Coolidge was a salty, original character, an unmistakable home-grown, native, American product,

and his was one of those typically American careers, which begin on the sidewalks, or on the farm, and prove to the youth of the nation that this is still the land of unbounded opportunity.

Notes

CHAPTER 1

The Lippmann quote is from Walter Lippmann, *Men of Destiny* (New York: Macmillan, 1927), p. 12–13.

CHAPTER 2

The basic sources for Coolidge's youth are Ernest C. Carpenter, *The Boyhood Days of President Calvin Coolidge* (Rutland, VT: Tuttle, 1925) and Hendrick Booraem V, *The Provincial: Calvin Coolidge and His World*, 1885–1895 (Lewisberg, PA: Bucknell University Press, 1994). The remark by Hennessy is in his book, *Four Decades of Massachusetts Politics*, 1890–1935 (New York: G.P. Putnam, 1935), p. 282. For the Bradford quotation, see Gamaliel Bradford, *The Quick and the Dead* (New York: Houghton Mifflin, 1931), p. 26. Coolidge's recollections about Vermont are in Calvin Coolidge, "Books of My Boyhood," *Cosmopolitan*, October, 1932, p. 19. The impact of Abbie Coolidge's death on Coolidge is in Robert Gilbert, *The Mortal Presidency: Illness and Anguish in the White House* (New York: Basic Books, 1992), p. 22. For Coolidge at Amherst see Claude M. Fuess, *Calvin Coolidge: The Man from Vermont* (Boston: Little Brown, 1940) and the same author's *Amherst: The Story of a New England College* (Boston: Little Brown, 1935). Coolidge's letter to his father is in Grace Coolidge, "The Real Calvin Coolidge," March, 1935, p. 25. The John Coolidge quote regarding his son's love of learning is in Alfred Pierce Dennis, "The Man Who Became President," a 1924 essay in Edward Lathem, *Meet*

Calvin Coolidge: The Man Behind the Myth (Brattleboro, VT: Stephen Greene, 1960), p. 24. For Charles Garman, see Former Students of Charles Edward Garman, *Studies in Philosophy and Psychology* (Boston: Houghton Mifflin, 1906) and Anonymous, *Studies in Philosophy and Psychology, by Former Students of Charles Edward Garman* (Boston: Houghton Mifflin, 1906). Coolidge on Garman is in Coolidge, *Have Faith in Massachusetts*, (New York: Houghton Mifflin, 1919), p. 320. Coolidge's letter to his father is in Edward Lathem, ed. *Your Son, Calvin Coolidge: A Selection of Letters from Calvin Coolidge to his Father* (Montpelier, VT: Vermont Historical Society, 1968), p. 73.

CHAPTER 3

The best source for Coolidge's law studies, early practice, and political career is Fuess, *Calvin Coolidge*. Fuess interviewed many of those individuals who knew Coolidge in this period, who of course are no longer alive. The statement about Coolidge's qualities is from Edward Elwell Whiting, *President Coolidge: A Contemporary Estimate* (Boston: Atlantic Monthly, 1923), p. 57. Coolidge's letter to his father are in Lathem, *Your Son, Calvin Coolidge*, p. 80–81. For Grace Coolidge, see Ishbel Ross, *Grace Coolidge and Her Era: The Story of a President's Wife* (New York, Dodd Mead, 1962); Grace Coolidge, "The Real Calvin Coolidge," *Good Housekeeping*, March, 1935, p. 243; and Bruce Barton, "The Silent Man on Beacon Hill, *Woman's Home Companion*, March, 1920. Coolidge on progressive thought is in Howard Quint and Robert Ferrell, eds. *The Talkative President: The Off-The-Record Press Conferences of Calvin Coolidge* (Amherst: University of Massachusetts Press, 1964), p. 9. The Murray Crane biography for which Coolidge wrote the preface is Solomon Bulkley Griffin, *W. Murray Crane: A Man and Brother* (Boston: Little Brown, 1926). For more on Crane, and a study of Massachusetts politics in this period, see Richard M. Abrams, *Conservatism in a Progressive Era: Massachusetts Politics 1900–1912* (Cambridge, MA: Harvard University, 1964), especially Chapters 1 and 2, and Michael E. Hennessy, *Four Decades of Massachusetts Politics 1890–1935*. The Sawyer quote is from

Roland D. Sawyer, *Cal Coolidge, President* (Boston: Four Seas, 1924), p. 98.

CHAPTER 4

The basic sources are Fuess, *Calvin Coolidge*, and William Allen White, *A Puritan in Babylon* (New York: Macmillan, 1938). The Coolidge letters are in Lathem, *Your Son, Calvin Coolidge*. For an understanding of state politics in this period, the best sources are Abrams and Hennessy. Coolidge's refusal to attend the San Francisco Exposition is in Robert A. Woods, *The Preparation of Calvin Coolidge* (Boston: Houghton Mifflin, 1824), p. 33–34, and the mayoralty is discussed in p. 59–64. His contribution to the 1914 state platform is in Hennessy, p. 86, and Woods, p. 35. The John Coolidge remark on his son's inauguration is in Lathem, *Your Son, Calvin Coolidge*, p. 126. The Coolidge speech at Wheaton College is in Coolidge, *The Price of Freedom: Speeches and Addresses* (New York: Scribner, 1924), p. 390–91. Stearns's letter to Maynard is in *Meet Calvin Coolidge*, p. 27. The Coolidge, Taft, and Lodge letters are in Lathem, *Your Son, Calvin Coolidge*, p. 126–27. The Stearns and Grace Coolidge statements are in Ross, *Grace Coolidge and Her Era*, p. 42 and 46. Mrs. Coolidge's comments on Stearns are in Grace Coolidge, "The Real Calvin Coolidge," May 1935, p. 247–248. For details on Samuel McCall, up to but not including the 1915 election, see Lawrence B. Evans, *Samuel W. McCall: Governor of Massachusetts* (Boston: Houghton Mifflin, 1916). The material on Coolidge's second term is from Michael E. Hennessy, *Calvin Coolidge* (New York: Putnam, 1924). The statement to Dwight Morrow is from Harold Nicolson, *Dwight Morrow* (New York: Harcourt Brace, 1935), p. 87.

CHAPTER 5

The Hemenway material is in Ralph W. Hemenway, "His Law Partner Looks Back," in Lathem, *Meet Calvin Coolidge*, p. 163–73 and Fuess, p. 151. The Coolidge correspondence is in Lathem, *Your Son, Calvin Coolidge*. Fuess and Donald R. McCoy, *Calvin*

Coolidge: The Quiet President (New York: Collier-Macmillan, 1967) offers the best treatments of the 1918 gubernatorial election. Coolidge's speeches during the campaign are in *Have Faith in Massachusetts*. The Coolidge gubernatorial record during his first months in office is discussed in McCoy, Chapter 8. There are several fine books in which to discover background information on the early post–World War I period: Mark Sullivan, *Our Times*, Vols. IV and V (New York: Scribner, 1935); Jules Abels, *In the Time of Silent Cal* (New York: G.P. Putnam, 1969); Joseph Huthmacher, *Massachusetts People and Politics*, 1919–1933 (Cambridge, MA: Harvard, 1959); Frederick Lewis Allen, *Only Yesterday* (New York: Harper, 1931); and William Leuchtenberg, *The Perils of Prosperity* (Chicago: University of Chicago, 1958). The material dealing with the labor unrest of the period may be found in the *New York Times*, the *New York Herald*, the *New York Tribune*, and the *New York World* for January–October, 1919. The A. Mitchell Palmer quotation is from his article, "The Case Against the 'Reds'" in the *Forum*, February 1920, p. 185. Mayor Hanson was discussed in the *New York Times*, August 29, 1919, and his obituary on July 8, 1940. General Wood's activity on the strike front in 1919 is in Herman Hagedorn, *Leonard Wood: A Biography* (New York: Harper, 1931), p. 333–37.

CHAPTER 6

The most complete account of the Boston police strike is in Chapter XI of Fuess's *Calvin Coolidge*, which is favorable to Coolidge. See also Francis Russell, "The Strike that Made a President," *American Heritage* (October, 1963), p. 44–47 ff., which savages Coolidge, Peters, and Curtis, and is pro-union. McCoy deals with the strike in Chapter 9 of his book. William Allen White, who alternates between criticizing and praising Coolidge, deals with the strike in *A Puritan in Babylon*, Chapter XV. The story of the jitney conflict is in Hennessy, *Calvin Coolidge*, p. 112–13. The veto of the alcohol measure conflict is in Calvin Coolidge, *The Price of Freedom*, p. 407. The AFL speech is from Woods, p. 163, and the Timilty view of Coolidge is on p. 33. The Fosdick review is in *Outlook*, February 2, 1921, p. 187–88. The French Strother observation is from "Calvin Coolidge," in *World's Work*, April 1924, p. 579. The message to Gompers is in Calvin Coolidge, *Have Faith in Massachusetts*. The Coolidge statement indicating he was prepared to lose the election rather than give in to the strikers appears in many places and several forms; this one is in Cameron Rogers, *The Legend of Calvin Coolidge* (Garden City, NY: Doubleday, Doran, 1928), p. 143. The political speech is from Edna M. Colman, *White House Gossip: From Andrew Johnson to Calvin Coolidge* (Garden City, NY: Doubleday, Page, 1927), p. 408. FDR's opinion of Coolidge is in White, p. 144. The analysis of Coolidge by a neighbor is in "Coolidge: A Governor Who Makes No Mistakes and Never Lost an Election," *Current Opinion*, January 1920, p. 37.

CHAPTER 7

The background for the 1920 Republican Convention is derived from Fuess, McCoy, and White, as well as the *New York Times*, the *New York Herald*, and the *New York Tribune*. The *New York World* reporter's observations are in "Coolidge: A Governor Who Makes No Mistakes and Never Lost an Election," *Current Opinion*, January 1920, p. 37. Coolidge's relations with his stepmother are in Lathem, *Your Son, Calvin Coolidge*, p. 22, 58, 106, 159. The Lippmann quote is from Walter Lippmann, "The Logic of Lowden," *New Republic*, April 14, 1920, p. 204. The use of money in the 1920 GOP campaign is discussed in Louise Overacker, *Money in Elections* (New York: Macmillan, 1922). The best source for information on Lowden is William T. Hutchinson, *Lowden of Illinois: The Life of Governor Frank O. Lowden* (Chicago: University of Chicago, 1957). For the conventions and election, see Wesley M. Bagby, *The Road to Normalcy*. Francis Russell's *The Shadow of Blooming Grove: Warren G. Harding in His Times* (New York: McGraw-Hill, 1968) is sometimes inaccurate but is still useful. Better for the Harding campaign is James N. Giglio, *H.M. Daugherty and the Politics of Expediency* (Kent: Kent State University Press, 1978). There is a mine of information regarding the wheeling and dealing in Mark Sullivan, *Our Times*, Vol. VI. Daugherty's prediction of a Harding nomination is in the *New York Times*, February 21, 1920, and his analysis of the race with Harding is in Harry Daugherty with Thomas Dixon, *The Inside Story of the Harding Tragedy* (New York: Churchill, 1932), p. 18–19. Samuel Hopkins Adams, *Incredible Era: The Life and Times of Warren Gamaliel Harding* (Boston: Houghton Mifflin, 1939), is marred by the author's antipathy for his subject, but contains material new for the times on the convention. Claude Fuess's quote regarding the Senate group's control of the convention is in Fuess, p. 258. The Penrose offer to Wood is in Bagby, *The Road to Normalcy*, p. 87. Johnson's refusal to accept the vice presidential nomination is in several works, among them Ray Tucker and Frederick Barkley, *Sons of the Wild Jackass* (Freeport, NY: Books for Libraries, 1969 ed.), p. 98–100. The Carpenter statement is in the *New York Times*, January 9, 1922. The Morris–Smoot encounter is in Charles Willis Thompson, *Presidents I've Known and Two Near Presidents* (Indianapolis: Bobbs-Merrill, 1929), p. 326–27. The Mencken story is in H.L. Mencken, *A Carnival of Buncombe*, edited by Malcolm Moos, (Baltimore: Johns Hopkins, 1956), p. 134.

CHAPTER 8

Material for the 1920 campaign was drawn from the *New York Times* and the *Boston Globe*, and where indicated magazine articles of the time. Coolidge's gubernatorial speeches were not covered carefully in the Boston newspapers of the period. This changed once he received the nomination. The Lynds' quotation from the Muncie woman is in Robert and Helen Lynd, *Middletown: A Study in Modern American Culture* (New York: Harcourt Brace & World, 1956 ed.) p. 28–29. There is no book dealing specifically with the Coolidge vice presidency, and the best on the subject are Fuess and McCoy. The incident involving Norris and Kellogg is in McCoy, p. 135–36. Coolidge's letters to his father are in Lathem, *Your Son Calvin Coolidge*. His views on Lodge are in White, p. 219. Coolidge's speeches as vice president are collected in *The Price of Freedom*. His speeches as president are in *Foundations of the Republic* (Freeport: Books for Libraries, 1968 ed.) Theodore Roosevelt, Jr.'s, comments on Coolidge in the cabinet come from his diary, as quoted in Gilbert, *The Mortal Presidency*, p. 27. The Ladd story is in Duff Gilfond, *The Rise of Saint Calvin: Merry Sidelights on the Career of Mr. Coolidge* (New York: Vanguard, 1932), p. 152. While Gilfond embroiders many of the stories he told, versions of many appeared elsewhere. The fire marshal story is in George Pepper, *Philadelphia Lawyer: An Autobiography* (Philadelphia: Lippincott, 1944), p. 202. The talk of a Coolidge replacement on the 1924 ticket is in Russell, *The Shadow of Blooming Grove*, p. 571. Much of the other material dealing with Harding comes from this source and Robert K. Murray, *The Harding Era: Warren G. Harding and His Administration* (Minneapolis: University of Minnesota, 1969). Muscle Shoals is covered in Richard Lowitt, *George W. Norris: The Persistence of a Progressive, 1913–1933* (Urbana: University of Illinois, 1971), p. 203 ff.; George Norris, *Fighting Liberal: The Autobiography of George W. Norris* (New York: Macmillan, 1945); and Allan Nevins and Frank Hill, *Ford: Expansion and Challenge, 1915–1933* (New York: Scribner, 1957). The material on the economy during the early 1920s is from Robert Sobel, *Herbert Hoover at the Onset of the Great Depression, 1929–1930* (Philadelphia: Lippincott, 1975). For the Coolidge taxation program, see Benjamin Rader, "Federal Taxation in the 1920s," *Historian*, Spring 1973, p. 415–435.

CHAPTER 9

In addition to the aforementioned basic Coolidge biographies, see Duff Gilfond's fanciful *The Rise of Saint Calvin*. Harding's reaction to the ship collision is in Russell, *Shadow of Blooming Grove*, p. 588. The incidents regarding the Coolidge swearing in can be found in Vrest Orton, *Calvin Coolidge's Unique Vermont Inauguration* (Rutland, VT: Academy, 1970). Bruce Barton's discussion of Coolidge in the White House is in Grace Coolidge, "The Real Calvin Coolidge," March, 1935, p. 221. Gilbert Fite, *George N. Peek and the Fight for Farm Policy* (Norman: University of Oklahoma, 1954), Chapter 1, contains a good analysis of the farm problem. Tax policies during the 1920s are covered in W. Elliot Brownlee, *Federal Taxation in America: A Short History* (New York: Cambridge,

1996). For the Coolidge press conferences and other valuable material, see Sheldon Stern, "The Struggle to Teach the Whole Story: Calvin Coolidge and American History Education," in *The New England Journal of History*, Fall 1996, p. 38–52. Coolidge's first thought on learning of Harding's death is in Pepper, *Philadelphia Lawyer*, p. 195. Press reaction to Coolidge's accession to the presidency are in Bruce Barton, "Calvin Coolidge As Seen Through the Eyes of His Friends," *American Review of Reviews*, September 1923, p. 273–78; "The New President Calvin Coolidge," *Outlook*, August 15, 1923, p. 580–81; Sullivan, "Coolidge and Congress," p. 202–3. A profile on C. Bascom Slemp is in Clinton Gilbert, *"You Takes Your Choice"* (New York: Putnam, 1924). Coolidge's speech writing is in Everett Sanders, "Calvin Coolidge: A Profile," *Saturday Evening Post*, December 6, 1930, p. 5. Fuess on Coolidge's speeches is in Arthur Fleser, *A Rhetorical Study of the Speaking of Calvin Coolidge* (Lewiston, NY: Edwin Mellen, 1990), p. 29. John Coolidge's observations are in Lathem, *Your Son, Calvin Coolidge*, Introduction. Coolidge's outreach to La Follette is in Murray, *The Harding Era*, p. 502. His relations with the congressional Republicans is from McCoy, p. 197. Coolidge's statement to Christian regarding the coal strike is in Pepper, *Philadelphia Lawyer*, p. 196. The story about Walsh and the river is in Sullivan, *Our Times*, p. 282–83. The Daugherty dismissal is in Giglio, *H.M. Daugherty*, Chapter 13. The story of the Montana road is in Burton K. Wheeler, *Yankee from the West* (Garden City, NY: Doubleday, 1962), p. 205. The *New Republic*'s remarks on McAdoo are in the March 5, 1924, issue.

CHAPTER 10

McCoy, Fuess, and White are the basic sources for this chapter, with White a trifle better than the others. The standard biography of Dwight Morrow is by Harold Nicolson, *Dwight Morrow*. The tax statistics are from the *1929 World Telegram Almanac and Book of Facts* (New York: World Telegram, 1929), p. 199. Thomas Silver, *Coolidge and the Historians* (Durham, NC: Carolina Academic Press, 1982), Chapter 4, is a remarkable dissection of the tax issue during the 1920s and a good corrective for the conventional wisdom on the subject. See also Andrew Mellon, *Taxation: The People's Business* (New York: Macmillan, 1924). The Lowden candidacy in 1924 is in Hutchinson, *Lowden*, Chapter 22. For the 1924 conventions, see Robert K. Murray, *The 103rd Ballot* (New York: Harper & Row, 1976); Kenneth McKay, *The Progressive Movement* of 1924 (New York: Octagon, 1972); and Bascom Timmons, *Portrait of An American: Charles G. Dawes* (New York: Henry Holt, 1953), Chapters 13–17. The Klan issue is best covered in John Higham, *Strangers in the Land: Patterns of American Nativism, 1860–1925* (New Brunswick, NJ: Rutgers, 1955). A good general work on the events that year is William Allen White, *Politics: The Citizen's Business* (New York: Macmillan, 1924). For the death of Calvin Coolidge, Jr., see Gilbert, *The Mortal Presidency*, Chapter 2, which also has material on Coolidge's subsequent health problems. The Brown statement is in Grace Coolidge, ed., "The Real Calvin Coolidge," *Good Housekeeping*, May, 1935, p. 248. Coolidge on the radio is in Fleser, *A Rhetorical Study... of Calvin Coolidge*, p. 63. His ranking in the poll is from the *New York Times* of September 4, 1927. The Davis campaign is covered in William Harbaugh, *Lawyer's Lawyer: The Life of John W. Davis* (New York: Oxford, 1973), Chapter 15. The Starling story is in Edmund Starling, *Starling of the White House* (New York: Simon & Schuster, 1946), p. 224.

CHAPTER 11

The basic sources again are Fuess, White, and McCoy. Lippmann on Coolidge frustrating politicians is in Lippmann, *Men of Destiny*, p. 15. The Coolidge speech to the editors is in Coolidge, *Foundations of the Republic*, p. 183–90. Silver's *Coolidge and the Historians* is a scathing attack on historians who denigrate Coolidge, especially Schlesinger, Jr., and contains a presentation and analysis of such matters. The Lane letters are in Anne Lane and Louise Wall, *The Letters of Franklin K. Lane, Personal and Political* (Boston: Houghton Mifflin, 1922), p. 448–54, 464–65. Coolidge's views on education and business are in Calvin Coolidge, *The Price of Freedom*, p. 9. For Mellon's analysis of the impact of the Coolidge tax plan, see Mellon, *Taxation*, p. 56 ff. The 1927 tax data can be found in the *New York Times*, January 2, 1928. Coolidge's speech on the economy is in Coolidge, *Foundations of the Republic*, p. 39–47. The "Toleration and Liberalism" speech is there as well, on p. 287–304. His speech on the need for government, and the desirability of a separation of government and business, "Government and Business," is to be found on p. 317–32. For Coolidge and the negroes and the Sargent statement, see Grace Coolidge, "The Real Calvin Coolidge," June, 1935, p. 202–3, and "Coolidge and Colored Candidates," *Literary Digest*, August 30, 1924, p. 13. The best study of the Mississippi River flood is John Barry, *Rising Tide: The Great Mississippi Flood of 1927 and How It Changed America* (New York: Simon & Schuster, 1997). Fuess covers the Warren nomination well, but see also Timmons, *Portrait of an American*, p. 246–7, and Harry Barnard, *Independent Man: The Life of Senator James Couzens* (New York: Scribner, 1958), p. 175–77. For Lane's views on Warren, see Lane and Wall, *Letters of Franklin K. Lane*, p. 367. The Lippmann analysis is in Walter Lippmann, *Men of Destiny*, p. 15. The president's views on spending are in Quint and Ferrell, *The Talkative President*, p. 111–12. Coolidge's radio experiences are in Robert Sobel, *The Manipulators: America in the Media Age* (New York: Doubleday, 1976), p. 151. The selections from the Coolidge press conferences are to be found in Quint and Ferrell, *The Talkative President*, p. 28. The Coolidge quotations regarding the press can be found in *Editor and Publisher*, August 11, 1923, and the Coolidge *Autobiography*, p. 183–84. The Hoover quotation is in Herbert Hoover, *The Memoirs of Herbert Hoover: The Cabinet and the Presidency, 1920–1933* (New York: Macmillan, 1952), p. 55–56.

CHAPTER 12

Of the general biographies, McCoy covers foreign affairs better than do Fuess and White. The Root remarks are from Philip C. Jessup, *Elihu Root* (New York: Dodd Mead, 1938), II, 433. Herbert Feiss, *The Diplomacy of the Dollar: First Era, 1919–1932* (Baltimore: Johns Hopkins, 1950) is most useful. For Coolidge's reading habits, see "Books the President Reads," *Outlook*, September 1, 1923, p. 33. Fears of running out of oil are discussed in Hoover, *The Cabinet and the Presidency*, p. 69–70. Mexican history in this period is well covered in Robert Quirk, *The Mexican Revolution and the Catholic Church, 1910–1929* (Bloomington: Indiana University, 1973); Ramon Ruiz, *The Great Rebellion: Mexico, 1905–1924* (New York: Norton, 1980); and James Wilkie, *Revolution in Mexico: Years of Upheaval, 1910–1940* (New York: Knopf, 1969). For Coolidge's attitudes toward Mexico, see C. Bascom Slemp, *The Mind of the President as Revealed by Himself in His Own Words*, (Garden City, NY: Doubleday Doran, 1926), p. 46, 47. Coolidge's views toward Mexico are also in White, p. 282. Borah and Mexico are in Claudius Johnson, *Borah of Idaho* (New York: Longmans, Green, 1936), p. 338. The Stoddard statement is in Grace Coolidge, "The Real Calvin Coolidge," June 1935, p. 250. The best source for Morrow's ambassadorship is Nicolson, *Dwight Morrow*. The Kellogg statement regarding Bolshevism in Mexico is on p. 307. For China policy, see Wesley Fishel, *The End of Extraterritoriality in China* (Berkeley: University of California, 1952). The Wilbur speech is in Charles and Mary Beard, *The Rise of American Civilization* (London: Jonathan Cape, 1930), Vol. 2, p. 705. American banks and Germany business are covered in Robert Sobel, *The Life and Times of Dillon Read* (New York: Dutton, 1991), Chapter 6. Kellogg's foreign policy actions and attitudes are from David Bryn-Jones, *Frank B. Kellogg: A Biography* (New York: Putnam, 1937). The Kellogg statement regarding China is in McCoy, p. 341. For U.S. business's foreign investments, see Cleona Lewis, *America's Stake in International Investments* (Washington: Brookings, 1938), and the statistics on American petroleum investments are on p. 588. Material on criticisms of government–bank–corporation relations is found in Joseph Brandes, *Herbert Hoover and Economic Diplomacy* (Pittsburgh: University of Pittsburgh, 1962), especially Chapter 10. Mira Wilkins, *The Maturing of Multinational Enterprise: American Business Abroad from 1914 to 1970* (Cambridge, MA: Harvard, 1974), offers an excellent account of American business's overseas activities in the 1920s. For further information on American investment overseas, see Robert Sobel, *ITT: The Management of*

Opportunity (New York: Weybright & Talley, 1982), and the same author's *RCA* (New York: Stein & Day, 1986).

CHAPTER 13

Fuess and McCoy are the background sources for Coolidge's last year in office. White has fanciful interpretations marred by second guessing, but it is generally good. The Lippmann quotes are from Lippmann, *Men of Destiny*, p. 18–34, 24–25. The Ripley story is in Fuess, McCoy, and White. See also William Z. Ripley, *From Main Street to Wall Street* (Boston: Little Brown, 1927). The recitation of the Coolidge decision not to run is best handled by Fuess, and unless otherwise indicated, so are the quotations. The Clark recollections are in Grace Coolidge, "The Real Calvin Coolidge," April 1935, p. 198–99. Coolidge's letters dealing with securities are from Laphem, *Your Son, Calvin Coolidge*, p. 86–108. The Hoover material is in Hoover, *The Cabinet and the Presidency*, p. 190–93. Quint and Ferrell, *The Talkative President*, p. 135–38, is the source for Coolidge's statements on Fed actions and brokers' loans in early 1928. For the market itself, see George Soule, *Prosperity Decade* (New York: Holt, Rinehart & Winston, 1947); Robert Sobel, *The Great Bull Market* (New York: Norton, 1968); and Alexander Dana Noyes, *The Market Place* (Boston: Houghton Mifflin, 1938). The allegations against Coolidge and Mellon come from Anonymous, *The Mirrors of 1932* (New York: Brewer, Warren & Putnam, 1931), p. 66–67. The Cole story is in White, p. 406–7.

CHAPTER 14

The account of Coolidge's last days in office is derived from Fuess and McCoy. Fuess is particularly valuable for Coolidge's retirement and last days. The *New York Times* was used for the securities markets and the economic news of the period. The business scene was well covered in the old but still useful George Soule, *Prosperity Decade*. See also Alexander Dana Noyes's memoir, *The Market Place*, for the views of the *New York Times* financial editor on the late 1920s. The Shotwell analysis is in the *1929 World Telegram*

Almanac and Book of Facts, p. 129. The Cook quotation is from *Torchlight Parade: Our Presidential Pageant* (New York: Minton Balch, 1929), p. 247–48. Edward Lathem, *Calvin Coolidge Says* (Plymouth, VT: Calvin Coolidge Memorial Foundation, 1972) is good for Coolidge's last years, and in addition is a collection of his newspaper columns. James C. Clark, *Faded Glory: Presidents Out of Power* (Westport, CT: Praeger, 1985) supplements Lathem. Ralph Waldo's comments are in Grace Coolidge's article, "The Real Calvin Coolidge," in *Good Housekeeping*, February, 1935, p. 21, 181. The Sanders article is in the *Saturday Evening Post*, March 25, 1933. Andrews's meeting with Coolidge is in Grace Coolidge, "The Real Calvin Coolidge, *Good Housekeeping*, June, 1935, p. 209. The Mencken quotes are from *A Carnival of Buncombe*, p. 61–64. The Day selection was widely reprinted, but is most accessible in Lathem, *Meet Calvin Coolidge*.

Selected Bibliography

1929 World Telegram Almanac and Book of Facts. New York: World Telegram, 1929.

Abels, Jules. *In the Time of Silent Cal*. New York: G.P. Putnam, 1969.

Abrams, Richard M. *Conservatism in a Progressive Era: Massachusetts Politics 1900–1912*. Cambridge, MA: Harvard University, 1964.

Adams, Samuel Hopkins. *Incredible Era: The Life and Times of Warren Gamaliel Harding*. Boston: Houghton Mifflin, 1939.

Allen, Frederick Lewis. *Only Yesterday*. New York: Harper, 1931.

Anonymous. *Boudoir Mirrors of Washington*. Philadelphia: Winston, 1923.

Anonymous. *The Mirrors of Washington*. New York: Putnam, 1921

Anonymous. *The Mirrors of 1932*. New York: Brewer, Warren & Putnam, 1931.

Anonymous. *Studies in Philosophy and Psychology, by Former Students of Charles Edward Garman*. Boston: Houghton Mifflin, 1906.

Bagby, Wesley M. *The Road to Normalcy*.

Bailey, Thomas A. *Presidential Greatness: The Image and the Man from George Washington to the Present*. New York: Appleton-Century, 1966.

———. *Presidential Saints and Sinners*. New York: Free Press, 1981.

———. *The Pugnacious Presidents: White House Warriors on Parade*. New York: Free Press, 1980.

Barnard, Harry. *Independent Man: The Life of Senator James Couzens.* New York: Scribner, 1958.

Barrett, Laurence I. *Gambling With History.* Garden City, NY: Doubleday, 1983.

Barry, John. *Rising Tide: The Great Mississippi Flood of 1927 and How It Changed America.* New York: Simon & Schuster, 1997.

Beard, Charles and Mary. *The Rise of American Civilization.* London: Jonathan Cape, 1930.

Blaisdel, Donald. *Government and Agriculture.* New York: Farrar & Rinehart, 1940.

Blumenthal, Sidney. *Our Long National Daydream.* New York: Harper & Row, 1988.

Booraem, Hendrik, V. *The Provincial: Calvin Coolidge and His World, 1885–1895.* Lewisberg, PA: Bucknell University Press, 1994.

Booth, Edward T. *Country Life in America as Lived by Ten Presidents of the United States.* New York: Knopf, 1947.

Bowden, Robert. *Boies Penrose: Symbol of an Era.* New York: Greenberg, 1937.

Boylan, James, ed. *The World and the '20s.* New York: Dial, 1973.

Bradford, Gamaliel. *The Quick and the Dead.* New York: Houghton Mifflin, 1931.

Brandes, Joseph. *Herbert Hoover and Economic Diplomacy.* Pittsburgh: University of Pittsburgh, 1962.

Brownlee, W. Elliot. *Federal Taxation in America: A Short History.* New York: Cambridge, 1996.

Bryn-Jones, David. *Frank B. Kellogg: A Biography.* New York: Putnam, 1937.

Burner, David. *Herbert Hoover: A Public Life.* New York: Knopf, 1979.

Butler, Nicholas Murray. *Across the Busy Years.* New York: Scribner, 1939.

Cannon, Lou. *President Reagan: The Role of a Lifetime.* New York: Simon & Schuster, 1991.

Carpenter, Ernest C. *The Boyhood Days of President Calvin Coolidge.* Rutland, VT: Tuttle, 1925.

Clark, James C. *Faded Glory: Presidents Out of Power.* Westport, CT: Praeger, 1985.

Colman, Edna M. White *House Gossip: From Andrew Johnson to Calvin Coolidge*. Garden City, NY: Doubleday, Page, 1927.

Combs, James. *The Reagan Range: The Nostalgic Myth in American Politics*. Bowling Green State University Popular Press, 1993.

Commonwealth of Massachusetts. *Messages to the General Court, Official Addresses, Proclamations, and State Papers of His Excellency, Governor Calvin Coolidge for the Years 1919 and 1920*. Boston: Commonwealth of Massachusetts, 1920.

Cook, Sherwin L. *Torchlight Parade: Our Presidential Pageant*. New York: Minton Balch, 1929.

Coolidge, Calvin. *Foundations of the Republic*. New York: Scribner, 1926.

———. *The Price of Freedom: Speeches and Addresses*. New York: Scribner, 1924.

———. *The Autobiography of Calvin Coolidge*. New York: Cosmopolitan, 1931.

———. *Have Faith in Massachusetts*. New York: Houghton Mifflin, 1919.

Coolidge, Grace. *An Autobiography*. Worland, WY: High Plains, 1992.

Curtis, Jane and Will and Frank Lieberman. *Return to These Hills: The Vermont Years of Calvin Coolidge*. Woodstock, VT: Curtis-Lieberman, 1985.

Daba, John Cotten. *Plymouth: Story of the Old Home of President Coolidge*. Woodstock, VT: Elm Tree, 1925.

Daugherty, Harry, with Thomas Dixon. *The Inside Story of the Harding Tragedy*. New York: Churchill, 1932.

Davenport, Walter. *Power and Glory: The Life of Boies Penrose*. New York: Putnam, 1931.

Dawes, Charles. *Notes as Vice President, 1928–1929*. Boston: Little Brown, 1935.

Dennis, Alfred. *Gods and Little Fishes*. Indianapolis: Bobbs-Merrill, 1931.

Derbyshire, John. *Seeing Calvin Coolidge in a Dream*. New York: St. Martin's, 1996.

Dubofsky, Melvyn and Van Tine, Warren. *John L. Lewis: A Biography*. New York: Quadrangle, 1971.

Dugger, Ronnie. *On Reagan: The Man & His Presidency*. New York: McGraw-Hill, 1983.

Edel, Wilbur. *The Reagan Presidency: An Actor's Finest Performance*. New York: Hippocrene, 1992.

Evans, Lawrence B. *Samuel W. McCall: Governor of Massachusetts*. Boston: Houghton Mifflin, 1916.

Feiss, Herbert. *The Diplomacy of the Dollar: First Era, 1919–1932*. Baltimore: Johns Hopkins, 1950.

Fishel, Wesley. *The End of Extraterritoriality in China*. Berkeley: University of California, 1952.

Fite, Gilbert. *George N. Peek and the Fight for Farm Policy*. Norman: University of Oklahoma, 1954.

Fleser, Arthur. *A Rhetorical Study of the Speaking of Calvin Coolidge*. Lewiston, NY: Edwin Mellen, 1990.

Former Students of Charles Edward Garman. *Studies in Philosophy and Psychology*. Boston: Houghton Mifflin, 1906.

Fuess, Claude M. *Amherst: The Story of a New England College*. Boston: Little Brown, 1935.

———. *Calvin Coolidge: The Man from Vermont*. Boston: Little Brown, 1940.

Garman, Eliza Miner. *Letters, Lectures, and Addresses of Charles Edward Garman: A Memorial Volume*. Boston: Houghton Mifflin, 1909.

Giglio, James N. *H.M. Daugherty and the Politics of Expediency*. Kent: Kent State University Press, 1978.

Gilbert, Clinton. *Behind the Mirrors: The Psychology of Disintegration at Washington*. New York: G.P. Putnam, 1922.

———. *"You Takes Your Choice."* New York: Putnam, 1924.

Gilbert, Robert. *The Mortal Presidency: Illness and Anguish in the White House*. New York: Basic Books, 1992.

Gilfond, Duff. *The Rise of Saint Calvin: Merry Sidelights on the Career of Mr. Coolidge*. New York: Vanguard, 1932.

Green, Horace. *The Life of Calvin Coolidge*. Burlington: Duffield, 1924.

Greene, J.R. *Calvin Coolidge: A Biography in Picture Postcards*. Athol, MA: Transcript, 1987.

Griffin, Solomon Bulkley. *W. Murray Crane: A Man and a Brother*. Boston: Little Brown, 1926.

Hagedorn, Herman. *Leonard Wood: A Biography*. New York: Harper, 1931.

Harbaugh, William. *Lawyer's Lawyer: The Life of John W. Davis*. New York: Oxford, 1973.

Hawley, Ellis. *Herbert Hoover As Secretary of Commerce, 1921–1928: Studies in New Era Thought and Practice*. Iowa City: University of Iowa, 1981.

Hennessy, Michael E. *Calvin Coolidge: From a Green Mountain Farm to the White House*. New York: G.P. Putnam, 1924.

———. *Four Decades of Massachusetts Politics, 1890–1935*. New York: G.P. Putnam, 1935.

Higham, John. *Strangers in the Land: Patterns of American Nativism, 1860–1925*. New Brunswick, NJ: Rutgers, 1955.

Hoover, Herbert. *The Memoirs of Herbert Hoover: The Cabinet and the Presidency, 1920–1933*. New York: Macmillan, 1952.

———. *The Memoirs of Herbert Hoover: The Great Depression, 1929–1931*. New York: Macmillan, 1952.

Hoover, Irwin. *Forty-Two Years in the White House*. New York: Macmillan, 1948.

Hughes, H. Stuart. *History as Art and Science: Twin Vistas on the Past*. New York: Harper Torchbooks, 1964.

Hutchinson, William T. *Lowden of Illinois: The Life of Governor Frank O. Lowden*. 2 vols. Chicago: University of Chicago, 1957.

Huthmacher, Joseph. *Massachusetts People and Politics, 1919–1933*. Cambridge, MA: Harvard, 1959.

Jessup, Philip. *Elihu Root*. New York: Dodd Mead, 1938.

Johnson, Claudius. *Borah of Idaho*. New York: Longmans, Green, 1936.

Johnson, Haynes. *Sleepwalking Through History*. New York: Norton, 1991.

Judah, Charles and George Smith. *The Unchosen*. New York: Coward-McCann, 1962.

Kent, Frank. *The Great Game of Politics*. Garden City, NY: Doubleday Doran, 1923.

Keynes, John Maynard. *Economic Consequences of the Peace*. New York: Harcourt Brace, 1920.

Lane, Ann and Louis Wall. *The Letters of Franklin K. Lane, Personal and Political*. Boston: Houghton Mifflin, 1922.

Lathem, Edward, ed. *Calvin Coolidge: Cartoons of His Presidential Years featuring the work of syndicated cartoonist John N. "Ding" Darling*, August 1923–March 1929. Plymouth, VT: Calvin Coolidge Memorial Foundation, 1973.

———. *Calvin Coolidge Says*. Plymouth, VT: Calvin Coolidge Memorial Foundation, 1972.

———. *Meet Calvin Coolidge: The Man Behind the Myth*. Brattleboro, VT: Stephen Greene, 1960.

———. *Your Son, Calvin Coolidge: A Selection of Letters from Calvin Coolidge to his Father*. Montpelier, VT: Vermont Historical Society, 1968.

Le Duc, Thomas. *Piety and Intellect at Amherst College, 1865–1912*. New York: Columbia University, 1946.

Leuchtenberg, William. *The Perils of Prosperity*. Chicago: University of Chicago, 1958.

Lewis, Cleona. *America's Stake in International Investments*. Washington: Brookings, 1938.

Lippmann, Walter. *Men of Destiny*. New York: Macmillan, 1927.

Lowitt, Richard. *George W. Norris: The Persistence of a Progressive, 1913–1933*. Urbana: University of Illinois, 1971.

Lowry, Edward. *Washington Close-Ups: Intimate Views of Some Public Figures*. Boston: Houghton Mifflin, 1921.

Lynd, Robert and Helen. *Middletown: A Study in Modern American Culture*. New York: Harcourt Brace & World, 1956 ed.

Mazur, Paul. *American Prosperity: Its Causes and Consequences*. New York: Viking, 1928.

McBride, Mary M. *The Story of Dwight W. Morrow*. New York: Farrar & Rinehart, 1930.

McCoy, Donald R. *Calvin Coolidge: The Quiet President*. New York: Collier-Macmillan, 1967.

McKay, Kenneth. *The Progressive Movement of 1924*. New York: Octagon, 1972.

McKee, John H. *Coolidge Wit and Wisdom*. Burlington, VT: Stokes, 1933.

Mellon, Andrew. *Taxation: The People's Business*. New York: Macmillan, 1924.

Mencken, H.L. *A Carnival of Buncombe*. Edited by Malcolm Moos. Baltimore: Johns Hopkins, 1956.

Merriam, Charles E. and Louis Overacker. *Primary Elections*. New York: University of Chicago, 1928.

Murray, Robert K. *The Harding Era: Warren G. Harding and His Administration*. Minneapolis: University of Minnesota, 1969.

———. *The 103rd Ballot*. New York: Harper & Row, 1976.

———. *The Politics of Normalcy: Government Theory and Practice in the Harding-Coolidge Era*. New York: Norton, 1973.

Murray, Robert K. and Tim Blessing. *Greatness in the White House: Rating the Presidents*. University Park: Pennsylvania State University Press, 1994 ed.

Nevins, Allan and Frank Hill. *Ford: Expansion and Challenge, 1915–1933*. New York: Scribner, 1957.

Nichols, Beverly. *The Star Spangled Manner*. New York: Doubleday Doran, 1930.

Nicolson, Harold. *Dwight Morrow*. New York: Harcourt Brace, 1935.

Norris, George. *Fighting Liberal: The Autobiography of George W. Norris*. New York: Macmillan, 1945.

Noyes, Alexander Dana. *The Market Place*. Boston: Houghton Mifflin, 1938.

Orton, Vrest. *Calvin Coolidge's Unique Vermont Inauguration*. Rutland, VT: Academy, 1970.

Overacker, Louise. *Money in Elections*. New York: Macmillan, 1922.

Parrish, Michael. *Anxious Decades: America in Prosperity and Impression, 1920–1941*. New York: Norton, 1992.

Pepper, George. *Philadelphia Lawyer: An Autobiography*. Philadelphia: Lippincott, 1944.

Peterson, Houston, ed. *Great Teachers, Portrayed by those who Studied Under Them*. New Brunswick, NJ: Rutgers, 1946.

Pollard, James. *The Presidents and the Press*. New York: Macmillan, 1947.

Pringle, Henry F. *The Life and Times of William Howard Taft*. New York: Farrar & Rinehart, 1939.

Quint, Howard and Robert Ferrell, eds. *The Talkative President: The Off-The-Record Press Conferences of Calvin Coolidge*. Amherst: University of Massachusetts Press, 1964.

Quirk, Robert. *The Mexican Revolution and the Catholic Church, 1910–1929*. Bloomington: Indiana University, 1973.

Rader, Benjamin. "Federal Taxation in the 1920s." *Historian*. Spring 1973.

Reeves, Richard. *The Reagan Detour*. New York: Simon & Schuster. 1985.

Ripley, William Z. *From Main Street to Wall Street*. Boston: Little Brown, 1927.

Roberts, Kenneth. *Concentrated New England*. Indianapolis: Bobbs-Merrill, 1924.

Rogers, Cameron. *The Legend of Calvin Coolidge*. Garden City, NY: Doubleday Doran, 1928.

Ross, Ishbel. *Grace Coolidge and Her Era: The Story of a President's Wife*. New York: Dodd Mead, 1962.

Ruiz, Ramon. *The Great Rebellion: Mexico, 1905–1924*. New York: Norton, 1980.

Russell, Francis. *The Shadow of Blooming Grove: Warren G. Harding in His Times*. New York: McGraw-Hill, 1968.

Sawyer, Roland D. *Cal Coolidge, President*. Boston: Four Seas, 1924.

Schaler, Michael. *Reckoning With Reagan*. New York: Oxford University Press, 1992.

Schieffer, Bob and Gary Paul Gates. *The Acting President*. New York: E.P. Dutton, 1989.

Schlesinger, Arthur, Jr. *The Age of Roosevelt: The Coming of the New Deal*. Boston: Houghton Mifflin, 1958.

———. *Cycles of American History*. Boston: Houghton Mifflin, 1986.

Shriftgiesser, Karl. *The Gentleman from Massachusetts: Henry Cabot Lodge*. Boston: Little Brown, 1944.

Silver, Thomas. *Coolidge and the Historians*. Durham, NC: Carolina Academic Press, 1982.

Slemp, C. Bascom. *The Mind of the President as Revealed by His Own Words*. New York: Doubleday Doran, 1926.

Sloan, Irving J. *Ronald W. Reagan, 1911–* . Dobbs Ferry, NY: Oceana, 1990.

Slosson, Preston. *The Great Crusade and After, 1914–1928*. New York: Macmillan, 1937.

Sobel, Robert. *The Great Bull Market*. New York: Norton, 1968.

——. *Herbert Hoover at the Onset of the Great Depression, 1929–1930*. Philadelphia: Lippincott, 1975.

——. *The Life and Times of Dillon Read*. New York: Dutton, 1991.

——. *The Manipulators: America in the Media Age*. New York: Doubleday, 1976.

Soule, George. *Prosperity Decade*. New York: Holt, Rinehart & Winston, 1947.

Starling, Edmund. *Starling of the White House*. New York: Simon & Schuster, 1946.

Stoddard, Henry. *As I Knew Them*. New York: Harper, 1927.

Sullivan, Mark. *Our Times*, Vols. IV–VI. New York: Scribner, 1935.

Thompson, Charles Willis, *Presidents I've Known and Two Near Presidents*. Indianapolis: Bobbs-Merrill, 1929.

Thompson, Robert, ed. *A Collation and Co-Ordination of the Mental Processes and Reactions of Calvin Coolidge, as Expressed in His Addresses and Messages, and Constituting a Self-Delineation of His Character and Ideals*. Chicago: Donahue, 1924.

Timmons, Bascom. *Portrait of an American: Charles G. Dawes*. New York: Henry Holt, 1953.

Tucker, Ray and Frederick Barkley. *Sons of the Wild Jackass*. Freeport, NY: Books for Libraries, 1969 [first printed in 1932].

United States. Department of Commerce. *Historical Statistics of the United States, Colonial Times to 1970*. Washington: USGPO, 1975.

Villard, Henry. *Prophets True and False*. Freeport, NY: Books for Libraries, 1969 [first printed in 1928].

Washburn, Robert. *Calvin Coolidge, His First Biography*. New York: Small Maynard, 1923.

Weisberger, Bernard. *The La Follettes of Wisconsin: Love and Politics in Progressive America*. Madison: University of Wisconsin, 1994.

Wheeler, Burton K. *Yankee from the West*. Garden City, NY: Doubleday, 1962.

White, William Allen. *Calvin Coolidge*. New York: Macmillan, 1925.

———. *Politics: The Citizen's Business*. New York: Macmillan, 1924.

———. *A Puritan in Babylon: The Story of Calvin Coolidge*. New York: Macmillan, 1938.

Whiting, Edward Elwell. *Calvin Coolidge: His Ideals of Citizenship*. Boston: W.A. Wilde, 1924.

———. *President Coolidge: A Contemporary Estimate*. Boston: Atlantic Monthly, 1923.

Wilkie, James. *Revolution in Mexico: Years of Upheaval, 1910–1940*. New York: Knopf, 1969.

Wilkins, Mira. *The Maturing of Multinational Enterprise: American Business Abroad from 1914 to 1970*. Cambridge, MA: Harvard, 1974.

Woods, Robert A. *The Preparation of Calvin Coolidge*. Boston: Houghton Mifflin, 1924.

Index